America's Revolution

PATRICK GRIFFIN

New York   Oxford

OXFORD UNIVERSITY PRESS

Oxford University Press is a department of the University of Oxford. It furthers the University's objective of excellence in research, scholarship, and education by publishing worldwide.

Oxford   New York
Auckland   Cape Town   Dar es Salaam   Hong Kong   Karachi
Kuala Lumpur   Madrid   Melbourne   Mexico City   Nairobi
New Delhi   Shanghai   Taipei   Toronto

With offices in
Argentina   Austria   Brazil   Chile   Czech Republic   France   Greece
Guatemala   Hungary   Italy   Japan   Poland   Portugal   Singapore
South Korea   Switzerland   Thailand   Turkey   Ukraine   Vietnam

Copyright © 2013 by Oxford University Press.

For titles covered by Section 112 of the US Higher Education Opportunity Act, please visit www.oup.com/us/he for the latest information about pricing and alternate formats.

Published by Oxford University Press
198 Madison Avenue, New York, NY 10016
www.oup.com

Oxford is a registered trademark of Oxford University Press.

All rights reserved. No part of this publication may be reproduced, stored in a retrieval system, or transmitted, in any form or by any means, electronic, mechanical, photocopying, recording, or otherwise, without the prior permission of Oxford University Press.

Library of Congress Cataloging-in-Publication Data
   Griffin, Patrick, 1965–
   America's revolution / Patrick Griffin.
      p. cm.
   Includes bibliographical references and index.
   ISBN 978–0–19–975480–9 (acid-free paper)   1. United States—History—Revolution,
   1775–1783.   2. United States—History—1783–1815.   3. Founding Fathers of the
   United States.   I. Title.
   E208.G828 2012
   973.3—dc23
   2012023300

9 8 7 6 5 4 3 2 1
Printed in the United States of America
on acid-free paper

For Mary Hope
Yesterday, and today, and tomorrow

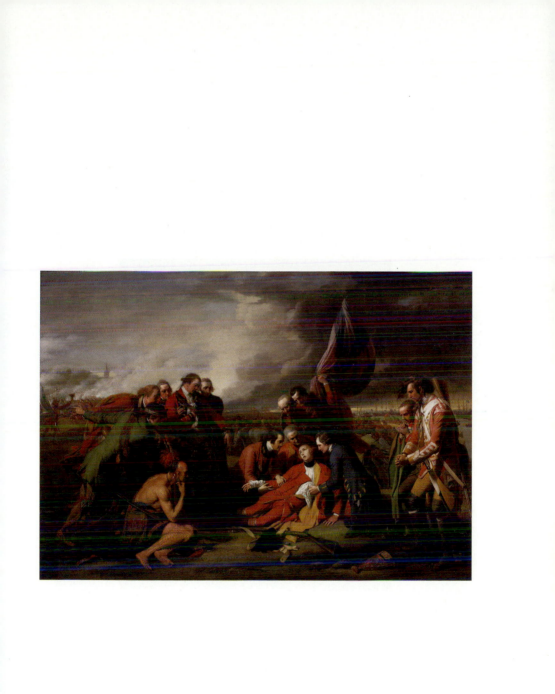

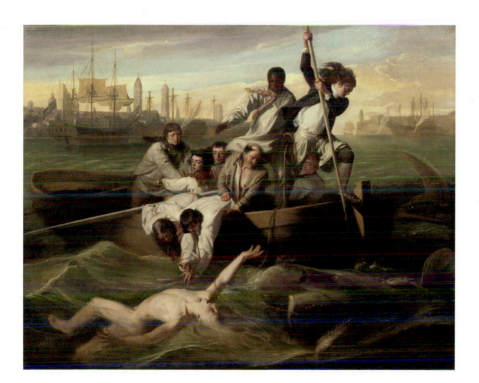

CONTENTS

≫

From Vanishing Point to Triptych

America's revolution had a beginning, a middle, and an end. Such a claim may appear self-evident. What revolution does not start and finish or have something happening in between? But the simple observation drives home a point often forgotten or missed when we study the "American Revolution." That term, usually unbounded by quotation marks, is freighted with a great deal of cultural baggage. It conjures up images ranging from tricorne hats and "the pursuit of happiness" to muskets and Thomas Jefferson. More importantly, the American Revolution has always occupied the center of national discourse. As it did for Americans in the nineteenth and twentieth centuries, it still distills who we are and structures what we would like to become. The idea of the "American Revolution," however, fails to capture what made it a revolution.

Understandably so. Americans have a difficult time gaining proper perspective on the event. It is the point where present and future confront the past. Since the nineteenth century, Americans conceived of themselves as a people of contradiction, a people of principle who sometimes failed to live up to the vaunted promise of foundational ideals found most notably in the Declaration of Independence, the closest thing to "American scripture."[1] In the years leading up to the Civil War, debate began and ended, literally and metaphorically, with the principles of the American Revolution. In their famous debates, Stephen Douglas and Abraham Lincoln drew inspiration from the same document and the founders to create two distinctive visions of what America, and freedom, represented. Memorialization of the founders and their revolution also justified the brutal warfare that neither Lincoln nor Douglas could avoid. And, of course, by beginning his Gettysburg Address with the words "four score and seven years ago," drawing a line back to 1776, Lincoln would consecrate the horrific violence of war by invoking "our fathers."[2]

Americans today, like their forebears, have a fascination with the founders. Many still venerate the founding generation as civic saints, especially on the holy day of the Fourth of July.[3] Americans may no longer use Washington as an example of honesty for children, but they still see the revolution as the founders'. The popularity of the HBO special on John Adams speaks to this simple lesson. So too the shelves at bookstores that groan with new books on founders such as Franklin. The men may have had their flaws, but they presided over an American Revolution that would be remembered for the principles of 1776, principles that would be enshrined as the nation's sacred heritage and highest aspirations. It was the central event in American history. After the revolution, not all persons could enjoy their rights to life, liberty, or the pursuit of happiness. But, as some historians suggest, it would be churlish and unfair—as well as anachronistic—to have expected the founders to have done anything differently. In any event, their vision of human equality—the notions enshrined in the Declaration—would be vindicated with time. Men and women would gain their rights as full citizens. Americans owe these victories to the vision of the founders.[4]

Another vision of the founders goes hand-in-hand with this understanding. From time to time, but especially when the United States has foundered, historian and citizen alike have cast a jaundiced eye on the American experiment by invoking the American Revolution. In the tense years before the Civil War, the runaway slave turned abolitionist Frederick Douglass chastised his fellow-citizens for bringing "our humble offering to the national altar" on the Fourth of July. "The rich inheritance of justice, liberty, prosperity, and independence bequeathed by your fathers is shared by you, not by me," he declared. Hypocrisy, "which would disgrace a nation of savages," defined that anniversary. "The character and conduct of this nation," he thundered, "never looked blacker to me than on this Fourth of July."[5] During the economic and social crisis of the turn of the twentieth century and the Great Depression, scholars questioned the motives of the founders, arguing that their avarice and self-interestedness explained the limitations of citizenship in the United States. In the wake of Watergate, their collective reputations suffered further blows. These flawed men, according to some, tried and succeeded in reining in the true promise of an American Revolution that could have—or should have—liberated the lower class, minorities, and women. Men such as Franklin, Adams, and Jefferson may have helped free the nation from Britain, but they did little to enhance the status of women. They did not free slaves. Far from it. In the same room where they signed the Declaration of Independence, the founders would draft a constitution that codified slavery as an American institution. At the same time, they relegated Indians to reservations, wiped them out, or forced them to embrace white ways. And lower-class whites still clung to the margins of society, be they in cities or on the frontier. The revolution steered by the founders failed. Americans may have won home rule but lost the fight over who was to rule at home.[6]

Both of these narratives speak to truths. Yet these contradictory understandings of the "American Revolution" represent flip sides of the same coin. Making sense of the founders' role, both camps suggest, offers a key for unlocking the meaning of the historical American Revolution and what it still portends for contemporary society, either in its principled yet flawed success or its hypocritical failure. In the twenty-first century, even, as men and women march in protest of Barack Obama's policies, they claim to act in the name of the founders. As one puts it, "If you read our Founding Fathers, people like Benjamin Franklin and Jefferson, what we're doing in this country now is making them roll over in their graves." Another, a 26-year-old engineer, believes "that we are carrying on their tradition." If the founders "were around us today they would be in the streets with us, leading us, and they'd be even angrier than we are." He hastened to add, "I imagine we'd have to politely ask them to leave their muskets home."[7] These modern-day tea protesters, upset by taxes and the perceived growth of government, style themselves modern Samuel Adamses, standing against what they regard as tyranny as Adams once did. They take their inspiration from the memory of 1776 and of such men in an almost religious sense. Perhaps, as some scholars argue, the Tea Party gets the founders wrong. Franklin and Jefferson would not recognize themselves in what one prominent historian calls a movement defined by religious and political "fundamentalism."[8]

Such criticisms, however, miss the point of how and why these men and this date still serve as reference points for Americans of all stripes, including those who oppose the modern Tea Party movement. As another scholar suggests, the Tea Party conflates memory with history, in much the same way all Americans do, even prominent historians. That point of conflation centers on the founders.[9] Barack Obama himself makes the point in his book *The Audacity of Hope*. Obama writes that the words "We hold these truths to be self evident, that all men are created equal" stand as "our starting point as Americans." The Declaration lays out "not only the foundation of our government but the substance of our common creed." The document "orients us, sets the course, each and every day" despite the fact that the "Spirit of Liberty didn't extend, in the minds of the Founders, to the slaves who worked their fields, made their beds, and nursed their children." Frederick Douglass was right. The framers laid out the agenda but did not finish the task at hand. Each generation of Americans, Obama suggests, has to take up the mantle of freedom.[10] If Americans grasp the American Revolution, they understand who they are and what they should become.

America is not exceptional in this regard. All national histories contain any number of totemic dates and figures that we could liken to "vanishing points" in a painting. During the Renaissance, master painters began experimenting with perspective, eschewing older approaches and attempting to characterize depth on the canvas in three dimensions. They developed the idea of the vanishing point to represent the spot on the canvas where all three-dimensional points converge. At it, all space on the horizon created by the painter meets and disappears. It gives a piece a greater, more realistic, sense of depth. But greater perspective comes with a price. The older methods allowed the viewer to see the whole more effectively. The eye could wander. Not so for the vanishing point. It commands attention to fixed places on the canvas, making other aspects of experience unseeable. The "American Revolution" serves as a national vanishing point, and within that story, all meaning converges at 1776. All debate about what it means to be an American revolves around this date and the men who brought it into being. Narratives and the arguments historians create to make sense of events and processes begin and end here, as the year becomes a problem to be explained, a riddle to solve. All experience in the distant past beckons to it, and all subsequent experience emerges from it. The year 1776 as America's historical vanishing point proves alluring and difficult from which to escape, and as such, the founders play disproportionately large roles in American civic life, standing in as proxies for the vanishing point.[11]

The preoccupation with vanishing points comes at a cost. It blinds the viewer to what America's revolution was. While the "American Revolution" focuses the eye on historical and enduring ideas, conflict, and tensions, America's revolution revolved—literally—around a dynamic process, one with a starting point, an endpoint, and an uncertain middle. These phases or aspects were not isolated. Indeed, one only makes sense in light of the others, since each was informed by all, and all were animated by each. The origins and progression of revolution shaped possible outcomes. The ends reflected the ways revolution started and how it unfolded. The way it began and how it ended were bridged by the nature of what occurred between the two. Vanishing points cannot do justice to such complexity.

Understanding America's revolution as revolution requires a different perspective. Fortunately, the world of art provides another useful model. During the Middle Ages, painters employed the form of the triptych to convey the idea that the individual parts only made sense within the entire composition. The triptych consists of three distinct images, divided by folds but bound together as one. Each image retains its own integrity. Juxtaposed, however, the pieces take on deeper significance, and the meaning of one can only be comprehended within the context of the others. In this way, the unity of the images as a whole is always offset by the division along the folds into three, adding to overall complexity of what should be seen as a panorama. Thus, the central painting animates those on either side of the fold, while those on the side make the central image intelligible.[12]

This book charts a simple narrative of revolution by drawing an American triptych. It examines three aspects of America's revolution—a British beginning, an uncertain middle, and American endings—as well as the ideas, tensions, and conflict implicit in each. These aspects can stand alone; but when viewed together, they take on new meanings and force us to reconsider the whole. This book explores how the beginning, middle, and end of America's revolution, each phase in dynamic relationship with the others, brought the idea of America into being.

Seeing America's revolution as a triptych points toward a more hidden, contested history, one less self-evidently about enduring preoccupations. The significance of focusing on revolutionary process does not lie in resurrecting the fortunes of the forgotten or unknown people who fought, suffered, and sacrificed during the revolution. We know these "other" founders exerted power. The question process forces us to confront is how and why and to what effect men and women negotiated a turbulent era and struggled with forces that threatened to overwhelm in a moment between the fall of British and the rise of American authority. Viewing revolution as triptych helps illustrate how America would travel full circle from one set of animating ideals and myths to another. In other words, this does not mean that we have to ignore vanishing points, far from it. For those mythic moments that people took to be realities lay at the heart of the origins and outcome of revolution. Although British and American vanishing points, they still demand explanation. In other words, only by seeing revolution for what it was can the viewer make sense of the difficult transition from British subjecthood to American citizenship, as well as the myths associated with each.

In one sense this book will explore the enduring tensions over how Americans define themselves by moving beyond them. It will try to separate out the content of revolution—the powerful ideas that animated actors and the contradictions that consume Americans even today—from process. Between 1763 and 1800, Americans tossed on a tempestuous sea of uncertainty and violence. Class conflicts erupted. Armies marched through cities and countryside. New voices emerged, proclaiming new ideas about liberty. Men killed each other. Some regions descended into the violent abyss. In others, bloodshed mattered less than principled battles between haves and have-nots. Americans confronted and created such chaos as sovereignty collapsed in America. The years 1763 to 1800 marked the start and end of a process by which Americans struggled to act in a world without limits.

The revolution began over an idea, the idea of sovereignty: the shape or form ultimate power should take, where it was to be located, and just as importantly, the justifications for each. It ended there as well. All sorts of ideas, many contradictory, supported the idea of sovereignty, and fueled and reflected the nature of the revolutionary process. It did not remain unchanged. In the 1770s, American subjects embraced a notion of sovereignty that could not sustain authority or contain social reality. By about 1800, they had created the conditions for a notion that could. The tensions did not go away. But the ways of ordering those tensions had changed.

This is all understandable. After all, revolution, certainly as early modern men and women understood it, meant revolving from one point of reference back to it. Johannes Kepler first used the term to describe the elliptical movement of celestial bodies around the sun. By the eighteenth century, men and women still understood the term this way. In his famous dictionary of the English language, Samuel Johnson defined revolution as the "course of any thing which returns to the point at which it began to move."[13] Revolution, of course, transformed the cultural and social landscape. The journey began and ended with sovereignty.

Such a process defined American experience from 1763 until 1800. Men and women living during those years witnessed—and participated in—the fracturing of British sovereignty, the competition to remake it, and the reimposition of American order. Americans have focused on labels with which to identify villains and heroes or winners and losers: American vs. British; founder vs. common folks; patriot vs. loyalist; Federalist vs. anti-Federalist; black vs. white; men vs. women; Indian vs. settler. Reliance on these labels as the bases to understand the sum total of the revolution, however, obscures what was really at work. Lost are the period's uncertainties, chaos, dismembering violence, and vacillation. Lost also are ways to account for the staying power of foundational myths. Only by examining the revolution's process can we make sense of what looks to us like an ambivalent settlement that would make America appear exceptional. In general, all revolutions are created equal; the particulars—the ways sovereignty breaks down, the nature of competition to remake it, and the settlement that follows—cohere to the distinctive characteristics of the society in which the process takes place. As do the myths of a revolution's origins and its outcomes. In other words, the readiest explanations of what is conventionally called exceptionalism come into focus by viewing revolution in an unexceptional light.

The revolutionary process, therefore, figures as the forgotten centerpiece of an American triptych. From the perspective of either side of the folds, origins and outcomes can stand alone, but in light of the middle, each takes on more elaborate meanings. The simple themes of each panel collide or merge with the others, creating a narrative. The upshot is that viewing America's revolution in such a light challenges the search for conventional vanishing points.

What follows are many of the conventional stories of America's revolution told in unconventional fashion. The book begins with how sovereignty crumbled in America in the years leading up to 1774. Over the course of the eighteenth century, Americans were rooting their collective sense of self in the ideals of Britishness, the sets of ideas and practices that men and women in the British Isles invoked to conceive of themselves as distinctive. What they failed to make sense of were its complex underpinnings and political implications. The distance between cultural realities and political expectations fractured British authority. Moreover, different regions in America experienced the process of becoming British in different ways. British identity, in other words, could obscure distinctive tensions lurking beneath. Finally, the process was not consensual or straightforward. The archipelagic template officials would employ to make America British—or how Ireland, Scotland, and England became Britain—was underwritten through a history of conquest. On one level, the years of crisis before the Declaration of Independence witnessed a transatlantic dialogue over what it meant to be British and how Americans would become part of the British nation. Local social controls and institutions foundered in the process, exacerbating tensions in American communities. Imperial sovereignty collapsed amid the din of domestic turmoil.

The second part of the book explores the ways in which American society fell apart at its seams, as men and women, many before voiceless, began to act in self-sovereign ways in a world without meaningful political sovereignty. As people took on the role of actors, distinctive and competing programs to reestablish sovereignty in a fallen world emerged. The war years revolved around this competitive and complex process. The War of Independence did not only represent a distinct phase of America's revolution; it also brought coherence to ideas and social tensions. In some regions, it ordered violence. In other regions, it muted violence. In others still, it amplified violence. Men and women from different regions, with distinctive fault lines, experienced the maelstrom of revolution differently. The disorder of revolution took on different guises as social controls melted away in a world without sovereignty. Ideas mattered a great deal, insofar as men and women used the principles available to make sense of what was happening and to offer prescriptions for tumult. Ideas and social tensions were not at odds. They went hand in hand as Americans negotiated uncertainty and chaos.

To be a revolution, as Kepler and Johnson appreciated, means that orbits must come to an endpoint. Tensions do not vanish, like points in a painting, but are given new justifications or are reordered. The third and final part of the book examines the negotiations—some spirited and violent, others less pronounced—to bring order back to a society that had ceased to be. The end of the process witnessed broad consensus emerging on the meanings of citizenship, political economy, the role of regional variation within the whole, the limits of political discourse, and, of course, the nature of sovereignty. Agreement over these broad issues entailed writing some out of the national narrative. Although the so-called founders played critical roles in this end-game, this is not a simple story of wealthy overawing the lower sort, or of white over black. Nor is it a story of the triumph of the virtuous and their ideals. Both of these stories comprise part of a broader whole. The tale of how Americans arrived at the vanishing point of the founders' 1776 proves as tangled as anything that came before. It is an enigmatic story, less of triumph, than of a settlement becoming truly American, a settlement that captured and canonized the new nation's many contradictions. This was as much America's revolution as the "American Revolution."

ACKNOWLEDGMENTS

Because this book is not your standard monograph but, to borrow a phrase from the great historian of Atlantic revolution R. R. Palmer, aspires to be at once a work of "historical synthesis" and narrative history, it relies on the rich scholarship done over the past generation on the American Revolution, Atlantic revolutions and the Atlantic world, global history, provincial culture, colonial America, the early republic, Native American history, and the Irish and British early modern period. I owe my colleagues in all of these fields—and many more—a great debt. I also owe a word of thanks to Jim Martin. A number of years ago, Jim approached me to work together on revising a book he had written a few decades earlier on the American Revolution and asked me to work on a first draft. When that work began to take the shape of the present book, after I had written some chapters, and it did not appear that it would stand as a revision, we decided to part ways amicably. I thank Jim for his kindness, generous spirit, his thoughts on the project, and his graciousness. I apologize to him for any misunderstandings. A number of people helped me shape the narrative for the book. The broad outline and idea of revolutionary process are loosely based on my book *American Leviathan*, but the first chance I had to amplify my ideas and apply them to the broader Revolution was in a class on Atlantic Revolutions that I co-taught with Sophia Rosenfeld at the University of Virginia. Sophie was patient enough to listen to some of my more silly formulations (as were the students), but more critically she encouraged me to think about revolution comparatively. At UVA I profited immensely from the insights of a number of scholars who offered their thoughts on my project at earlier stages. These include Brian Balogh, Gary Gallagher, Paul Halliday, Andrew O'Shaughnessy, George Van Cleve, and most especially my dear friend Peter Onuf. The inspirations that Peter's thoughts provided are strewn throughout these pages. A group of historians and friends at Notre Dame commented on sections of the manuscript, for which I am most grateful. Kathleen Cummings, Tom Cummings, John McGreevy, and Mark Noll offered solid, critical ideas that helped me frame the questions I was pursuing. At Notre Dame, I was fortunate to work with a number of talented graduate students, three of whom offered to serve as research assistants for the project. My deep appreciation goes to Myles Beaupre, Peter Choi, and Joshua Kercsmar. I cannot say enough about each of these fine, young scholars, but Josh deserves a special word of praise. His work on this project was extraordinary and his enthusiasm was infectious. The institution that hires him will be a lucky one indeed. In addition, Nicholas Canny, Bruce Steiner, and most particularly Tim Breen and Robert Ingram offered their thoughts over the years on a number of themes that I flesh out in the narrative. At times, I fear I have tried Tim and Robert's patience. The book would not be what it is without their thoughtfulness, their sound scholarly judgment, and their friendship.

Many of the arguments of *America's Revolution* were presented at various professional meetings and other venues. I also gave talks at the following institutions where I discussed themes that I develop in the book: the Institute for Historical Research at the University of London; Trinity College Dublin; the Moore Institute at the National University of Ireland, Galway; University of Oxford; the University of Aberdeen; Northwestern University; Ohio University; the University of Virginia; and my home institution, the University of Notre Dame. Oxford University Press proved a wonderful outfit with which to publish a book. I thank Brian Wheel especially for his patience and sound judgment and David Wharton for his work with the production team. I also owe a debt to the (many) readers of the manuscript, expert in a great many subfields, for their comments and criticisms: Kathryn Braund, Ben Carp, Edward Crowther, Rebecca Goetz, Sally Hadden, David Porter, Walter Sargent, Scott Smith, and Donna Spindel. Ben's comments were especially thoughtful. I thank him for the time and energy he put into the manuscript.

It has been a joy to see my family grow as this book developed. My thanks to Michael, Liam, Maggie, and Annie in ways that are impossible to put into words. Each of them is a delight, though a trying delight at times, and I am the proudest of fathers. So as to avoid the risk of seeming maudlin (which, as a rule, I eschew), I'll stop there. They know what they mean to my work and my life. I'd also like to give a special shout-out to my nieces, Reagan and Cailyn. I did not leave you out of the acknowledgements this time! I am also grateful for the good counsel and support of their mother—my sister Joan—and, of course, the example my mother, Johanna Griffin, has provided. The dedication speaks for itself. It does not require another syllable, except to tell you, the reader, that the woman to whom the book is dedicated is my wife.

PNG

꙰

PART I

The Beginning

Britons

In 1771, an American painter living in London hoped to turn a myth into reality, and in so doing, produced something revolutionary. In that year, Benjamin West unveiled at the Royal Academy a piece called *The Death of General Wolfe*. On the sprawling canvas, West cast a diminutive 32-year-old British commander, James Wolfe, as national messiah. In 1759, Wolfe had fallen defeating the marquis de Montcalm in the Battle of Quebec, a moment that secured for the British supremacy of North America in the Seven Years' War. For dying in such heroic fashion and winning a North American empire, the British public canonized Wolfe. In this regard, West did not choose a daring subject or event to portray. Yet by portraying the scene in the manner in which he did, West caused a sensation in England. King George III considered the painting unseemly, as did the reigning doyen of epic painting, Sir Joshua Reynolds, who thought it ill-conceived. The costumes gave pause. In the painting, West dressed Wolfe and the figures surrounding him in contemporary clothing. George III, clinging to conventions of the day, argued that a man of Wolfe's heroic stature should be clothed in classical garb. Advocating a sense of aesthetics based on what could be called a philosophical history, one that rested on general principles of the "grand" and eschewed "the detail of particular," Reynolds went so far as to advise West as he was painting the piece to change the costumes. Wolfe had, after all, literally embodied the "comprehensive" or universal virtues of sacrifice and loyalty that Britons believed had animated the Roman Republic and hoped would animate their nation.[1]

West ignored Reynolds's warning. *The Death of General Wolfe* made the startling point that for virtue, honor, and sacrifice, Britons had to look no further than their own nation at the present moment. So his figures look as if they emerged from the classical world in the military fashion of the day. As West argued, "the same truth that guides the pen of the historian should govern the pencil of the artist." In "undertaking to tell this great event to eye of the world," he wondered if he needed the inspiration of the classical world: "If instead of the facts of the transaction, I represent classical fictions, how shall I be understood by posterity?"[2] Britons, West suggested, had taken up the civilizing mantle of ancient Rome. Eventually George III and Reynolds became enthusiastic supporters of West and his painting. With time, West became a court painter, as well as the king's confidante, and George III would commission his own copy of *The Death of General Wolfe*. Reynolds came to believe it would usher in a new approach for graphically interpreting the past. With the grand reception of *The Death of General Wolfe*, West became eighteenth-century Britain's most celebrated artist. He helped usher in a new generation of artists whose work focused on imperial and public themes and less on the mercantile, a sensibility that led also to the founding of the Royal Academy. More to the point, in memorializing Wolfe as he had, West had struck a deep cultural chord in a nation, whose people believed that—perhaps—Britons had bettered the Romans in achieving empire without losing their virtue.[3]

It took an American to make this point. West, who came from relatively modest beginnings, had left provincial Pennsylvania years earlier to make a name for himself in the teeming metropole. In Pennsylvania, he enjoyed the patronage of William Smith, the Scottish born professor at the Academy in Philadelphia, as well as of the city's leading light, Benjamin Franklin. But in London, he could ply his trade in the service of men who ran an empire, including the king who eventually sat for him. Like many provincials, he yearned to establish his reputation in the center, hoping to demonstrate that the Britain he captured on the canvas included the subjects who, like him, lived in the peripheries.

The Death of General Wolfe revolves around a vision of Britishness as seen from the margins. If the painting resembles a Pietà, it is a secular and nationalist one. Wolfe,

Figure I.1 Benjamin West, *The Death of General Wolfe*, 1770. National Gallery of Canada, Ottawa.

almost like a fallen Christ beneath the cross of St. George on the King's Colors, lies at the center of the composition. Around him stand three figures cradling the fallen general almost like Mary held the dead Christ: the Irishman Isaac Barré; a Scottish physician named John Adair; and Hervey Smyth, an English aide. Barré, a member of Ireland's established Protestant Church, would sit in Britain's parliament. Adair presumably would have been educated in Edinburgh or Glasgow, the leading universities for medical training in the British Isles, and as such would most likely have been a Presbyterian lowlander.[4] The Englishman Smyth served as an officer in the war and would after it produce well-known prospects of British-ruled Quebec. Britannia in the person of Wolfe, then, is upheld by the three kingdoms that comprise the nation: England, Scotland, and Ireland. Each of these characters embodies the ideals that lay behind Britishness at the moment West was painting. To be an Irish Protestant or an educated Lowland Scot entitled one, in theory, to the full rights of subjecthood that an English elite enjoyed. In 1770, these were a people Protestant, commercial, maritime, and free, the ideals that made Britons a distinctive and chosen people, virtues that would be reborn in their fullness in the wake of Wolfe's sacrifice.[5]

At the right of the painting stand an English Grenadier and Wolfe's servant. In one sense, the positioning speaks of status and what we could call class today. The battlefield did not break down the hierarchies that animated British society; indeed, life in the army brought differences in status into even sharper relief. To be an officer, or to occupy the center of the canvas, entailed being a gentleman. The grenadier and the servant are separated, yet also heir to British liberties. Although not part of the political nation—neither would have held enough land to vote for parliamentary elections, for instance—they were virtually represented and so merited inclusion in the painting. Britain did, after all, grow from England in the past, and the ideas of Englishmen, as well as the sacrifice of the common sort, lay at the heart of the ideas that made Britain what it had become.

In another vein, this grouping plays a critical role in the balance of the piece. For, to the left West has gathered in front of an English brigadier a few Americans and a highlander. General Robert Monckton, an Englishman with an Irish title, had helped suppress rebellion in Highland Scotland before serving in North America during the war and playing a leading role in the conquest of Quebec. During his time of service, he had the responsibility of clearing Nova Scotia of its Acadian inhabitants. Those former French subjects, who would acquiesce to British authority, such as the Catholics of conquered Quebec, could with time be considered British subjects. Not so for the Acadians. The British initiated a plan to "destroy all those settlements by burning down all their houses, cutting their dykes, and destroying all the grain growing," after which the Acadians would be "transported they know not whither."[6] Scattered throughout the North American colonies because of their refusal to swear loyalty to a Protestant British king, these French Catholics were deemed beyond the bounds the subjecthood and thus beyond redemption.[7]

Two of the men before Monckton chose a different path. The highlander wears a Fraser tartan, and most likely is Captain Simon Fraser. Simon Fraser came from Inverness, a center of Jacobitism. Earlier in the eighteenth century, Jacobites, as they were labeled, had supported the exiled and Catholic King James II, who as a Stuart was a fellow Scot. During the Glorious Revolution, many highlanders including

Frasers had rallied to the cause of James as he fought for the British Crown against his Protestant Dutch son-in-law William of Orange. Twice during the eighteenth century, Highland clans had risen against the state to reinstitute Stuart rule. And in 1745 and 1746, they were crushed—indeed, some would say massacred—by that state right near Fraser's hometown. Fraser was, therefore, an outlier in Britain. For many, highlanders, as supporters of other claimants to the throne and as uncivilized men and women, lay beyond the Pale of subjecthood. In many respects, they were the Acadians of Great Britain, a people separated from civilized England by culture and in some cases religion. And many of these people had been cleared off their lands in Scotland for their political allegiances and backwards ways in the years leading up to the Seven Years' War. The Fraser portrayed here, however, has opted to surrender his Highland customs, at least most of them, for loyalty to king and nation and had fought valiantly throughout the Seven Years' War for the British state.[8]

So, too, the man portrayed next to the Scot. On his powder horn West inscribed the name William Johnson.[9] Born a Catholic in Ireland to a Jacobite family dispossessed by the English conquest of the kingdom, William Johnson migrated to the American frontier, established himself as a fur trader, and converted to Protestantism. Through a shrewd cultivation of connections, he had created a network of powerful patrons stretching from New York to London. Johnson would then gain renown in the war, becoming its first public hero for leading a combined Indian-British force in the battle for Crown Point, in the process, earning a baronetcy. This man born to the wrong Irish faith tradition had made the transition to Britishness. Presumably, Sir William Johnson's former coreligionists in Ireland could as well. The fruits of empire could be theirs if they chose the path of Fraser and Johnson rather than the one of the Acadians. This was no idle promise. Indeed, more than half of Britain's American army in the French and Indian War was comprised of Irish and Scots.[10]

The Indian sits in an enigmatic pose at the bottom of the canvas. We could think of him as the proverbial "noble savage" striking a thinkerlike pose. Or we could see him as a potential subject as well. The Indian represented in the painting is most likely modeled on a Mohawk named Hendrick, who had been killed a few years earlier in the war. Although two Hendricks lived during the eighteenth-century, West conflated them, creating an image of an Indian warrior allied to William Johnson. The imagined Hendrick had traveled with a Mohawk delegation to England early in the century and met Queen Anne. He was also Protestant, had died fighting for the British during the Seven Years' War, and was often portrayed wearing British clothes. He was, in essence, created as a British Indian and an icon for the war.[11] If the path to British subjecthood lay open to others beyond the Pale so long as they reformed their ways, in theory Indians could become subjects. Although considered at the time savages, and portrayed this way by West, they in fact differed little from Irish Catholics and highlanders. Look again at Fraser and Johnson. Each wears the clothing of what the viewer could consider "wood's dwellers," that is savages, or barbarians. While Fraser is adorned with the kilt, the symbol of the clan and of the pastoral economy, Johnson wears Indian leggings, the kind of clothing ideally suited for warfare and travel in the woods, and the outfit of an American ranger, the sort of light infantry that the British developed over the course of the war. Wearing a green coat, not a red one, for camouflage, with his tricorne shorn of its brim, he is dressed for irregular warfare. But his savagery, like Fraser's barbarism, is turned to the benefit of the state. The same holds true for the Mohawk. Although seated at the bottom of the scene, he can presumably ascend the ladder of civility to the level of the Irishman and then the Scot, both of whom stand above him.[12]

The lesson is clear. The promise of Britishness can be theirs as well. Note how the brightness comes from their direction, pushing the smoke of war away from the English grouping on the right. Here ships lie waiting to resume their civilizing trade once more. A steeple appears in the background. The tools of war lay strewn on the ground. Peace will bring British order, stability, and civility. The images and figures portend what is to come as they canonize the present and sanitize the past. The figures of Johnson and Fraser point not only to the herald delivering news of victory but also to the empire's glorious future. These men may have served as savages or barbarians in the service of empire, but in so doing, and by surrounding the soon-to-be risen Wolfe, they earn a place that the lower sort on the right have already secured.

The only subjects missing are typical American colonists of English descent, the sort of men and women who accounted for the majority of people who lived in Britain's North American colonies from New England as far south as the Caribbean. Then again, West himself, the man who presents the viewer with this mythic conception of the new British nation, best represents the place of Americans within the nation. Indeed, as Britain's most celebrated painter, his experience would suggest that Americans, as much as Protestant Irishman and Lowland Scots, had earned a place in the mythic scene. Or, to put a finer point on it, they did not merit it on their own; Wolfe's redemptive death secured their place. West's whole backdrop, of course, is America. British valor, and Wolfe's sacrifice, had won a continent. America was the future, and an American Briton memorializes this hope.

For West, this painting spoke to what he regarded as profound truths. No doubt, he took liberties with the actual account of the battle. Some of these participants, like Johnson, had not fought at Quebec. Barré, shot in the eye during the attack, was nowhere near Wolfe as he fell. But searching for literal accuracy misses the fact that for Barré, Fraser, Johnson, Wolfe, and West, this representation of the recent past shed light on present realities. In 1763, the year the Treaty of Paris was signed formally ending the war, to be British could be summed up in West's masterpiece. It laid out the present realities, as well as the bright future, one that included America at its center. In the painting, and in Wolfe's historical imagination, England's past confronted a British present and an American future. As much as his daring use of contemporary dress, this vision proved revolutionary.

CHAPTER 1

O Happy Country! Happy Kingdom!

The origins of the American Revolution would seem self-evident. After 1763, British officials finally took notice of American colonies 3,000 miles away that they had ignored through an official attitude of "a wise and salutary neglect," an approach underscored by the idea that "the colonies owed little or nothing to any care of [Britain's]."[1] Corrupt ministries saw opportunities for tapping underexploited wealth and so trampled on the liberties that Americans believed they were entitled to. Colonists, then, stood up for their rights against a corrupt Parliament and eventually a corrupt Crown. Doing so required nothing more than "simple facts, plain arguments, and common sense." After all, "there is something very absurd, in supposing a continent to be perpetually governed by an island."[2] The two men who uttered these famous phrases—the Irish-born parliamentarian Edmund Burke and the English corset-maker turned professional radical Thomas Paine—would grow to hate each other, especially after the opening stages of the French Revolution. But in the 1760s and 1770s, the two agreed upon a great deal, particularly the rights and status of Americans within the British system. As Paine argued, "From the part Mr Burke took in the American Revolution, it was natural that I should consider him a friend to mankind."[3] Both believed that before the Seven Years' War, Americans had enjoyed a virtual independence and that their status became increasingly constraining after the war.

If we start our exploration of revolution from this premise and from this moment, it is easy to assume that Americans arrived at independence almost inevitably, that Paine's plea for "common sense" naturally sprung from Burke's idea of "salutary neglect," punctuated only by the seemingly inevitable litany of act after intolerable act. In fact, such a telling of the great imperial fracture with its breaking point at 1763 is an American tale, mixing myth and reality. The British did not neglect the colonies, certainly not during the eighteenth century. Nor did Americans consider independence commonsensical—quite the opposite, in fact. In the eighteenth century, most Americans celebrated their ties to Britain. Britishness was self-evident. Understanding the crisis that would lead to independence, therefore, entails explaining not how and why the colonies were primed to break away from Britain

but how and why Americans were connected to Britain before 1763. Ironically, probing these connections requires turning from considerations central to American
identity—the quest for independence—to how Americans were coming to resemble
subjects in West's painting, a narrative far more complex than the simple story of
Paine and Burke.

Take the case of a famous family of planters in the colonies. In 1704, the Byrds
from Virginia found themselves in the midst of a transition that was gripping each of
the colonies. In that year, William Byrd I died, and his son, William Byrd II, inherited his estate. The death marked the transition from an English to a British Virginia.
William I, who had come to Virginia in the 1660s from England and received a
grant of land through London connections, comprised part of a generation of planters and traders that had tried to transform an American wilderness into something
resembling an English society. He soon made the most of his opportunity, earning a
small fortune by investing in the fur trade with Indians from the piedmont region of
Virginia and the Carolinas. Like many of his neighbors, who had survived the early,
difficult phase of settlement, he also imported indentured servants from England to

Figure 1.1 Hans Hysing, *William Byrd II*. ca. 1724. Virginia Historical Society.

work on his tobacco plantation. The Virginia of William I was English, a corrupted one in terms of metropolitan standards, but English nonetheless. From these relatively rough-hewn beginnings, William II then steered a course for polite gentility. Byrd traveled to England for his education, studying at Middle Temple where he was admitted to the bar. He collected the latest books published in the metropole on a dizzying array of subjects, and before he died, he had amassed the largest library in the colonies. Eventually, William Byrd II became one of Virginia's most influential men and perhaps the colony's leading devotee of all things British.

William Byrd II tried as best he could to turn his Virginia into Britain. While his father had helped create an English world in an America isolated by an ocean, the son tried to reestablish the transatlantic connection by turning a saltwater barrier into a highway and tapping into the cultural currents uniting the kingdoms of England, Scotland, and Ireland.[4] He and Virginia emerged from a planter phase to one defined by Atlantic dynamics and British cultural standards.[5] He emulated all things English like other British provincials, particularly the Protestant Irish and lowland Scots. He wore the latest fashions from London, employing a consignment agent in London to ship his tobacco to England and to send the latest consumer goods to him. For decades, he maintained a correspondence with some of the keenest minds in England. He even published a few books, one a humorous piece of his work drawing a dividing line between Virginia and North Carolina. He dabbled in science and on a daily basis read Latin and Greek. Eventually, in recognition of his interests and accomplishments in science and natural history he was named a fellow of Britain's Royal Society. His contributions, he hoped, would "benefit my country" and prove "useful to Great Britain."[6]

With time, he styled himself a natural leader of the colony, serving for a short time in the House of Burgesses and for a much longer spell on the Royal governor's council, the one institution that more than any other represented the Crown in the colony. A man of the British Enlightenment, he represented a generation of rising elites in the colonies, men who by birth and inclination stood poised to bring a rustic America more securely into a British cultural orbit. He took these cultural responsibilities seriously. The rising tide of Irish migration into his colony troubled him, leading him to fear that they would overtake English stock like "the Goths and Vandals of old."[7] On the other hand, he encouraged "industrious" Germans to settle on lands that he owned, hoping that their arrival would drive up the prices of his lands. With time, he believed they would "be accounted the kings natural subjects."[8] He also believed that a simple, unadorned and unenthusiastic Anglicanism—the sort favored by England's elite—should serve as the official religion of the colony, and he tended to look down on effusive expressions of religiosity, especially those associated with a growing number of itinerant ministers preaching redemption through Christ.

Byrd may have wanted to style himself British, but he was also an American patriarch. He constructed his great brick house, Westover, to demonstrate his status as a wealthy Virginian and as a Briton. Like wealthy Irishmen and Scots, Byrd modeled Westover on English Georgian great houses of the period. Situated on the James River near Virginia's first English settlement, it conveyed permanence. Fittingly, Westover, unlike similar houses in England, was surrounded by "dependencies," small structures dotting the landscape built to house his slaves.[9] Byrd owned more slaves than nearly any other Virginian; in fact, during his lifetime Virginia and other colonies in the South would change from societies with slaves to "slave societies," colonies in which the institution of slavery and the repression of slaves dominated economic, political, and cultural life. And he could be a cruel master. On one occasion, when a slave named Eugene was caught wetting the bed, Byrd had him drink "a pint of piss" as a remedy. He slapped his slave Jenny for throwing water on the couch. He also reported that his wife burned Jenny "with a hot iron" and beat her with tongs.[10]

Byrd also ruled over the women of his life as a patriarch. While he elevated his wife on a pedestal, he also ensured that on his plantation woman's work would be performed by slave women. He frequented brothels and preyed on maidservants. Earlier in his life, when he had traveled to England, trying to entice well-born English women to take his hand in marriage, he also trolled the streets at night for prostitutes. Moreover, he took advantage of the slave women in his midst, a pattern that more conspicuously defined relations between master and slave in South Carolina and Jamaica.[11]

In 1744 when he died, most in his small world regarded him as one of Virginia's leaders and the epitome of a refined British provincial subject. His son, William Byrd III, initially followed the path laid out by his father. True to his station, he served in the Virginia House of Burgesses and as a colonel in a Virginia regiment in the Seven Years' War. While one of Virginia's elite, he too considered himself a Briton.

Over the course of the eighteenth century, America followed the course set out by the Byrds. About the time the first William Byrd arrived from England, the colonies up and down the coast resembled English settler societies more than anything else.[12] By and large, the descendants of Englishmen and women had peopled the colonies. Moreover, English-style social structures, religious traditions, law, and markets, as well as English cultural assumptions characterized the colonies, stretching from New England in the north to places like Barbados in the south. Although Dutch, Germans, and Irish also sailed to the colonies, the movement of English people and traditions across the ocean dominated the seventeenth century. Settlers like William Byrd I did not succeed in re-creating England in the New World, however hard they tried. Rather, they fashioned local variations on an English rule, each different from the other and with its own distinctive tensions but bound together by the same broad English settlement dynamic. Not so for the eighteenth century.

Although William Byrd II inherited a world that appeared in some fundamental form English, his Virginia little resembled the English colonies of Massachusetts, New York, or Pennsylvania. It even differed a great deal from South Carolina and Jamaica. But he would live to see the day when distinctive English colonial legacies were being reforged into more uniform provincial British identities. In many ways as the eighteenth century progressed, the American colonies would differ little from Scotland or Ireland. In fact, a process of what we could call "becoming British" defined America's eighteenth century, as English colonies up and down the Atlantic coast and into the Caribbean, yoked to one another through the English center, would be integrated into a larger Atlantic world and bound together as never before. The ideas and behaviors that had allowed the kingdoms of England, Scotland, and Ireland to coalesce as one state began to traverse the Atlantic, tying what were becoming American British provinces to the archipelago as never before.[13] This occurred for many related reasons. Migration from the peripheries of the Atlantic world—from Ireland, Scotland, and Germany—rose to unprecedented levels. By and large, these people moved to the Middle Colonies. To the South, societies that had slaves in the seventeenth century became slave societies, as planters imported men and women in chains directly from Africa to work tobacco and rice plantations. This forced labor integrated the colonies more fully into Atlantic trading networks and allowed masters to style themselves provincial Britons. Americans also became part of a broader consumer world, as they bought goods produced in the metropole and began to fashion themselves—literally—as British men and women. Americans also participated in a British world of ideas. To make sense of all these changes, Americans were embracing a new religiosity in much the same way some British men and women had. Finally, at the same time, their political structures were maturing and beginning to resemble British institutions.

It is tempting to see evangelical sensibilities and a tradition of revivals, what we could call vital piety, as peculiarly American forms of religiosity. Similarly, we can make the leap of viewing conspicuous consumption as something essentially American. Or democratically based political institutions. And, of course, slavery would seem a peculiarly American institution. In reality, each of these phenomena animated the broader Atlantic world of which America formed one part. Britain's institutions may not have been as democratic as, say, those of Massachusetts. However, the forms and tone appeared much the same. The consumer revolution first gripped England before it reached America. In a similar vein, itinerant preachers enjoyed great success in England, Scotland, and even Ireland, as did those who railed against them. Finally, Britain had few slaves, and in this regard was much like New England. But the slave societies of the Chesapeake and South Carolina had a great deal in common with Britain's Caribbean colonies. In fact, because the vast majority of work in the colonies and in the British Isles was done by bound labor in some form or another, America easily fit into the British Atlantic labor system.[14] Like all British societies, America was rife with social divisions. And like all British societies, America had its own peculiar tensions that defined it and with which it had to contend.

That said, in some ways America remained a place apart, owing by and large to the peculiar histories of settlement and the choices settlers made in the seventeenth century. For one thing, because of the past, race, not only class, represented a defining fissure in American society. This owed a great deal to vexed relations with Indians and the fact that planters bought Africans to work on plantations. Vital piety seemed to resonate more fully with Americans, especially those of a particular class or status caught in the grips of change in the cities and on the frontier. Moreover, the broad appeal of religious revival—indeed, the mania for it—could be construed as a distinctive American response to an Atlantic-wide process of becoming British. Similarly, goods had greater meanings beyond mere utility. They came to epitomize how many Americans fashioned themselves, not only in terms of status but also in terms of affiliation with the British state, and because of the basic parity in American society, a product of history, British goods appealed to nearly all. So broad dynamics resonated in a distinctive way in America. Finally and most critically, men and women experienced and articulated these trends differently in different colonies. Regional variation, a product of history, tempered Britishness.

The ties that bound America to Britain in 1763 were not political per se. Rather, they appeared, as Burke famously put it, like threads of affection and commerce "light as air."[15] By the time Wolfe defeated Montcalm on the Plains of Abraham, America was not so much an amalgamation of outposts in the English Atlantic as British provinces much like Ireland and Scotland, places separated from England and the archipelagic provinces politically yet part of that cultural world. By the end of the Seven Years' War, breaking away from Britain proved unthinkable; rather, celebrating Britishness made sense. Shared Britishness was not a veneer. It was deeply felt and widely articulated. Yet it did overlay regional variations, as well as local social tensions rooted in the seventeenth century, tensions neither reordered nor newly rationalized by making America British.

We often talk of America as a place. But "America" really resembled more a collection of places in the eighteenth century. True, each of these places had changed a great deal since their founding, but "America," aside from a geographic term, had little meaning. And "American," unless one was visiting the British Isles, had no meaning at all. The men and women who lived in the colonies called themselves Virginians, New Englanders, Pennsylvanians, and Barbadians. Many still referred to themselves by what could be called ethnic labels or the place they had left in the Old World: Dutch or Irish, for example. They called themselves and each other by their religious denominations: Presbyterian or Quaker. They even thought of themselves by the type of areas in which they lived—frontier, city, town—or by their status or by the sort of work that they did.

Although diverse, each of the colonies shared a similar past, and the gap between the commonalities and distinctiveness of earlier histories would have implications for how each would become British. Most English settlers hoped to build their own visions of English society in the New World. But the regions they landed in differed from one another in terms of climate and the indigenous peoples they encountered. Moreover, English settlers came over for different reasons with different assumptions, and different goals in mind. As English colonies sprang up in America and became stable, each was defined by distinctive tensions, divisions, and fault lines that would endure as English settler colonies became British provinces. American colonists, then, had many histories within a shared settlement process that would both shape who they were in the eighteenth century and would determine how they understood their sense of Britishness. In fact, aside from the example of the Irish, English, and Scots, one would be hard pressed to find groups of people, having a common political allegiance and cultural heritage, and who lived next to each other, who appeared so different.

England's earliest and most important colonies most closely resembled the metropole; they also diverged the most from metropolitan standards. Barbados, Jamaica, and the smaller islands of the Lesser Antilles, such as Nevis, Montserrat, St. Christopher, and Antigua, were dominated both by black enslaved labor and a tiny caste of wealthy whites who ruled over their slaves. Early on, settlers mainly from England, many working as indentured servants, struggled to produce an exploitable commodity until they fastened on sugar. Sugar transformed the islands.

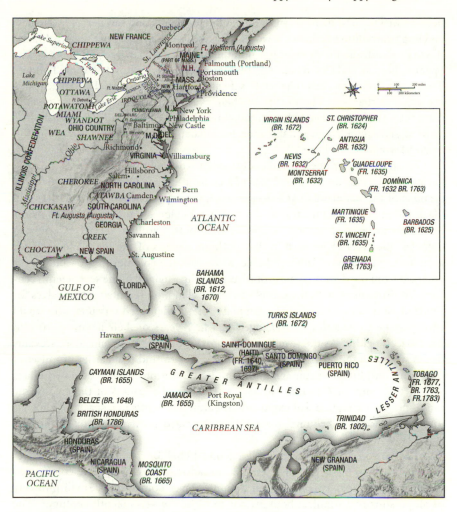

Map 1.1 The American Colonial World in the Eighteenth Century.

By the mid-seventeenth century, the voracious demand for manpower to work the fields and sugar factories led to the transformation of the labor force. Planters in Barbados began looking to Africa for the labor supply, and the other islands followed suit. Whereas other English colonies that would become slave societies had areas peopled by poorer whites, most of whom did not own slaves, the Caribbean did not.[16]

These became the richest New World holdings of the British, made integral to the metropolitan economy by the cultivation of a product consumed by nearly all Englishmen and women. The Caribbean was England's New World center. As writer Daniel Dafoe put it, "No *African* Trade, *no* Negroes; *no* Negroes, *no* Sugars...*no* Sugars, &c.; *no* Islands; *no* Islands, *no* Continent; *no* Continent, *no* Trade; that is to say, farewell all your *American* Trade."[17] However ruthless planters became, they hoped to transform tropical islands into genteel English societies. Or they hoped to become wealthy and then return to England. Hospitality and savagery, recklessness and English tradition defined the world they fashioned. Because of their wealth and ties to England, and the strategic position the islands played in a region populated by Spanish, French, and Dutch holdings, planters wielded substantial power in London. They employed agents in Whitehall to safeguard their interests, and absentee planters sat in Parliament. The duality of their existences underscored their greatest fears, fears that were related: that the small number of whites could be overrun by a growing slave population; and that their personal, military, and commercial links to England would be weakened.[18]

Far from outliers, these colonies defined broader colonial patterns. At the most basic level, the islands comprised part of a Greater English Caribbean that included sections of the mainland.[19] At a deeper level, the experience of white settlers and black slaves created templates for the mainland colonies, and the story of places like Barbados echoed in the Chesapeake and South Carolina. Like the Caribbean colonies, the early experience in the southern regions of the mainland revolved around the problems of labor and race. Moreover, the colonies in the Chesapeake emerged from the demographic problems gripping England in the seventeenth century. Virginia, along with the Caribbean and Ireland, represented safety valves for England. Masterless men could be shipped over as indentured servants, who would earn passage to America in exchange for 4 to 7 years of their labor, to work in the tobacco fields.[20] As the seventeenth century wore on, more and more servants began surviving the terms of their indentures only to find that earlier promises of land went unfulfilled, encouraging them to look west into regions held by Indians and in 1675 and 1676 to lash out against Indians, the leaders of the colony, the king, and a labor regime that exploited indentured servants in a spasm of violence known as Bacon's Rebellion.[21] Instability encouraged planters to look for a more stable labor force.

The period around the time of Bacon's Rebellion changed older arrangements, and Virginia began to resemble Barbados more closely. The colony also established its most salient cultural divides. Slaves comprised a small minority of all persons in Virginia, about 5% for most of the seventeenth century.[22] The late seventeenth century witnessed the transformation of Virginia into a slave society. The planters in Barbados, who were increasingly looking to Africa for slaves and who had instituted black or slave codes to privilege whites over blacks, seemed to have solved the labor issue. In 1684, William Byrd I hoped to import "men or lusty boys" from England but feared the price would be "too dear." Like other planters, he set his sights on Africans.[23] The Africanization of slavery, and the turn to a labor force dominated by slaves, seemed a logical solution to the colony's many woes.[24] The complex process also created a society of haves and have-nots based on race. Common whites now had a stake in society and tended not to challenge the wealthy elite rising in their midst. William Byrd II would live in a stable world, yet this stability would be achieved at a massive social and human cost.[25]

Farther south, the Greater Caribbean pattern of animating tensions held. South Carolina, founded by Caribbean planters—mostly English—who had left the islands to try to emulate the lives of their fathers and who had brought slaves with them, did not have a staple crop to exploit, until they fastened on rice. Rice initiated a plantation revolution in South Carolina, allowing and requiring planters to purchase increasing numbers of slaves from Africa. Soon regions of South Carolina, especially the low country around Charleston, were defined by the "black majority" toiling on rice plantations. Although the work regimen here was notoriously brutal, slaves also had enough physical distance from their masters—unlike the Chesapeake—to develop an African-American culture unmediated by a white world. In this region, despite the inhumanity of the institution of slavery, men and women adapted African folk and religious ways to create a sense of community among the uprooted from Africa.[26]

Relations with Indians in the southern colonies were also fraught. Virginians relentlessly destroyed Algonquian-speaking people in their midst, so that by 1700, few Indians lived east of the Mountains. In the Carolinas, similar patterns played out. As more and more planters and slaves entered the colony, Indians contested the movement, staging wars against the colony and against other groups of Indians who sought to take advantage of the arrival of the newcomers at the expense of others. North and South Carolina seized with Indian wars in the early eighteenth century, as settlers moved onto lands claimed by Indians, as aggressive traders vied with one another for access to Indians to the west, and as militias from the colonies fought side-by-side with new Indian allies against former trading partners. Throughout these tumultuous years, groups such as the Creeks sold captured enemies off as slaves to English settlements, and in doing so, engrafted English avarice onto Indian custom. These dislocations also helped pay for the transition to the enslavement of large numbers of Africans.[27] The tensions caused by war, European migration, and African forced migration led to the creation of new amalgams of people, such as the Catawbas, a group that survived the tumult of the period by uniting remnants of groups shattered by colonial and Indian aggression, as well as by diseases and dependency on fur traders.[28]

The colonies comprising New England—Massachusetts, including its outpost in the district of Maine and what had been Plymouth Plantation, as well as New Hampshire, Connecticut, and Rhode Island—were the outliers in the broader English Atlantic.[29] Here too settlers hoped to fashion English societies in new places, but in ways unlike the Greater Caribbean. By and large, the descendants of Puritans who had fled England in the early to mid-seventeenth century to create a "new" and more reformed version of England peopled the colonies.[30] They and their many descendants soon spread to adjacent regions, leading to bloody struggles between native and newcomer.[31] Yet with time, the New England settlements came to resemble the other colonies. As settlers moved beyond Massachusetts and as the population in the region grew through natural increase, more people meant rising prices for land and more demand for consumer goods.[32] At the dawn of the eighteenth century, the descendants of Puritan settlers had become, much like men and women in England, a rather "polite and commercial people."[33] By 1700, ships from New England were sailing about the Atlantic basin, bringing food, fish, and livestock grown, caught, and raised on New England's farms and seas to Europe and the Caribbean. With time in New England a series of port towns had developed that were supplied by farming hinterlands serving both the needs of such towns, as well as the places to which they traded. Further out, a few wealthy families ruled vast swaths of land almost like company towns. In town, country, and baronial frontier, as the eighteenth century dawned, wealthy men connected to a broader world of trade controlled the politics of the colonies. New England commercial success also spurred shipbuilding, insurance, and banking. Sending grain to the Caribbean also established the links that would make New England one leg of the infamous triangle trade involving sugar and slaves between Africa, the Caribbean, and New England.[34]

New England had become an English society with distinctive divisions. As affluence grew, so did incipient conflicts over status and wealth, particularly in port towns.[35] Port towns, which employed a mix of different people, represented the most diverse places in all of New England. Black slaves rubbed shoulders with Irish sailors, poor English-descended laborers, and the wealthy descendants of original Puritan settlers. Moreover, as changes gripped the region, the most fundamental assumptions about how society functioned began to change. Nowhere was this more pronounced than in the household. In the early years of settlement, men and women worked together in an economy centered on the household and one premised on subsistence and barter. In this system, women enjoyed visibility; their work had intrinsic meaning as it was valued by society. Following English metropolitan patterns, with the rapid shift to a market-based economy, and the attenuation of face-to-face community relations in favor of more impersonal forms, women lost their visibility.[36] New England, therefore, was becoming a world of opportunity and of looming tensions. Conflict remained rare, but with difficult times, it would not take much to unleash the pressures that were becoming more and more apparent as New England was becoming more and more prosperous. Although the original settlers had left the Old World to create a new England, their descendants had, in fact, fashioned a society that looked like old England.

The Middle Colonies—New York, New Jersey, Pennsylvania, and Delaware— proved even more fractious and energetic. Originally settled by the Dutch and controlled by the English after a series of mid-century wars, New York seethed with friction between English settlers and the Dutch who lived in the city and up the Hudson.[37] Following the New England model, as these places became English, fault lines became apparent. Up and down the Hudson River, families held land as tenants, as great patroons and English-speaking proprietors resisted selling land. Compared to other colonies, few were freeholders. New York was also embroiled in slave conspiracies, and in one horrific episode, a number of slaves were executed, accused—wrongfully—of helping to burn the town of New York City to the ground in 1741.[38] Tensions exploded from time to time, most memorably during the Glorious Revolution when King James II was deposed and the throne was assumed by his daughter Mary and son-in-law William of Orange. While the archipelago reeled with a crisis of sovereignty, in New York at issue were status, ethnicity, access to power, and regional differences.[39] After the Glorious Revolution, New York remained divided by factions, the most powerful of which were led by the merchant-landowning governor James DeLancey and his Presbyterian nemesis William Livingston.[40]

Relations on the frontier complicated a diverse cultural picture, particularly because the Iroquois, who enjoyed a virtual hegemony in the region, inhabited the edges of the colony. No group rivaled the Five Nations that had banded together into a confederation before Columbus had even landed, and they claimed much of the east as theirs by conquest. New Yorkers recognized the Five Nations or Iroquois League as power-brokers by signing onto what was called the "covenant chain." The covenant chain mandated that colonial governments not negotiate with smaller tribes but only with and through the Iroquois. In exchange, the Iroquois would police the frontier and keep it quiet. From time to time, the frontier seethed with violence, particularly between French allied Indians and their Iroquois enemies, but after 1701, with the signing of what was called the "Great Peace" ending that warfare, uneasy peace came to the frontier.[41] Because of endemic warfare in the Carolinas, the Tuscaroras would become the sixth nation of the Iroquois confederation. The Iroquois also attacked the strongest group in the region, the Cherokees. Nonetheless, the peace in Iroquoia underwritten by the covenant chain made the Iroquois the third great power in North America behind the English and the French. The strength of the Six Nations also amplified colonial New York's influence.

As in England, fractious politics defined the Middle Colonies. Pennsylvania, founded in 1681 by English Quakers as part of a "holy experiment," typifies this theme. This colony, which presented yet another aspect of seventeenth-century English culture, thrived because of an extraordinary network of merchants through-out the Atlantic world and a vast amount of land that could be sold to migrants from England, Ireland, and Wales, as well as the German Rhine Valley.[42] As one visitor put it, the taverns of the colony "buzzed" with many languages. "I dined att a taveren with a very mixed company of different nations and religions," he remembered. "There were Scots, English, Dutch, Germans, and Irish; there were Roman Catholicks, Church men, Presbyterians, Quakers, Newlightmen, Methodists, Seventh day men, Moravians, Anabaptists, and one Jew."[43] Diversity did not bring peace, but it did sustain stability. Like Englishmen at the time, Pennsylvanians were renowned for the bumptious quality of their political squabbles. As merchants in Philadelphia and settlers from the rich farming region of Bucks County grew wealthy from the trading connections to many parts of the world, poorer Quakers in Philadelphia, derisively called "the leather aprons" challenged rule by "their betters."[44]

Indians fared better in Pennsylvania than in nearly any other English colony. William Penn, the founder of the colony, made it his mission to treat Indians with respect, and although he and his successors especially placed increasing demands on Indians to sell land, Penn would be remembered by Indians in the region, particularly the Delaware, as a just man. Indeed, the Pennsylvania native Benjamin West wove Penn's legendary generosity into myth in a famous painting entitled *The Treaty of Penn with the Indians*. In it, the colony's founder, standing before bright skies and the fruits of civility, treats with Delawares emerging from the woods. Imagery aside, West's painting spoke to some truths. Penn welcomed Indian refugees from other regions, particularly groups that the Iroquois had displaced, offering them lands on which to settle so long as they cooperated with fur traders who worked for the wealthy officials of the colony. Soon groups like the Shawnees from the west and Nanticokes and Conoys from the south were settling along the Susquehanna River, all with the blessing of officials and the Iroquois, who extended the covenant chain to Pennsylvania in the early eighteenth century.[45]

Figure 1.2 Benjamin West, *Penn's Treaty*, 1771. Pennsylvania Academy of the Fine Arts.

By the first decades of the eighteenth century, the English New World colonies comprised a series of distinctive societies strewn up and down the Atlantic coast and extending into the Caribbean, hemmed in by the Appalachian Mountains to the west, that had little in common save their common English origins, the desire of settlers to try to re-create Old World customs in the New World, and the hybridized English societies that had emerged. Places ranging from Massachusetts to Montserrat still resembled settlement societies, and although they had negotiated similar crises in the seventeenth century that would define what sorts of societies they were poised to become in the eighteenth century, a recent past during which settlers believed that they were trying to civilize a savage natural world haunted them. West's painting of Penn and the Indians recognized these seventeenth-century legacies, though sanitizing anxieties with eighteenth-century myth. But as English aspirations encountered the challenges of a New World, these older visions began to metastasize into something different altogether, as American colonies had become bastardized almost archaic visions of an England that was quickly ceasing to be.[46] Nonetheless, they had grown stable, especially as the issues swirling around land and labor were resolved. Stability entailed authority and often oppression, and each society from New England, to New York and Pennsylvania, to the Chesapeake and the Greater Caribbean, was developing its own patterns of political relations and a homegrown elite. No doubt, tensions lurked beneath the surface. But one would have been hard-pressed to find what appeared to be more generally prosperous and orderly places anywhere in the world.

Over the course of the eighteenth century, these distinctive settler societies would become British. To some extent, the mainland colonies would follow the example of the Caribbean once more in becoming more closely tied to the center. In the mainland colonies, the transformation would begin with peoples, goods, and ideas. And it would end with the war that Benjamin West memorialized. The great transformation of an English America happened almost imperceptibly and is not the history of mythic events or great crises. The history of the eighteenth century entailed processes.

Although migration in the seventeenth century to mainland America and the Caribbean was dominated by Englishmen and women, in the eighteenth century those on the margins of the Atlantic world comprised the lion's share of peoples crossing the ocean. From 1717 until the American Revolution, at least 100,000 German-speaking men and women traveled from their homelands in the Rhine River Valley first to Dutch port towns, and then after reboarding ships in England to the Middle Colonies. While most Catholic Germans from the Palatinate traveled east to Hungary, Protestants—reformed, Lutheran, and members of smaller sects— looked to Pennsylvania, which offered opportunity for a people who lived in a world wracked by recession and war; it also offered religious toleration.[47]

Of course, these German-speakers were not British in an ethnic sense. But their local worlds already intersected the broader Atlantic world. In periods of peace, the goods they produced and the surpluses they grew were traded throughout the Atlantic via the artery of the Rhine, and they too had become consumers of New World goods such as sugar and tobacco. Moreover, members of smaller sects had a great deal in common with Penn's Quakers. In other words, while not British, these Germans were fellow travelers. They had another reason to venture to America. Penn knew that the Rhineland, tied to America by Atlantic shipping networks, would provide people who would populate his province. Unsurprisingly, he recruited settlers from such regions.[48] Upon landing in Philadelphia, these people made an oath abjuring foreign princes and swore allegiance to their new king, the king of England. They promised to be "faithful and bear true Allegiance to his present MAJESTY KING GEORGE THE SECOND, and his Successor Kings of Great Britain."[49] In many respects after swearing an oath to the Crown, they had become Britons.[50]

Other groups had an easier time of it. In the eighteenth century, most migrants from the British Isles left from the margins. Some also began to imagine a future in America. Scottish migration was light during the early eighteenth century, as Scots traditionally looked to Ireland or the Continent to migrate, but accelerated by mid-century. Between 1701 and 1780, approximately 80,000 Scots ventured to America, the majority arriving between the end of the Seven Years' War and 1775. More than two out of every three came from the Lowlands. Among these lowlanders were merchants, teachers, doctors, clergymen, and military officers, the sorts of people who would have a profound effect on colonial society. More lowland migrants, however, arrived as indentured servants. Lowlanders came as their economy was integrated into a greater Britain's and, with the resulting disruptions, as settlement opportunities in Ireland were drying up.[51]

Highlanders, many of whom spoke Scots Gaelic and some of whom confessed to be Catholics, began pouring into the colonies in the 1730s as part of a plan to settle

Georgia with a people who would act as a hedge against Indians and the Spaniards. After the Seven Years' War, most highlanders settled in ethnic enclaves in North Carolina, especially in the Cape Fear region, and in New York near the holdings of William Johnson in the Mohawk River Valley. Highlanders came in the mid-eighteenth century as the clan system and pastoral economy came under assault. With population outstripping the ability of the land to provide and sheep displacing people, traveling to the New World seemed reasonable. Many highlanders, moreover, had served in the British army in America during the recent war. Going to America did not require an unprecedented leap of imagination.[52]

Although Englishmen and women would also travel to America in the eighteenth century, and many Scots would come especially after the 1750s, the greatest numbers to sail from the British Isles came from Ireland. Perhaps 200,000 arrived from 1717 until the American Revolution; in fact, with the exception of slaves from Africa, they represented the largest group to sail to America over the course of the eighteenth century. Of course, they already recognized the king as their sovereign, whether they liked it or not. Most who came, moreover, were Protestant, who for many years had produced one of the most important commodities shipped across the Atlantic: linen. Most left from those regions that had been immersed in a British world of politics and commerce—Ulster—explaining why Protestants predominated. We usually refer to these people as Scots Irish or Scotch Irish. By and large, however, the migrants would not have recognized these labels. Moreover, the use of the term Scotch Irish obscures the fact that Catholics came too, albeit in smaller numbers, largely because relatively few lived in regions that were affected by rapid commercialization. Most of these would become Protestant in America. Contemporaries referred to the men and women from Ulster as "Irish."[53]

Although many Irish settled in the cities (and Philadelphia, in particular, would have a strong and visible Irish presence), many more traveled to the frontier. Here they squatted or tried to buy land from Pennsylvania officials, who saw the Irish as a perfect barrier against potentially dangerous Indians to the west. Waves of Irish came over in the late 1720s, early 1740s, and 1750s. As the century progressed, more and more of these arrivals came as indentured servants, most of whom hoped to work for a master for a few years, and then find land to the west.

As waves of migrants crested, officials struck deals with the Six Nations to purchase additional land for settlement. Famously in 1736, the Iroquois sold a whole swath of land on the west side of the Susquehanna River, land on which Delaware and Shawnee refugees lived. A chief of the Delawares named Teedyuscung complained that the Iroquois called the Delawares "women...[and] took us by the Hair of the Head, and removed Us off of the Land."[54] Evicted, these Indians moved west into the Ohio country. As the Indians left, settlers arrived. Eventually, migrants and their children would move from and through Pennsylvania into the Great Valley of Virginia down the so-called Great Wagon Road. Along the way, they turned wilderness areas into settled societies.[55] They could only do so because, for the most part, the first half of the eighteenth century was marked by peace between Indians and whites. Germans too settled on the frontier, usually in enclaves together. In fact, the Shenandoah was almost divided into two separate sections, one dominated by the Irish, the other by Germans.[56]

To a great extent, these newcomers both challenged established settlers and remade the face of the colonies. Benjamin Franklin worried over the Irish infecting the body politic like a disease. He also fretted over the Palatine migrants "herding together." "Why should Pennsylvania, founded by the English," he wondered, "become a colony of aliens, who will shortly be so numerous as to Germanize us, instead of our Anglifying them, and will never adopt our language or customs any more than they can acquire our complexion."[57] Franklin, in particular, was terrified of what these newcomers would do to the English world that he had grown up in. Nonetheless, as they moved across the frontier, and established businesses in places like Philadelphia, they became important contributors to the Atlantic economy. Eventually, crop surpluses would make their way up the Great Wagon Road to fill the hulls of ships owned by Quaker merchants, who then sent this produce all over the Atlantic. In this regard, they also epitomized another Atlantic-wide trend that was bringing the colonies closer to Britain: a consumer revolution. For as grain went out, people born in Europe and goods manufactured in Britain came in.

Over the first half of the eighteenth century, Britons experienced an explosion in demand for the finer things in life. Before this time, luxury goods—silverware, fine china, wigs—remained the province of the gentry. Now, those sorts of people joining the ranks of the middling sort, especially prosperous farmers, merchants, and manufacturers, hoped to emulate their social superiors. Before the eighteenth century, goods demonstrated one's station in society, but as status became blurred so too did the meanings of consumption. In this regard, Americans proved just as enthusiastic as the British.[58] The Caribbean experience typified what would happen throughout America from mid-century on. As sugar prices soared in the mid-eighteenth century, after a period of stagnation, uncertainty, and warfare, planters enjoyed a golden age of prosperity. By 1750, sugar had become Britain's largest import, accounting for more than 10% of all British trade. With more spending power, planters tried to make their societies examples of British gentility. Unsurprisingly, they personified the exciting yet shallow nature of consumer culture. Self-fashioning was liberating for planters, yet with time they became parodied symbols of the vacuity of material excess. More critically, slave labor underwrote their ability to consume.[59]

Men like William Byrd II, who saw himself as English, demanded the latest fashions produced in England. But even the self-consciously egalitarian Benjamin Franklin was not so self-conscious in this regard. He too sought to wear the clothes in season in England and ordered fine china, at one point sending to his wife "something from all the China Works in England" to show "the Difference in Workmanship"[60] George Washington was an especially discerning shopper. He sent letters to his consignment agent requesting bedsteads, curtains, furniture, carpets, cloth, riding gloves, wine, knives, silk hose, shoes, and books on architecture, giving exact directions of the styles he wanted. Above all, he desired what was "fashionable."[61]

Franklin used goods, like Byrd and his fellow Virginia planter George Washington, to try to set himself apart from those he regarded as his social inferiors. Wearing the latest and most expensive clothing would allow all to see, especially those who did not know such men intimately, that these were the natural rulers of society. With more goods moving to and fro, more slaves to work fields, general peace in the colonies, these men became some of America's wealthiest and most influential.

Figure 1.3 John Singleton Copley, *Mary and Elizabeth Royall*, about 1758. Museum of Fine Arts, Boston.

Befitting their newfound status, they assumed positions of control in their respective colonies. Franklin rose from a printer to a businessman, to a landholder, and then to a gentleman of leisure. As he did so, he had portraits painted with him donning the latest finery. Soon he became a political and civic leader of the colony. The same held true for Byrd, as it did for wealthy New Englanders, such as Thomas Hutchinson, who would rise in prominence to become governor of Massachusetts.

Portraiture offers a window onto this broader Atlantic dynamic. Painters moved through the colonies hiring themselves out to an emerging elite that itself was coming of age through changes gripping the Atlantic system. And they were hired to allow America's *noveaux riches*—slave owners, merchants, and professionals—to display and fashion themselves, their dependents, and their possessions. One such painter, the Bostonian John Singleton Copley, for instance, focused his efforts not on the faces of his subjects but on what they wore. His painting of Mary and Elizabeth Royall is a perfect example. These daughters of a prominent rum merchant in New England, an industry fueled by Atlantic trade networks and slave labor in the Caribbean, look at the viewer amid yards and yards of expensive satin. Fabric dominates the canvas, but by design. The cloth itself, of course, was imported from England, and the sisters wear their sleeves in a style fashionable in England. The hummingbird and the King Charles spaniel tell a tale of exoticism, wealth, status, and connections to Britain. The painting, therefore, sells an image, one carefully cultivated by the father of the girls, Isaac Royall, but one that speaks to the need to be accepted in the metropole and be perceived as dominant in the provinces.[62]

Trends in building most visibly reflected British patterns of consumption. During the eighteenth century, Americans began emulating British architectural styles. Beginning in the late seventeenth century, English elites were fascinated by the work of late Renaissance continental architects such as Andrea Palladio. Like the Italian master, they began to design their homes and public buildings along classical lines and through the adoption of classical perspective, symmetry, and what were regarded as harmonious mathematical ratios. Although William Byrd II owned three editions of Palladio's works, most Americans learned of his influence by way of England. America did not have trained architects. Instead, carpenters, master builders, and gentlemen amateurs drew up plans from pattern books that arrived from England, many of which advocated what scholars have called an Anglo-Palladian perspective. Pattern books discussed both design principles and practical building issues, distilling what British builders had learned in the previous decades of classical elements. In fact, American Georgian architecture, so named because of the reigning British monarchs, mimicked Anglo-Palladianism style almost slavishly. Other provincials, particularly members of the Irish Ascendancy, did the same.[63]

As such, American Georgian style illustrated the provincial nature of American society. The colonies, after all, were provinces of Britain. They also dimly reflected metropolitan norms. American public buildings such as the Governor's mansion in Williamsburg, the "old statehouse" in Philadelphia—what later would be called

Figure 1.4 John Trumbull, *An Anglo-Palladian Villa*, 1777. New York Historical Society.

Independence Hall—as well as churches like St. Michael's in Charleston and the Old North Church in Boston, followed in an almost overly correct fashion reigning norms in Britain. Churches looked exactly like those designed by Christopher Wren and James Gibbs. Public buildings displayed the symmetry of the Italian neoclassical forms popular throughout Britain. Yet, provincial Americans also chose specific elements that worked for what they wanted to achieve. In architecture, provincial style reflected the healthy tension between metropolitan norms and local variation. Private residences as well followed this rule. Wealthy merchants in Newport, Rhode Island, relied on the amateur architects Richard Munday and Peter Harrison to make their homes look British.[64] Similarly, wealthy planters like William Byrd hoped their homes would demonstrate how British they were and how they ruled all that they surveyed. Such buildings, then, spoke to the confidence and self-consciousness of men such as Byrd.[65]

These men did not act alone in making America British. Men and women read of the things they could purchase in a growing number of newspapers, which also filled them in on the news of the broader British world that they were feeling increasingly connected with. And by the mid-eighteenth century, the wealthy and the middling sort in America were importing unprecedented amounts of British goods. Virginia offers a good example of this dynamic. Consignment agents in London made it their business to send over the very latest things to the colony's elite. These agents picked up the tobacco of the great planters who lived on navigable rivers. They then sold the tobacco in London, took their cut or commission from the sale, and purchased consumer goods to bring back to Virginia. Similar agents or factors from Scotland set up local offices in Virginia to satisfy the demand of the not-so-wealthy. Here they purchased tobacco from smaller producers who lived further to the west and far removed from the rivers of the Tidewater, and in exchange, procured British goods for them. Some even established stores for consumers. Indeed, the influence of Scottish factors in American led to the explosive growth of the city of Glasgow, which soon became a center of transatlantic trade.[66] Americans rich and poor alike demanded the stuff of empire: silk, wines, and tea. They also wanted the stuff of Britain and Ireland: iron goods, such as nails, horseshoes, axes, and hoes, as well as hats and linen.

Goods had an inherently democratic effect because all one needed was money. Even men and women on the rough-hewn frontier participated in this broader world of goods. As soon as roads were built to frontier enclaves and crop surpluses were transported out, merchants came peddling goods, including watches, wigs, and clothes produced in Britain. And women, of course, participated as vigorously as men. Indeed, one did not even have to be free to consume. Advertisements for runaway slaves, for instance, often included the sorts of clothes worn by the slave, and in some instances, they proved themselves to be discerning shoppers. One slave named Jack, who had run away from William Moore of Chester County, Pennsylvania, was described in a newspaper notice as wearing "a new Ozenburg shirt, a pair of strip'd home-spun Breeches, a strip'd ticking Waistcoat, an old dimity Coat of his Master's with Buttons of Horse teeth set in Brass, and Cloth Sleeves, a felt Hat almost new."[67] As goods served as a leveler in America, perhaps covering up real distinctions of wealth and status, they made all Americans part of a broader British cultural world.

Goods came in ships and in wagons. So did ideas. Americans, too, engaged in Britain's enlightenment, albeit in an emulative fashion. The American Enlightenment, if we can call it that, was personified by brilliant men such as Franklin, who tended to make ideas useable. Nonetheless, participating in a British intellectual world also made them more British. Like Byrd, Americans up and down the coast were enthralled with the new ideas that Englishmen like Newton had introduced. And they enjoyed some successes in this regard. David Rittenhouse developed an orrery, a mechanical model of the solar system. Cotton Mather, a minister from Massachusetts, became an early proponent of inoculation from smallpox. A number of these, like Byrd, became members of the Royal Society. Americans were also avid consumers of cutting-edge British political thought. They read in serial and book form the work of writers such as John Locke, John Trenchard, and Thomas Gordon, and even the Irish-born Francis Hutcheson, figures associated with the British Enlightenment of the eighteenth century. The American Enlightenment, if we could term the belief in the power of reason to improve man's condition, also dimly reflected its metropolitan equivalent and something was often lost in transatlantic translation. The Caribbean offers a good example. Planters adopted British humanitarian ideals and reform impulses associated with Britain's Enlightenment to ameliorate the plight of their slaves. They did not do so for altruistic reasons but because it made financial sense. "Amelioration" also promised to allay their fears over slave insurrection.[68] America had Franklin, but Franklin for all his justifiable notoriety was no Newton. No doubt, Americans contributed to the British world of ideas—Franklin's experiments on electricity and his charting of the Gulf Stream serving as two prominent examples—but their expertise lie in practical applications of new theories. Once again, Franklin's work epitomizes the trend. He developed bifocals, a new stove, and the lightning rod, the sorts of things that made life more comfortable.[69]

Ideas affected every aspect of colonial life, especially churches. Churchmen, particularly those trained in universities in New England and Scotland, championed new forms of polite piety that were concerned more with reason than with vital faith. Some latitudinarians called on their congregations to see Christ not only as savior but also as a moral exemplar and man of reason. In fact, Franklin's favorite preacher, a Presbyterian named Samuel Hemphill, was born in Ireland and trained by some of Britain's leading intellectuals in Scotland. Hemphill preached to an affluent and polite Philadelphia congregation, where Franklin came on Sundays to hear the young man's sermons. Hemphill's Christ appeared much like Franklin's, one who, like Socrates, served more as a model of humility to be followed and less as a savior.

The colonies, therefore, were caught in the grips of profound changes in the first half of the eighteenth century. The creation of a provincial elite, the wide dispersal of goods, the arrival of new peoples from Atlantic peripheries, and the emulation and adaptation of British ideas were remaking the face of whole societies in a very short period of time. If they were becoming "provincial," they did not take it to mean parochial and backwards. To be a provincial Briton meant that one participated in the cultural and economic life of Britain.[70]

In fact, a deeper pattern of change was gripping the colonies. The process of becoming British was really a regional variation of a common Atlantic theme, one that defined the experiences of other settler societies in the New World. The transition to slave-based economies, the expulsion of Native Americans from productive land tied by networks into the Atlantic economy, the rise of creole elites, and the integration of the economies of Old and New Worlds through advanced shipping, migration, and news created a consolidated Atlantic system. The transition from self-consciously English settlements into British provinces, driven by peoples, goods, and ideas, then, represented the American experience of a much broader change. From this Olympian perspective, becoming British, as well as the resulting provincial dilemma, was a response to the creation of an integrated Atlantic world, a world connected not divided by an ocean.[71]

If such changes stemmed from a re-immersion into a broader British Atlantic world, so too did the response. Historians have long tried to make sense of a startling phenomenon that developed throughout the mainland colonies in the decades before the Seven Years' War. Starting in the 1730s, colonists in New England began rediscovering God. They did not do so in the Puritanism of their ancestors, though the process of finding God bore a certain resemblance to an earlier form of religiosity. Rather, New Englanders were embracing "enthusiasm." Like the Calvinists of old, many New Englanders began turning their back on theological arguments that stressed the role of man or works in the salvation story. Only Grace saved. Unlike old-line Calvinists, they often did so in an emotional way. Men and women fainted during sermons. Some seemed to fall into deep depressions. Others babbled.[72] Such behavior reminded older ministers of the witchcraft hysteria that had gripped New England in the early 1690s. Then, many were convinced, the devil was abroad in the world. But as more and more people embraced a vital piety, most increasingly believed that God was at work in their lives and in their community.[73]

Some of the earliest "awakenings," for this was how people regarded the mass revivals of the times, took place in the meetinghouse of a New England minister named Jonathan Edwards. Edwards, who avidly read and wrote on most of the important topics of the Enlightenment, was no latitudinarian. A man of reason, he believed that reason met its limit in God. Formalism in religious worship and expression led to a deadening spirituality. Reason did not make man God's equal; reason only showed the unrelenting depravity of the human condition, a depravity that only God could remedy. "The God that holds you over the Pit of Hell," Edwards warned, "much as one holds a spider, or some loathsome insect, over the fire, abhors you, and is dreadfully provoked."[74] All one had to do was recognize sinfulness, call on God's mercy, and accept Grace. Edwards struck a chord, and soon men and women from meetinghouses all over New England including those in Boston were clamoring for revival.[75] And Congregationalists were divided over the merits of vital piety. Divisions tended to run along social fault lines. In general, the New Englanders who supported revivals were younger and a bit poorer than their parents or tended to be people on the move, those on the margins of society who would have to look elsewhere for opportunity. In cities, they tended to be debtors. As such, revivals represented both a reaction to theological innovation and the changes gripping society.[76] But we would be wrong to consider these merely conservative, or backward looking, reactions to change. Edwards, after all, epitomized the age of reason. And people did not so much embrace vital piety to reject change as to comprehend it.

As revivals spread, following the course of change, this pattern became even more pronounced. As Edwards was winning over souls to Christ further north, men and women in the Middle Colonies were also experiencing an awakening. A number of Presbyterians in the area around Newark, New Jersey, the sons and daughters of émigrés from New England including the minister Jonathan Dickinson, clamored for God's saving grace. But the nature of Middle Colony revivals reflected the ethnic diversity of the region. A Dutchman named Theodore Frelinghuysen was preaching a new message of salvation among his people. He soon drew the attention of the Irish-born father and son William and Gilbert Tennant. William had been born a member of the established Church of Ireland and converted to Presbyterianism before sailing for America. Settled in New Jersey, he founded a small academy for training ministers, a place his enemies would later dub the "Log College." Gilbert, his star pupil and also an advocate for the message preached by Frelinghuysen, soon electrified meetinghouses in his region. Moving throughout New Jersey, Pennsylvania, and New York, Tennant preached a nondenominational message of saving faith, especially targeting what he considered a corrupt and learned ministry and suggesting that unless awakened, they were leading their charges to hell. Because of "Letter-learned and regular Pharisees...the People were as Sheep without a Shepherd," he charged.[77] In doing so, he ripped the fledgling American Presbyterian Church, then centered in the Middle Colonies, in two.[78]

Revivals did not represent a peculiarly American response to change. America exploded when the most electrifying revivalist of the day, an Englishman named George Whitefield, arrived. Whitefield, a minister for the Church of England and devotee of John Wesley, the father of what would later be called Methodism, believed in the merits of the new birth. He led revivals throughout the British Atlantic world, travelling to Scotland numerous times, as well as Bermuda. Only in Ireland did he receive a less than courteous welcome. Here, as he put it in 1757 during a trip to Dublin, "Satan's children"—Catholics, in other words—tossed "Vollies of hard stones."[79] In America, the "grand itinerant" traveled to every colony, holding open-air revivals of many thousands and enjoying resounding success.[80]

Even the hard-to-impress Franklin could not help but be overwhelmed by Whitefield. "I happened soon after to attend one of his sermons," he wrote after one of Whitefield's visits to Philadelphia, "in the course of which I perceived he intended to finish with a collection." Franklin did not want to get swept up in enthusiasm and "silently resolved he should get nothing from me. I had in my pocket a handful of copper money, three or four silver dollars, and five pistoles in gold." He soon gave in: "As he proceeded I began to soften and concluded to give the coppers. Another stroke of his oratory made me ashamed of that and determined me to give the silver; and he finished so admirably that I emptied my pocket wholly into the collector's dish, gold and all."[81] No doubt, Franklin made a great deal of money off of the preacher, as his paper covered his travels and advertised his next stops. But he also admired the man for charisma.[82]

Although Whitefield's preaching tore congregations apart, it revealed deep patterns of change in British American society. The patterns in New England held throughout the colonies. Those more established, the older, more settled, and the wealthier, tended to oppose revivals. Younger men and women and the poorer and more mobile embraced what they regarded as a liberating message. Although itinerants seemed to rail against the excesses of an increasingly consumer-oriented culture, they also preached a message of individual salvation. These were products of their time as well. The revivals that gripped Virginia are a case in point. At first, following the pattern of the Middle Colonies, Presbyterians in the colony were sponsoring revivals, most notably Samuel Davies. But soon, as enthusiasm spread to more outlying regions of Virginia, another group untethered to any formal church structure spread the message. Baptists, originally from New England, traveled to the Virginia frontier to preach a message of individual salvation as they denigrated formal church hierarchies and trumpeted the idea of liberty to challenge established church structures. Understandably, these Baptists caused fits for the established church in the colony.[83]

Yet the divisions caused or exacerbated by revivals obscures something more fundamental at work. Awakenings, in fact, represented the first common experience that many Americans had, and they experienced them as provincial Britons. For Whitefield, denomination did not matter. As he put it, "Don't tell me you are a Baptist, an Independent, a Presbyterian, a dissenter, tell me you are a Christian, that is all I want."[84] However British Atlantic in their scope, revivals represented distinctive provincial responses to the process of becoming British. In much the same way Scots embraced their universities and Irish Protestants championed an ideal of "improving" a backward kingdom, Americans too had to grapple with what it meant to be a province of Britain. On one level, revivals were creative responses by a people overwhelmingly Protestant caught in the grips of Atlantic-wide change. On another level, however, they reflected the tenor of the times. Ministers such as Jonathan Edwards embraced many of the new ideas of the eighteenth century, even if he rejected their premises. And revivals on the scale they occurred would have been unimaginable without the British dimension or the networks created by and sustaining an integrated Atlantic world. All this said, although vital piety served a social function, people found God through a common experience. The Great Awakening, therefore, was and was not a response to the process of becoming British.[85]

A shared cultural sense of Britishness also gave colonists a newfound appreciation of the ways that their political institutions mirrored those of the metropole. Nearly all American colonies, including those of the Caribbean, emerged from the seventeenth century as royal colonies. The king appointed a royal governor, who acted as his representative in the colony, much like the lord lieutenant acted as the king's viceroy in Ireland. The governor or the king's Privy Council usually selected the members of the upper house of the legislature, generally called the Council. Really more like councilors to the governor, these men also enjoyed some of the prerogatives of Britain's House of Lords. Beneath them sat the popularly elected assemblies, which performed much the same function as the House of Commons in Britain, the lower house of Parliament. In Barbados, for instance, freeholders elected the first General Assembly in 1639. Within 10 years, the Assembly was initiating legislation that could be signed into law by a royal governor, assisted by a council he appointed. As soon as Jamaica became an English colony in 1655, it followed suit. Like most colonial lower houses, its assembly prided itself on functioning like England's Parliament by protecting local and traditional rights.[86]

Entrenched elites like William Byrd, or those who were newly rising in a changing world like Benjamin Franklin, controlled politics, even what we would consider more popular bodies like assemblies. Like Britain, therefore, colonists also had a government of mixed constitution. Power was divided in each colony, not by function, but along the natural divisions of society. Each strata of society—the Crown's interest, the established elite, and the more common sort—had representation, if not actually then at least virtually. Provincial institutions, of course, proved just as corrupt as Britain's Parliament. But, in theory, the interests of one body balanced the interests of the others and, in so doing, protected liberty. As Britons, Americans believed that such arrangements ensured that power would not destroy liberty. As Dr. William Douglas of Boston put it in 1751, government in America consisted "of three separate negatives" that served as "checks upon one another." He saw in these British style arrangements "trinity in unity."[87]

That said, American political structures took on a provincial caste, with all that that ambiguous word implies. As a rule, because of the availability of land, more American colonists had the right to vote than did Britons. Indeed, nearly three-fourths of all adult white males in the colonies voted, a far larger percentage than could in Britain. In Virginia, men needed to own 100 unsettled or 25 settled acres to vote. In North Carolina and Georgia, 50 would do. In New York, holding a lifetime or permanent lease entitled one to the franchise. As Thomas Hutchinson said, "anything with the appearance of a man" could vote in the colonies. Yet, voter participation varied from colony to colony, and most colonists proved apathetic. Often candidates ran unopposed, and participation usually only spiked because of local circumstances. However democratically responsive provincial assemblies were, in other words, they were not fully utilized. Nonetheless, the tenor of political life differed from Britain. Americans deferred to their betters to represent them, but they participated in politics vigorously when they chose to do so. Strife within increasingly stable structures is the best way to characterize what made American institutions American. The power of patronage was weak, and assemblies were strong. Governors possessed great powers, but relied on colonists for their maintenance. People regarded their representatives as their agents, but elites held the reins of political power.[88] These assemblies also jealously guarded their prerogatives. They had a history of ignoring or skirting laws passed by Parliament or instructions from the King's Privy Council. They also bullied royal governors. In this regard, the American practice of politics diverged from the British theory of politics. The constitutional centers of power in America were the legislatures; in fact, assemblies enjoyed some powers that Parliament would have envied. As such, most Americans were used to the idea of dividing sovereignty.[89]

Those colonies that were established by charter, and remained that way like Connecticut and Rhode Island, or were founded as proprietary colonies like Pennsylvania and Maryland, retained a British mixed structure, as well as American distinctiveness. Nonetheless, in the immediate aftermath of the Seven Years' War, some were clamoring for new political arrangements. Reformers did not ask for independence; rather, they called for royal government. In fact, Franklin made the argument that Pennsylvania should become a royal colony like most of the others, to save it from the crippling factionalism that seemed to engulf it from time to time. He saw each of the colonies as spokes attached to a British hub, and he wanted to make those connections more uniform and more conspicuous. Franklin wanted to give cultural realities an institutional or political manifestation.[90]

The process of making America British reached its apogee with history's first world war. Americans usually refer to the epic conflict between the world's greatest superpowers of the time as the French and Indian War. And since British regulars and American colonists were fighting the French and their Indian allies in the backwoods of America, the term seems to fit. Europeans and the British called the conflict the Seven Years' War, counting the years from the formal declaration of war in 1756 until its formal conclusion with the Treaty of Paris in 1763. Both of these names, however, fail to convey what was at stake for Britain, America, and the world. From 1754, when hostilities in America commenced until the signing of the treaty in 1763, the British and their colonists engaged in battles on every known continent. In this "Great War for Empire," America for the first time lay at the center of a European power struggle that had global implications.[91] The winner—Britain—would rule a global empire the likes of which the world had never before seen. And Britain itself, as well as it colonies, which had become full-fledged British provinces, would never be the same again.

The war fittingly began on the very edge of Britain's domains in America, the Ohio country, on lands disputed between Britain and France. As population in the colonies was growing, as migration to them was adding to numbers every day, and as places like the Shenandoah Valley were already becoming populated, well-connected speculators believed that the next big landgrab would occur beyond the Appalachian Mountains. In 1747, a number of wealthy Virginians—the friends, neighbors, and associates of William Byrd III—had founded the Ohio Company. If they could claim the region, legalize those claims, and divide the territory in saleable plots, they would stand to make a fortune.[92]

Time, population pressure, and precedent were on their side. Virginians had a charter dating back to the seventeenth century that on paper at least granted the Ohio country to the colony. More important, fur traders had traveled for some time to the region to do business with Native Americans. The areas west of the mountains were home to a great many Indian groups. The Iroquois, the strongest group of Indians in all of eastern North America, claimed the region through conquest. A century before, or so the reasoning went, Iroquois raiding parties had depopulated the Ohio country in search of captives to replenish a declining Iroquois population through adoption. Colonial governments and the British Crown had followed the example of New York and recognized the supremacy of the Iroquois to this and other eastern regions by signing onto the covenant chain. Through the covenant chain, eastern governments could purchase land from the Iroquois without having to treat with the smaller tribes who lived on it.[93] Throughout the 1730s, the Six Nations ceded territory to governments east of the mountains that were peopled by groups such as the Delawares and Shawnees. In exchange for the land, these groups were allowed to settle in the Ohio country, as vassals of the Iroquois. The Six Nations let these groups know, in no uncertain terms, that "you are our women; our forefathers made you so, and put a petticoat on you, and charged you to be true to us and lie with no other man." They were as a nation, in other words, not to do the things associated with men: go to war and engage in diplomacy.[94] Once there, however, Delawares, Shawnees, and other groups—even Iroquois living in Ohio such as the Mingoes— more or less declared their independence from the Six Nations, and as they did so, traders from the east traveled to the region, which now teemed with deer. The presence of the traders—some from Pennsylvania, others from Virginia—soon attracted Indians living to the west and the north in French-dominated regions, groups such as the Miami. Although before the 1750s no settlers had moved out to the Ohio country, traders seemed to be preparing the table for prospective settlement.[95]

The French saw the British traders who had moved through the region as the vanguards of British claims and settlement. If Pennsylvanians or Virginians pushed over the mountains, they could threaten the integrity of the French empire in North America, one connected by the Great Lakes and Mississippi River system. The Ohio River and its tributaries, although no French lived along it, pointed like a dagger into the heart of France's empire. As traders tried to pry Indians in the Great Lakes region away from their traditional allies, the French officials decided to make good on their claims to the region. They dispatched troops to overawe Indians who were trading with the British and to post lead plates at strategic points alerting all that the French considered the Ohio country their sovereign territory. They also tried to woo native newcomers to the region, such as Delawares and Shawnees. Finally, they constructed forts at strategic points in the region, the largest called Fort Duquesne at the head of the Ohio River.[96]

The Virginians acted to protect their interests. The royal governor of the colony, Robert Dinwiddie, had little choice but to dispatch a militia officer named George Washington to let the French know of British claims. The young Virginian, the brother of an investor in the Ohio Company, had cut his teeth as a surveyor and styled himself an aspiring British gentleman. Washington traveled to the West in 1753, where he was informed by a French commander that they would not relinquish possession of the Ohio country. The following year, he set off again in the company of Iroquois from the region to warn the French out of Fort Duquesne. The ill-conceived mission led to a brief skirmish a few miles east of the fort, culminating in the killing of a young French ensign at the hands of an Iroquois half-king. With the French pursuing, Washington holed up in a small resupply station dubbed Fort Necessity. Here, soon surrounded by enraged French troops and their Indian allies, Washington was forced to surrender. The terms of surrender, which he signed, included an admission that he had arranged the assassination of the young French ensign.[97]

As soon as Washington marched back to Williamsburg after the embarrassing surrender at Fort Necessity, France and Britain were at war. Although a formal declaration lay 2 years on the horizon, the British hoped that colonists would be able to prosecute the war. At the behest of Benjamin Franklin and Massachusetts governor William Shirley, representatives from the prominent old North American colonies met in Albany in June and July 1754 to coordinate plans for dealing with the French. Franklin proposed that the colonies band together in a union that, he hoped, would tie all the colonies together through the Crown in a confederation and provide defense for their common frontier. As his and other newspapers put it, the colonists like a dismembered snake had to "unite or die." A president-general would be appointed by the Crown, a post akin to Ireland's lord lieutenant, and the colonists would elect a Grand Council, which would almost serve as America's Parliament. The council and the president-general would make plans for "mutual defence and security, and for extending the British Settlements in North America." Colonies would be taxed to raise troops and build forts. Each colony retained its constitution, but yielded its rights to conduct treaty negotiations with Indians. The covenant chain would become a relic of the past.[98]

Because the colonies had no basis of unity beyond the Crown, the plan failed. Representatives squabbled over claims to the west and the historic right to treat with Indians for the interests of their colonies. New York, or better a faction led by William Johnson and his close ally Governor James DeLancey, did not want to cede its influence with the Iroquois to New Englanders. Representatives fought over who would pay for defense. Individual colonies would not or could not come up with the troops, supplies, or money requested by the Crown to fight the French. A Quaker-dominated assembly in Pennsylvania, which was bearing the brunt of Indian raids, did not even provide for its own defense. And commissioners struggled with the idea of compromising their sovereign rights. The assemblies of some colonies rejected the plan, others ignored it, and still others lingered over it. One Pennsylvanian went so far as to call the commissioners "arrant Blockheads" for devising such a half-baked plan. Not above self-interest, Franklin realized the union he proposed would help him secure his land claims in the West. Indeed, the young lieutenant governor of Massachusetts, Thomas Hutchinson, appeared one of the few disinterested commissioners. Then again, New Englanders, with a long exposed frontier and little access to the Iroquois to police it, stood the most to gain by a union.[99]

Eventually, the ministry in Britain understood that to win this war required a new approach. In fact, as colonial representatives were meeting in Albany, officials in Whitehall were already devising a new approach to the war in North America.[100] Soon the ministry dispatched a veteran commander named Edward Braddock to put a swift end to the war in America. The plan was simple. Braddock would lead veteran troops out west to the forks of the Ohio and attack and destroy the wooden fort under construction there by the French, Fort Duquesne. Although fur traders like George Croghan warned Braddock that he needed the support of Indians skilled at guerilla warfare to accomplish such a feat in the difficult terrain of the American wilderness, Braddock thought he knew better. As Benjamin Franklin recalled, Braddock declared "these savages may, indeed, be a formidable enemy to your raw American militia but upon the king's regular and disciplined troops, sir, it is impossible they should make any impression."[101] Indians would never in his mind inherit the west, not even groups who already lived there like the Delawares and Shawnees. They could never stand up to troops tested by European warfare. The British, he assured the traders, would and could go it alone.

As he prepared to move west by cutting a road through the wilderness to Fort Duquesne—following George Washington—the French assembled Indians from throughout the Great Lakes region and the Ohio country. With sappers slowly cutting a road, the French and the Indians waited for the right moment to attack. They fell upon Braddock with devastating results. Even hardened veterans quaked as Indians attacked and shot from the trees. They formed lines, as they had been trained, but such maneuvers did not work in the woods of America. It was a rout. One soldier recalled the terror of the ambush. "The Indians, a merciless Crew that compos'd Part of the French Army," he remembered, "began immediately to scalp the Dead and Wounded." He called them "ravenous Hell-hounds."[102] Braddock, as well as much of his command, fell. The defeat of Braddock set the tenor for the first few years of the war, as Indians rallied to the French from as far west as the Mississippi, and the British, who could not even retain the allegiance of the Indian allies they started with, continued to lose. Even the Iroquois, who were bound diplomatically to the British and to many of the eastern colonies, chose to remain as neutral as they could rather than back a loser. For the first 3 years of the war in America, the British steadily lost ground to the French in the Hudson River corridor. The British were in no position to try to take Fort Duquesne again. After the defeat of Braddock, the nations of the Ohio country cast their lot if not with the French at least against the British and their colonists. Soon raiding parties were fanning out over the mountains to strike isolated settlements to the east.

The tide finally turned in 1757 in a place later made famous by the novelist James Fennimore Cooper in his book *The Last of the Mohicans*. In that year, the British were poised to lose yet another fort near the Hudson River. Fort William Henry was besieged by the French, and with no hope of relief, the British commander decided he had to surrender. He did so under gracious terms. He and his troops would be allowed to leave the fort with their honor, arms, and standards intact. Although the terms comported with European norms of warfare, the Indians allied with the French were incensed. Many who had marched a great distance for booty and war trophies such as scalps did not fight for pay but for honor. As the British marched out, the Indians ran into the fort and killed a number of the British left behind in the infirmary. They also attacked the departing column. The "massacre" at Fort William Henry would awaken the British to the type of warfare they were confronting in America, and from this point forward, they would adapt to it. Most visibly, they created ranger units well-schooled in the rigors and tactics of American warfare. More significantly, this episode also represented the last time so many Indians would ally themselves with the French.

About the same time as the "massacre," the ministry in Britain came up with a new strategy for the war. With battles raging all over the globe, officials decided that the larger war would be won or lost in America. British Secretary of State, William Pitt "the elder," designed a strategy to maximize Britain's strengths and exploit France's weaknesses by advocating the use of Britain's superior navy to strangle France's attempts to resupply its troops in America. Hoping to exploit the manpower of the colonies, Pitt also promised to reimburse American colonial governments for supplying British forces and for raising their militias to fight and support the war effort. Pitt understood that American colonists had to be full partners in the struggle if Britain was to win. Famously, British regulars and militia from Massachusetts took the French fort at Louisbourg, which commanded the approach to the St. Lawrence Seaway. With the French bottled up, they could not dole out the goods necessary to keep Indians fighting with them. Nor could they resupply their troops.

It was only a matter of time before the end came. In 1758, the new British commander General John Forbes made a renewed push west against Fort Duquesne with British ranger units leading the way. With few Indian allies, the French saw they had no chance. They evacuated the fort and burned it to the ground even before the British arrived. Some months later, the British pressed up the Hudson River Valley and down the St. Lawrence to squeeze the epicenter of Frances's New World holdings. In September 1759, under the leadership of General James Wolfe, the British—with many Irish and Scots in the ranks—defeated the Marquis de Montcalm at Quebec in a battle on the Plains of Abraham, the scene that West immortalized. Soon they took Montreal as well. By 1760, the French and Indian War, the American chapter of the Seven Years' War, was over. Three years later, the Treaty of Paris formally ended the world war.

When news came of the defeat of Montcalm by Wolfe at Quebec, colonists lit bonfires in nearly every major American city. As the British now rejoiced at a

Figure 1.5 Charles Wilson Peale, *George Washington*, 1772. Washington and Lee University, Lexington, Virginia.

complete victory over their hated rivals, the French, Americans now rejoiced that the threat to their north and west was gone, hopefully for good. No longer would men and women from Massachusetts fear that Catholics to the north would send raiding parties to their outlying settlements. No longer would settlers from Pennsylvania fear that the French would lead Indians to settlements up and down the Susquehanna. Virginians now hoped that the greatest obstacles to expansion west were removed.

But colonists celebrated something more. They gloried in their Britishness. The painter Charles Wilson Peale, who had studied with Benjamin West and who earned a living producing images of America's provincial elite, painted a portrait of George Washington resplendent in his Virginia militia uniform from the Seven Years' War. Completed the same year—1772—as West's *Death of General Wolfe*, Peale's portrait tells a similar story. In it, Washington wears the blood-stained sash of the fallen British general, Edward Braddock. For the provincial Washington, Braddock had been all that Washington aspired to be.[103]

A minister from Boston named Jonathan Mayhew gave voice to such sensibilities, waxing rhapsodic about the savior Wolfe storming the hellish gates of Quebec: "Behold, there falls their valiant Leader!…Behold this place, renowned for its strength, the power and pride of the enemy, against which so many fruitless attempts had been made, now surrender'd to his Britannic Majesty, whose colours, yonder, wave over the devoted city."[104] Like West, Mayhew saw a new age dawning of British manifest destiny. "Great Britain," he foresaw, "must of course, in a little time, be possessed of a territory here in North-America, extending and continued from [Hudson] Bay…as far as Florida to the southward." The realm would stretch "as far back to the westward, almost, as we should desire." Indians would gladly live in peace west of the Mississippi. East of it, Mayhew believed, would arise "a mighty empire…in numbers little inferior to the greatest in Europe, and in felicity to none." He hastened to add he did not mean "an independent" empire. It would be British to the core. His new New World would thrive with "mighty cities," ports, and fleets of ships "alternately sailing out and returning, laden with the produce of this, and every other country under heaven." Valleys would be covered with corn, and the hills would "rejoice." Religion here would be "professed and practiced…in far greater purity and perfection, than since the times of the apostles." "O happy country! Happy kingdom," he declared.[105] As Mayhew suggested, the process of making America British, thus far, had been a story of consensus. He could not reckon otherwise, nor could he imagine how America's seventeenth-century English past, and Britain's for that matter, could haunt British America in the eighteenth century.

CHAPTER 2

꙳

Reduce the Savages to Reason

Rarely has a family drawn the course of empire. In the seventeenth and eight-eenth century, one English family did it twice. In 1656, William Petty, the phy-sician-general of Oliver Cromwell's army of conquest in Ireland, surveyed the whole of the kingdom to administer the confiscation of land from Catholics. Cromwell had invaded Ireland in 1649, a little after he had defeated the forces of King Charles I in a grisly civil war. Once the king was executed, Cromwell turned his attention to bringing order to the edges of his commonwealth: Scotland and Ireland. Catholics in Ireland had proved particularly vexing to English rulers. They had staged a bloody rebellion against English authority and the policy of Protestant plantation in 1641. Most had then supported the now headless king. And all embraced a faith that the Puritan Cromwell considered anathema. After savaging the country through siege and massacre, he hoped to reshape the landscape.[1]

Although Petty was trained as a physician at Oxford, he had a great interest in the relationship between space, economy, and politics, what later would be referred to as the science of political economy. In fact, his pathbreaking work on the subject would have a lasting influence on such luminaries as the Scot Adam Smith. Petty also studied with Francis Bacon, the father of the modern scientific method who famously believed that the world could best be perceived through experimentation. Petty did his mentor proud, becoming one of the founding members of the Royal Society. The act of mapping, Petty knew from his varied training, entailed control and precision.

Although not trained as a surveyor or a mapmaker, Petty accomplished the her-culean task of mapping Ireland in little over a year. The result remade Ireland, liter-ally and figuratively, laying the basis for British order in Ireland. In the north, east, and south of the country, Protestants displaced Catholics, and the survey laid out the best lands to settle. He did not bother mapping a number of western counties, as these were set aside for displaced Catholics. As an act that was based on the survey declared, "for the better security of all those parts of Ireland which are now intended to be planted with English and Protestants," Catholics had to "remove and transplant themselves into the Province of Connaught, and the county of Clare." Those who

Figure 2.1 Isaac Fuller, *Sir William Petty*, ca. 1649–50. National Portrait Gallery, London.

transgressed the line of the River Shannon could be considered spies and could be summarily executed.[2] While the rest of the country would be brutally anglicized, here would be a world beyond the pale, a place for the barbarous Irish to exist for the time being in any event. The survey, then, paved the way for the total conquest of a kingdom that had been imperfectly controlled by England.

Fittingly, Petty had studied with the political philosopher Thomas Hobbes. Hobbes, of course, had written his famous tract *Leviathan* to chart how a society and a state come into being. Indeed, he wrote the piece as Ireland had descended into chaos.[3] The island with its violence and factionalism, its seething disorder and uncertainty, was a case study in what happened in a vacuum of sovereignty. Petty, then, lived during one of the most tumultuous periods in England's history and the history of the neighboring kingdoms. Yet his work helped to deliver the region from its state of war and to create an oppressive but effective sense of sovereignty. As an Englishman who helped project English power into Ireland and Scotland, he served as a midwife of British history.

For these efforts at mapping an English imperium, as well as for his work in science and economics, Petty earned a baronetcy. Sir William would go on to live out his life in England and on his huge estate in the south of Ireland. He would also serve in the English parliament and had some involvement with the tobacco trade between Virginia, Ireland, and England.[4] By the time he died in 1687, England had gained control over its troubling neighbors Scotland and Ireland, a process that would reach its apogee only a few years after Petty's death with the Glorious Revolution. In fact, just before he died, Petty laid out what he thought was his final solution for the Irish problem. He urged the English government to dilute and eventually destroy the Catholic Church in Ireland "by transporting a million people to England." Prefiguring arguments for the Union of 1801 between Britain and Ireland, Petty argued that if Protestants predominated on each side of the Irish Sea, Catholicism would wither away and with it the barbarous manners of the people.[5] Although his plea was ignored, the family prospered. Through shrewd marriages and an astute cultivation of connections, the Pettys became one of the most prominent families in the British Isles. Eventually, Sir William's direct descendants would earn Irish and British noble titles, first becoming earls and then marquises.

What Petty did for the British Isles, his great-grandson would do for America. William-Petty Fitzmaurice was born in Ireland, living on lands that his great-grandfather had earned through his surveys. By the time he was born, the seventeenth-century crisis of sovereignty for the British Isles had come to an end. Scotland and England had been joined together, and Ireland had been effectively yoked to the two kingdoms, through the institution of Parliament. Now integrating America loomed as a new challenge for the British state. The Earl of Shelburne, as the younger William came to be known, sat in the Irish and British parliaments after serving under Wolfe during the Seven Years' War. At the end of the war, he entered the ministry and would become a patron of thinkers such as Adam Smith and members of Parliament such as Isaac Barré. Eventually, he would also lead a government and invest heavily in Britain's chief global concern, the East India Company. But in 1763, one of his chief tasks was to head up a group called the Board of Trade. The Board did a great deal more than supervise trade within the British empire. It also had responsibility for suggesting and formulating policy for the colonies in America. In the wake of the war, the most pressing issues, ironically, were similar to those his great-grandfather had contended with in Ireland: how to manage space and govern diverse peoples. In this case, however, Shelburne had to try to make sense of the greatest territorial empire the world had ever seen while Britain reeled from the financial fallout of the global war just ended. Far from the British Isles, the holdings the British had gained through the terms of the Treaty of Paris included the eastern half of North America, a region stretching from the Arctic Circle to the Gulf of Mexico, and from the Atlantic to the Mississippi.[6]

In 1763, Shelburne helped devise a survey in which North America would be divided in two. The so-called Proclamation Line running up and down the Appalachian Mountains was drawn up to cut America into two imperial zones. This line, much like the Irish survey, would become the basis for British rule. As he wrote a few years later, the Royal Proclamation was "to be understood a system of bounding not particular provinces but our American settlements in general."[7] To the west, outside America's pale, lived Indians. And this area, much like the counties reserved to the Irish a century before west of the Shannon River, would be an area beyond the bounds of civilization. East of the line, Shelburne and the other men who had a hand in governing Britain believed, lived men and women who bore the rights and responsibilities of subjects. The questions Shelburne and other members of other ministries confronted here was how to conceive of America within the British state. How, for

Figure 2.2 Joshua Reynolds, *William Petty, 1st Marquess of Lansdowne*, 1766. National Portrait Gallery, London.

instance, did American colonies compare to Ireland, Scotland, and England? Could they be considered the equals of societies in the British Isles? Did equality even have any meaning within a British state composed of distinctive kingdoms?

Together this family story speaks to the ways English power extended to the marches in the seventeenth century and how British power would envelop America in the eighteenth century after the colonies had become British provinces. The parallels point to the fact that what had happened in the seventeenth century served as a blueprint for the eighteenth century. In 1763, then, Shelburne was doing for the Atlantic what his great-grandfather had done for the British Isles. But these stories tell us more. Maps bring an illusory sense of control. For on the spaces they represent live people. The English in the seventeenth century and their British heirs in the eighteenth century would struggle to come up with ways of governing space and bringing diverse peoples within the state, what we could call a process of state formation. In many ways, the process was the same, but the scope and scale changed in profound ways.

No doubt, great-grandfather and great-grandson had to govern two increasingly different worlds. In 1763, Britain was in the midst of a great transition. During the lifetime of William Petty, the English did not so much rule over a centralized empire as struggle to comprehend the kingdoms in the North Atlantic archipelago within one state, as well as oversee an assemblage of colonies in an unsystematic way on the other side of the Atlantic. By the eighteenth century, the British controlled more holdings, including a number of trading towns, or factories, in West Africa and

India, as well as strategic garrisons in and around the Mediterranean. But sovereignty and formal authority, as well as the laws and institutions that gave these abstractions meaning, were focused on the British Isles. By 1763, with the signing of the Treaty of Paris, British policymakers like Shelburne had to systematize this diverse collection of holdings, which included vastly expanded territory in North America. As they did so, they had to come up with notions of how they would extend the reach of formal authority in an effective way to the edges. They did not invent ideas of how to govern out of thin air; rather, they relied on their experience governing Ireland and Scotland.[8]

British ministers in 1763 had templates at hand to create not one but two distinctive worlds in America, templates that Benjamin West had wrought into simple myths of consensus. One blueprint of governance suggested that American colonists could and should be incorporated into the British central state in some way. Americans could be treated like other provincials, Protestant Irish and Lowland Scots, albeit in ways that spoke to the distinctive characteristics of the American colonies and the great physical distance between these peripheral regions and the metropole. Both Protestant Irishmen and lowlanders in Scotland were considered, in theory, full subjects with all the rights of Englishmen. The kingdoms they inhabited, however, were not treated the same. Although constituent parts of one British state, Ireland and Scotland had different constitutional arrangements with England. Such arrangements created tensions, but they also revealed the dynamic and flexible nature of the British state, that one size could not and did not fit all circumstances.[9]

Another set of precedents, one more suited to the western regions of America peopled by Indians, suggested a different approach. In the West, in the newly acquired regions beyond the Appalachian Mountains, the peoples there seemed much like the barbarous peoples who had inhabited the "Celtic fringes" of the British Isles: the Catholic Gaelic Irish and Highland Scots. These diverse peoples, whether in the west of Ireland, the north of Scotland, or the Ohio Valley, seemed uncivilized to the English, men and women beyond the pale of full rights. These peoples could not be governed like civilized Protestant subjects.[10]

This archipelagic blueprint for America had a tangled and fraught history, one of conflict and accommodation, as well as inclusion and exclusion. Yet, though they were contending with the meaning of new peoples, goods, and ideas, colonists had not had to contend with the struggles that defined the parameters of Britishness in the seventeenth century. Of course, Americans knew of the mythic events that remade the British Isles, even considering them their birthright as well. They understood, in theory, that sovereignty was rooted in the King-in-Parliament, as well as the fact that the Irish and the Scots had distinctive relationships to England. They even could wrap their minds around the tensions that defined relations among the kingdoms of the British state. But the crises of the seventeenth century had not restructured the colonies, nor did they transform the relationship between colonies and the British state. They lived, in a way, under a separate roof, albeit a structure without walls, open to the influences of the metropole.[11] Becoming British culturally, but not yet British politically, Americans still considered themselves loyal subjects, albeit subjects enjoying relative autonomy. Such an amphibious identity represented a common marker for colonists with distinctive pasts. But the Scots and the Irish

lived amphibious lives as well, and for them hybrid status obscured a past of compromise, accommodation, and trauma. Theirs was not a story of simple consensus,
the sort that West enshrined.

Just as critically, the process of British state formation shaped the provincial
imaginations of all Americans. The dates and events of Britishness were their cultural
vanishing points, where history and memory intersected. They too embraced the
language of power and liberty, as well as the myths, that had sustained the creation of
Britishness. Events and discourses stemming from the archipelagic process defined
how they conceived themselves and how they saw the world. What Americans could
not imagine were their roles in a drama in which Britain's seventeenth century would
be reprised in America in the eighteenth century. In other words, the keys to understanding America in the eighteenth century lay in the seventeenth century in the
British Isles.

Shelburne could not have known that, at the most abstract level, 1763—the *annus
mirabilis* for Britain—would touch off a crisis of global scale and complexity. The
Seven Years' War presented states around the world with puzzling questions about
sovereignty that would eventually lead to the French Revolution and the loss of
Spain's New World empire. The Seven Years' War initiated not only an era of Atlantic
revolutions, but a global one as well. The world war placed extraordinary burdens
on states whose institutional structures were almost still medieval. Problems were
exacerbated by the collapse of multiethnic empires outside of Europe, including the
Ottomans, Safavids, and Mughals. In the midst of greater demands on insufficiently
powerful states, the threat to worldwide trade networks would prove a daunting
challenge for Europeans, pressing them to look for new outlets for commerce and
for new regions to conquer. Because of these many tensions, stresses were felt at
home and on the peripheries of empire, necessitating reform and streamlining of
governance. The British case revolved around commerce, debt, and new lands. And
it involved territories around the world. During the Seven Years' War, the East India
Company, one of Britain's oldest trading concerns that had its own army and administrative apparatus, won large holdings in southeast and eastern India. The population in Bengal that the company would claim suzerainty over topped 20,000,000.
Although the East India Company ruled, the British state would have an interest
in seeing the company thrive. Making the American peripheries British, therefore,
represented one facet of the British chapter of a global response to a worldwide crisis
of sovereignty.[12]

Each European empire faced the prospect of extending sovereignty or at least
reforming the relationship between center and periphery. The consolidation of an
Atlantic world challenged European states to imagine authority in what the Spanish
called the ultramarine possessions. The Seven Years' War itself represented a moment
when states were imposing sovereignty onto an integrated system, in which they had
become competitors. After the war, the pressure to imagine this system anew and
to rethink the relationship between colonies and metropole grew even more insistent. So Spanish officials announced plans for fundamental "reform," in much the
same way the French, though losers in the game of empire, sought to integrate their
Caribbean holdings, particularly Saint-Domingue, into a coherent imperial structure

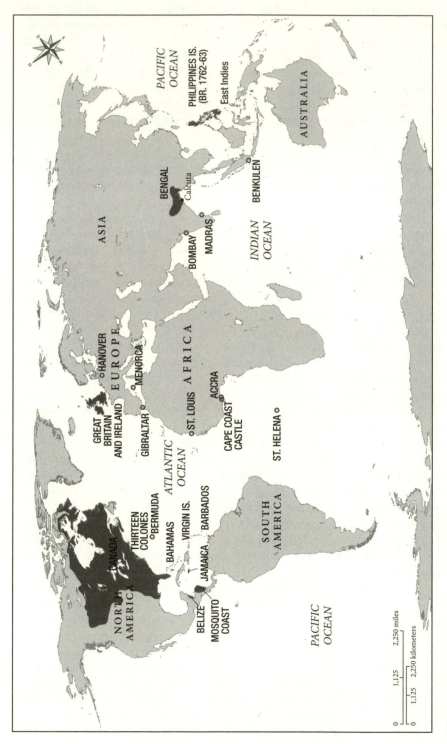

Map 2.1 British Global Holdings after Seven Years' War.

as they sought to reconceive reform at home. What the British won, not lost, forced officials to think in a conscious way of how far-off places would and should be governed, reformed, or imagined. The imperative to rethink what authority meant and where it was situated and how it would function now extended beyond the archipelago and even the consolidated Atlantic. It was global in scope. Ultimately, the British would look to the institution of Parliament to manage a complex world.[13]

These global issues, which formed a broad, silent context of pressures framing British plans for America, lay over the horizon for most Americans.[14] From the point of view of what they knew and what they saw, Americans in 1763 had every reason to be hopeful about their status within the British world; in fact, being British was a straightforward and simple affair. It meant first and foremost honoring the king as sovereign. For Americans, through parade, poems, and pageants, had elevated the Crown to nearly sacrosanct status, in some cases literally. In 1748, Benjamin Franklin described an electrical contraption called the "magical picture" of the king. The device delivered an electrical shock to anyone trying to remove the crown from the image's head. As he put it, if one's fingers touched a metal strip "and with the other hand endeavour to take off the crown, he will receive a terrible blow, and fail in the attempt." He added that "if the picture were highly charged, the consequence might perhaps be as fatal as that of high treason." If a group tried together, the experiment was called "The Conspirators."[15] The king served as a conductor of a unified culture. American colonists, particularly after the Seven Years' War, nearly venerated the Crown as they rejoiced in "the best of all kings." From elite to lowest, from Massachusetts to Georgia and the Leeward Islands, the idea of the Crown tied Americans together, a fitting cap to a simple sense of Britishness that had transformed English colonies into British provinces.

The monarch underscored what Americans were, as much as he ensured peace and stability. In this way, the Crown represented no mere abstraction. Of course, the idea that the Crown maintained stability amounted to a mixture of myth, useful fiction, and invention. Nonetheless, what we could call the cult of the Crown in the colonies united what had been disparate places in a shared world of Britishness and underscored an important lesson about sovereignty. It depended above all else on a tacit agreement in society, a compact about the legitimacy of authority. Elites and the local institutions they governed, then, in many ways dimly reflected the glory of the monarch. And in this way, they gave concrete substance to often-vague and sometimes contradictory understandings of how the Crown was the glue that held America together and kept myriad tensions in check.[16]

Chief among these tensions was the balance between *imperium* and *libertas*, power and liberty. George III, in theory, served as an umpire between each opposing force that classical history taught usually rose or fell at the expense of the other. The most troubling transition point when history turned hinged on the moment when republican Rome had become an empire, a moment that eerily resembled the years after 1763 for Britons. Ideally, the king had to play the role of an Augustus, in that he was responsible for managing a pivot point in history when empire could corrupt or civilize. Through his deeds or misdeeds, a king, then, could encourage historical processes to tend toward virtue or toward corruption. The emperor Marcus Aurelius, a philosopher king, had—at least in British memory—most effectively ruled an

Figure 2.3 Benjamin West, *George III*, 1783. The Cleveland Museum of Art.

empire that had safeguarded liberty. He served as an ideal model of a crowned leader reigning in a period of peace and security, epitomizing an ideal of Roman society before the fall. America's Britons believed in the years after the war that George III was succeeding in ensuring order while protecting rights. Britons in the Old World may have been confident, as West was, yet anxious about achieving empire without sacrificing liberty, so much so that many denied the tension. In fact, their history suggested that sometimes even kings could move history in the wrong direction. But the same anxiety did not grip Americans—not yet, that is.[17]

By 1763, then, as Americans celebrated a great victory over France, they considered themselves to be British, enthusiastically so. They were bound less to each other than to Britain through the Crown, by loyalty and an invigorated Protestant culture, as well as by increased trade and consumption. These made political ties meaningful, and gave some, like Franklin, the impetus to imagine a new British nation, decentralized but more tightly drawn together, as a key component of America's future. And there is the irony that defines the years before the War of Independence. It would be difficult to find a province of the British state in which men and women had such an abiding sense of their participation in the British system or a people more attached, in an unquestioning way, to the person the king.

Americans were not alone in venerating "the best of all kings." Englishmen and women believed they were united to the person of the patriot king in an almost mystical union. In fact, this belief proved more durable than any faith in empire.[18]

Other provincials placed their faith in the Crown as well. But their reasons for doing so were complicated. The Scots and the Irish, through their difficult pasts, were tied to England by bonds more sturdy than threads of affection. More critically, both kingdoms were part of a broader British state, the creation of which had proven a complex and difficult endeavor.[19] Although Protestant Irishman and lowlanders also considered themselves British, and this identity grew more pronounced over the course of the eighteenth century, they knew from their bloody history and the tensions that still lurked in each society that only parliamentary sovereignty could hold the whole together or could guarantee British ideals. No doubt, the English benefited more than most in this regard. Yet all recognized that Parliament, not only the Crown, underscored peace. Not so in the colonies. Colonists shared a culture with those in the metropole but had a different history. Peace was maintained not by Parliament but by local political arrangements, the availability of land, and the stability of the labor force, all of which, colonists believed, were protected by the Crown. Sovereignty for the British state was bound up in Parliament, as much as it was the silent superstructure of identity.[20]

The story of why Parliament would emerge as Britain's sovereign answer to a global crisis is multilayered and far from self-evident. But first and foremost that story depended on history. Like all Europeans, British officials relied on Enlightenment principles—or the latest ideas about politics, economy, and society—and on the lessons of classical antiquity or their imagined heritage to reform the empire that had taken shape in the wake of the world war. As a parallel, Spanish imperial reforms drew from such ideas. And officials came to an understanding and set of policies that could reorder institutions and relationships that spanned an ocean to ensure that empire functioned in a way to maintain civility in the peripheries while safe-guarding virtue in the center. The Spanish, because of their distinctive history, relied on their Crown to play this role. British experience pointed toward another institu-tion to play the reformist role. At its heart, the reason why Parliament became the vehicle for extending sovereignty outward arose from the history of the archipelago, when the kingdoms of England, Scotland, and Ireland had "become British."[21]

West's image of Britishness and empire, therefore, obscured a much more com-plex dynamic. More to the point, becoming British was not simple. On one level, the mythic events of the seventeenth century and the political ideas they spawned created a common cultural currency, a common history for Britons on both sides of the ocean. Not only did the events and memory of the seventeenth century pro-vide blueprints for British officials to govern America, they also offered means for Americans to make sense of what was happening to them.[22] But at another level, the memories of the seventeenth century obscured a troubling history that would also encompass America.

The English experience that would shape the blueprints for nation and empire revolved around the problem of how to incorporate diverse peoples within a mul-tiple monarchy, or resolving the enigma of making three kingdoms into one com-monwealth.[23] For that's what Britain was before the Seven Years' War. The English, with the help of elites in Ireland, Scotland, and Wales, ruled over the kingdoms of Scotland and Ireland and the principality of Wales. They did so, of course, through one crown: the king of England, Scotland, and Ireland. They also did so through a

Map 2.2 The Early Modern British Isles.

parliament in London. Crown and Parliament had been transformed over the previous two centuries. Many reasons accounted for a unified crown and parliamentary supremacy. But at the heart of this history lay two ideas: creating a stable notion of sovereignty for England; and then using this idea to rule the distinctive places of the British Isles with one centralized set of institutions. The Crown may have provided enough of a veneer for Americans to comprehend their British identity before 1763; however, the often-sordid history of the archipelago, with Parliament at its center, would serve as the blueprint for integrating America into the British state system after 1763.

Throughout the early modern period, English leaders had struggled with living on the same island as the Scots across the border to the north. By 1707, the two had become one with an act of union creating Great Britain. Separating these earlier struggles from the Union of 1707 were epic events that would have dramatic effects for how the British would rule, and just as significantly, for how they justified rule. Englishmen and Scots had warred with each other throughout the late Middle Ages, so much so that the borderland between them had become a rough, almost ungovernable place. Successive monarchs had worried over the Scots forming alliances with traditional enemies Spain and France. The English had tried to encourage their nobles living in the wild north to marry the daughters of Scottish nobles to encourage unity. They had tried sending armies to coerce the Scots. None of these strategies had worked.[24]

Uniting the kingdoms was fraught with difficulties. In 1603, as the unmarried Queen Elizabeth, lay dying, her closest advisers fretted over who was to succeed her. Ultimately, her relative, King James VI of Scotland, was chosen. In deciding on the Scot, the members of Elizabeth's Privy Council figured they could secure the violent border to the north and ensure that Catholic powers on the continent would not see Scotland as a backdoor through which to attack England. Less than 15 years after the battle with the famed Spanish Armada, these fears were very real. While most lowlanders were Protestant, civilized, and acculturated to English social norms, the Highlands proved a different matter altogether. Many highlanders retained an allegiance to Rome, embraced the clan system, and had durable links to their relatives and coreligionists in the north of Ireland. They appeared to be a barbarous people of backwards manners, who spoke a foreign language—Gaelic. And they had a history of creating alliances with England's enemies.[25]

The Lowlands also presented complex issues. Although the English Privy Council hoped to create a unified state between England and Scotland, Scottish Lowland elites refused to surrender their autonomy, political and economic, to what they regarded as an English-dominated parliament. Instead, they retained their own parliament that met in Edinburgh, voiced their allegiance to King James VI of Scotland—not James I of England—and held tight to their own cultural traditions. James ruled over two distinct kingdoms. Peace came between the two not because the Scots and the English saw eye-to-eye, but because they were united in a dynastic union. Over the course of the seventeenth century, this fragile sense of unity would be sorely tested.[26]

The experience with the Scots points to a defining pattern of the early modern period: the extension of English power into the marches or edges of the British Isles. At the same time that English leaders were struggling to incorporate Scotland, they were also dealing with rebellion in Ireland. Like the Scots, the Irish were divided. Cities like Dublin and the area surrounding it called "the Pale" were ruled by the descendants of Englishmen and women who had peopled the kingdom in the Middle Ages. These almost amphibious men and women called Ireland their home but spoke English and considered themselves culturally to be English. In fact, they regarded the king of England as the king of Ireland as well. They had their own parliament in Dublin, which in theory ruled the entire island. The Pale was surrounded by what contemporaries called the "mere" or "Gaelic" Irish, men and women very much like highlanders who spoke Irish, a language nearly indistinguishable from Scots Gaelic. They too had a pastoral economy and had a warlike culture rooted in a clan system. The "mere" Irish were Catholic, perhaps mainly in name, but certainly not Protestant. These people also had tried to use their estimable connections on the Continent to forge alliances with England's enemies.[27]

In much the same way the English tried to control the Scottish border, officials in England during Elizabeth's reign set their sights on conquering Ireland. Doing so was no mean task. Under Elizabeth, adventurers like Walter Raleigh and Humphrey Gilbert tried to establish plantations in Ulster and then Munster. In doing so, they touched off a series of brutal guerilla campaigns. More troops were dispatched to the rebellious island to put down the Irish and to confiscate land for those men who could secure the island for England. And they perfected terror tactics in order to do so. Gilbert, who would like Raleigh become one of England's chief proponents of settlement in America, believed that to civilize the Irish entailed killing them.[28] As a memorialist argued after Raleigh's death, he "was a man of great Courage and Industry, but of equal Severity of Temper, which he particularly exercised towards the Irish."[29]

While some English settlers devised chilling theories of racial subordination and conquest, English attempts to subdue the island under the Tudors failed. Under James I, the policy would become more insistent. James put the backing of the English state, now united with Scotland, behind a new plan of plantation for Ulster, the most rebellious and Gaelic of all the Irish provinces. In so doing, he was also proposing to sever the cultural and military link between the Scottish Highlands and Ireland.[30] In less than one generation, tens of thousands of English and Scottish Protestants propelled by the same demographic forces that spurred migration to the Caribbean and the Chesapeake left Britain to confiscate the lands of the Irish. All in all, English plans for Ireland teetered between two poles: conquest and an almost racialized understanding of the Irish, on the one hand, and reform and a belief that the Irish could be civilized, on the other. This pattern would be replayed in Ireland time and again and replicated throughout the marches, including Scotland and America.[31]

The seventeenth century witnessed a series of events that would create vanishing points for all Britons in the eighteenth century. Some stemmed from England's rivalry with Continental Catholic powers, such as the foiling of a conspiracy to blow up the Houses of parliament in 1605, the so-called Gunpowder Plot. This and other events would structure how men and women made sense of their place within a broader Britain. They also structured how they would understand sovereignty. In part, this is the case because most of the vanishing points emerged from related crises that began and ended over the issue of sovereignty. To rule Scotland and Ireland effectively required a large administrative apparatus and a great deal of money. In other words, the Crown may have claimed sovereignty over the whole of Britain and Ireland, but only a parliament could make that sovereignty meaningful. Parliament had emerged in the Middle Ages less as a discrete law-making body than as an appendage to the Crown, almost like a cabinet. It met rarely and was more an event than an institution. Nonetheless, because only Parliament could raise money, it possessed one vital prerogative the Crown did not have. As the state's powers grew, manifest in the person of the monarch, so too did the demand for laws and money, both realized in Parliament. This dilemma as to where English sovereignty ultimately resided set the stage for an epic struggle between the two that would become the defining story of seventeenth-century English, Irish, and Scottish history and would have enormous implications for eighteenth-century America as well.[32]

The crisis began, fittingly enough, in the marches and would eventually become a civil war engulfing the three kingdoms.[33] In 1641, Gaelic Irish warlords staged a brutal rebellion throughout the kingdom against foreign Protestants who had confiscated lands. The uprising begot massacres perpetrated by both Catholic and Protestant. In one notable instance, an Indian named John Fortune who had settled in Ireland and become "a Christian" was mistaken for an English Protestant and robbed of his cattle and sheep.[34] Fortune was lucky. Many "poore protestant prisoners," as one deponent declared, were "like sheepe to the slaughter."[35] For the next generation, the "Irish"—a term increasingly encompassing both the "mere" Irish and Catholic English Pale's men—would try to reclaim the kingdom from the increasingly aggressive and Protestant English state. To the English settlers in the kingdom and many English at home, the Irish were "the most barbarous *Caniballs*." In the 1640s, "it is just the State and Condition of *Ireland* as then of *Canaan*; and they must looke for the like measure of punishment by the English and Scotish Nation, as Canaan did by the *Israelites*."[36]

About the same time, Scots launched a rebellion against English control but for a very different reason. Lowland Protestants objected to the attempts of King Charles I, the son of James who assumed the throne in 1625, to impose an English episcopal church model on Calvinist congregations. The so-called Bishops' Wars would lead Charles to try to extort money from Parliament, which controlled the power of the purse strings. Ever jealous of their prerogatives and increasingly impatient with the crises that they believed Charles had manufactured, members of Parliament refused to help unless Charles reined in his centralizing tendencies. In the eyes of many, Charles was a dangerously power-hungry monarch who wanted to dictate to Parliament. Eventually, the two sides would go to war over a number of issues, all revolving around the prerogatives of rule. Scottish Calvinists would send troops to Ireland to protect Scottish settlers there and settle old scores with the Irish. They would also sign a Solemn League and Covenant to become allies of the parliamentarians and to ensure that the Catholically inclined Church of England would have no future in Scotland. The covenant railed against popery, as well as the prelacy, that is the unscriptural adherence to a church structure premised upon the rule of bishops. The Crown, they feared, was infected by both. Lowland Scots combined with England's Parliament for "the Extirpation of poperie, prelacie...Superstitions, Heresie, Schism, Prophanesse, and whatsoever shall be found to bee contrarie to sound Doctrine, and the power of Godlinesse."[37]

The British Isles reeled from a vacuum of legitimate authority, and as it did men and women discovered the wherewithal to press for their rights. Indeed, some groups, the most famous of which known as the Levellers, suggested that all social distinctions should be done away with. These people were, in the words of contemporaries, turning "the world upside down." In this volatile context, Charles would lose his head in 1649, as England, along with Scotland and Ireland, was declared a commonwealth. Oliver Cromwell, who assumed control of parliamentary forces and rule after Charles's execution as a virtual dictator, restored a semblance of order and also attempted to subjugate the wild Irish by massacring a people he considered savages. He also pressed English ecclesiastical norms on a less than enthusiastic Scottish Presbyterian Church, as he began the reformation of the Highlands both religiously and culturally. In other words, the king lay dead, but the English agenda remained much the same, and indeed became even more insistent.[38]

The crisis did not end even when the monarchy was restored in 1660. After nearly 20 years of instability, most members of Parliament agreed that the commonwealth experiment had failed. And in 1660, the son of Charles I assumed the throne. Although Charles II condemned those rebels who had put his father to death, and would die a Catholic on his deathbed, he more or less followed the middle course laid out by his grandfather James. But as Charles was growing older without a legitimate heir, many worried over the succession. Indeed, the next in line was his younger brother, James, the Duke of York, an avowed Catholic. In the 1680s, some members of Parliament, fearing the instability that would follow in the wake of James's accession, tried to have him excluded from the throne, but to no avail. In 1685, after Charles died, James II assumed the throne. As many had predicted, his accession once more plunged England into the abyss.

The tensions, however, that had animated the fight between Crown and Parliament a generation earlier, and had embroiled the marches, remained the same. The archipelago formed the basis for establishing meaningful sovereignty, and aside from authoritarian rule, only Parliament could fulfill such a complex task. James II, like his father, sought to centralize his authority at the expense of Parliament. A Catholic, who looked to Louis XIV of France as a natural ally and as a model monarch, James also repealed disabling legislation against Catholics in Ireland, promised dissenters rights on par with churchmen in England and Scotland, and seemed poised to re-grant Catholics lands that they had lost in all the kingdoms. As Parliament set itself against the king, a committee engaged in secret negotiations with James's son-in-law, the Protector of the United Provinces of the Low Countries William of Orange, offering him a share of the crown, so long as he was willing to hold it with James's Protestant daughter and William's wife, Mary. William agreed, hoping to use English forces against his French enemies, and in 1688 landed in England with an invasion force. James, then, fled, first to the Continent and then to Ireland, where he hoped to rally Irish and Scottish forces for a fight against William and his Dutch and English armies. In 1690, James's forces lost to William's at the Battle of the Boyne. England, Ireland, and Scotland were now ruled by William and Mary.[39]

Out of what contemporaries called a Glorious Revolution, a final settlement between Crown and Parliament emerged that would have dramatic implications for how the English would understand governance. With James's defeat, Parliament declared itself supreme. No doubt, the Crown still retained estimable powers, and Parliament could only rule with, and never against, the Crown. Yet, members of Parliament insisted that the new king agree to the drafting of a Bill of Rights, which by and large guaranteed the rights of Parliament against the king.

Theorists now came up with sophisticated and sanitized justifications not only for William's right to assume the throne but also to make sense of the instability of the seventeenth century and the promise of stability that finally emerged with the idea of parliamentary supremacy. Most famously, John Locke wrote that governance was not premised on the will of a dictator to power but took shape through a social contract signed between free individuals and their appointed rulers. And any time a ruler stepped beyond the limits of consent, the people, in their chief institution Parliament, had a right to depose that ruler. Locke's famous *Second Treatise*, of course, laid out the rights of a subject. All people were created equal with rights to life, liberty, and property. Individuals surrendered a portion of these rights to the government for protection. Governments existed "by the consent of the people." And the role of government was "limited to the public good of the society...and therefore can never have a right to destroy, enslave, or designedly to impoverish the subjects."[40] Good government, the type that most believed was achieved through the Glorious Revolution and its attendant ideal of parliamentary supremacy, ensured tranquility. Through the tumult of the seventeenth century, therefore, Englishmen had come to some sort of consensus of how sovereignty had to work and where it was ultimately located. This, they believed, made England distinctive, different than, say, absolutist France. It also made England stable.[41]

Fittingly, West captured this sentiment beautifully in his *Battle of the Boyne*. Here the heroic William, in the saddle and striking the pose of the Roman Marcus Aurelius, stands for the classical virtues rescued by his defeat of the despot James II, virtues, presumably, still alive in Britain throughout the eighteenth century and manifest in the parliamentary authority William had defended.[42]

This notion of parliamentary supremacy also promised to bring an end to the disorder that defined England's relations with its near neighbors. In 1707, a year after the Scottish parliament voted itself out of existence, England and Scotland were yoked together through Parliament. From this point forward, what would now be called "Great Britain" would have one parliament, which would meet in Westminster. The Scots retained control of their schools and universities, their legal system, and the Church of Scotland, which would be organized along Presbyterian lines. In some ways the process was consensual. Lowland Scots, now as provincials in a broader Britain, struggled with their status, but they did so most visibly by pouring their energies into intellectual endeavors. In fact, the dynamic commonly called the "Scottish Enlightenment" can be construed, in part, as an expression of their attraction and repulsion to and from all things English.[43]

The consensual image, however, obscures a more complex history. The process of state formation did not take place without a hitch. The novelist Daniel Defoe, the author of *Robinson Crusoe*, argued that union "agitated the whole Kingdom." Defoe, who took a job promoting the Union, understood what happened in a society when order broke down. *Robinson Crusoe*, after all, is a study of the state of nature. In the immediate aftermath of the Union, Scotland resembled that place where fear prevailed. Common men and women flew "in the Face of their Masters, and upbraid the Gentlemen, who managed it, with Selling and Betraying their Country, and Surrendering their Constitution, Sovereignty and Independency to the *English*." Defoe reported how people gathered in the streets of Edinburgh and accosted those considered "Treaters," or those pressing for the Union. In one instance, rioters "assaulted" one such traitor's house "with Stones and Sticks" and sledge hammers.

The "Rabble" grew on such occasions, roving "up and down the Town, Breaking the Windows of the Members of Parliament." Only troops could restrain them and restore order. In fact, rioting was not uncommon in the cities of Scotland after Parliament passed unpopular laws.[44]

The process of British state formation proved even more troubling in the Highlands. Many highlanders, who supported the deposed King James, were more or less excluded from this settlement, and it was understood that so long as they did not recognize the new status quo, they would be considered enemies of the state. And the English, along with their Lowland allies, would hammer the Highlands relentlessly, especially when clansmen championed the cause of James's descendants to the throne. Eventually, the Highlands and the "Jacobites" would be conquered in much the same way Ireland was, by clearing the people off the land and crushing and reforming what they regarded as a barbarous culture. The marchland pattern of conquest and reform prevailed in Highland Scotland. In 1746, British troops "slaughtered" highlanders at Culloden Moor and in the regions surrounding it. The Duke of Cumberland, the son of King George II, cut down a broadsword charge of highlanders with volleys of grapeshot. He then oversaw the hunting down of those who fled. The man known as "the Butcher" led an officer corps that likened the rebels to "vermin" and wild beasts, a subhuman species that merited no quarter.[45] As one witness to the slaughter put it, "the late victory had obtain'd over the Clans of the Canaanites, a sort of Highland Army . . . or a Banditti of Robbers, that were left to prove Israel."[46] The massacre of highlanders was followed by a policy of reform, which some hoped

Figure 2.4 Benjamin West, *Battle of the Boyne in 1690*, 1778. Private Collection/The Bridgeman Art Library.

would civilize the Highlands. Reformers advocated schools to undermine the Gaelic language, outlawing Highland clothing, including the kilt, and clearing men and women off the land for more productive agriculture. The Highlands would be civilized and anglicized, with all that the terms connoted. The upshot for Scotland, and for a wider Britain, was this: what had been a dynastic union was now, literally, a sovereign union, manifest in Parliament.

Parliamentary sovereignty presented all provincials with dilemmas. The Irish, too, came to recognize British parliamentary supremacy. Unlike the Scots, the Irish would retain their parliament in Dublin, now peopled exclusively by Protestants. In Ireland, after all, Protestants had stood shoulder-to-shoulder against James's Catholic army. Nonetheless, they would have to recognize the right of a British parliament to legislate for Irish affairs, though the Irish did not consent to such measures. Catholics were now excluded from the polity and from the land. Penal laws were put in place that would not destroy Catholic culture but would destroy Catholic power. Members of the established Church of Ireland would rule the kingdom, but only so long as they recognized that Britain could dictate for it.[47] By the late seventeenth century, Irish writers began to question if "an Act of Parliament made in England shall bind the Kingdom and People of Ireland without their allowance and acceptance of such Act in the kingdome of Ireland."[48] In 1698, William Molyneux, a friend of Locke's, would write a treatise on this issue, declaring that Parliament could not justify legislating for Irish affairs. "To tax me without my Consent," he famously wrote, "is little better, if at all, than down-right Robbing me."[49]

By the eighteenth century, this line of questioning became more insistent. Some such as Jonathan Swift, the famous clergyman who wrote *Gulliver's Travels*, would write against the British conceit to rule Irish affairs without the consent of

Figure 2.5 David Morier, *Culloden*, 1746. The Royal Collection, Her Majesty Queen Elizabeth II.

the people. "Am I a *Free-Man* in England, and do I become a *Slave* in six Hours by crossing the Channel," he asked.[50] Free persons enjoyed all the rights of Britons, especially that of consent. Slaves did not. As he wrote in the wake of English attempts to coin money for Ireland, "our Ancestors reduced this Kingdom to the Obedience of ENGLAND, for which we have been rewarded with a worse Climate, the Priviledge of being governed by Laws to which we do not consent, [and] a ruined Trade." Yet with a disgruntled Catholic majority and a growing dissenter presence in the country, there was only so far that churchmen like Swift could go in protesting British parliamentary supremacy. For his part, Swift denied inferences that he would "dispute the King's Prerogative" or that the Irish had "grown ripe for Rebellion, and ready to shake off the Dependency of Ireland upon the Crown of England."[51] Like Scottish lowlanders, members of Ireland's Ascendancy lived with enemies of the state that ever threatened the revolution settlement. Moreover, England was tied to Ireland through dense networks of patronage. Fear and proximity, much as in Scotland, influenced the dynamic of state formation.[52]

To drive home this lesson, Parliament passed in 1719 the "6ᵗʰ of George I," the so-called Declaratory Act. In exactly the same language that would be used decades later in America in the wake of disturbances over Parliament's attempts to legislate for the colonies, the Act mandated that although Ireland had its own parliament and was a fully constituted kingdom, the parliament in Westminster could determine Irish affairs "in all cases whatsoever." Declarations of parliamentary supremacy did not bring an end to Ireland's provincial dilemma. In fact, they enflamed the kingdom. An apothecary named Charles Lucas took up Swift's mantle in the mid-eighteenth century. Unlike Swift, however, Lucas appealed to the masses to question parliamentary sovereignty. Lucas called on "Freemen" to defend their rights like "Sons of Liberty." Emulating English writers of the seventeenth century, and well-known serializers John Trenchard and Thomas Gordon, Lucas took the ideas that sustained the British state to challenge the second-class status of Irish Protestants within the constitutional arrangement. "Ireland is," he declared, "by Right and by Law; a Perfect, Free and Independent Kingdom." With good reason, Lucas was called the "Wilkes of Ireland." The famous agitator John Wilkes lambasted officials whom he believed betrayed an English legacy of freedom. Wilkes styled himself a patriot by arguing that although Britain's form of government was ideal, its ministers had to safeguard liberty. More of a reformer than a revolutionary, Wilkes used publicity and self-promotion to try to make the English system more responsive to English subjects. Politicization of the people could bring pressure for reform. Lucas did the same with the same methods for Ireland. Lucas, who did not want to declare independence from the Crown, only contested the idea of British parliamentary supremacy. He also whipped up the populace, for which he was banished by the state to the Continent for 10 years. Parliament could enforce its will in Ireland.[53] For all the sound and fury, Protestant Ireland made peace with the revolution settlement. Fears of Catholics and the presence of British garrisons in the kingdom resolved any sort of dilemma.

Others in the kingdom negotiated the provincial dilemma in ways that spoke to their distinctive status in the kingdom. Dissenters, concentrated in Ulster, believed they had merited inclusion into the political nation by their support of the Protestant cause. Disappointed at their exclusion from political life, some petitioned Parliament for a full enjoyment of their rights. Some voted with their feet, opting to sail to America when the economy failed, thereby becoming part of the process that was making America British. Movement and a stubborn belief in their rights as Protestant Britons defined the ways Ireland's dissenters made sense of their place in post-revolution Britain.[54] Catholics, for their part, struggled with increased disabilities. They, too, came to terms with the settlement and tried to carve out niches for themselves in constrained circumstances. Some tried to revive the Irish language, particularly those who had supported the failed Jacobite cause. Others, especially a wealthy merchant class, came to see the British Parliament as a potential patron and protector against an Irish Parliament that continued to pass disabling legislation. The poorer sort tried to make the best of a difficult situation. Rural insurgents created secret organizations to protect their traditional rights to land. Urban Catholics rioted if their betters overstepped their bounds or hounded priests to an unreasonable degree.[55]

It is at this point after the Glorious Revolution settlement took a final shape in the kingdoms of England, Ireland, and Scotland when we can say that British history meaningfully begins. Other features animated the now invigorated British state, features that did not revolve around markers like ethnicity or race. Britons prided themselves on being a people tied to the sea, and trade to some extent defined who they were. The experience of state formation and the crisis of sovereignty in the seventeenth century encouraged Britons to focus their sense of self upon the sea. They regarded themselves as an island—or islands—people, divorced from the Continent by history and their mythic readings of it, but tied to other parts of the world through trade.[56] Protestantism, likewise, played a central role in making them a people and in determining who was a subject and, just as significantly, who was not. As Britain was engaged with Catholic France in a series of wars over the course of the eighteenth century, these tendencies would grow even more significant. And the idea of loyalty to the Crown bound the peoples living in Ireland, Scotland, and England together. English, Irish, and Scots could consider themselves British so long as they championed these ideals. Living within the realm and rejecting any of these markers placed one beyond the pale.

The new central role that Parliament had assumed over the course of the seventeenth century buttressed this whole arrangement. Indeed, Parliament made it its mission to protect the three foundations of Britishness: Protestantism, commerce, and the loyalty of a "free" people to the Crown. These ideals became both the bases of identity for Britons and became the stuff that animated sovereignty. As Wilkes's career demonstrated, these ideas also sustained arguments for reform. Patriots defined themselves by championing British liberty. But in the British Isles, they meant little without a Parliament that sustained them. The ideology of empire and notion of identity as Britons that took shape in the period also papered over the more troubling aspects of state formation within the British Isles, a history of conflict that included riot, rebellion, repression, conquest, and reform, as well as acquiescence.[57]

The British arrangement emerged from the incorporation of the Scots and Irish within the state under the concept of parliamentary sovereignty, an arrangement that would be tested by events in America. After 1763, a process of state formation that had integrated the three nations of the British Isles would be extended across an ocean in the wake of a global war between empires. A system that was flexible enough to incorporate non-English men and women would face the daunting task of making sense of a growing and dynamic population of white colonists, black slaves, and Native Americans an ocean away. Officials also confronted colonies with diverse histories and social hierarchies, ranging from New England to the Leeward Islands. Finally, they had to contend with large numbers of former French subjects who were Catholic.[58]

American colonists in the old English settlements assumed the process for them would be different. Although they had contributed as much as they believed they could, or nearly as much as the British had come to expect, Americans could now revel in a victory that they thought they had some hand in. The war was won in America, and militia had served alongside British regulars. They may not have liked all that they saw—British troops were cruel and haughty and their commanders were consumed with discipline and hierarchy—but colonists could now regard themselves too as Britons, heirs to a legacy of commerce, liberty, Protestantism, and loyalty.[59] The war was, in effect, their Glorious Revolution. With the victory in the Great War for Empire, they could believe that this too was their empire, that America formed an integral part of Britain. In fact, as Franklin prophesied, American population would double every 20 years. Eventually, "the greatest number of Englishmen will be on this side of the water." Britain's glory would grow. "What an accession of power to the British empire by sea as well as land!" he gushed. American devotion to the Crown ensured as much and united all the provinces: "The inhabitants of them [the colonies] are, in common with the other subjects of *Great Britain*, anxious for the glory of her Crown, and extent of her power and commerce, the welfare and future repose of the whole *British* people." Like Mayhew, Franklin saw great possibilities for British America without any cost. "Happy as we now are," he declared, "under the best of kings...happy too in the wisdom and vigour of every part of administration, particularly that part whose peculiar province is the British plantations." Happy consensus would prevail.[60]

Franklin was wrong. Americans could not escape British history, though try as they might. They too would be privy to a process of state formation no less fraught than Ireland and Scotland's. The first signs that Americans would grapple with the metropolitan models appeared in the wilderness. Like the Irish and Scottish experiences, the process did not start because of any grand plan. It did so through necessity. The lasting legacy of the war revolved around two related issues, debt and land. Since the colonists showed little initiative in leading the war effort—and because Britain shouldered the whole burden—the national debt doubled from its prewar level of £72 million to £146 million.[61] Financing the interest of the debt alone seemed a staggering prospect. And the level of debt showed no signs of diminishing. In fact, the obverse was the case. Britain now controlled nearly all of France's New World holdings. As well as the trans-Appalachian West, the British now ruled the island of Grenada in the Caribbean, the Floridas, and most dauntingly, the province of Quebec. They also had achieved mastery over France in India. Each presented its own challenges. Justifiably fearing that the French would regroup to try to win back the lands they had lost, the British realized that they would have to maintain a sizeable regular force in America, which would cost £225,000 per year.[62]

If past was prologue, America would be fought over again. And those fears appeared to be realized no sooner than the French had lost in America. In 1763, after the British had garrisoned the forts the French had held in the West, the Indians throughout the Midwest rose. The immediate impetus stemmed from British treatment of Native Americans. Unlike the French, who had sought to create a middle ground between European and Native American ways, the British under their commander Jeffrey Amherst determined that they would dictate the terms of peace. The French had regarded Indians as partners. The British would not. Indians would be allowed little freedom to trade and would have to do so under rigid British terms. Most gallingly, Indians would be considered dependents. As the "rebellion" against established authority unfolded, some argued that only stern measures could "reduce the Savages to Reason."[63] Amherst called for the most pernicious means to do so, infamously proposing that items, such as blankets, infected with smallpox be sent as presents to Indians besieging a British fort, hoping they would touch off an epidemic.[64] In short, he advocated any means "to Extirpate this Execrable

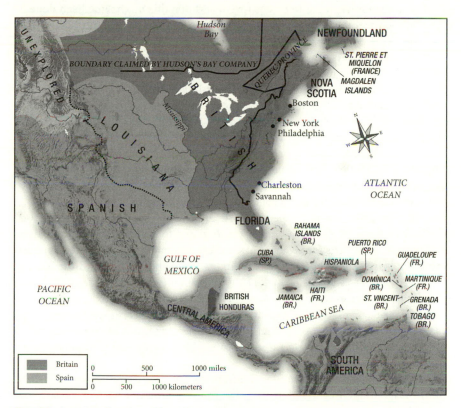

Map 2.3 America after Seven Years' War.

Race."[65] Amherst, a veteran of Culloden, advocated the same methods for dealing with people on the marches as had been used in the Highlands and beyond the pale in Ireland. Savages, like barbarians, had to be conquered.[66]

Under the leadership of a charismatic Ottawa war chief named Pontiac and the spiritual leadership of a Delaware named Neolin, Indians throughout the West attacked British troops at forts they had just secured from the French. Most worryingly for the British, Pontiac was encouraging other formerly French-allied Indians to take up arms against the British. Indians were besieging the newly constructed massive masonry structure they had built on the ruins of Fort Duquesne, the cornerstone of western plans now named Fort Pitt. To the British, who could not even entertain the idea that Indians would rise on their own, Pontiac's War signaled the dangers of ignoring the West and of believing that the French were gone for good. The war, instead, ignited fears that the French were secretly coordinating Native American attacks, that they were unleashing "savages," although such was not the case. The war drove home the point that peace would not be cheap and Indians would have to be placated.[67] More critically, the ways that the war played out signaled that this war was less a distinctively American crisis—one pitting whites against Indians—than a British crisis in America. Echoing characterizations of the Irish and of the Scots, frontier settlers believed that the Indians "were the Canaanites, who by God's commandment were to be destroyed; and that this not having been done by them at the time, the present war might be considered as a just punishment from God for their disobedience."[68]

The war and fears of a French resurgence, in part, led to an ambivalent approach to Quebec, further complicating British plans for governance of American holdings. The Treaty of Paris stipulated that former French subjects there could enjoy "the liberty of the Catholick religion ... as far as the laws of Great Britain permit." The sticking point was that the laws of Britain did not permit Catholics to enjoy their civil rights as subjects. Just as significantly, administrators of Quebec were encouraged to anglicize the people and to persuade them to become members of the Church of England. Official policy mandated that Quebec would become a British province, one in line with the ideological character of the archipelagic settlement. Unofficially, those working on the ground recognized the infeasibility of such an approach. As a military governor put it, the people were "extremely tenacious of their Religion." Catholics were even allowed to name a bishop and to send him, after some delay and wrangling, to Paris for ordination. Officials negotiated the difficulties supporting Catholicism raised by recognizing him as the "Superintendent of the Romish Church." Catholics would enjoy a de facto toleration in an empire defined by a de jure anti-Catholicism. While they were ostensibly being transformed into good subjects, the British would rule the province with garrison government, under which the people would not enjoy political rights. Quebec, then, was an imperial work in progress, one in which officials decided to establish vague and provisional ruling mechanisms.[69]

Quebec proved the exception. Confronting the twin issues of land and debt, the British variation of the global fallout from the Seven Years' War, would lead the British to create a twinned plan for the rest of America, one scheme for the region west of the Appalachian Mountains and another for the colonies east of the mountains. In essence, part of America would become part of a British territorial empire; the other parts, which already enjoyed the fruits of government, would be incorporated into the British state. These plans did not emerge as some sort of grand, well-articulated strategy. Rather, they took shape as the British tried to bring order to its New World holdings and to ease the debt of war. If Americans reveled in the idea that they too could claim the rights of Britons, they would have to learn quickly that they would have to shoulder the responsibilities of Britons as well. The new system would hinge, literally, on a line in the wilderness. Although its rationale would take shape from Britain's seventeenth-century experience of bringing stability to England and extending sovereignty to Scotland and Ireland, the origins of the line lay in the American West.[70]

In the midst of Pontiac's War, British officials realized that the garrison form of government and racist attitudes of its military commander, Sir Jeffrey Amherst, were largely to blame for the debacle. Following the marchland pattern, officials advocated reform of Indians. Long-term stability required that they be civilized. Amherst was recalled, and as he was, officials reorganized the ways that the new acquisitions to the west would be administered. Thomas Gage was appointed as the new military commander in America. In addition, the Board of Trade made it its business to direct affairs in America. The first order of business was to bring a semblance of stability to America. The Board did so by laying out a line along the spine of the Appalachians, the so-called Proclamation Line, to divide America between a settled East and an Indian-dominated West. These Lords of Trade also appointed two superintendents for Indian affairs, one north of the Ohio River, the other for the south. For this task, they chose an Irishman, Sir William Johnson, and a Scot, John Stuart. Both had experience with subject peoples, in Johnson's case the Iroquois, in Stuart's the Cherokee, the most powerful group in the southeast. Perhaps just as critically, both lived for some time beyond the pale of Britishness: Johnson was born a Catholic, and Stuart a highlander. But both had embraced the markers of Britishness since, becoming civilized, loyal, Protestant subjects.[71]

They would serve as exemplars of all that made the new arrangement west of the Proclamation Line function. The Royal Proclamation, which established the line, mandated that settlers were not to move west of the line. "We do hereby strictly forbid," the Proclamation read, "on Pain of Our Displeasure, all Our loving Subjects from making any Purchases or Settlements" west of the line. Nor could speculators claim land there. Indians, although under the sovereign authority of the British Crown, were to live unmolested on the land.[72] Officials did not do so for what we could call enlightened reasons; rather, they were transfixed with managing the West as cheaply as possible. It was understood that the West was a region in which subjects could not live. It was to be a region beyond government, a place more like a state of nature. Without government, civility could not flourish. Indians, therefore, were subject to British authority but were not subjects. They would, in effect, be considered along the lines of the barbarous wild Irish and Scottish highlanders.[73]

Selecting Johnson and Stuart as superintendents, therefore, made a great deal of sense. Along with the considerable experience both brought to their tasks, as well as their connections with Indians, they also had made the transition from barbarism to civility. In other words, they had firsthand experience with both blueprints of

Britishization: the model that was implemented for the Protestant Irish and Lowland Scots; and the one that was playing out in the West and that had defined the incorporation of Irish Catholics and highlanders. And each hoped that with time, Indians too could be pacified and reformed. But until then, their land was not to be settled—in theory at least. Johnson and Stuart advocated sending missionaries and traders to civilize the Indians. Even on the marches, provisions could be made for creating a people Protestant, maritime, commercial, and free in the wake of conquest. In the meantime, the Proclamation Line ensured peace. Did officials, and people like Johnson and Stuart, really believe this reasoning? It is impossible to say. But this much is clear. The idea of making the West a "no-man's land," with the need for few troops and few resources, reflected the new fiscal restraints the British confronted after 1763. Governance without government in the West meant sovereignty on the cheap.[74]

To make the system work meant that Johnson and Stuart and their deputies had to keep Indians peaceful, and they were to use their connections and leverage to encourage responsible trade and the work of missionaries among the Indians. Their responsibility included adjudicating disputes between Indian groups. The Lords of Trade ordered small numbers of troops to be stationed at key points in the West, such as Fort Pitt and Fort Chartres on the Mississippi, where former French subjects still lived. Here troops would provide a basis for garrison government, keep an eye out for French intrigue and an eye on French *habitants*, make British sovereignty manifest, and warn off those types of peoples—settlers, squatters, and speculators—who could imperil the arrangement. Their job, therefore, was to keep the West quiet.

East of the line lay a different world. We have been taught that Americans would be treated as second-class citizens by the British after 1763, that America would reluctantly become part of a British "empire" with all that that word implies. We usually think of the dreaded Stamp Act as the beginning of the end of British rule in America. In fact, it marked the beginning of British rule in America. After the Seven Years' War, as we shall see, American colonists would be treated much like other provincial groups, especially as Parliament passed a series of duties for America and the Caribbean colonies. Indeed, while officials created the new empire in the West for nonsubjects, regions east of the Proclamation Line were to be incorporated into the British state. American colonists, civilized, loyal, and Protestant, would be treated much like Lowland Scots and Protestant Irish. The distinction between state and empire mattered a great deal. While centralizing control over space transfixed officials out west, even if they did so by the cheapest means possible, establishing control over subjects concerned them in the East. Stabilizing these holdings in these ways offered the surest means of negotiating the many tensions, stemming from strapped treasuries at home to new opportunities around the world, that all imperial states had to confront after the Seven Years' War. With the process of state formation, officials had a great deal of experience, more than two centuries' worth, and so could address new issues with old tools. Although the days of "salutary neglect" were about to end, this did not mean that American rights would be trampled by an empire. Rather, what had been colonies would now become new British provinces of a unitary state. The year 1707 marked a formal storting point of British history in the British Isles. The year 1763 would mark its beginnings in America, as well as the end of colonial history.

It seemed that, at first glance in any event, Americans would not take issue with becoming members of the state. They celebrated victories over the French, as did other provincials. They considered British freedoms to be their birthrights as well. They had demonstrated their loyalty. They too enjoyed the fruits of commerce. And with the exception of some small numbers of Catholics in Maryland, Delaware, and Pennsylvania, nearly all professed themselves to be Protestant. The victory over Catholic France, then, represented a victory for Americans as well, a coming of age. In other words, they knew as well as any people in the British Isles what it meant to be British. They knew how Ireland and Scotland had been pacified and incorporated. They knew also that epic battles had been fought to safeguard the liberties of Britain both abroad and in Britain itself.

Americans considered themselves British culturally. What about politically? The Crown tied Americans to England. But the idea of parliamentary sovereignty meant less to them than to other provincials. For although land and the need to raise money represented the critical issues that officials had to grapple with after 1763 because of global stresses, the answer that they would come up with would be the extension of a notion of sovereignty based on Parliament's right to rule that made England, Ireland, and Scotland as a whole governable. Britons had suffered through the complex tumults of the seventeenth century convinced that only a Parliament in Westminster could hold them together. Although Americans had not been privy to that history, they hoped to be considered on a par with other Britons. They should have been careful for what they wished for.

CHAPTER 3

﹌

Such a Power Should Be Watched with a Jealous Eye

O ne final story of Britons, this one less well documented than the charting of empire and the rise of a planter. During the height of the Seven Years' War, an Irish-born migrant to Pennsylvania's frontier, James McCullough, catalogued the fortunes of men and women in the area around a place called Paxton, a region that Indian raiding parties visited and revisited. McCullough was not captured or killed, but in July 1756, his sons John and James were. "Weep not for the dead neither bemoan him," he cried, "but weep sore for him that goeth away for he shall return no more nor see his native country." A month later, he recorded "a verey great Slaughter...by the indins Wherin 39 persons killed and taken Captives." In November, John Woods, his wife, mother-in-law, and John Archer's wife—McCullough's friends and neighbors— were killed, along with 8 or 9 other men. Four children were also "Carried off." The reported carnage continued for years, including "11 persons killed at paxton by the indins" in May 1757 and "a very great Slaughter" near Opequon in the Shenandoah in which, as McCullough alleged, "60 odd killed and taken captiv."[1]

Other fathers would lose sons on the bleeding frontier. In 1763, after it was reported that a groups of Indians had "cruelly butchered" settlers on the northern border of Pennsylvania near a place called Wyoming, a group from a settlement right next to McCullough's place decided that they had had enough.[2] The provincial government in Pennsylvania had not protected them during the Seven Years' War. The British were failing to protect them during Pontiac's War. They then decided they had to protect themselves. Amidst a failure of authority, this meant launching a preemptive strike against the Indians in their midst. An unfounded rumor set them off. Near Paxton, at a place called Conestogoe Manor, lived a group of "domesticated" Indians, who were peaceful and lived amicably with their white neighbors. Nonetheless, word was out that one of them named Will Sawk had given information about the defenses and location of settlements to belligerent Indians to the West who had been raiding in the region. Frontiersman arrived at Conestogoe Manor on a snowy day in December. There they found six Indians but not Sawk. The rest were away selling brooms to their neighbors. The raiders killed all six, including children.

Pennsylvania authorities were dumbstruck when they heard of the atrocity, rounding up the rest of the Conestogoes and sending them to the workhouse in the town of Lancaster for safekeeping. Undeterred, the frontiersmen, now growing in number and calling themselves the Paxton Boys, rode off to the workhouse, where they killed 14 Indians in horrific ways, smashing skulls, hacking off limbs, and blowing heads to smithereens. They spared none. They then resolved to march on the city of Philadelphia, to bring down the government that in their eyes had failed in its most fundamental task, protecting its inhabitants. The Paxton Boys and their followers argued that all they were doing was acting as good British subjects. One of the leaders professed the group to be "loyal Subjects to the best of Kings." They were "firmly attached to his Royal, Person, Interest and Government." But they lived in a world in which "the Blood of our many murdered Brethren [was] tamely covered, but out poor happy Friends abandoned to Slavery among the Savages."[3] The negligence of government had driven them to act. The Paxton Boys, too, were heirs to the Glorious Revolution. But they did not enjoy the rights of subjects. With no protection, there was no government. As John Locke had argued, the state existed to safeguard inalienable rights. If it did not, the people had a right to take things into their own hands. After all, "a Right to *demand*, and to *receive* Protection" was the privilege of all "*free born Subjects of Britain.*"[4]

While they portrayed themselves as Britons, the British in their midst found these arguments preposterous. Troops stationed nearby were dispatched not to protect the settlers, but to ensure that the Paxton Boys stood down. Under threat of being fired upon, the frontiersmen left for home. Members of Parliament were likewise incensed and supported the measures of Thomas Gage, the military commander of North America, to put this rabble in its place. The British had no great love for Indians, but they also could not make heads or tails of vigilantes trying to set the standard for what it meant to be British, or see how settlers could make the case that by killing Indians they were safeguarding their rights.

The story says a great deal about the looming gap between metropolitan and provincial ideals of British identity. Men and women on both sides of the ocean used the same sets of ideas to characterize their position within the nation. But it seemed the words carried different meanings in different regions. For the British, parliamentary sovereignty should have also held the transatlantic system together. For Americans, this was not the case. Americans conceived of the markers of Britishness in much the same way other provincials in the British Isles did; however, American ideas were leavened and complicated by other issues. For starters, they had an abiding sense that the king maintained stability. Like all Britons, they understood that the King-in-Parliament was the site where ultimate authority was located; however, through their history, they privileged one over the other. The Crown, safeguarding provincial autonomy and the imagined balance typifying provincial political institutions, trumped a parliament intent on more centralized authority.

The story of the Paxton Boys says something more. Frontier disturbances were nothing new. Nor, alas, was Indian killing. Some Americans, however, were beginning to equate such practices with their rights. Scottish understandings of Britishness were complicated by region and culture and revolved around whether one was a rude highlander or civilized lowlander. Irish conceptions centered on religious confession, whether one were a Protestant or a Papist. Americans struggled with these same tensions, but race and region—both aspects of America's diverse seventeenth-century pasts—along with the sorts of fissures that divide any society, such as socioeconomic status, represented the salient fault lines in the colonies. And unsurprisingly, these categories colored any understanding of what it meant to be British. The Paxton Boys were not the only ones who equated their rights as subjects with the color of their skin or their status within their colony.[5]

Officials took this from the episode: the threat of British sovereign force had saved the day. Nonetheless, throughout the colonies, east and west, Americans would begin to question the nature of that authority. On one level, as the Paxton Boys and their apologists argued, the British did not seem to appreciate the distinctive pressures Americans had to contend with. At a deeper level, Americans would begin to see that although both British and Americans used the same language of British identity, they were harboring different sets of assumptions as they defined Britishness.

With the Seven Years' War, and its attendant global pressures, the question of sovereignty could no longer remain an abstraction nor could the nature of the relationship between Britain and the colonies. At last, Americans would confront issues that Scots and the Irish had grappled with for generations. The state had the reach to hold tensions in check in both these kingdoms as they were incorporated into the state. If not the reach, each kingdom that comprised part of Britain was held in check by fear, fear of economic insignificance and highlanders for the Scots, and fears of Catholics for the Irish. Not so for America. Levels of debt, the distance to the colonies, and the historic virtual independence of colonial political institutions ensured that making sovereignty manifest, especially a version rooted in Parliament, would prove difficult. As events took on a life of their own, it would prove impossible. To be sure, Americans rioted, wrote resolutions, and made impassioned pleas in print about their status as they negotiated the process of state formation. This does not mean that a revolution was in the offing in 1765. All provincials did the same things, especially the Irish. But in the American case, Parliament's attempt to bring the colonies into the British national fold entailed a weakening of local authority. Parliament, moreover, aside from a massive infusion of money and troops across 3,000 miles of ocean, could not fill the void of authority. As Americans rebelled, sovereignty began to crack. In other words, the transatlantic cleavage did not only lead to misunderstanding and blundering; it also pointed to fundamental contradictions that could not be squared in America.

The British cause to make the colonies in the East part of the nation, which began as part of an effort to reform the relationship between center and periphery, would founder on these issues, as would the attempt to make the West part of an empire. In fact, failure would occur at an accelerated pace in the West. And ironically, Americans would base their resistance on the very ideals that underscored British identity for all. The ideas of John Locke more or less summed up the reasonable ways that Britons imagined the origins and maintenance of their state. The social contract to leave an inconvenient state of nature, and which mandated that some measure of rights had to be surrendered to ensure tranquility for all, lay at the heart of the political consensus that held Britain together during the eighteenth century.

Americans too had a fondness for Locke. But after the early 1770s, they would look to the last few sections of his *Second Treatise*, those chapters that argued that the subject did not have to tolerate a magistrate who overstepped his bounds. In such instances, the people had a right to rebel. Americans were not only contesting a British notion of nation or empire. They were also questioning the bonds of sovereignty. And as they did so, they began to leave a world described by Locke for a world described by another social theorist named Thomas Hobbes. Hobbes's world without sovereignty was not "inconvenient." His was "nasty, brutish, and short." This was the nature of the world in which authority collapsed.

The beginning of the end of sovereignty marked the beginning of revolution. The Revolution's origins, of course, had a great deal to do with seminal ideas and tensions within America between haves and have-nots. However, the crisis that pushed the colonies into the vortex of revolution revolved around questions of sovereignty and authority, making that crisis, in essence, a transatlantic British civil conflict. When American colonists and British officials differed over what it meant to be British—and especially Parliament's position in that equation—sovereignty was compromised. At that point, socioeconomic and racial tensions, rooted in the distinctive characteristics and history of each region, bubbled to the surface, further attenuating authority.

Like most momentous events, the incorporation of the colonies into the British state began in an inauspicious fashion and it did not exactly begin by design. In 1764, Parliament passed what is called the Sugar Act. The Act, which did not propose anything new for the colonies, was designed to enforce old laws on the books enacted to regulate the flow of trade, in this case an Act that laid a duty on the importation of foreign molasses into the colonies, a measure that, if enforced, would help the wealthiest of Britain's colonies—the sugar islands of the Caribbean—as well as the Treasury. Colonists, and New Englanders in particular who distilled rum from molasses, knew of such laws. They just ignored them. So did customs officials. In fact, everyone colluded to allow the smuggling of Dutch and French molasses into the colonies. Rhode Island distillers, for instance, purchased four fifths of their molasses from the French, and officials gladly took the bribes offered by merchants.[6]

The ministry, however, realized that this corrupt practice took coffers out of a treasury emptied by the world war and the provisional steps taken to address new responsibilities. The 1764 Act reduced the duty on foreign molasses, setting it below the amount used to bribe officials. Customs duties would be collected by better-paid officials in the colonies, ones less reliant on bribes for making a living. Parliament, it seemed, was trying to streamline administration to raise revenues. Americans complained, especially merchants who fretted over the enforcement of the duty. Some grumbled about Parliament overstepping its bounds. But then again, any protester had to know that the 1764 Act merely was put in place to put teeth in laws already passed, which in effect stemmed in the first place from the Navigation Acts. Colonial trade, or so the mercantilist logic of the Navigation Acts went, should benefit England and its balance of trade, not foreign powers. The impetus for angst stemmed from economic, as well as principled, grounds. Distillers worried the Act would put them out of business. And Americans also blamed the wealthy West Indian nabobs, not only the ministry, for the passage of the Sugar Act.[7]

The following year, protest grew to a fevered pitch. In 1765, George Grenville, the first minister, proposed that the colonies of the mainland and the Caribbean pay an excise duty on stamped paper that was to be used for 15 classes of documents needed for court proceedings, licenses, diplomas, mortgages, indentures, the papers for ships to leave harbor, deeds for land, leases, and contracts. Along with the documents that allowed society and government to function, the paper used for newspapers, pamphlets, even dice and playing cards was to be embossed with a stamp by the Treasury Office. The stamped paper was then to be shipped across the ocean in merchantmen, where it would be warehoused and sold. Grenville hoped that levying a stamp duty would help defray the costs of stationing troops in America. Subjects in Britain and Ireland would service and manage the debt. In other words, the rationale for passing a Stamp Act for the colonies did not seem unreasonable at the time.[8]

The Sugar and Stamp Acts represented the first attempts—admittedly groping attempts—of the British to reform the consolidated Atlantic. They were groping for two reasons. First, at this point officials were reacting to the immediate pressures of the period: the pressing need to govern space, rule peoples, and manage debt in the face of what they considered to be continuing imperial rivalry. Second, the state finally had the capacity to project its authority, in a substantive way, across the ocean. War-making on a global scale had amplified the reach of the British state.[9] Although they had not devised a formal reform agenda up to this point, officials were suggesting through these Acts that informal arrangements of the past were not up to the task of imperial management in the wake of war.

The ministry passed other measures as well that also addressed—again gropingly—the pressures of the period. As well as attempting to regulate a British system of trade premised on mercantilist assumptions, officials also tried to regulate the money supply. Passed in 1764, the Currency Act was designed to tighten the money supply, prohibiting colonies from issuing further paper currency, as the ministry did not want to encourage inflation within the empire or devalue any currency. Another parliamentary initiative, the Quartering Act, was really an amendment to a measure passed annually in Parliament called the Mutiny Act. The Quartering Act was suggested as a way of helping defray the costs for the new American military establishment. The troops, which now safeguarded the extended empire, could be housed and fed at colonial expense. New York, where many troops were stationed, balked at complying.[10]

But it was with the Stamp Act that local tensions exploded, fissures in societies became apparent, principled positions were staked out, and what should have been discrete issues merged, further fueling discontent and focusing anger. For these reasons, it merits close attention, first in terms of understanding what happened and then exploring the complex how and why of the crisis. The story of the crisis involves not only those who rebelled but also those who did not, those who were struggling to compete in a changing world of labor, those who were striving to lead the colonies, those who were clamoring for their rights as religious dissenters, and those who saw in the eighteenth century the specter of the seventeenth century. Americans, it should be noted, were not exceptional, though the grievances they gave vent to during the crisis were distinctive.

Bostonians seemed to harbor the greatest grievances against the stamp duty. Young up-and-comers like Samuel Adams, men on the make but outside the colony's governing elite, clamored for a repeal of the tax even before it was enacted. An aspiring provincial leader who like the Royall sisters also sat for John Singleton Copley, Adams considered the stamp duty an "unconstitutional tax." It infringed "the most essential Rights of British Subjects," rights that Americans could claim.[11] Poorer men and women rioted. With the encouragement of Adams and John Hancock, groups attacked the house of Andrew Oliver, who would be appointed to collect the hated tax, as well as the warehouse they supposed would house the paper once it arrived from London. Under the leadership of a cobbler and veteran of the Seven Years' War named Ebenezer Mackintosh, they then set their sights on the man they thought was behind it all, the all-too-well-connected lieutenant governor Thomas Hutchinson. Mobs ransacked his house after he had ordered a clever effigy of Lord Bute torn down: a boot with a devil climbing out of it. In vilifying the Scottish Bute as a traitor, these men and women were tapping into a powerful early modern English prejudice. Only a Jacobite could pursue such a course. Hutchinson was terrified of the fury he confronted. "The hellish crew," as

Figure 3.1 John Singleton Copley, *Samuel Adams*, about 1772. Museum of Fine Arts, Boston.

he put it, "fell upon my house with the rage of devils." They even tore the wainscoting off the walls. "Such ruins," he lamented, "were never seen in America."[12] What was happening was unnatural. Later, assembling under what they called "a liberty tree," the rioters demanded that the collector appear and publicly and ritualistically announce his resignation, which he wisely did. Parliament, it seemed, stirred a hornet's nest of resentment in Boston.[13]

The mayhem in Boston struck a responsive chord. Educated but provincial men like James Otis wrote pamphlets excoriating Parliament for passing a tax without the consent of the colonists. "No less certain is it that the Parliament of Great-Britain has a just and equitable right, power and authority, to *impose taxes on the colonies*," he wrote. Otis did not find it "reasonable this right should be practised upon without allowing the colonies an actual representation. An equal representation of the whole state is, at least in theory, of the essence of a perfect parliament, or supreme legislative." The stamp duty flew in the face of Britishness. He asked, "Is it to be believed, that when a continent of 3000 miles in length, shall have more inhabitants than there are at this day in Great-Britain, France and Ireland, perhaps in all Europe; they will be quite content with the bare name of British subjects, and to the end of time, supinely acquiesce in laws made, as it may happen, against their interest, by an assembly 3000 miles beyond [the] sea"?[14]

Soon disturbances spread to other colonies, as locals demanded that the men who were to collect the stamp duties in their respective colonies resign. Elsewhere, colonists also issued scathing indictments of Parliament's presumption to tax the colonies. Patrick Henry, a self-trained and ambitious lawyer of modest background from the backcountry, composed a series of resolutions that he presented to Virginia's Assembly, echoing the case that Bostonians were making. Having cut his teeth championing the rights of Baptists to enjoy toleration in a colony with an established church, Henry displayed the same passion and sensibilities in championing the rights of the colonies, arguing that the colonists did not surrender their rights because they lived across the ocean from Britain. They possessed "all the privileges, franchises, and immunities that have at any time been held, enjoyed, and possessed by the people of Great Britain," the same rights as "natural-born subjects." Taxation by ones representatives was "the distinguishing characteristick of British freedom." It followed for Henry and his Virginia allies that "the General Assembly of this colony have the only and sole exclusive right and power to lay taxes and impositions upon the inhabitants of this colony, and that every attempt to vest such power in any person or persons whatsoever, other than the General Assembly aforesaid, has a manifest tendency to destroy British as well as American freedom."[15] Marylander Daniel Dulany went so far as to suggest that the actions of Parliament violated the foundations of Britishness it was supposed the safeguard. By what right did members of Parliament suppose to betray the central tenets of the constitution? The colonists were only claiming "the privilege, which is common to all *British subjects*, of being taxed *only* with their own consent given by their representatives." As he put it, "To give property not belonging to the giver, and without the consent of the owner, is... [an] evident and flagrant injustice."[16]

Every colony did not resist. In general, the planters of the West Indies complied with the Stamp Act, by and large because of their distinctive relationship to

Britain, as well as their rather distinctive social structure. Whites on the Leeward Islands of Nevis and St. Christopher rioted, burning stamps at the door of a distributor, but their opposition to what they called "badges of slavery" is the exception that proves the rule. Planters on these islands were tied most closely to the North American colonies through trade, and an interruption of commerce, which the Stamp Act promised, could bring famine or slave insurrection. In Antigua, whites paid the duty, as the King's 68th Regiment ensured no demonstrations took place. Planters from Barbados and Jamaica, like colonists on the mainland, viewed the tax as "an invasion... of the constitutional Rights of English Subjects," decried taxation without their consent, and petitioned Parliament for repeal. But they complied. They needed British sea power and markets to sustain their trade and their lifestyles. And the fear of slave rebellion, which British military presence muted, drove planters to acquiesce. Although North Americans like John Adams condemned planters for their "base Desertion of the Cause of Liberty" and their "tame Surrender of the Rights of Britons," the white planters of what one newspaper called "the SLAVISH Islands" had little incentive to go the way of Massachusetts.[17] Moreover, Scots who had settled in the Caribbean used the occasion of the Stamp Act to try to demonstrate their loyalty to the Crown. Anxious to remove the taint of Jacobitism that haunted them, they hoped to demonstrate that they were as British as their English Caribbean neighbors.[18]

Other colonists on the mainland also demonstrated similar restraint, albeit for different reasons. South Carolina's planters also proved reluctant to support resistance. For example, Henry Laurens, a rice planter, thought the Stamp Act ill-considered, but he weighed his options carefully. His was a complex society, more complex than Barbados. Managing a slave society with a large free white population in a town that depended on trade with Britain caused him fits once the process of state formation began in earnest. South Carolinians, who had a lobby in London second in influence only to the West Indies planters, understood the interest-based politics of the metropole and they associated themselves with modest reformers. Moreover, elites in South Carolina had optimism for the future. The relatively rapid growth of their slave-based economies gave them confidence in the economy, even if what they regarded as British meddling irritated them. For these practical and confident men, not driven by ideology or the fear of imagined threats, resistance represented a last resort. They worked more effectively within the dictates of a system that responded to symbolic provocation and timely concession. Those living around Laurens did not appreciate such subtleties. For his caution, the lower sort in his midst tarred him a supporter of the Act and even accosted him, searching his house for stamps. Reluctant patriots such as Laurens, who preached moderation, found themselves in an awkward position.[19]

Not only those living in slave societies demonstrated ambivalence. Pennsylvania's local officials also preached moderation. A lawyer named John Dickinson worried that the colony's reputation was tainted by charges of anarchy and tumult and wanted to avoid such charges in the future. As Boston reeled, he and other well-off Pennsylvanians hoped to demonstrate that Philadelphia was not Boston, even if they opposed the Stamp Act. Dickinson also feared the overt resistance, particularly on the part of the Assembly dominated by Quakers, would lead the British to send troops, a move that he reckoned would lead to anarchy and then repression. For their own part, the members of the Assembly showed little inclination to support radical calls for resistance, and soon those who opposed such measures began to equate the Assembly with Parliament. Those out of power in Pennsylvania, the so-called proprietary faction, tried to foster opposition to the Stamp Act outside the Assembly. Radical opposition coalesced out of doors, trying to goad the Assembly to act in the name of the people, making it more difficult for men like Dickinson to steer any sort of middle course.[20]

Parliament, now under the leadership of Lord Rockingham—a man more attuned to pleas for provincial liberty than Grenville—repealed the Stamp Act. He had ample reason to do so. Merchants in England, afraid of what unrest would mean for their businesses, put pressure on the ministry to reverse course. Rockingham and his followers could console themselves with the idea that they were standing up for the liberty of the subject. One of Benjamin West's subjects, Isaac Barré, argued in Parliament about the shortsightedness of a stamp tax, calling the colonists championing their rights "sons of liberty" who were "actuated by Principles of true English Lyberty." Let their assemblies pass taxes and send the revenues to Britain, he urged.[21] At this juncture, therefore, it seemed that the system worked. Officials had responded appropriately, when they were brought back to their senses. Certainly, English radicals like John Wilkes and more tradition-inclined Britons like Edmund Burke thought this was the case. Rioting when the natural leaders of a society forgot their obligations or overstepped rightful bounds could, in fact, protect the fabric of society.[22] This is the way Bostonians interpreted repeal. When word reached Boston, riot turned to celebration. Colonists considered the repeal of the Stamp Act to be no less a momentous event than the foiling of the gunpowder plot in England in 1605.

Nonetheless, from the British perspective, the ideal of parliamentary sovereignty was as important, if not more so, than a specific piece of legislation. The only way to raise revenues in the long term and incorporate America or reform the bonds that tied the colonies to Britain involved expanding the scope of Parliament's authority, the basis of state formation for the archipelago. Britons of all stripes believed the Americans subject to Parliament. Parliament had supremacy in America by virtue of the fact that Britain was sovereign in America. Subjection had nothing to do with exercising one's rights, even if doing so served as a hallmark of Britishness. This seeming contradiction, after all, energized the successful blueprint of state formation. And at this juncture, with heavy tax burdens at home, it proved expedient to elevate Parliament's authority as absolute in raising revenue in the colonies.[23] So no sooner had they repealed the Stamp Act, than members of Parliament passed the Declaratory Act for America. The "sixth of George III" was modeled directly on the "sixth of George I," Ireland's Declaratory Act. Through the measure, Parliament assumed in law what it already claimed entitlement to: that it had the right to legislate for American affairs "in all cases whatsoever." The Act did not represent a piece of punitive legislation, but a logical course of action given the process of state formation. Rioting and remonstrating led Parliament to back away, with good reason. Parliament now pushed back to safeguard its prerogative as it had done in Ireland decades earlier, a prerogative that had been won at great expense of blood and treasure over the course of the seventeenth century. For the British, sovereignty had become an unambiguous concept. Although constitutionally, different provinces had different relationships with England, ultimate power was indivisible and resided in one place. As the famous jurist Sir William Blackstone put it in the very year the Stamp Act was passed, "there is and must be" in each government "a supreme, irresistible, absolute, uncontrolled authority, in which the *jura summi imperii*, or the rights of sovereignty, reside." History had chosen Parliament.[24]

It is easy to believe that what was happening in America was somehow unique. In fact, the American case is better considered a variation on a common rule. Just as it had in Ireland and Scotland, the process of British state formation exacerbated tensions historic in nature and deeply rooted in the culture of each province. The process also gave discontent a legitimate channel of grievance. Look at how the breakdown of authority in New England reflected the distinctive fissures in that society, as well as its economic fortunes. The poorer sort—men like Mackintosh—found themselves in difficult straits in the years after the war. Different groups viewed the American economy with confidence and fear. While South Carolina's planters had hope for the future, the postwar years proved especially difficult in Boston. Boston's economy had languished for decades; the war had brought prosperity to well-connected merchants and to ship-builders. But distilling and fishing, two key industries for the city, had suffered. Luckily, men who would have been unemployed were off fighting in the war, but as it ended, they returned. True, the depression was harder felt in other cities, but only because Boston's economy was so stagnant to begin with, and the war turned the city into one of haves and have-nots. While merchants emulated Georgian British rituals, such as horseracing and by staging elaborate weddings, poorer artisans were becoming paupers. In fact, the "Loyal Nine," the men who had been behind the riots in Boston, worked as craftsmen and had suffered especially from the postwar recession. They were, therefore, giving vent to frustrations not only to the tax but also to the class of men who had profited most from the recent war.[25]

Unrest gripped other American cities for, once again, distinctive reasons. Many workers in America's other port towns suffered as well. The development of New York and Philadelphia during the Seven Years' War, when work had been plentiful, had led to a moment of opportunity for many. Workers had flourished during the war years throughout the colonies but especially in cities like New York and Philadelphia. Soldiers and materiel streamed into New York, and merchants underwrote privateers who attacked French shipping. Some found that smuggling, even to the enemy, paid well. Young men found ample work for good wages. Philadelphians similarly enjoyed the fruits of wartime demand and supply. This phenomenon may have been temporary, a product of the shortage of labor and explosion of demand during the war; nonetheless, when the postwar recession hit, workers—not the owners—were suffering. The resumption of migration from Ireland and Germany in these years, as well as the movement of young people into the cities after the war, exacerbated the problem.[26] Cities, then, were rife with tensions.

American colonists had a number of lenses to try to make sense of what was happening to them. Most would have agreed with pamphleteers like James Otis that Britishness, based on commerce and liberty, was at stake. Americans, in general, as Britons saw the world through the prism of oppositional politics in the seventeenth century. They fretted, as the English had, over unfettered power, of institutions that stepped over their prescribed bounds and trampled on the liberties of people. Pamphleteers gave voice to these beliefs—these mental switchboards, really—by casting Parliament in the way English writers had portrayed the Stuarts a century earlier. Local tensions found articulation through these switchboards.[27]

Most Americans also harbored a sense of history that encouraged them to see what was happening in providential terms. One agitator in Boston believed that in using stamped paper, colonists would "receive the mark of the beast." The experience of the Seven Years' War, in which colonists played a role in fighting the forces of Catholic France, strengthened the idea that history was defined by the contest between virtue and vice, liberty and tyranny. Religious ideals that hinged on beliefs of the role of God in history saw the swing between these two poles as more than a secular pattern. Seventeenth-century English history, from which many of their political ideas had emerged, was animated by similar patterns. The Glorious Revolution, and the struggle against tyranny and popery, did not just represent a distant past but was part of the fabric of the present. Otis made such a case in his pamphlet *The Rights of the British Colonists Asserted and Proved* by arguing the Americans were heir to a Glorious Revolution that delivered "this kingdom from popery and arbitrary power." By 1765, "popery" meant more than anti-Catholicism and had political implications. It raised the specter of any form of tyranny, anything that threatened the subject's God-given rights. As Presbyterians in Pennsylvania charged in the wake of stamp disturbances, they were apt to recognize "No King but King Jesus."[28]

This sensibility was heightened by other disturbances in the 1760s. Indeed, a people embracing such a politico-religious understanding of past, present, and future had many issues to fasten on in the 1760s. In Virginia, Baptists saw their persecution in providential terms and were quick to draw political implications. Many small landholders in the colony had become Baptists during the Great Awakening. Rejecting the idea of infant baptism on theological grounds, these men and women also believed that laypersons had the right, if inspired, to preach. Baptists challenged laws that mandated that clergy have licenses, as well as the idea that dissenters had to support the established Episcopal Church. For their pains, Baptists were liable to be imprisoned or fined, and ministers endured scores of attacks during the 1760s and 1770s. Most gallingly, they believed that they too should enjoy rights to the enjoyment of toleration. Nonetheless, they flourished in Virginia.[29]

In some ways, discrimination allowed them to make sense of their plight in a changing world. Dissent gave poor whites a powerful lens with which to view political controversies and through which to understand economic difficulties and debt. In their minds, the established church, whose members were the colony's elite, stood for hierarchy and arbitrary power. With time, they also applied those sensibilities to the British, further placing elites in compromised positions unless they also resisted British encroachments on "liberty."[30] In these years, they suggested that their participation in the struggle for colonial rights would be contingent on basic reform of Virginia's confessional state. They premised their cooperation with the Anglican better sort on toleration, the ending of the tithe, and the ability to conduct marriage ceremonies and to own church property.[31]

The religious issue fused with the provincial response to the process of state for-mation, each fueling the other. The question of whether Anglicans could and should have a bishop for America offers perhaps the best example of how social tensions had political and religious outlets in America. In the wake of the Treaty of Paris, as British officials struggled to cobble together a plan for imperial sovereignty, bishops of the Church of England attempted to formulate a plan for an American religious establishment. Mirroring the struggle to define the ambiguous status of America within the British state, the question of what sort of establishment should be created for the colonies engendered all sorts of debate. The Church of England had been established in the southern colonies, as well as the counties around New York City. The other Middle Colonies did not have an established Anglican church. And New England's established church was congregational. The Great Awakening only added to the religiously plural nature of American society. The Archbishop of Canterbury, Thomas Secker, hoped to install a bishop in America to bring the colonies into Britain's ecclesiastical orbit. To Secker, church and state had to be united, and unity could only occur once more than 25 percent of the population professed the creed of an established church. He, therefore, hoped to reform American manners, to revital-ize its culture, and ensure "an orderly Discipline exercised in the Churches." He also wanted the installation of a bishop for practical matters. Bishops ordained clergy and confirmed parishioners. A number of Anglican clergy in the colonies, many of whom had converted to the Church of England and who now ministered to congre-gations in the Middle Colonies and New England, seconded Secker's calls. In their eyes, the Church represented the purest manifestation of the early Christian com-munity. Moreover, some hoped that creating an American bishopric would also ease the way for the conversion of Quebec, as an active bishop, they hoped, could help transform Catholics into loyal Anglicans. Finally, some colonial Anglicans suggested that a bishop's firm hand could repair the rift caused by the Stamp Act disturbances and end dissent.[32]

Most Americans would have nothing to do with the idea. In fact, it struck a nerve. The same Jonathan Mayhew who waxed rhapsodic about the glories of a British America challenged Secker on the issue of bishops. Mayhew saw episcopacy leading to popery and arbitrary government. "People have no security against being unmercifully priest-ridden," he declared, "but by keeping all imperious Bishops, and other Clergymen who love to lord it over God's heritage, from getting their foot into the stirrup at all." Both the Stamp Act and even murmurings of establishing an American episcopate, he reckoned, stemmed from the same fatal errors. In general, colonists in the North and South equated episcopacy with political power, particu-larly in the person of a royal governor. And they interpreted pleas to create a bish-opric in light of the struggle against the Stamp Act. Given their worldview, Secker's attempts represented part of a broader conspiracy that challenged the rights of a British Christian people. The state wisely did not pursue the course.[33]

In many ways, therefore, rioters and those who resisted ascendancies—both British and colonial, religious and otherwise—were voicing pent-up frustrations about their place in a rapidly changing society and used the languages and ideological blueprints at their disposal to do so. So too were Samuel Adams and John Hancock. Although less vulnerable than the poorer sort, these men sensed a proverbial glass ceiling above them: the ruling elite of society, which was linked to England by lines of patronage and influence and wedded to a British national agenda with Parliament at its center. They too lived in a fluid society. Because the economy was so fickle, so too was confidence in political leadership. These sorts of men, too, expressed their frustrations with the status quo. And they hated those who assumed power through family connections and influence with those in high office. They reserved most of their hatred for the man who epitomized everything they struggled against: Thomas Hutchinson. With connections to the Caribbean, London, and markets to the west, Hutchinson and his family had "very ambitious and avaricious dispositions." John Adams sneered at "the amazing ascendancy of one family, [a] foundation sufficient on which to erect a tyranny."[34] Throughout the British Atlantic world, men like John Adams struggled against ascendancies. In England, John Wilkes—also regarded as a rabble-rouser—lambasted the well-connected who thrived as insiders on corruption. Similarly, the Irishman Charles Lucas decried the influence of Ireland's Ascendancy, tied as it was to patronage networks in England and that attempted to keep the middling sort like Lucas on a lower rung of the status ladder.[35]

America had many Hutchinsons. Dr. Thomas Young, a physician born of Irish parents in New York's Hudson River Valley, despised the landed elite who dominated politics in the colony. Livingston was his Hutchinson. Young later became a self-styled radical like Adams, a man Hutchinson called one of "the most flaming zealots" and one of "the incendiaries of the lower order." Richard Henry Lee from Virginia had a different yet similar story. Born to one of the most prominent families in the colony, Lee imagined a life of leadership and prosperity. Although as a third-born son, he would have to create such a life for himself because his eldest brother would receive the lion's share of the family lands and wealth. Slipping into debt, he also slipped below the glass ceiling that men such as Adams saw above them. Lee also became a radical leader, who enjoyed the reputation—literally—as a rabble-rouser.[36]

As a prominent official in Massachusetts named Peter Oliver put it, such rebellion was "unnatural." Men like Adams, whom he viewed as a Satan and "a Machiavilian," could "turn the Minds of the great Vulgar." What was happening in the colonies was done to "gratifye the Pride, Ambition and Resentment, of a few abandoned Demagogues." Oliver, who hated the up-and-comers, overstated his case; yet, he fastened on a dynamic that was gripping the colonies. With the riots, some fundamental cleavages in American colonial society were revealed. And disturbances were spreading. Massachusetts to Oliver "was the Volcano from whence issued all the Smoak, Flame, and Lava which hath since enveloped the whole British American Continent."[37]

On the other hand, some seemed to be suggesting that such issues mattered naught, that principle was at stake. After all, pamphleteers and orators like Patrick Henry believed that this fight should be waged with the very ideas that underscored the British state. If Britons argued that their nation was premised upon the notion of liberty, on the protection of Protestantism, and on the virtues of commerce, then Parliament should live up to those ideals. The case was simple. The Crown existed, most Americans believed, to safeguard such rights. Parliament was butting in where it was not welcome, and in so doing, was stamping on the rights of freeborn

Americans, no less British for living 3,000 miles away. The notion of "no taxation without representation," after all, went to the heart of what made Britons distinctive. Ultimately the idea drew from certain assumptions that had animated seventeenth-century English history, that power and liberty were at odds and the men and women had to remain vigilant against those intent on compromising their rights.[38]

The Bostonians, it seems, had won a victory for liberty. In fact, the protesters embraced Barré's term "Sons of Liberty," adding it to the American revolutionary lexicon. But these men, in fact, were doing little more than other provincials had done as they were incorporated into the state. Scots debated the terms of their inclusion, lamenting what the demise of their parliament meant for their liberties. Their proximity to England, but more significantly the fears of further economic marginalization, swayed most to accept the terms of Scottish parliamentary surrender and British parliamentary supremacy. The Irish proved a more nagging problem. They too protested, wrote pamphlets, and resolutions. They even boycotted. As Jonathan Swift famously put it after the passage of Ireland's Declaratory Act, that. "Ireland *wou'd never be happy 'till a Law were made for* burning *every Thing that came from* England, *except their* People *and their* Coals."[39] In effect, such negotiation, however spirited, proved the norm not the exception.

The same applies to rioting. We are all too conditioned to see the Stamp Act crisis as the first act of an inevitable drama about home rule or who was to rule at home. Insurmountable tensions emerged between center and periphery or between classes of subjects. Or so the story goes. But if we look around the British world, and to the American past, a different picture comes into focus. Rioting was nothing unusual. Men and women commonly took to the streets in England, Scotland, and Ireland to protest the measures that governments took, especially when such measures impinged on their abilities to get ahead or to keep body and soul together, or when liberty and security were threatened. In 1759, to cite just one instance, a crowd of 3,000, some armed with swords, marched to the Irish parliament house to protest what turned out to be a rumor that Ireland was to become part of the union and would lose its Parliament. The crowd forced a number of the Lords and Commons to declare their support "for the country and against the union." One English official found it hard to imagine "a Protestant multitude attack[ing] a Protestant government." Such actions were, however, not unusual within the archipelago. Indeed, Parliament had warmed to the idea of taxing Americans, in part, because Englishmen and women had raised a furor over a proposed cider tax.[40]

Riot, then, played a useful function in society, alerting leaders to moments when they crossed the line. Bostonians, in particular, had a long and distinguished history of rioting, defining who they were, their status, their attachment to neighborhoods, and their credentials as good British subjects by taking it out on each other. Each November 5, for instance, north-enders and south-enders took to the streets to protest Guy Fawkes's attempt to blow up the houses of Parliament in 1605. Bostonians drank and reveled too much on such occasions. And Pope's Day usually degenerated into an ill-defined brawl between the two ends of the city. In other words, it allowed those on the margins to blow off steam and to serve notice to their leaders that the people could if necessary act for themselves. Moreover, the symbolism of the Stamp Act riots was unexceptional. By the 1740s, colonists in New England and New

York deployed English symbols of treachery in processions and rituals. Effigies of the Pretender, the Pope, and the Devil were carted throughout cities and towns and then burned by revelers on commons. In 1765, men and women fashioned effigies of British officials, or made use of the boot and the devil to represent Bute. In this way, they tried to make the case that their struggle resembled the one that gripped England a century earlier, and they used the language and symbols of that earlier crisis to speak to their crisis. In this way, Lord Bute, the "treacherous" Scot and long assumed a closet Jacobite, or supporter of the exiled Stuarts, served as the perfect foil. Symbols revealed the integrity and applicability of seventeenth-century English political imagery and popular anti-Catholicism.[41]

The tensions unleashed or revealed by the riots, therefore, were not uniquely American. Every society, of course, is riven with tensions, be these ethnic, racial, class or status-based, or religious. During difficult times, relations become especially tense, and conflict erupts along society's fault lines. Thus, protest in America often followed predictable patterns, and fractures appeared along predictable lines. What was happening in places like Boston differed little from similar events that occurred throughout the British Atlantic world. In such instances, tensions often below the surface emerged, especially as authorities struggled to keep order. Officials then had a number of strategies at hand. They could wait for tensions to dissipate. They could placate rioters. Or they could repress them. The final option, it should be noted, worked in Georgia. Here the Stamp Act was enacted, but only because the royal governor had direct control of British troops in a colony that was isolated and newly settled.[42] Georgia, however, was the exception that proves the rule. In Boston's case, the British chose the second option: placation; and given the geographic distance from Britain to America, doing so made the greatest deal of sense. Nonetheless, officials understood that the principle of parliamentary sovereignty mattered. Even Lord Rockingham, who had a great deal of ideological sympathy with the aggrieved Americans, accepted the fact that this had to be the glue that would bind America to Britain. Americans would remonstrate and riot. The lower sort would set themselves against authority and ascendancies, political and religious. Men on the make would see their main chance and try to take it. Local authority would be shaken. Such was the nature of the process of state formation.

In the midst of the Stamp Act furor, the ministry asked Benjamin Franklin, in London at the time, to appear before Parliament to answer some questions about the behavior of Americans. Franklin addressed the House of Commons on the issue by arguing that colonists were not contesting Parliament's right to legislate but the particular issue on which it decided to legislate. Parliament, he declared, made the mistake of levying an "internal" tax, one normally passed only by provincial assemblies. Colonists did not dispute Parliament's right to regulate commerce. "External" taxes, those that regulated trade within constituent parts of the British realm, he argued, could be levied by Parliament. The stamp duty ran afoul of this principle.[43] In fact, Franklin misunderstood and misspoke. Colonists, like all subjects, did not want to be taxed at all.[44] Internal or external, it did not matter. Moreover, many Americans did not believe that Parliament had sovereign authority to do such a thing. In this way, Americans probably believed the same things the Irish and Scots did. They too did not like to pay duties. In both of these instances, however, Parliament had the coercive means at hand to persuade provincials in the British Isles to accept taxes and the principles that underscored them.

Parliament, eager to raise whatever money it could to defray expenses, followed Franklin's advice. More or less, that is. Rockingham's administration did not last, and in the merry-go-round of British politics, an ailing William Pitt, since elevated to the nobility as the Earl of Chatham, was asked to form a government. He turned much of his leadership in the House to his Chancellor of the Exchequer, Charles Townshend. With experience on the Board of Trade, Townshend now assumed leadership for dealing with the crisis in the colonies. The younger brother of George Townshend, soon to be the lord-lieutenant of Ireland and who had fought with Cumberland at Culloden and Wolfe at Quebec, Charles advocated levying a series of duties on goods produced in Britain or its dependencies and shipped to America, goods such as lead, paint, glass, and tea. Unlike the tax on stamped paper, the Townshend Duties were not designed to raise money for the British establishment on American soil or for the troops stationed in the West. Townshend had far more ambitious plans. Judging Franklin's distinction between external and internal taxes "an absurdity," Townshend believed that Parliament had to be supreme and that sovereignty had to be unified under it. Much like his brother would do for Ireland when he tried to institute more direct rule from London by undermining the powers of local officials and so to unify sovereignty, Townshend hoped to undo the corrupting influence of local assemblies by making appointed officials answerable directly to the ministry. The immediate impetus was the failure of the New York Assembly to comply with the Quartering Act. Revenue from import duties, he reckoned, could be used to pay royal governors, judges, and customs officials, in the process rendering them independent from local officials. By doing so, he could make regional assemblies subservient to Parliament by undercutting corrupting influences. Townshend saw that fundamental reform along these lines was necessary for the empire to rule over an integrated Atlantic. Townshend also hoped that reform in the Atlantic system could alleviate a problem further afield. The tax on tea could also be used to shore up the East India Company, while providing Americans with tea at a cheaper cost than smugglers could offer. Townshend, therefore, was a visionary, though one not destined to win over the hearts and minds of Americans.[45]

In many respects, Townshend was attempting to resolve the animating ambiguities that defined Britain's imperial constitution. Although the archipelago was ruled by one Parliament, Ireland and Scotland had different, and in Ireland's case convoluted, relationships to the center. The colonies even more so, as did the company-state that was the East India Company. The British empire was defined by multiple power arrangements, authority was plastic, and legal local rights were understood to be part of the fabric of constitutional tradition. Over time, governance had evolved, of course, and within the British Isles had developed into the ideal of parliamentary sovereignty, with the sharing of powers and spoils in the marchlands, to make the arrangement palatable. But Americans had not been privy to those arrangements, encouraging them to understand that power could be shared because in the past the plasticity of sovereignty had allowed for that belief. Townshend shattered the illusion of this belief the moment he characterized Franklin's distinction as absurd and the moment he tried to unify sovereignty.[46]

Predictably, the colonies exploded once more. In this instance, they moved beyond mobbing to more concerted and efficacious resistance. Sons of Liberty argued that Americans should refuse to allow the importation of British goods so long as the duties remained on the books. Up and down the coast, local groups published promises not to consume British goods. The lists of proscribed items included goods ranging from gloves to anchors and glue to silks.[47]

To make this manageable, radical groups from cities along the coast established committees to coordinate efforts, to keep each other appraised of what was happening in their communities, and most critically to ensure that the merchants of each town were not circumventing the others. So they nervously watched each other. If one city failed, they all would fail. Committees policed their own neighborhoods by creating committees of safety, the sorts of groups that had emerged in England in the seventeenth century to monitor behavior. The members of these bodies intimidated those suspected of supporting or abetting ministerial measures.[48] In some instances, merchants who failed to abide by the wishes of local committees saw their businesses covered with "Hillsborough paint," a mixture of mud and feces named after the Earl of Hillsborough, one of the chief men responsible for Britain's American policy.[49] They even turned back ships. In coordinating their efforts, Americans were acting as true Britons. "Let us," the *Pennsylvania Gazette* implored, "as a Patriot said, when the liberties of England were in like danger from James the first, *petition and petition the King again, as we usually do to God, and without ceasing, till he hear us.*"[50]

Although riots were not surprising, the creation of such networks was. Americans were creating networks of trust as sovereign authority in America was faltering and as local authorities seemed unable or unwilling to step into the breach. Emulating forms of association prevalent throughout the British Isles, these "patriots"—meaning those willing to sacrifice individual interest for the common good—made the same sorts of arguments they had made in the wake of the Stamp Act.[51] In this instance, they wore homespun to demonstrate their contempt for Parliament's presumption to tax them directly or indirectly, internally or externally. They refused to drink tea exported from Asia via England, instead brewing their own homemade concoction called Labrador tea, by all accounts a bitter and wretched substitute for the real thing. More critically, they created committees or councils to ensure that merchants kept up their promises not to import. Vigilance, to use a watchword of the day, was required by all. Some, such as John Adams, read and admired Swift. Others did not. But they certainly were emulating the things that he had proposed when Ireland found itself in similar straits.[52]

The American response, and the Irish one for that matter, also revealed the local parameters of Britishness, that it was always articulated in the vernacular. Swift, of course, as a member of the established Church in Ireland, made his arguments conscious of how they would play out in a society riven by confessional differences. In his kingdom, religion served as more than a badge of identity; it was a marker of power. Naturally enough, he framed his arguments in terms of religious confession, which structured power relations in the kingdom. Americans did the same with their animating tensions. Eerily enough, many American parvenus, men just like Swift, who hoped to make a mark on the British world and the sort to write pamphlets and remonstrate, argued that unless the British government practiced what it preached, they would be transformed into slaves. Pamphleteers asserted Americans would be "reduced to the most abject slavery." James Otis argued that "in no case are the essential rights of the subjects inhabiting the subordinate dominions to be destroyed. This would put it in the power of the superior to reduce the inferior to a state of slavery; which cannot be rightfully done even with *conquered* enemies and *rebels*." Even rebellious Irish or Jacobite Scots could not be enslaved.[53] The turn of phrase was not empty rhetoric. Throughout the colonies, from Boston to Savannah, race entailed power. Americans had within eyeshot living examples of what happened to persons bereft of liberty. The use of such a discourse did not encourage Americans to embrace the cause of abolitionism—at least not yet—but it pointed to what we would consider a contradiction. As a New Hampshire newspaper pointed out, "many among us, who call themselves Sons of Liberty, are asserting the natural Rights of Mankind, and their peculiar priviledges as Englishmen...and ingrafted into the British Constitution, that each Individual has the sole Right of disposing of his own Property." It asked "Is it not surprizing to find many of those very Persons tyranizing over some of their fellow Creatures, and making them Slaves in the fullest sense of the Word!"[54] Many white Americans decried infringements on their liberty while they held their fellows in bondage. Nonetheless, Americans, especially those from the South, lived quite comfortably with paradox.

Through all the tumult, it appeared that no power could restore order in the colonies, certainly not local governments. The protesters appeared to have the most promising chances of doing so. At least they had acquired a sense of purpose, coordination, and cohesion, prerequisites for effective rule. New Englanders especially had traditions of self-governance that they could fall back on to make decisions for the whole quickly. Committees formed to correspond with other colonies could rely upon a growing number of newspapers to get the word out about common action. So, for instance, the Stamp Act Congress, which met in New York to discuss the idea of common resistance, included representatives from eight colonies, all of which had committees based on models of local governance and which learned of what was happening in other places through reporting in newspapers and pamphlets.[55] The older guard, by contrast, seemed impotent. Royal governors harangued rioters and their assemblies, but to no avail. Few were listening.

The pleas for principled resistance grew as yet more pamphleteers added their voices to the chorus, most conspicuously John Dickinson. The "Farmer," as he called himself, made the same types of arguments that others before him had made. Parliament had no right to do what it proposed and was betraying the principles of the British state. Americans understood the Crown to be sovereign. And Americans possessed the right and the obligation as trueborn Britons to make a stand for their rights. "If *Great-Britain* can order us to come to her for the necessaries we want," Dickinson declared, "and can order us to pay what taxes she pleases before we take them away, or when we land them here, we are as abject slaves as *France* and *Poland* can shew in wooden shoes, and with uncombed hair."[56]

Such voices were heard yet again. Not by Townshend—he was dead and gone—but by Lord North, the latest in a series of first ministers. Under North's watch,

Parliament repealed all the duties Townshend had passed save one, the duty on tea. It seemed that Americans and Britons could not understand one another. It also appeared that Americans were a tad paranoid.[57] To be sure, it did not help matters that the ministry amounted to little more than a revolving door, or that ministers proved shortsighted, incompetent, or corrupt.

But what was at issue was how the processes of reform and of state formation, which successive ministries supported, were going terribly awry in America for more prosaic reasons: interest, fears, and distance. Hutchinson's interests were rooted in England. Not so for men such as Samuel Adams and a rising group of men coming of age who did not have Hutchinson's firm connections to British power. Placemen, pensioners, and undertakers may have yoked Ireland and Scotland to Britain, but such bonds did not bind as many prominent Americans. For generations, their politics had thrived by standing up against governors, not being co-opted by them. Decrying those tightly bound to the center, then, struck a deep chord of American political culture.

Moreover, fear would not encourage people to deliver over to the state what they regarded as God-given rights. Worries over rebellious Catholics and highlanders drove the men who ruled Ireland and Scotland into Parliament's arms, even if they did protest too much. The only analogous threat for much of mainland America, the French, was a fleeting memory. So long as the colonists and the British had a common foe in France, one that served as a potent bogey of all things British, looming conflicts between center and periphery could be muted. That possibility was gone. Similarly, fears of slave insurrections may have given Caribbean planters pause as they considered the effects of the Stamp Act upon their liberties and fortunes.[58] But they too were more directly tied to the metropole than many mainlanders; and even for those North Americans living in slave societies, the percentage of slaves in their midst did not match that of the Caribbean. Mainland societies, with large numbers of poorer whites, had more complex social structures than the sugar islands. Complexity, in this instance, muted fears.

Finally, geographic distance dictated that repressing riot or rebellion would pose daunting problems. It would prove massively expensive to dispatch regulars to eastern cities, and the ministry knew provincial Americans, so intent on celebrating their British liberties, would bridle at the appearance of a standing army in their midst. Sending troops, therefore, could exacerbate tensions. Still, after the repeal of the Townshend Duties, this option had to be weighed against the necessity of waiting for things to quiet down or placating Americans. The first two did not seem to be working.

One further issue complicated the bumpy process of making America British politically: the challenge to local authority. Parliament, of course, by trying to establish its sovereign role in America, threatened to emasculate colonial assemblies. Governors also lost some of their latitude, as they were now forced to align themselves much more closely with British policy. In these instances, it became that much more difficult to steer a course between local interest and British directives. Under normal circumstances, such an act required political genius. Now, as the case of Hutchinson demonstrates, it proved impossible. Most troublingly, local institutions could not maintain order. Wave upon wave of civil disobedience and petty violence strained governmental legitimacy. Efficacy and legitimacy during such crises did not necessarily conflict. Efficacious government, after all, provided the basis for legitimacy.

The ever-loyal Peter Oliver saw a pernicious pattern at work. "As for the People in general, they were like…perfect Machines, wound up by any Hand who might first take the Winch." He used a grim analogy all Americans could appreciate. "They were," he found, "like the poor Negro Boy, who, in the Time of the late Stamp Act, was bid by his Master, in the Evening to fetch something from his Barn; but did not move at the Command. His Master spoke to him with Severity, & asked him why he did not go as he was bid? The poor Wretch replied, with Tears in his Eyes, 'me fraid Massah Tamp Act he catch me.'" Through manipulation and fear "The Mob again triumphed." And government teetered on the brink.[59] Some amount of riot was acceptable. As Hutchinson put it, riots did not "strike the mind with so much abhorrence as some other offenses do." But if they were not confronted by legal authority, they would "sap the foundation of all government."[60]

To put it in eighteenth-century parlance, American officials may have argued that power and liberty were at odds; but they articulated such ideas as authority was faltering. The theory they looked to in order to make sense of their plight certainly argued that liberty and power conflicted. Indeed, this was one of the defining tropes of the seventeenth-century British experience. Social realities suggested different understandings. Power was not the problem. A lack of it was. Unable to stand up to intimidation, by and large because of distance from Britain, the absence of an "other" to fear, and compelling bonds of interest and patronage, local authority withered.[61]

The issues that stymied order in the East did not bedevil the West. There settlers and Indians had their own ghosts to contend with. The grisly work of the Paxton Boys and their march on Philadelphia sent shockwaves through the British Atlantic. In 1764, the ministry condemned the butchery, fearing that it would unleash more Indian "rebellions" and possibly entice the French back into North America. Franklin, who argued that it was he, not British troops, that sent the Paxton Boys home packing, proclaimed them "Christian white Savages." As he put it, "The barbarous Men…committed the atrocious Fact, in Defiance of Government, of all Laws human and divine, and to the eternal Disgrace of their Country and Colour."[62] Leaders in other colonies, even New Jersey, feared that settlers would kill Indians in their midst. Pennsylvania's officials, however, reacted with the greatest amount of indignation. The murders set off a firestorm in Philadelphia, as "Quakers" condemned the Paxton Boys for their murderous spree and frontier settlers applauded or tried to justify the actions of the vigilantes. Franklin would use the event as fodder for discrediting proprietary rule in favor of royal rule for the colony.

Much more significantly, the murders signaled something amiss with British western policy. Policymakers hoped that the Proclamation Line would hold through a combination of deference and self-interest. Settlers, if they dared to stray west, would not be protected. The West, after all, was conceived as a nonsubject region, a place in which government and subjects by definition could not exist. The normal rules of social intercourse, therefore, did not apply. Officials believed that prospective settlers would recognize the peril of moving onto lands that were reserved for Indians. Instead, men and women would, or the ministry hoped, move to regions where government was or would be established, such as Nova Scotia and the Floridas.[63] Since both lay on the littoral, new settlers could then engage in trade with the mother country. If they moved west—even if they survived—they would be lost to the Atlantic economy. If people would not or could not move west, the same would hold for speculators. If they had no prospects for profit, they would look elsewhere. Moreover, they could never hope to establish good title so long as the line remained inviolate.

The plan proved a disaster from the start. In fact, the erection of the line increased pressure on it. Demographic changes contributed to its failure. In the years after the Seven Years' War, common men and women were streaming into colonial ports from Europe. Population was booming, both through migration and natural increase. Land in many places was going for a premium. The Valley of Virginia, for instance, a place unoccupied by Euro-Americans 30 years before, was filling or had become too pricey for the poorest in society.[64] A bit further to the east in the colony, settlers tried their hands at growing tobacco. These are the people who would rely on Scottish factors for loans and for consumer goods. By the 1760s, they had become so well established that they were putting pressure on eastern elites for a greater share of political power. Energized by the Great Awakening, particularly Baptists preachers, these up and comers—men just like Patrick Henry—argued that they too were entitled to a say in governance.[65] In other words, the western reaches of Virginia were no longer prime destinations for poorer settlers.

Further south, in the backcountry of the Carolinas, chaos reigned. In the years of the Seven Years' War, men and women had settled on land claimed by the Cherokees, who with the end of hostilities demanded the return of their land. When authorities refused, they attacked. Ironically, Scottish Highland regiments dispatched to pacify the Cherokees employed a scorched earth policy. Some Highland commanders followed their orders reluctantly. The irony was not lost on them. Jeffrey Amherst, who had cut his teeth as an officer at Culloden and who now dispatched the highlanders, had no such qualms.[66] The region, like many others on the frontier, seethed with violence. In the midst of the collapse of order, unruly men and women, many of them hunters, had established themselves on the far reaches of the colonies. The middling-sort among frontier settlers, those who wanted to create settled societies and establish slave-based commercial agriculture, saw themselves trapped between lawless "banditti," who had little regard for the law, and eastern officials, who cared little for frontier governance. Some settlers argued that in such a context, they had no choice but to "regulate" affairs on their own. With no authority willing or able to restore order to chaotic communities or to establish courts of law, these "Regulators" would. In this Hobbesian world, the Regulators believed that "many among Us have been obliged to punish some of these Banditti and their Accomplices, in a proper Manner—Necessity (that first Principle) compelling them to Do, what was expected that the Executive Branch of the Legislature would *long ago*, have Done." They were "*Free-Men*—British Subjects—Not Born *Slaves*."[67] And they whipped miscreants, burned houses, and forced the idle to work. The discourse of Britishness proved pliable enough to speak to local concerns that did not resonate in Britain. The language also spoke to concerns any Briton would recognize. In calling themselves, Regulators, South Carolinians were employing a seventeenth-century English term, one used as local authority proved unable to maintain order.[68]

North Carolina proved even more volatile. In the wake of the wars with and against Indians in the early eighteenth century, settlers began peopling the back-country regions of the colony. By the 1760s, after they had created settled societies, the middling sort, who had achieved a competency, clamored for greater political participation and a fair shake from eastern merchants and officials. They also did not see eye-to-eye with local officials who sacrificed the interests of Piedmont communities for eastern elites. Rallying behind a British understanding of their rights and a firm Protestant belief in the righteousness of their cause, North Carolina's "Regulators" hoped to reform local governance and create a more just society. Ultimately, they would fight a pitched battle at a place called Alamance in 1771 against the corrupt governor William Tryon and the colony's militia. Nearly 20 regulators would be killed, and 6 executed after the battle.[69] In North Carolina, therefore, regulators lined themselves up against eastern indifference and avarice. In South Carolina, they established vigilante bands to wipe out nests of unruly squatters. In both places, they made the claim that if government failed to do its duty, they had the right to regulate their own affairs.

The Carolina backcountry was hardly the type of place that invited new settlers. Settlers were fighting settlers. East confronted West. The Cherokees were nursing heavy grievances. But west of the Proclamation Line, opportunity beckoned. No government, to be sure, meant no protection. It also meant no courts to evict, few troops to warn off, and no magistrates to fine. In other words, the fact that the West had no government ensured that the poorer sort enjoyed an umbrella of protection against the law. Beginning in the years just after the Seven Years' War and Pontiac's War, therefore, even as the West still proved dangerous, men and women began traveling along the roads that had been laid out by armies to besiege French forts to remote locations beyond the line. If patterns of frontier development that had defined earlier frontier regions like southeast Pennsylvania and the Shenandoah Valley prevailed, this movement meant that the earliest to settle on a plot and improve it could expect to claim land later on. And they did not pay heed to Indian claims or Crown directives. The Indians, Sir William Johnson lamented, "complain Grievously of the Want of the Boundary Line or their having met with no redress about their Lands, of their not obtaining Justice on the frontiers, of the Insults & Murders committed by the Inhabitants at the back of the Settlements."[70]

Pressure also grew from speculators. Far from impeding speculative schemes, the line seemed to invite them. At first, traders and land jobbers set their sights on Illinois. With a number of former French subjects settled there, it appeared to be a place that fell between the cracks. After all, even if they were Catholic and perhaps disloyal, they were not "savages." Government, therefore, would have to be established there because if "subjects" lived in a region, government had to exist to order society. Speculators seized on this exception to the wider western rule and established companies, such as the Illinois Company, to foster settlement. For an eastern elite that had fewer prospects of trade with Britain, or in debt to English and Scottish merchants, land seemed the most likely vehicle for making money.

Unsurprisingly, men like George Washington and Benjamin Franklin cast their lots with Illinois investment schemes. Meanwhile, these and others also formed companies for investing in lands in Ohio. Even though Ohio was not slated to be a subject region, Americans knew that it was only a matter of time before a ministry came to power that would recognize their claims. In expectation of this event, Americans such as Franklin lobbied Parliament and the ministry, and they also invited leading English politicians to invest in these schemes. Corruption, after all, made this world go round. Unsurprisingly, officials working for British imperial aims in the West, such as William Johnson, an architect of the western plan and a British superintendent of Indian affairs, also invested. Conflict of interest was a foreign concept in the British Atlantic.[71]

The results were predictable. As more settlers arrived and as more traders tried to pry lands away from Indians, Indians struck back. Much of the West, then, descended into a period of tit-for-tat murders, not only complicating British plans to keep the region peaceful but also stymying attempts to have prisoners returned after years of captivity in Indian settlements. In other words, in these circumstances, old hatreds could not and did not dissipate. Some took advantage of the chaos. Richard Henderson, a trader from North Carolina, for instance, used debts that Indians had accrued to extort land in the Kentucky country from Cherokees. Others saw disorder as a license to kill. Members of a Maryland militia murdered a Shawnee negotiator who was supposed to be returning prisoners. To make matters worse, they paraded his severed head around as a trophy for members of militia from other colonies to gawk at.

Although officials tried as best they could to patch up quarrels, pressures and events kept intruding. In the wake of the murder of the Shawnee deputy, Crown officials scrambled to make amends. In early 1765, they dispatched George Croghan, an old hand at the Indian trade and deputy to William Johnson, to travel west with goods to "cover up" the death. Croghan was to engage in a Native American ritual of mourning and amendment. He also hoped to use the meeting as an opportunity to initiate trade with tribes in the Illinois country so as to pave the way for speculation. British goods would be sent along with goods financed by a Philadelphia trading firm. As Croghan stopped off at Fort Pitt to confer with British commanders, the goods followed. Yet they never made it to Fort Pitt. As drivers traveled over the Appalachians at a place called Sideling Hill, men who had recently settled in the region beyond the line stopped the train. With blackened faces, they ordered the drivers to turn their horses around or to suffer the wrath of the people. When the drivers hesitated, the "Black Boys" shot a number of their horses and burned the goods. They saw the goods as part of a plan to placate Indians, who the Black Boys argued had killed and captured settlers. That the goods were also being sent to establish a trade with Indians, and that guns and powder were among the things on the train, especially galled them. Settlers would die, they suggested, to make men such as Croghan and his absentee financiers in Philadelphia rich.[72]

British troops stationed at a nearby fort tried to capture some of the Black Boys. They dragged one back to the fort, but as soon as they did, a mob appeared outside the walls, opening fire on the troops. The commander quickly released the prisoner to the local magistrate to the East, arguing that since no government existed in the West—civil or military—he had no jurisdiction. He also suggested that the crowd threatened to burn the fort around his ears. Once the rioter was handed over to the magistrate, he was released. No jail would hold him. The Black Boys were never brought to justice, nor could they be. British authority, tied to an ideology that justified meager troop levels, was not up to the task. Eastern officials, already hated for their failure to protect settlers, knew better than to intervene. With no power in the region willing or able to impose order, violence festered. "The outrages committed by the frontier people are really amazing," Benjamin Franklin declared. He saw the West in much the same way Peter Oliver saw the East. This was unnatural rebellion that enfeebled government. He found that "impunity for former riots has emboldened them. Rising in arms to destroy property, public and private, and insulting the King's troops and fort, is going great lengths indeed." He concluded that "I can truly say, it gives me great concern. Such practices throw a disgrace over our whole country that can only be wiped off by exemplary punishment of the actors, which our *weak* government cannot or will not inflict."[73] The Paxton Boys had been sent home because of British authority. The Black Boys would ride again because of the absence of such authority. More settlers arrived, and speculative schemes mushroomed, creating a vicious cycle, further attenuating authority.

The attack of the Black Boys occurred just days before Grenville proposed a Stamp Act for the colonies. One spoke to tensions and the issue of authority in the West, just as the other would initiate a similar crisis in the East. Sir William Johnson, the official most responsible for western policy and the one who complained about unrestrained settlers, saw similar sensibilities defining the East. He blamed "a few pretended Patriots but in reality Enemies to the British Constitution," for whom a "Democratical system ... is their sole aim."[74] The West, therefore, was eerily like the East. It too suffered from a failure or lack of authority, which further encouraged vigilantism and popular tumult. The rituals that went along with riots also looked a great deal like those employed by rural insurgents throughout the British Isles. The Black Boys were the American frontier version of the Whiteboys or Oakboys of Ireland, for instance, rural insurgents who houghed cattle, intimidated landlords, and protected the interests of their group.[75] But whereas membership in such groups in Ireland often followed along sectarian lines, in America they broke down according to race. What also made the West distinctive was the speed with which order unraveled, itself a product of the decision by officials in London to create an empire on the cheap, one without government. The ideology that animated the western empire reflected these real world constraints.

In this way, both the need to rule the West and the failure of sovereignty in the West also stemmed from the crisis initiated by the Seven Years' War and the pressures on resources and imagination it generated. And as authority was failing, tensions exploded, reflecting the salient dividing lines in each region. So in the East, officials tied to London vied with local up-and-comers, and each had to manage the discontent of the working poor in their midst, a group made especially vulnerable after the Seven Years' War. In the West, Indians and settlers lived in a tense state of seething violence. In this competition, settlers saw the British as a threat. As did Indians, albeit for different reasons. And each set of these actors confronted the speculating elite and their jobbers. Even though the pace of change was faster out West—and this would not be the last time in American history in which eastern patterns were replicated in compressed time frames in the West—the dynamics mirrored those apparent in the East.[76]

As the crises deepened, British officials would chart two different courses in America. In the West, they first tried to ease tensions by placating Indians. This was failing. They now resolved to bend the Proclamation Line. To be sure, some called for government in the West. Others preaching economy knew that imposing a firmer form of sovereignty to so large a region proved impossible for the British at the moment. Treating with Indians to surrender land seemed like the most sensible solution. It also promised to enrich speculators. In other words, "everyone" could be happy at the expense of Indians who lived on the land. This idea was the brainchild of William Johnson. In 1768, John Stuart met with Cherokee officials at a place called Hard Labour. Here he won concessions for land for white settlement in regions north and east of the Ohio River, much of the present state of West Virginia. At the same time, realizing that his plan for the West was in tatters, Johnson revived the covenant chain and contacted Iroquois leaders to arrange a meeting at Fort Stanwix, a site in the middle of Iroquoia. The Six Nations would not be surrendering vast swaths of land on the borders of New York where they lived. Rather, they would be setting aside their claim to lands in the Ohio Valley, most of the present state of Kentucky. The Iroquois, of course, did not live here. But they claimed some notion of sovereignty over it because of their fictive position of supremacy over the people that hunted there, the Shawnees and the Cherokees. At Fort Stanwix, with Johnson's knowing approval, the Iroquois ceded Kentucky to white settlement.[77]

Officials in London did not approve. Most notably, the head of the Board of Trade, Lord Hillsborough, condemned the treaty, which, he believed, was "contrary to the opinion of His Majesty's Servants on this side." The new line would "not only probably produce jealousy and dissatisfaction amongst the Cherokees, but will also tend to undo and throw into confusion those settlements and agreements for the other part of the Boundary Line." He said the British would not pay for the "gifts" that the Iroquois requested for the cession. Hillsborough declared that the line would stand inviolate.[78] This is not to say that Hillsborough did so out of principle. He epitomized the eighteenth-century trimmer, one who could trim his sails to the prevailing political winds in pursing his interests. In fact, Franklin claimed that Hillsborough stood in the ways of speculative schemes, such as Franklin's Grand Ohio Company, because they threatened to depopulate his estates in Ireland. Hillsborough, therefore, did not want the availability of American land to impinge on his rental income. Despite Hillsborough's refusal to countenance the concession, American speculators and squatters, as well as British officials on the frontier, acted as if the sordid treaty were law. They understood that it would only be a matter of time before Hillsborough was gone; indeed, Franklin made it his mission to undo Hillsborough, a man he personally detested.

The East required a different approach. Successive ministries had tried a wait-and-see approach, placation, and bluster. Nothing had worked. Quite to the contrary, local authority was shaken to its foundations. The blueprints that officials had in hand to comprehend America within a state system had a darker side, one that had been employed in Ireland with great effectiveness and in Scotland only a generation earlier. The British could send troops to make sovereignty manifest. Peter Oliver argued that such an approach should become general policy. "The Time was approaching," he declared, "which promised some Degree of Protection to those who wished for the Restoration of Government."[79]

Two British regiments arrived from Halifax. Or to be precise, two regiments full of Irish soldiers who had sailed from Cork to Halifax arrived in Boston. Like the highlanders who were called on to put down the Cherokees, those who had experienced the darker aspects of British state formation would extend that process to America. The troops, according to the commander of British forces in America Thomas Gage, would ensure "that the Hands of Government in His Colonies should be further strengthened." Gage, who like his nemesis Samuel Adams sat for John Singleton Copley, believed they had little choice. "A determined Resolution," he believed, was necessary "to inforce at all Events, a due Submission to that Dependence on the Parent State, to which all Colonies have ever been Subjected." As he put it, "Warm and Spirited Resolves with Speedy Execution in Consequence thereof, will be the only Effectual means to put a

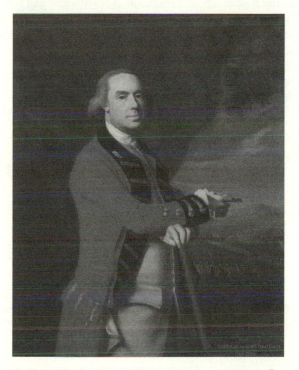

Figure 3.2 John Singleton Copley, *General Thomas Gage,* ca. 1768. Yale Center for British Art.

Stop to the Seditious Spirit, and daring Threats of Rebellion so prevalent in this Country." Force might be necessary: "The Moderation and Forbearance hitherto shewn by Great Britain, has been Construed into Timidity, and served only to raise Sedition and Mutiny, to a higher Pitch." The lesson was simple. "Quash this Spirit at a Blow," he argued, "without too much regard to the Expence and it will prove oeconomy in the End. Such Resolute and determined Conduct, will Astonish the rest of the Provinces, and damp the Spirit of Insurrection, that may lurk amongst them."[80]

No doubt, officials understood the limitations of such an action, as well as its provocative implications. Americans were bound to see the arrival of British regulars as yet another instance of a British violation of essential British liberties. Standing armies, as the Stuarts had taught, symbolized tyranny. "A standing Army," Samuel Adams intoned, "however necessary it may be at some times, is always dangerous to the Liberties of the People." Troops were harbingers and agents of tyranny. "Soldiers are apt to consider themselves as a Body distinct from the rest of the Citizens," he chided, and "They have their Arms always in their hands. Their Rules and their Discipline is severe." He warned that "such a Power should be watched with a jealous Eye."[81] Moreover, dispatching troops, who had to be billeted and fed, to America would prove costly. And after all, one of the chief reasons to make America part of the state and to reform imperial relations was to ease debt. But Americans now were protesting not only British legislation; they were chafing at the very foundations of British stability, the sovereignty of Parliament. The ministry sent troops to Boston. They did not take the decision lightly. If the Americans continued to act like the Irish, they would be put down like "a Dublin mob."[82] It was now clear that earlier plans had failed.

PART II

✐

The Middle

Actors

In the middle of the war years, another American was painting in London. John Singleton Copley, the artist who had painted the Royall sisters in their lavish satin dresses, was born and raised in Boston, the son of Irish immigrants. His father from Limerick died in the West Indies while John was quite young, and he was raised above the tobacco shop on Long Wharf that his mother from Clare owned. While his mother ran the business, she remarried an Englishman who introduced Copley to literature and to the basics of painting. Portrait-painting provided an excellent living for someone so talented, and eventually Copley would marry the daughter of a prominent merchant and purchase a home on Beacon Hill. Although perfectly suited to his life as a chronicler of a consumer-oriented British American culture, Copley lamented his status. Provincial success did not allow his creativity to flourish. He, too, hoped to become a celebrated painter.[1]

In 1765, in the midst of what he called "the noise and confusion amongst us Americans," he sent to Benjamin West and Joshua Reynolds a portrait of his half-brother Henry Pelham.[2] In it, his brother, shown in profile and dressed in the latest fashion, looks away from the viewer while in his right hand dangles a gold chain attached to a New England flying squirrel eating a nut. Between his hand and his pet lies a glass of water. *Boy with a Squirrel*, as it came to be known, centers on that tumbler of water. The water separates two distinct worlds. On one side is the disorder of nature; on the other lies order and civility. The water also punctuates Old World and New, representing the ocean that divided the colonies from Britain. Yet the chain, the light fetters that Burke spoke of, binds them together. With the chain in place, the New World is tethered to metropolitan standards and taste. Without the chain, it will revert to its natural state, the state of nature. These bonds, Copley knew, were straining when he sent off the painting. The chain, of course, also bound Copley to Britain. So in this sense the painting is autobiographical and speaks to Copley's provincial dilemma: the son of Irish immigrants living in provincial America yearning to be accepted in the center, tied to the metropole yet separated by water.[3] The painting captured West and Reynolds's imaginations, and they invited Copley to London,

Figure II.1 John Singleton Copley, *Boy with a Squirrel*, 1765. Musuem of Fine Arts, Boston.

although the invitation arrived with a barb. They regarded his work as descriptive and harsh. It was, according to Reynolds, notable for "a little Hardness in the Drawing, Coldness in the Shades, An over minuteness." West worried it appeared "too liney." They feared his technique would degenerate or be "corrupted" unless he moved from the peripheries to the center. Like West, Copley made the provincials' trek and traveled to England in 1774 as Boston reeled with uncertainty. He became a protégé of the great West, staying with him for a while in London. No sooner had he arrived, then he viewed West's masterpiece. "I have seen Mr. West's Death of General Wolf," he recounted, a painting he regarded as "sufficient of itself to Immortalize the author of it."[4]

In 1778, now living in London, John Singleton Copley completed his most famous and puzzling piece, *Watson and the Shark*. On the face of it, *Watson and the Shark* would seem to have nothing to do with revolution. Yet, the painting proved as revolutionary as anything West had done. Although Copley remained within the paradigm of epic history painting, his subject proved anything but epic. In London, Copley had befriended a prominent merchant named Brook Watson, who told the young painter of how he had lost a leg years before in a shark attack off the coast of Havana when he was serving as a crewman on a British ship. Watson would eventually serve in the House of Commons and become Lord Mayor of London and a chief investor in the East India Company. When he commissioned Copley to paint the story he told, he hoped to inspire young boys to overcome obstacles much as he had. He wanted the painting to recount a narrative.[5]

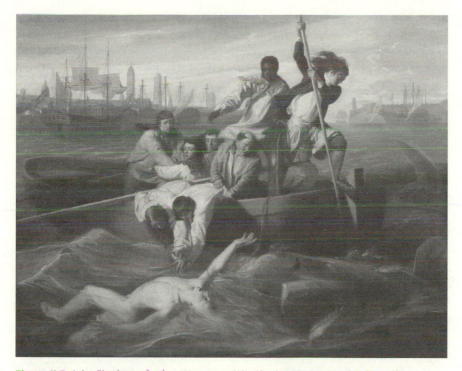

Figure II.2 John Singleton Copley, *Watson and the Shark*, 1778. National Gallery of Art, Washington, D.C.

Copley reinvented the scene, giving it as much gravity as any of the pieces painted by West. Prominent Britons do not appear. Copley's men strike heroic poses but are anonymous, a motley mix of men and boys who worked for a living. The painting does not so much celebrate the everyday as memorialize it. These people Copley captures on canvas are caught in a drama of life and death no less significant than those who directed armies. Copley's piece is not a morality play pitting success against failure. Nor does it mix the elements of myth and reality. Instead, it places unromanticized common men at the center of a personal struggle, one of free and slave, black and white, trying to keep an unnatural-looking beast at bay. In other words, the painting works within the conventions of the history-painting genre while subverting those same conventions.

The painting has an enigmatic quality. Indeed, tension defines it. Art historians have argued that it tells a story of perdition and redemption, good and evil, as man struggles with leviathan, the shark serving as actual and metaphorical threat.[6] It can be seen to represent uncertainty and chaos. Only the violence of man can overcome the nature of beast. Calculating and impassioned men confront an indifferent and cruel natural world that has its own logic. Copley presents the viewer with a dark vision, in which the protagonists struggle alone. Instead of furled flags, the young man brandishes a harpoon. No nation reigns here, as its barbed end plunges toward the shark much like St. Michael's sword vanquished Satan.[7] A ship lies at anchor, in the choppy haven that is not a haven, but a place of violence. The sails lie at half-mast; whether the ship is entering or leaving port is impossible to say. The signs of civilization—a city's church steeples, ships loaded for trade—are bathed in the light of dawn, but are unreachable and unnoticed. The viewer and the subjects are trapped in the dark moment.

Disruption defines the piece. The young man in the water is naked before forces that threaten to overwhelm, helpless in the sea. Apparently, he will leave this life as he entered it. At the center of the painting, trying to extend the rope to young Watson, stands the black seaman. By placing him at the center, Copley suggests that hierarchies and conventions are inverted in this story. Common people are engaged in mythic and virtuous action, and a man who should stand on the margins, acts in the middle. The message is clear. In such moments, when self-preservation is paramount, social distinctions crumble and common people become actors. In the midst of upheaval—and the viewer has no idea how the scene will end—the anxiety seen on the faces of Copley's subjects expresses an idea that only uncertainty is certain.[8]

Watson and the Shark spoke to Copley's fears when the chain holding the squirrel snapped. Ultimately, the young man was dismembered. So too, of course was Britain, and Copley as well. Copley was torn by the war. Although he viewed himself as an American, he would not allow himself to be pigeonholed as a patriot or loyalist. He painted portraits of patriots such as Paul Revere and, of course, Samuel Adams and dined with loyalists such as Thomas Hutchinson. What he called a "civil war" ripped his family apart and plunged him into fits of depression. In 1775, after news reached him of the firefights at Lexington and Concord, he despaired that "the flame of civil war is now broke out in America, and I have not the least doubt it will rage with a violence equil to what it has ever done in any Country at any time." This was more than a war of independence. What was happening was unnatural. "Ocians of blood," he predicted, "will be shed to humble a people which they never will subdue." America would reel from "all the miserys of War, Sword, famine, and perhaps pestalence." As he learned from reading Proverbs, "when the Sword of Rebellion is Drawn, the Sheath shall be thrown away."[9]

Like this portrayal of life on the boat in a choppy sea, the world of Copley was wracked by uncertainty, violence, and chaos. Although he would with time become a member of the Royal Academy and gain renown for portraying the patriotic through portraiture in commercial shows, almost fittingly the painter known for the use of emotion suffered from madness.[10] In most respects, *Watson and the Shark* does not memorialize the epic events of the day in a metaphorical way, but in other respects, it lays out the untidy and troubling aspects of what was happening to worlds public and private in the years the War of Independence raged, as men and women were both liberated and bewildered by the disruption of established social frameworks and cultural assumptions once the chain broke.

CHAPTER 4

֍

They Will Cast Your Sovereignty in Your Face

Through nonimportation, nonconsumption, and boycotting of British goods, Samuel Adams hoped to transform America into a "Christian Sparta," a place renowned for its austere virtue.[1] Americans, Adams hoped, would learn to do without British goods and in the process become like the mythic citizens of the republics of the classical age. In a word, he hoped to use the crisis at hand to reconceive America. Because resistance to Parliament entailed using the weapons of consumer choice, women necessarily had to play leading roles. Through their participation, women transformed a crisis over sovereignty into an opportunity to step out of doors and to claim a portion of the public sphere. And in doing so, "radicals" like Adams welcomed them.

One such actor was Elizabeth Murray, a complex person who led both a typical and exceptional life. Elizabeth Murray left the borders of Scotland in the company of an older brother, James, after her parents had died. She sailed to North Carolina, the Cape Fear region amid other Scottish migrants, and ran the household while James established himself as a leading merchant. The family shuttled back and forth across the Atlantic as James grew wealthier, eventually landing in Boston in 1749. Here Elizabeth decided to go into business for herself. With James's financial backing, and after the sale of slaves to establish her credit, Elizabeth opened a milliner's shop, where she imported and sold some of the latest British fashions, in the process becoming one of a number of women who owned their own shops outright. If a woman were married, under the laws of coverture only real property could belong to the husband. Many women nonetheless ran successful businesses under their husbands' names. Elizabeth worked in such a manner under her first husband. When he died, the business was hers again. So successful would she become that she would commission Copley for a portrait. The fruits she holds in her hands in the painting speak to the idea of bounty, the gifts her business bestowed.

She thrived in Boston during the war years. As a wealthy, well-connected woman tied into merchant networks, business was brisk. She also remarried well. Following the tried and true formula for wealth in eighteenth-century America—one exemplified by George Washington and Charles Carroll of Carrollton, both

Figure 4.1 John Singleton Copley, *Mrs. James Smith (Elizabeth Murray)*, 1769. Museum of Fine Arts, Boston.

of whom had married widows—Elizabeth would marry a rich widower. When he died, she became one of the wealthiest women in the colonies. With the Stamp Act crisis, Elizabeth found herself in no-man's-land. She revered Boston for all it had given her; then again, her life epitomized the forces that had made America British over the course of the eighteenth century. Although she lived in Britain during the worst of the crisis, she heard how disruptions to daily life and the pressures put on merchants to refuse to import or sell British goods ruined some friends. Others readily signed on to nonimportation agreements. Elizabeth lamented friends who went under. She also cheered those who resisted, those who saw it as "their duty to stand up for so valuable a country." "If I was in Boston," she declared, "I wou'd drink no tea." She would also advise her friends to sign agreements to boycott British goods.[2]

What Elizabeth Murray wanted above all else was stability for her family and to maintain her property. Many of her relatives, including her third husband, would remain loyal to the Crown. She shared his sentiments, especially after the region descended into disorder, but above all she wanted to preserve her world. As the region around Boston became a staging area for war in 1775, Elizabeth refused to leave her estate in Cambridge for fear it would be occupied by American militia or British troops. With her servants, slaves, and family around her, she ran the farm and looked after the financial dealings of the family, tasks normally reserved to a husband, who had fled to British-occupied Boston, a decision that vexed Elizabeth. Eventually, after a local committee of correspondence ordered her farm occupied, she made her way into Boston. Elizabeth Murray died in 1785 as the world she had known collapsed. The woman, who embraced patriotic principles in the 1760s and early 1770s and who flirted with loyalism in the years thereafter, pushed against some of the assumptions of the day as she tried to restore order to her life.[3] But her story was not a simple one of heroic ascent. Slaves helped pave the way for her independence, as did the connections her brother provided.

In the 1760s and 1770s, the economy depended on the production and consumption of women such as Elizabeth Murray. And as British sovereignty collapsed, they would play critical roles in maintaining a semblance of stability in a disordered society. As Murray's story suggests, women were pushing at the boundaries of acceptable gender roles while working within them. In this regard, Murray did not act alone. As wave after wave of protest gripped the colonies in the early 1770s, women like Murray stood on the front lines, asserting themselves publicly on the very edge of prescribed bounds. In 1770, for instance, women from Boston led a subscription drive for a binding nonimportation agreement. Collecting a few hundred signatures, the women asserted that they would not purchase or consume tea and urged others to follow their example, using their conventional prerogatives as domestic consumers and producers to make a political statement. Their plan worked. Word reached Connecticut of what the women in Boston were doing, and soon a petition was making its rounds there.[4] With authority in question, they stepped in to fill the void, acting as virtual police of patriotic sentiment. By their consumer choices, they played vital roles in fashioning what Adams hoped would become a republic of virtue, a virtual nation within the empire standing for all that the Glorious Revolution in theory was supposed to have guaranteed for all Britons. In this way, rioting and protesting, in both of which women participated, turned the colonies into a crucible, transforming older attitudes into new ones.

Rebellion, of course, was common enough in the early modern world. And for the most part, popular riots tended to be conservative in nature—that is, designed to recover a world that was being lost—rather than progressive in intent. Moreover, in the early modern world officials assumed that rabble rousers or men on the make were at the bottom of it all, that such conniving men sought to take advantage of discontent. What happened in America did not differ from the model of what happened in other places throughout the British Atlantic world. But what made events in America literally revolutionary was this: these riots were not only giving a voice to the normally voiceless but were also responding to the fears and hopes associated with a failure of sovereignty. As time wore on and as no single actor could make claims to authority legitimate, this tendency became even more pronounced.

Americans, as British subjects, knew of the critical significance of sovereignty. It represented society's lifeblood, or as Hobbes had put it during England's seventeenth century, sovereignty was "the Soule of the Common-wealth; which once departed from the body, the members doe no more receive their motion from it."[5] Men and women were entitled to rights, and the state—in this case Parliament—was empowered to uphold them. In this way, sovereignty was both created and made manifest.

Most Britons would have known at least the rude outlines of this Lockean social contract theory. And under normal circumstances, subjects could and did applaud governing arrangements. But there was a second Locke, one that did not curry favor among the British except in critical moments. Locke goes on to say that if a sovereign forgets his rationale for governing, and instead tramples on the rights of subjects, they have the right and obligation to stand up for their liberties. "Should either the executive or the legislative, when they have got the power in their hands, design, or go about to enslave or destroy them," Locke had argued, "the people have no other remedy in this, as in all other cases where they have no judge on earth, but to appeal to heaven."[6]

In a world where sovereignty was crumbling, these women began to take that step. The implications would be enormous not only for British rule but also for American societies. "Appealing to heaven," as Locke put it, did not only mean the people questioned the efficacy or legitimacy of the state. It also meant that in everyday life where authority was uncertain, men and women had to reckon with responsibility for their own lives and fortunes. As sovereignty crumbled, so too did the social and cultural structures that held tensions in check. These women, who led boycotting movements, were also giving voice to this reality.

What appeared to be deference across the board was teetering. At one level, into the vacuum of authority stepped some Americans for the first time. Of course, outsiders or arrivistes such as Samuel Adams and Patrick Henry would play such roles. These men were assuming positions of local authority, but they did not comprise part of a ruling elite for provincial America, the few whose names were known even in the metropole. Local leaders who did not have enduring ties or bonds of interest to Britain would see the crisis of sovereignty as an opportunity to rise to the top. At another level, those who by the unspoken rules that defined what could be considered deferential societies could not or should not play politically assertive roles in society were doing just that. As local authority faltered, so too did the structures that animated authority in the early modern world.[7] The end of deference, if it ever really existed, had not come at this time. Elites would still have power, or at least would try to use, manipulate, or channel popular forces for their own purposes. Nonetheless, the theoretically natural order of things was—for the moment at least—being turned on its head.

Americans, of course, were still tethered to Britain by an idea, a very powerful idea. Allegiance to the Crown, they believed, made them who they were. For many, however, that notion of sovereignty only had meaning so long as it could be manifest. The Crown's authority was premised most critically on local political institutions. These, by and large, were teetering on the brink. In other words, only an idea of British authority remained. Americans themselves had stepped in to fill the power vacuum, and as they were constructing their own imagined community out of the stuff of provincial protest, the possibilities of acknowledging the efficacy of the Crown were growing more and more remote. By 1774, it was beginning to become clear to some that the emperor had no clothes.

The relationship between the failure of sovereignty, the collapse of authority, and the insistence of a new elite in trying to channel social friction defined the period just after the Stamp Act. The women of Boston stood at the intersection of these dynamics, representing something new in American history: a group of people energized by shocks to the established order but also able to conceive of structural change to society. Even though their resistance to a changing world proved useful to the likes of Samuel Adams, women—and men—who participated in the rituals of consumption and resistance helped fashion new bases for meaningful relationships between citizens and society. Because of the networks from which nonimportation movements had sprung, resistance in one region could be joined to resistance in other regions, amplifying the actions of people normally cut out of the political process. Because of the associational nature of protest, networks that had emerged to air discontents could also begin to fill the void of authority. Print, of course, played a critical role, as did what we could call the creation of a common British identity. More to the point, in the years before the revolution common people had been empowered. But only as sovereignty began to crumble could they act upon it.

What was happening in the West serves as a useful model to understand what was happening throughout America. Although the British comprehended western territories under a distinctive plan, the crisis that gripped the region and the process of the dissolution of sovereignty had a great deal in common with the breakdown in the East. It only took place more quickly and perhaps more dramatically. Indeed, the Fort Stanwix Treaty accelerated the pace of events. As Hillsborough had expected, settlers streamed into areas ceded by the Treaty, alarming Cherokees and Shawnees who saw the region as their hunting ground. Also as expected, speculators saw their main chance and took it. In fact, with the prospect of millions of acres in and around the ceded areas before them, they created huge speculating conglomerates, such as the Grand Ohio Company, the brainchild of Benjamin Franklin, which combined the principals of a number of companies. Even defunct ventures found new life with the Treaty. With the ideology of the line in place, only certain sections of the West—in theory—lay open to speculation and governance. With the bending of the line, and the impeachment of the imperial ideology, the whole line lay in danger. The step, justified as a safety valve, turned a low simmer into a boil, and soon the West once more descended into violence.[8]

It was now becoming apparent that the region lay beyond the reach, financially and geographically, of the British to control it. Officials soon realized that they did not have the resources to cover mounting Indian deaths or the troops to restrain settlers. To complicate matters, common men and women were threatening the British with more violence if they continued to "appease" Indians. Officials in London were sending authorities such as Johnson and Stuart mixed signals. Some, such as Hillsborough held their ground; others assured them that it was just a matter of time before the claims of huge conglomerates would be recognized. And all the while, well-connected Americans, those who hoped that they could play the role of leaders in a new British America, such as Franklin, tried to use their influence with the ministry in Britain. More provincially minded elites—men on the rise with fewer connections to the metropole such as George Washington and George Mason—tried to make the most of their connections to colonial governments to see their schemes succeed. Land, then, was yet another variable in this contest over authority.

All too predictably, the whole British program for the West collapsed. It did so for the most ordinary of reasons. The Mississippi River was ruining the foundations of one of the forts in the West that the British had inherited from the French. Fort Chartres had been seen as a critical piece of the western plan, the point furthest west where British sovereignty would be made manifest. It also had critical symbolic importance for Indians in the area, announcing that the British had assumed the mantle of the French in adjudicating disputes and facilitating trade. Forts, therefore, were important features of the whole civilizing mission that had presumably under-scored the British approach to the West. With the ideology of that approach now in ruins, forts had less utility. And with the Mississippi wearing Fort Chartres away, British officials had a stark choice to make: either keep up the pretense of a western plan and pour more money and men into the fort; or abandon it. They chose the lat-ter course. With resources stretched even thinner with the national crisis in the East, commanders ordered troops out of Fort Chartres and to eastern cities.

As Thomas Gage worried, settlers would consider themselves almost independ-ent with the abandonment of Chartres unless the Crown could adopt some plan to assert sovereignty. It was not to be, and western authority came down like a house of cards. Fort Pitt existed as a key piece of the western plan, an important symbol of sovereignty, as well as a strategic lynchpin in the west, tying forts further removed to support and supplies from the East. But with Fort Chartres abandoned, it no longer had such a role to play. In 1772, therefore, officials decided to abandon it as well. General Gage gave the fort's commanding officers orders to sell off what they could, transport cannon to the east, and destroy the fort's mighty bastions. Even these tasks could not go well. Locals, such as George Croghan, colluded with one another to keep prices low at auction. While the bastions could not be destroyed only com-promised, the cannon proved too unwieldy to transport expeditiously; many were dumped in the rivers. In fact, this denouement was neither here nor there. By 1773, the British had effectively left the West.

In theory, the individual colonies would now bear some of the responsibility for the West. So Pennsylvania and Virginia dispatched agents—really bands of vigilantes—to lay claim to the region around Fort Pitt. Neither had a real mandate—sovereignty was still technically vested solely in the Crown not through the colonies—and neither could prevail. Speculative companies used the vacuum of authority to establish their own colony, exactly where Virginia and Pennsylvania officials laid claim, the greatest of which was to be called Vandalia, in honor of the Queen's putative Vandal ancestry. At first, as they pulled strings in London, agents for Vandalia had an edge. Indeed, so well-connected had American speculating schemes become that Hillsborough was toppled from power by their influence. As he fell from grace, even the pretense of British authority came crashing down. Vandalia had only a few legal hurdles to clear in the capital before its backers would turn their attention to the claimants from Virginia and Pennsylvania. As expected, settlers also streamed in, willing to be used as pawns in the looming struggle between colonies and companies. Most of these men and women banked on the notion that the older process of frontier develop-ment that rewarded the early and the lucky would apply to them in the West. In these years, young men on the make, such as George Rogers Clark from Virginia—those who resembled young Patrick Henrys—were drawn to the Ohio Valley where real opportunity lay. These and squatters were willing to risk their lives for competency and riches. As Clark wrote his brother, "this Cuntry Setels very fast."[9]

With British abandonment, the West, in fact, entered an abyss. Officials had rationalized the pullout from much of the frontier region by arguing that Indians would welcome the change, as they could regard forts as intrusive. They also tried to justify the Treaty of Fort Stanwix as a measure that preserved Indian interests. After all, the Iroquois had agreed. But Cherokees and Shawnees refused to recognize the validity of the treaty, especially younger men who saw their way of life and livelihoods threatened by the advance of squatters, surveyors, land jobbers, and speculators. The covenant chain, in their minds, could not justify such a naked landgrab. They and other groups saw, with good reason, a conspiracy to take their lands from them. As a Delaware delegation argued, "it will be out of the Indians' power to govern their young men, for we assure you the black clouds begin to gather fast in this country."[10] Understandably, Indians resisted. With the removal of authority, and with the early scramble to reconstitute it, the West was quickly becoming a Hobbesian world of all against all. In 1774, a settler named Michael Cresap, to cite the most prominent example, led a band that massacred men, women, and children. One official put the number he and others killed at 49. He exaggerated. But the point was that the West had become a lawless place.[11] Squatters and young men on the make refused to act in a deferential manner, ignoring both injunctions from colonial governments and the Crown. The same held for Indians. Deference to elders also made little sense in a world that was collapsing. No doubt, Indians and Euro-American notions of deference differed in profound ways. But the implications of a boundless world made for similar responses.

From the British perspective, the East also sorely lacked restraint. With the arrival of more British troops, who now had a more visible presence in eastern streets, it was becoming apparent that the British were abandoning an earlier approach of state formation. Troops were to fix in the minds of colonists the potentially coercive power of the state. Although commanders tried to ensure that violence was avoided, the appearance of redcoats sent a message to all as to where the ultimate power of the state lay. As had been the case in places like Boston before, the gap between metropolitan expectations and provincial realities manifested themselves through local tensions. The crisis of sovereignty had made a bad economy worse in the colonies. New York and Pennsylvania struggled with a tight money supply made tighter still by the Currency Act of 1764 that limited the authority of the colonies to issue paper currency. Local trade was constricted, and even the large merchant house Baynton, Wharton, and Morgan collapsed. In Boston, the years 1767 to 1769 proved especially difficult, so much so that John Hancock's brother lost his business. The early 1770s did not see much improvement across the board. The ebbing tide lowered many boats, driving small shopkeepers into bankruptcy and the poorer sort to the poorhouse. Indeed, the greatest public works projects of the period were for almshouses, cloth factories, and prisons, one of which held Ebenezer Macintosh who had been arrested for debt.[12] Nonetheless, the failure of a major London banking house frightened merchants, leading some to demand payments on debt from American traders and planters.

But even if the economy had not yet recovered, it was moving out of the post-war recession unevenly, leading to different interpretations on recovery. Planters in Virginia fretted over the tobacco market. Slaveholders from the smaller islands of the Caribbean also suffered economically during these years. Yet slaveholding South Carolinians and planters from the larger islands of the Caribbean, as well as some merchants from port towns in the North who had prospered during the war, saw hope for the future. Farmers in Pennsylvania also had reason to be optimistic. Their economy was diversified and fundamentally sound. Trade, they reckoned, would return to prewar levels, and they believed that they had much to protect. Some did not fear that parliamentary acts could impoverish; they worried, instead, that meddling could threaten a return to prosperity.[13]

Boston was not one of these places. British troops were competing with locals for scarce jobs in the cities, heightening tensions between these groups. Drunken soldiers treated men and women in unsurprisingly appalling fashion, and from time to time soldiers beat civilians. In one memorable case, after a number of tense incidents, a Boston rope maker told a soldier looking for work that he could clean out the rope maker's shithouse. The soldier punched the rope maker, but a gang gave him a beating. The soldier returned with his friends, igniting a street brawl. The following days, roving bands of young Bostonians and British soldiers trolled the streets looking for fights.[14] Tensions also mounted between the up-and-comers and the "mob." Samuel Adams preached restraint to the people, believing it his job to keep an "unthinking herd," as he put it, "awake to their grievances." A Frenchman believed that, because of the crisis, Adams had acquired a reputation throughout Europe as "one of the prime movers" of rebellion. Yet he was no anarchist or puppet-master. He despised Hutchinson and the present government but not the idea of government, declaring in the newspaper that he wanted "No Mobs—No Confusions—No Tumults."[15] As long as the common sort stayed within the bounds of pressing for their legitimate rights as they were traditionally defined and as long as violence remained at acceptable levels—and thereby could be channeled—Adams supported popular action.[16]

Adams, however, could not control men's passions. On the evening of 5 March 1770, only a few days after the brawl at the rope maker's, a group of young men gathered on King's Street and began harassing a sentry outside of the customs house. The crowd grew, and as more troops emerged, surrounded the customs house. One denounced the sentry as "damned rascally Scoundrel Lobster Son of a Bitch." Boys began firing snowballs and lobbing anything else they could find. As the tension mounted and as the sentry's comrades joined him in the street, the crowd dared the British to fire. The British opened fire, and three men lay dead. Two died of their wounds soon after.[17] A Boston silversmith and engraver named Paul Revere would produce a famous image of what would be remembered as the "Boston massacre."

Just as significant as the violence were the people involved. John Adams, who defended the soldiers, said at the trial that "we have been entertained with a great variety of phrases, to avoid calling this sort of people a mob. Some call them shavers, some call them geniuses." Adams had no such qualms. "The plain English is, gentlemen," he declared, "most probably a motley rabble of saucy boys, negroes, and mulattoes, Irish teagues and outlandish jack tars." The riot was directed by the down and outs of Boston society.[18] Indeed, a rope maker, a black sailor named Crispus

Figure 4.2 Paul Revere, *Boston Massacre*, 1770. Courtesy of the Massachusetts Historical Society.

Attucks, and an Irish immigrant were among the dead. They had been involved in brawls with British troops before. Ironically, the rioters were killed by Irishmen named Hartegan, White, and Killroy under the command of an Irish officer named Thomas Preston serving in the British army.[19]

Men such as Attucks had, of course, good reason to be upset about the status quo. During the Seven Years' War, their lives had changed profoundly. Before the war, most labor in America was bound. In the port towns, servants and apprentices and slaves all worked within a web of relationships. For servants and those on the artisanal ladder, progress proved slow but predictable. When times were flush, they did not see greater benefits; their masters did. But when times grew hard, working-men had security, as the master bore the brunt of economic dislocation. The steady rhythm of the system, which reflected the deferential nature of society, also provided basic security. With the war, things began to change. As port towns boomed with men and material coming in from Britain, demand for labor grew to such a height that the promise of wages and mobility—both upward and geographic—proved more alluring than a bound labor system. With good reason, working men—when they could—now worked for wages. Such a system functioned in a way inversely proportional to a bound labor regime. Wage laborers could expect to make good money during periods of prosperity, as could owners. But when recession hit, the owner had no obligation—financial or moral—to keep jobs for men or to keep wages fair. The worker bore the cost if an economy cooled. The experience of carpenters named Benjamin Morgan and David Falk is a case in point. In 1753, Morgan signed a contract with an employer named Isaac Norris for a monthly stipend plus food. In 1755, after the war had begun and as demand for building increased, he signed a new contract with the same employer for a wage, which would only be paid when he worked. Moreover, he would be responsible for his own food. Falk did the same a year later. A short time later, however, after a bout of misfortune, he asked for the older arrangement.[20]

With recession, wage laborers found themselves unemployed or their wages cut. Nonetheless, the men still believed that the economy and society, as well as the relationships that animated both, had to be constrained by moral laws—that an economy amounted to more than the sum total of supply and demand. The men who ran ports, owned ships, and built them did not agree. Working people did not yet comprise what we could call a class, a group with an enduring consciousness.[21] That does not mean that class sensibilities were not yet present. Consciousness proved, at this point, more episodic.[22] They still looked above and below them—not side-to-side—for the most salient relationships, still living in a society that was defined by the rituals of deferring to authority, even if deferential assumptions were questioned. More critically, they still articulated dissatisfaction with their lot in life by looking back, almost nostalgically, to a world that seemed to be drifting away. When they rioted, as they did throughout Boston in the years between 1765 and 1770, they were articulating a deep sense of frustration with the fortunes of their lives in a quickly changing world. At least that was the case for the time being.

And this was so not only in the port towns of America. In farming villages as well, where the vast majority of Americans lived, the lot of the young did not appear as promising as it had earlier. In the mid-eighteenth century, Americans experienced a baby boom of their own. Franklin, who believed that surging population would lead America to become the western seat of the British empire, reckoned that the population was doubling every 20 years. In coming up with his estimates, it should be noted, he was influenced by the work of Sir William Petty.[23] Natural increase meant that many sons would not receive enough land on which to raise and support a family of their own. Concord, a small farming village not far from Boston, epitomized these trends. More young men had to move out from older settlements for land or had to find professions of their own. Newcomers, and young men regarded as idle, were "warned out" by those who feared they were slipping down the social structure. The town, in other words, would not support them if they slipped into indigence. The tensions placed strains on the relationships between fathers and sons and mothers and daughters. Would young women find promising men to marry? Would or could young men gain their independence from their parents? The patriarchal structure teetered amid the population boom, as postwar recession limited opportunities further. In addition, the protests that stifled trade had also hit farmers hard. Boycotts, nonimportation, and nonconsumption attenuated the ties to the West Indian market, which had demanded livestock, lumber, fish, and rum from New England. Concord, like many small towns, suffered.[24] The consumer revolution had transformed the countryside as much as the city, enmeshing small towns in the hinterland of bigger cities within a web of markets. But the markets, as urban workers had learned, did not forgive. In the years after the war, as riots gripped American cities, men and their sons working on farms were also struggling to make ends meet. Their sons then began to wonder what the future would bring for them, as they looked back to the day when moral reasoning held as much sway as the market in determining fortunes.

Further afield still, the world of the great land magnates of the Connecticut River Valley, the so-called "River Gods," was fragmenting. The Connecticut River Valley also witnessed a boom in population, one that stressed an already divided region. Religious disputes between New Lights, usually the poorer sort who supported the Awakening, and the Old Lights, who opposed it, reflected the tensions that were gripping the region. Indeed, a series of revivals that spread through New England in the early 1760s heightened differences. With postwar economic stagnation, men and women began to contest the River Gods' justifications for authority. Much like the residents of Concord, they came to believe that an older, better world was unraveling, and the River Gods lay behind it. And they vented their frustrations as authority in America began faltering. The arguments used by radicals about the arbitrary nature of imperial authority found, in other words, fertile ground.[25]

Americans had been dealing with the idea of markets for years. Moreover, they were savvy enough to understand that market relations threatened older social systems, and that they had a hand in that transformation. They were not mindless victims, in other words. Resistance spoke to frustrations that most societies experienced from time to time. Yet resistance in this context—or even thumbing noses at authority—signaled something amiss in places like Boston. For more than 5 years, these sorts of men had engaged in riot and small-scale rebellion. Although these sorts of actions did not represent anything unusual for the period, in places like Boston at this time authority had become especially enfeebled, and the absence of authority had lifted the lid on a cauldron of resentment. To Peter Oliver, the issue was sovereignty. The "Hydra of Rebellion," he argued, only arose after men like James Otis and Samuel Adams "broke down the Barriers of Government." With protest following protest, "government was now pretty thoroughly dissolved."[26]

Locals like Samuel Adams were soon trying to make rhetorical use of the tragedy that took the lives of the "saucy" young men. He and a few other leaders sent out a pamphlet highlighting what had happened in the streets of Boston, arguing that the soldiers involved had to stand for trial and that the "massacre" was proof positive of the tyranny of a standing army. The pamphlet—a copy of which was sent to Lord Rockingham, Edmund Burke, John Wilkes, and Charles Lucas—also offered an interpretive reading of events, one that not only downplayed the local tensions implicit in the riot that led to massacre, but that also tried to rally opinion and support around men like Bowdoin, Hancock, and Adams. The pamphlet stated that the troops "fired upon the inhabitants promiscuously in King street." The writers suggested that soldiers conspired with officials in a "plot to massacre the inhabitants." Resistance heightened the appeal of patriotism, but a patriotism that privileged their places as interpreters of events and leaders of opinion. In other words, they recast resentments between haves and have-nots as the stuff of the crisis of authority, conflating two sets of tensions as they did so. As British sovereignty was reeling, the battle for America had begun.[27]

That battle would be fought in every city and town, and virtually every hamlet, as the crisis of sovereignty deepened. And as it did, ordinary Americans would play unprecedented political roles, energizing and threatening their betters, challenging presumptions of authority but also providing opportunities for channeling unrest.[28] The changing roles of women offer a great example. Without the cooperation or lead of women, boycotting, nonimportation, and nonconsumption did not stand a chance of working. Women regulated the household economy, where most consumption began and ended. Their roles in society may have become less visible in those American communities that had experienced the transition to a market economy. Nonetheless, as riots grew in intensity, as postwar recession gripped the colonies, and as popular demonstrations slowed trade, markets were disrupted. Even in places like Philadelphia, the most prosperous American city in the eighteenth century, colonial resistance strategies strained market relations. If dislocations were experienced here, they also were disrupting communities like Lexington and Concord, small farming villages that comprised part of the hinterland of Boston. Fewer market outlets privileged the household economy, and more significantly, the role of women.

Women took advantage of the turning back of the clock, standing established patterns on their heads. Indeed, the first political act of many women in the 1760s and 1770s involved saying "no." They said no to British goods. A group of women about to be married said "no" to their fiancés so long as the marriage licenses were printed on stamped paper. In 1770, 300 well-to-do women signed an announcement in the *Boston Evening Post* declaring they would not drink tea, as would women from North Carolina who called themselves the Edenton Ladies Patriotic Guild.[29] Women marched in demonstrations, styling themselves guardians of a moral economy, one less tied to market supply and demand and more to simple right and wrong. They ostracized merchants who sought to take advantage of the situation, those who would not cooperate with their neighbors, or those who were price-gouging. In some cases, this meant ostracizing other women. In 1768, for instance, a merchant named Jane Eustis signed a nonimportation agreement. A year later, she refused to re-subscribe and was listed in a newspaper. Discredited, she moved to England.[30] As fabrics such as linen were no longer entering the colonies from England and Ireland, wives, daughters, and mothers made their own clothes. Wearing homespun in many places did not only become fashionable; it became necessary. For caffeine-addled Americans, nonimportation of tea presented significant hardship. Women again stepped into the breach, brewing local concoctions. In other words, women's work had real value again, and their visibility grew accordingly. In some ways, the roles they played did not portend a looming battle of the sexes or even reveal deep-seated resentments; rather, they signaled how America's political crises and concomitant economic dislocations placed women at the center of colonial society.[31]

Many were anxious to have women play their new part. Patriot leaders organized petition-signing ceremonies, which featured women. Women took part in spinning competitions, yoking their leadership in the household to patriotic opposition to parliamentary sovereignty. A poem written by Milcah Martha Moore summed up the new roles women were taking up:

> Since the men, from a party or fear of a frown
> Are kept by a sugar-plum quietly down
> Supinely asleep—and depriv'd of their sight
> Are stripp'd of their freedom, and robb'd of their right;
> If the sons, so degenerate! The blessings despise
> Let the Daughters of Liberty nobly arise.[32]

In one memorable exercise, women added their names to a "Solemn league and Covenant" declaring that colonists would not consume British goods. The seventeenth-century imagery was no mistake. Scots had signed their own covenant to declare their opposition to Stuart tyranny, particularly attempts to expand English ecclesiastical practices northward. Although Boston's leaders were behind the signing, the participation of groups formally excluded from the levers of power gave the ritual more universal meaning. Although women in America, of course, were not protesting bishops, they were making the same essential point by their participation: without authority, the structures that gave life authority became less viable.[33]

After the "massacre" in Boston and waves of riots and new nonimportation agreements, places like Boston had changed. For a start, the British withdrew their troops from city streets. The troops still occupied the area but were now billeted on an island in the harbor, and commanders took pains to steer clear of provocative measures. In this, the British had stumbled onto a sensible approach. After 1770, tensions eased a bit in the colonies, as Parliament passed no new laws for America, troops stayed indoors, and Americans got back to their lives. Nonetheless, the 5 years from 1765 to 1770 had a profound effect on American society. For 5 years, men and women were out in the streets contesting not only British authority but also the changes that had gripped their lives. In so doing, they threatened the survival of local governance. "Government," Gage declared, "is at an End in Boston, and in the hands of the People, who have only to assemble to execute any Designs."[34] The British had not or could not demonstrate the resolve to make their sovereignty meaningful. Behind the years of relative peace in the colonies, therefore, lay new realities.

King Charles I famously said at the outset of the English Civil Wars, "no bishop, no king." Both the Crown and the episcopate relied on the same ideals of hierarchy and status. Rip one away, and the other lay vulnerable. For Americans, the watchwords had become "no authority, no deference." Ordinary men and women tipped the social order upside down from time to time in ritualistic ways in Europe, as for example when jesters became mayors for a day during "feasts of fools." On Pope's Day, ordinary Americans too inverted the social order, as they ruled Boston for a day. The Stamp Act crisis, and the riots that followed, fed into a similar pattern.

American society, like early modern European societies, was premised, in theory, on deference. Deferring to one's betters represented one strategy among many of making sense of power relations in local contexts. Americans negotiated with one another over how to understand and articulate power and status in varieties of ways. Doffing one's cap was one way of doing so. So was rioting. Both involved defining the relationship between groups of distinct status over issues like rule. Subtle and not-so-subtle forms of negotiation defined the give-and-take over authority. What we could call deference may have been weaker in America, given the unusual level of parity and the absence of titled nobility. Nonetheless, in much the same way most Americans conceived the Crown to be sovereign, they also had assumed that the age-old idea of status animated the nature of relations in their homes, towns, and cities. In the crucible of revolution, certain strategies for negotiating power, in other words, began to crack. Revolution, therefore, acted as solvent.[35]

Only the committees that had emerged in the early years of tumult could contain or constrain popular unrest. Committees based in New York, Philadelphia, and Boston had even proven effective in blockading the ports of cities such as Providence and Newport, both of which had tried to withdraw from nonimportation agreements.[36] While the many who considered themselves loyal to the Crown still believed that local assemblies and royal governors represented the local manifestation of sovereignty, for 5 years these had failed in their most simple tasks of keeping order and peace in society. And in the place of older regimes, new ones were emerging. Committees had begun to take over the reins of rule in many of the larger cities and towns of America. After all, they remained the only bodies standing that could channel the forces that had overwhelmed older structures. The power of committees, however, relied on the threat of the "mob" and the boycott, the tools of the lower sort and women, which epitomized those tensions. Even the hint of a new measure by the British unleashed a torrent of protest and spasm of violence.

Prolonged protest did not prove that the British were losing America; rather, it demonstrated that they had lost America. So, for instance, when a British customs ship, the *Gaspee*, ran aground off Rhode Island in 1772, it surprised few—save officials—that men burned it. This was not a provocative measure—quite the opposite in fact. It spoke to new realities. As the captain of the schooner had been preying on locals, who carried wood and provisions in small boats, rumors circulated how he had let his men steal cattle and pilfer firewood. The ship did not safeguard British sovereignty but represented a tyrannical but feeble attempt to foist sovereignty on a community that was learning to manage on its own. In these circumstances, any British measure would face stiff opposition. But the *Gaspee* affair accomplished much more. The affair strengthened colonial resolve to build continental institutions. In the wake of the incident, the British ministry appointed a commission to investigate, and the commissioners argued that the persons responsible for burning the *Gaspee* could be tried in England, an affront to an old English liberty of being tried by one's peers. What happened in Rhode Island reverberated in Virginia. Led by Thomas Jefferson, Patrick Henry, and Richard Henry Lee, the House of Burgesses commissioned a committee to open up communications with other colonies to address issues dangerous to all America. Only unity could maintain vigilance. Within 12 months, nearly all the other colonies had followed suit.[37]

In the years between 1770 and 1773, as the government left the colonies well-enough alone, one event after another demonstrated the tenuousness of maintaining even the appearance of British rule in an America that had already effectively been lost. In these years, for instance, the bishop's controversy erupted once more, this time in Virginia, leading many Americans again to fear that the government was intent on creating an established church for the colonies. Even some Episcopal clergy opposed the installation of a bishop because the possibility would further exacerbate tensions in America. The installation of an American bishop did not take place at this juncture for these reasons, especially as the increasingly politicized citizenry, many of whom were Baptist and already enraged by the idea of an established church, would use the issue to push for the toppling of the Anglican Church's ascendant status in Virginia. The House of Burgesses had no interest in pursuing the matter and congratulated those ministers who opposed "A Measure by which much Disturbance, great Anxiety, and Apprehension would certainly take place among his Majesty's Faithful Subjects." Dissenters, who one critic declared had grown embittered "against the very name of bishops, and all episcopal government," again played a prominent role in stymieing the creation of an American bishopric. In light of the years of tension, two Anglican ministers who opposed an American episcopate argued, any such move would "endanger the very existence of the British Empire in America."[38]

The renewal of the bishop's controversy demonstrates how policy and rumor could lead sentiment to change in unforeseen ways. The years 1773 and 1774 provided much more evidence of how during moments of uncertain sovereignty crises hinged on contingency. The story of the so-called Tea Party offers the best example of this reality. During the years of crisis, Parliament had a great many other issues to attend to, only a number of which revolved around the North American colonies, including, for example, India.[39] In fact, a looming fiscal crisis touched off by the impending insolvency of one of Britain's largest companies, the East India Company, preoccupied the North ministry. On paper, the company exported spices, silk, opium, and precious metals from the East. It was also the largest importer of tea from China. The company functioned more like a government than a business, ruling over the people of Bengal in an imperialistic fashion and maintaining an army and civil administration on the subcontinent, all to improve its bottom line. To support this infrastructure and the capital British elites invested in it, the company enjoyed a state-sponsored monopoly, allowing it to charge high prices for its tea. The arrangement proved unsustainable. Irresponsible company directors at home clashed with officials in India, who were mismanaging their holdings. Wealth had not followed the annexation of territories and, with war, deficits grew. The company, which could not compete with shippers from other nations and even from some smugglers in Britain, was teetering on the brink of bankruptcy by 1773. In the meantime, as Burke found, tea "was rotting in the warehouses of the company" in London.[40] Bankruptcy would not only destroy one of Britain's oldest joint-stock concerns; it also promised to throw the economy into a recession, the likes of which had not been seen since the 1720s in the wake of the South Sea Bubble, in which another company with global aspirations collapsed. In these circumstances, America offered an opportunity for the fortunes of the company.

North decided that the company should be allowed to sell tea in America without regulation or middlemen, promising to drive down costs for the consumer. The government also aimed at fundamentally reforming the way the company did business and in so doing sought to redefine the relationship between the company and the state. What ministers were attempting to do for America, much as their predecessors had done for the kingdoms of Scotland and Ireland earlier, they were beginning to extend now to India. As part of the reformist agenda, while Parliament gave the company a loan to stave off bankruptcy, the company could establish its own stores in British territories and sell its surplus tea directly to the consumer.[41] In pushing for the enabling legislation, North did not have America on his mind. Tea was the stuff of global empire. Burke argued that of all goods, "Tea is an object of other importance. Tea is perhaps the most important object, taking in with its necessary connexions, of any in the mighty circle of our commerce."[42] British merchants would now invest heavily in the tea bound for America, one, in fact, being Brook Watson, the subject of Copley's famous painting. Burke realized that as a byproduct of monopolization and investment, American consumers—avid drinkers of tea—would be able to purchase high quality tea more cheaply than they could by smuggling. Smugglers, however, who as Britons feared monopolies as much as standing armies, stood to lose boatloads of money. Not coincidentally, they tended to support, and in some cases direct, the patriot cause.[43]

Like Burke, Americans understood that tea mattered as a symbol. And because of its symbolic significance, the tea arriving in New York and Philadelphia was sent back to England. In Massachusetts, it was not so simple. Thomas Hutchinson believed he could hold onto the reins of authority while keeping disorder contained. On the one hand, Hutchinson did not want to precipitate a crisis. He knew once the ships entered Boston harbor, they could not leave until the duty on the tea had been paid. And he and his family had a personal stake in the East India Company. On the other hand, he invited the opportunity to demonstrate to all in Massachusetts that the British remained sovereign. "Surely," as he put it, "it is time this anarchy was restrained and corrected by some authority or other." After the ships entered, the duty had to be paid within 20 days—by December 17—or the tea would be subject to confiscation. He had time to wait the crisis out and would do nothing to exacerbate tensions, but he would not give in to what he saw a rabble-rousers. As people demonstrated in the streets against the arrival of East India tea, Hutchinson was under increased pressure to send the ships back to England. The captain of the *Dartmouth* pleaded with him to allow the ships to leave unloaded and without a customs clearance. Hutchinson refused.

John Singleton Copley, the painter, found himself in the middle of the controversy, torn by friends and patrons on both sides. In 1769, he had married the daughter of a leading Boston merchant named Richard Clarke who also served as chief agent for the East India Company. Clarke and his sons also were consignees to the tea that arrived in Boston in 1773. On November 29, 1773, Copley traveled to the Old South Meeting House, where at least 5,000, the "Body of the People" organized by the Boston Committee of Correspondence, were meeting to discuss what to do with the tea, and attempted to mediate the dispute. Copley saw ruin for his family in this "Political Storm," but although he "cooled the Resentment" of the people, he could not convince them that his family posed no threat to their liberties. He then met privately with men who had sat for him, John Hancock, Joseph Warren, and Samuel Adams, but to no avail.[44]

The "Body of the People" took matters into their own hands. On December 16, the day before the deadline, 100 to 150 of the Sons of Liberty assembled, dressed as Mohawks, boarded three British ships at Griffin's wharf in Boston, and used ropes to pull over three hundred 400 lb. tea chests from the holds. On deck, they smashed open the chests with hatchets and then shoveled the tea overboard. All told, they dumped £90,000 of tea from China into the harbor. Principal leaders, such as Samuel Adams and John Hancock, who were involved in planning, stayed away from Griffin's wharf, so as not to be accused of doing anything illegal.[45]

Arguably, the Tea Party proved the finest hour of the Sons of Liberty. At issue, however, was not just Parliament's presumption to meddle in American affairs. The Act, in fact, had the effect of targeting that very stratum of subjects in America that was now standing up for its right to rule in America. In many ways, men like John Hancock, who made a living by smuggling, were not only economically hamstrung by such legislation but were also politically disabled. During the previous decade, the middling sort had become the American equivalent of the "Third Estate." Years later, during a similar crisis in France, the Abbé Sieyès would write that the men of this station were the people who produced and consumed but who did not move the levers of power. Others, whose status was supported by a theoretical deference, held unwarranted privileges. Reverting to this literal status quo ante as Burke proposed, after a decade in which many Americans had stepped beyond their appointed roles on a consistent basis, would prove exceptionally difficult. Since 1765, the American third estate had grasped the levers, as crisis after crisis discredited and enfeebled an older local oligarchy. The masterless men who took to the streets then threatened not only the British; they also threatened the Hancocks of the world, who had tried to walk the fine line of confronting and coercing British officials without fomenting unfettered violence. In one vein, radicals in places like Boston hoped to use tumult to their advantage, to channel the justifiable anger of men—and women—who were beginning to imagine lives as actors freed from deferential fetters. But in another vein, they were playing a dangerous game. Societies could not function without order; and America appeared on the brink. In this instance, parliamentary sovereignty, in the form of the Tea Act, threatened to undo the arrival of their arrivistes, as it also would serve as the final act of the old order.[46]

Certainly, by now the British recognized the gist of what was happening. And they responded vigorously to the new series of riots. In the wake of the Tea Party, political enemies discredited North's policies. Hard-liners in the government, those who remembered how crises of sovereignty had been handled in Ireland and Scotland, argued that Americans had to be coerced. Although Burke warned "they will cast your sovereignty in your face," Parliament did not listen.[47] In response to the tumults over tea, Parliament passed a series of measures designed to make clear who was sovereign. Collectively known as the Coercive Acts, these measures closed the port of Boston until restitution was made for the tea. They also replaced the old leadership of the colony with garrison government, and General Thomas Gage was named the new governor. The popular assembly could no longer appoint the governor's council. The Crown now would do so. If any officials or soldiers were to be tried for a capital offense, they could now stand for trial in a more neutral site, say, Nova Scotia. Town Meetings were forbidden, except for electing local officials. In addition, Parliament passed a measure for quartering the troops who would be visible once more in American streets. The Coercive Acts, then, were designed not only to bring Bostonians to task for their misdeeds; they were also put in place to strike at the heart of alternative sources of authority. Neither the "people" nor the arrivistes would control courts, assemblies, or local meetings. Until proper order could be restored, made manifest by repayment for the tea, soldiers would see to order. Contrition, then, would serve as a barometer of American accession to British notions of state formation.

At issue, of course, was sovereignty. Most Americans still conceived the Crown as the place where ultimate power rested. Parliament and most other Britons had other ideas. But a difference over the location of sovereignty did not make for a crisis. Nor did a dispute over taxation or even colonial rights. Although these issues mattered, they became the stuff of revolution as authority teetered and as deference began to crack for a prolonged period of time. Sovereign authority, Americans argued, was designed to protect their birthright. They agreed with other Britons that they had rights that underscored their liberties, their commerce, and their Protestantism. At this juncture, it appeared that Parliament could neither protect these rights nor even provide for the preconditions for these rights to have meaning. In a world without authority, more fundamental issues of order and the very nature of society preoccupied colonists. Without order, there could be no meaningful society. Without society, rights to life, liberty, and property, as well as the ability to engage in commerce and worship as Protestants, could not be realized. Rights could not be manifest, as Locke said, when a people were "subject to the inconstant, uncertain, unknown, arbitrary will of another man." Parliament's meddling, many American Britons came to believe, had touched off the tumults that had brought society to its knees. Far from the solution, the Coercive Acts seemed the epitome of all that was wrong with parliamentary ideas about sovereignty. As Burke understood, "the cement is gone; the cohesion is loosened; and everything hastens to decay and dissolution."[48]

At this juncture, Americans began to imagine new possibilities for order. In fact, out of this crisis, Americans were constructing their own sovereign entities and the networks that made authority function. Far from curtailing alternative forms of authority, the Coercive Acts—or Intolerable Acts, as Americans called these and other measures—allowed new forms to flourish that had little to do with prevailing institutional structures. With the turn of events, Committees of Correspondence not only gained a new lease on life, they also had a new rationale. Some Bostonians refused to follow orders of anyone working under the auspices of General Thomas Gage, the new military governor installed by the Massachusetts Government Act. Outlying communities would not transfer their taxes to the new government. And locals forced councilors appointed under the new government to resign. Committees coordinated these actions.[49]

The committee network encompassing all of the colonies was now doing the stuff of government, providing for the common welfare by sending food, money, and moral support to what were seen as beleaguered Bostonians. The Boston Committee on Donations received hundreds of gifts from all over America. South Carolinians sent rice to feed the city. New Jersey sent rye. Others sent sheep, cattle, firewood, and honey, anything that could be transported by road with the closure of the port. East Hampton, New York, went so far as to levy a £100 tax on its people to relieve the Bostonians.[50] Committees were also beginning to provide for common defense as well, as they pried the militia structure away from failing governmental authority. In many places, they—not governors—controlled militia. Leaders of these networks believed that, given the provocative measures of the Intolerable Acts, they had little option but to create the conditions for order in their communities and throughout the colonies. As a British traveler to Virginia named Nicholas Cresswell recorded in October 1774, "everything here is in the utmost confusion. Committees are appointed to inspect into the Character and Conduct of every tradesman, and to prevent them selling Tea or buying British Manufactures." As militias formed, dissenters were tarred and feathered. "The King is openly cursed," Cresswell lamented, "and his authority set in defiance."[51]

Finally, in response to what appeared to be an impossible situation, members of these committees decided to meet together as a congress to discuss their common concerns. The first "Continental Congress," as it was called, would meet in Philadelphia to devise a concerted response to what were viewed as provocative measures. Convening in September 1774, representatives from the mainland colonies save Georgia met in the context of fear and uncertainty. No sooner had they arrived than rumors swept through the colonies of the British bombarding Boston. The rumors proved false but electrified proceedings. Paul Revere, who had published the famous print of the "Boston massacre," rode to Philadelphia with news of resolutions passed by committees in Massachusetts. The so-called Suffolk Resolves declared that the colonists had the right to nullify parliamentary legislation they deemed unconstitutional. The resolves also said that the colonists could wage a defensive war. As Americans wondered what was happening to their communities, Patrick Henry offered a clear, if frightening, vision. "Fleets and Armies and the present State of Things shew that Government is Dissolved," he declared. "We are in a State of nature." Self-preservation was at stake.[52]

The Continental Congress united Americans as never before. It also bound together the ad hoc network of governance that had emerged in the colonies. It did so most conspicuously in the form of "the Association." Congress debated how best to respond to the provocative measures but fastened on one tried and true approach. The representatives called for a boycott modeled on one just passed by an extra-constitutional "convention" of former members of the House of Burgesses that had met in Virginia.[53] The Royal Governor believed such bodies were "now enforcing throughout the country with the greatest vigour." The powers of committees and the Association were formidable. As he put it, they assumed the prerogative "to inspect the books, invoices and all the secrets of trade and correspondence of merchants." They "watch the conduct of every inhabitant without distinction

Figure 4.3 John Singleton Copley, *Paul Revere*, 1768. Museum of Fine Arts, Boston.

and to send for all such as come under their suspicion into their presence, to inter-rogate them respecting all matters which at their pleasure they think fit objects of their inquiry, and to stigmatize as they term it such as they find transgressing what they are now hardy enough to call the laws of Congress." Most disturbingly, he found that "every county besides is now arming a company of men who they call an independent company for the avowed purpose of protecting their committees and to be employed against government if occasion require."[54] The Association would be continental in scope but enforced at the local level through the recently empowered committee system. Congress called for committees of inspection or safety to be created by every village, town, and city. Men and women would police their neighbors, ensuring that the boycott worked. Some suspect groups were harassed. Northern Anglicans, recently arrived Scots, and small-scale merchants tended to be regarded as loyal to Parliament. Committees intimidated those on the fence, using terror and humiliation. Although their bark proved worse than their bite, these "hardy" bodies—not the British or those appointed by them—were gov-erning America.[55]

We could call these now "hardy" forms extra-constitutional or even extra-insti-tutional. In fact, they created the stuff of sovereignty in the imaginative space that existed between government and society, the space where association flourished.

Indeed, the decision to call their meetings a "congress" speaks to the ambivalent position of such structures. They were certainly not sovereign, nor did they pretend to be, hence the decision to use a value-neutral term that would not even suggest quasi-sovereignty. Yet, no one could deny that Congress was doing the stuff that sovereign authority did. America now existed in such a never-never land, a place between one entity that claimed authority but could not enact it and another that could not yet claim it but did enact it. True, through such extra-institutional life, Americans were relying on bonds of trust that had grown over the previous decade. Nonetheless, they were also attending to more elemental concerns. In the absence of viable authority, congresses and committees would begin to assert such a role.

The Quebec Act, a measure that appeared to be yet another innocuous-sounding Act that had precious little to do with the mainland colonies but that would occasion a flurry of protest, proved the final straw. It did three things. First, it recognized the practical difficulties of governing Quebec, a province peopled almost exclusively by Catholics and former subjects of an enemy, by providing the legal protection of worship that the Quebecois enjoyed in fact. The government would have oversight over ordinations and consecrating bishops but also exempted the people from the Test Act, which excluded Catholics in the archipelago from enjoying their civil rights. The Act also allowed the Catholic Church to collect tithes for its maintenance. The Catholic Church in Quebec, then, was put on a quasi-establishment basis.[56] Second, it installed a civil government for the region but one without democratic institutions. Third, it shifted the boundary of the province of Quebec to the Ohio River. All the region north and west of the Ohio, including the Illinois country, would now be subject to civil authority seated in Quebec. To a great extent, therefore, the Quebec Act recognized many of the problems that the British had encountered in the wake of the Seven Years' War in both the East and the West. The West, they learned, needed authority, and the Act provided for some in a region largely unpopulated by white settlers. It also spoke to the problems that had dogged the process of state formation by providing for a flexible notion of authority—one that could in this instance encompass even Catholics—by recognizing that social realities and authority had to go hand-in-hand for stability.

What made for order in one region meant disorder for another. In fact, the form that flexible notion of Britishness took for incorporating Quebec especially troubled Americans. In 1763, the British had added the former French colony of Grenada, transferred by the terms of the Treaty of Paris, to their Caribbean holdings. Grenada resembled the other Caribbean holdings in every respect but one: religion. The planters here were Catholic. The ministry had allowed planters in Grenada to practice their faith openly and even to vote for the members of the island's assembly. Although one of the central tenets of Britishness stipulated that faiths other than Protestantism would not be tolerated, policymakers proved flexible enough to understand that incorporating former French subjects required flexibility.[57]

An island in the Caribbean was one thing. Quebec, however, lay on the borders of the mainland colonies. For generations, it had served as a potent bogey, the sum of all fears. In the old mainland colonies, a place with few Catholics, granting Catholics any rights made no sense at all. In a world energized by the pan-Protestant religiosity of the Great Awakening, in fact, it proved especially troubling. A Pennsylvanian declared the Act "the boldest stride of despotism that has been made by any set of men since the restoration." A minister from New England suggested that the protector of the Constitution, King George III, was introducing policies that were unconstitutional in much the same way Charles I had in the seventeenth century. "The Quebec bill, as it is called," he argued, "establishing Popery, by Authority, in an American Province, is an Infringement on the constitutional Principles of our Kingdom and Government, and against the Principles of our holy Religion."[58] Coming on the heels of the so-called "Bishop controversy," during which some believed that the installation of an Anglican bishop in America would pave the way for popery, the Act stoked further fears of arbitrary government, especially since the ideological templates most Americans employed equated popery with tyranny.

The tone-deaf quality of passing such an Act, in other words, epitomized the bind that many Americans believed they were in. Americans hammered away at the Quebec Act because it threatened settlement of the West. They decried it because it gave rights to hated Catholics. They saw it as tyrannical because it did not give these same subjects the rights enjoyed by American colonists, the rights to have their own assembly. It occasioned, therefore, contradictory responses. No matter. What the responses to it revealed was the fact that Britain and America lay an ocean apart and, that by 1774, the process of state formation had failed, and failed miserably. Americans now fretted that the three bases of Britishness—liberty, commerce, and Protestantism—were imperiled, as the problems associated with the process of state formation had become a full-blown crisis over sovereignty. They believed what they did not only because the ideas of the seventeenth century created a mental switchboard, though true enough, but also because they found themselves in a crisis very much like England's seventeenth century.[59] In these circumstances, as the English had learned, ideas that underwrote stability could support rebellion. Ideas that animated the state could also be used to undo it.

The British-held islands in the Caribbean, of course, also struggled with similar issues. Nonetheless, while the cities of North America exploded in protest, the Caribbean remained quiet. Why? The answer is simple. To some extent, planters already had a secure place in the British system. In fact, one prominent planter from Jamaica named William Beckford would serve as lord mayor of London in the 1760s. Beckford was not exceptional. Wealthy planters increasingly lived lives tethered to London, not in a metaphorical way. Many planters, like Beckford, lived as absentee landlords in England and sent their sons for educations to Oxford and Cambridge. They comprised the most powerful colonial lobby in England, and the Society of West Indian merchants was one of the most cohesive English trade associations. Nearly all were Anglicans. Even residents of Montserrat, which had been peopled by Irish Catholics, attended Anglican services. More critically, they lived in societies in which worries about slave rebellion were always present. Upwards of 90% of the inhabitants of the islands toiled as slaves in awful conditions on sugar plantations. This was a world, nearly exclusively, of masters and slaves, a world with a negligible free white community. Planters, moreover, lived in a region studded with islands held by other nations, many inimical to them and Britain. Rebellion à la the mainland colonies was not an option.[60]

They, therefore, had a secure sense of their Britishness; however, they had little security in their lives, liberties, and property without the patronage of the British state. All the major islands complied with parliamentary legislation. In many ways, they were like the Ascendancy in Ireland, but with more money. With no hint of irony and understanding the full implications of what they were saying, colonists on the mainland saw the planters from "the Slavish Islands" in the years of crisis as a people apart.[61] Troops may have been unusual in the streets of Boston before the crisis of sovereignty. In places like Barbados where the threat of slave rebellion always loomed large, British troops were commonplace. As a visitor to Barbados found in 1774, "the militia...are well disciplined to keep the Negroes in awe. The Planters are in general rich, but a set of dissipating, abandoned, and cruel People."[62] Unsurprisingly, few planters complained of standing armies. Interests, fears, and viable ties of a ruling elite to Britain ensured they would remonstrate but would not push the issue of sovereignty. The ruling oligarchy, after all, however much it hated taxes, had ample reasons to keep the lid of authority firmly secured. As a minister from the Caribbean understood, "to resist *one* Evil, with not only the Hazard, but the Certainty, of bringing down *more* and *greater* Evils on our Heads" amounted to a fool's errand.[63]

The same, of course, could be said of places like South Carolina, a colony with a black majority. Yet the white population, especially in the western reaches of the colony, was growing. The low country may have been dominated by slave labor; the rest of the colony was not. South Carolina had experienced only one major slave revolt, the Stono Rebellion of 1739.[64] Given the nature of the men who participated in the revolt—Catholics from the Congo who had experience with warfare and with European weapons—it seemed to be an exceptional event. The militia had put down the rebellion, after which the colonial assembly passed punitive legislation. The colony had remained relatively quiet until the crisis of sovereignty.[65]

In the 1770s, rumors flew of slave insurrection that would plunge the colony into spasms of fear and violence. In 1775, two slaves fingered a free black named Thomas Jeremiah as the instigator of a planned slave rebellion, which the British were behind. However bogus the charge, wealthy planters acted upon it. Although Jeremiah worked as a pilot and owned slaves and he may well have been the wealthiest African American in the colonies, the same Henry Laurens who was accosted by a mob during the Stamp Act disturbances charged that Jeremiah's skin color excluded him from enjoying the rights of a Briton, even if he was Christian and free. Laurens, who had earned his wealth as a slave trader and styled himself a moderate, would later play a number of prominent roles in the patriot movement. He and other planters, practical men who found themselves trapped between slaves, the lower sort of white society, and British officialdom, with some reluctance edged into the patriot camp. The royal governor, William Campbell, a Scot and slave owner, was appalled by what was happening, especially that Jeremiah's so-called trial in a slave court would be held without jury or proper counsel. The Jeremiah affair ignited tensions in South Carolina. Incensed over the Intolerable Acts and Campbell's stance on Jeremiah, a patriot mob rose up against Campbell, forcing him to leave the colony. On August 18, 1775, Thomas Jeremiah was hanged and his body burned as an example. South Carolina's planters were surrounded by colonies that did not find themselves in this predicament. A Continental Congress, therefore, diluted such fears, and with time moderates such a Laurens became hard-liners. In this context, their practical stake in the slave system guaranteed as much.[66]

One man, more than most, understood the nature of what was happening in British North America. John Murray, the Fourth Earl of Dunmore, had been appointed royal governor of Virginia in 1771. From the get-go, he had butted heads with Virginians such as Patrick Henry, dissolving the popular assembly in 1773 and 1774 as its members voiced full-throated support for resistance to Parliament. A Scottish peer, Dunmore understood that to control the colony and buttress authority meant winning over the affections of Virginia's arrivistes, such as Henry and George Washington. The surest way of doing that was pandering to their pocketbooks.[67]

Dunmore knew that many wealthy Virginians were struggling with many issues. Dissenters, largely Baptists, were challenging the notion of an established church, suggesting that any alliance over political aims would hinge on toleration.[68]

Figure 4.4 Sir Joshua Reynolds, *John Murray, 4th Earl of Dunmore*, 1765. Scottish National Portrait Gallery.

Virginians reeled from debt, especially tobacco planters who owed great deals of money to London consignment houses and to Scottish factors. The consumption of all things British only exacerbated the problem. George Washington made the transition to wheat on Mount Vernon, in large part, because of how indebted tobacco planters were becoming. Debt almost destroyed the Byrd family. True to his station, William Byrd III, the son of the man who hoped to make Virginia British, served in the Virginia House of Burgesses. But he gambled the family fortune away. "This gentleman," a visitor to the region remarked, "from a man of the greatest property of any in America has reduced himself to that Degree to gameing, that Few or nobody will Credit him for Ever so small a sum of money. He was obliged to sel[l] 400 fine Negroes a few Days before my arrival." In 1768, unable to make ends meet in a period of postwar recession when many Virginians were falling into debt to English and Scottish merchants, William III parceled up the family lands and sold them off. He eventually committed suicide.[69]

Dunmore saw that a solution to his concerns and those of planters lay in the disorderly West. While the Proclamation Line, of course, still stood, its ideology was now discredited. Moreover, with British withdrawal the frontier was descending into a state of violence. Dunmore decided to restore order in the West on his terms in order to buttress his failing authority in the East. Two obstacles, however, stood in his way: Indians and settlers. Dunmore realized he would have to conquer one group with the manpower of the other in order to placate a Virginia speculating elite. So in 1773, he and his chief lieutenant in the West, a man named John Connolly, hatched a plan to make much of the region Virginia's. They believed that they had charter law on their side. The old seventeenth-century charter for the colony suggested that Virginia had no westward border, save in theory the Pacific Ocean. Dunmore knew, however, that he needed more than a charter. After all, speculators from a number of colonies possessed overlapping claims to much of the Ohio Valley. Sir William Johnson, moreover, had a signed treaty in his hands stipulating that the Iroquois had ceded the Kentucky country. Pennsylvanians claimed the region around Fort Pitt, as did boosters of Vandalia. He and Connolly decided that only conquest could win the West. Connolly manned the ruined Fort Pitt with militiamen from Virginia, renaming it Fort Dunmore. He demanded that settlers in the region recognize themselves as Virginians, even dispatching vigilantes to intimidate those who supported other claimants.[70]

Dunmore also tried to whip settlers into an anti-Indian frenzy. Much of the region he set his eyes on, the Kentucky country, served as hunting grounds to two groups: Cherokees from the South and Shawnees from north of the Ohio River. Although the Iroquois claimed sovereignty over both, young men from both groups refused to recognize that fictive supremacy, launching raids against settlements to win back the land. Dunmore tried to manage the fear that Indian raiding engendered. His agents sent back breathless reports of Indian atrocities, many of them false, all to win the people over to the idea that the West needed sovereign authority. Eventually, Dunmore fastened on the idea that the Shawnees would have to be conquered. Cherokees may have been causing the most trouble for settlers; but they tended to frighten the settlers too much. The thought of Shawnees attacking would elicit the right mixture of rage and fear.[71] Therefore, in 1774 Dunmore went to war against the Shawnees, assembling a sizeable army, largely comprised of men raised in frontier regions. He split the army in two. One force would march south the Ohio River, the other, which Dunmore personally led, marched north. The southern army fought a sizeable Shawnee force to a standstill at a place along the Ohio River called Point Pleasant. Meanwhile, Dunmore's contingent surrounded the chief Shawnee settlement called Chillicothe while its fighting men were away. Realizing their predicament, the Shawnees sued for peace.

Dunmore now claimed all of the Kentucky country for Virginia, as well as the area around what had been Fort Pitt. Other speculative schemes, such as the one behind the colony of Vandalia, withered away. He now asserted his newfound authority in a place that had almost descended into a state of nature. Squatters were warned off. He may have made use of settlers, but they would not inherit the earth. He also contested claims of North Carolinians and Pennsylvanians to the West. Although he did not have the blessing of the British government to do so, Dunmore understood better than any other that in a world without authority sovereignty could only be claimed by the person who provided order.

The western story of Dunmore offers important lessons for the nature of this period. Much of America, east and west of the line, was pulsing with disorder and floundering without authority. But there is another side to this coin. In many areas, east and west of the line, actors were trying to restore order on their own terms, as the social fabric was ripping apart. With masterless men, young farmers, women, Indians, and slaves seeing disorder as an opportunity to challenge their betters, others styling themselves society's natural rulers, or would-be natural rulers, were busy reknitting the stuff of authority. The process of revolution was not a simple sequence of one form of order to unbridled competition to a new form of order. Rather, it was characterized by the interplay of uncertainty and the search for order, occurring at different places at different times and sometimes reoccurring. If the crisis that led to revolution was complex, the period that followed promised to be kaleidoscopic. As men like Dunmore understood, the Furies had to be contained to bring an end to uncertainty and to violence. At this early juncture, just as Americans from many places were beginning to understand the nature of a world without authority, Dunmore believed that he could manage disorder, to use it for his own purposes. Men like Bowdoin, Hancock, and Samuel Adams, of course, harbored the same assumptions.[72]

By 1775, Britain had lost America. Some refused to believe this was the case. Edmund Burke made an impassioned plea for a return to the status quo ante, to a time when America was not held to Britain with the chains of authority but with bonds of affection and commerce "light as air." Speaking before Parliament on March 22, 1775, Burke argued that "salutary neglect" had defined the nature of the relationship between the two, and if it had worked in the past, why fix it now? Why not return to older conventions of peace and deference? Burke, of course, was wrong to believe that America had been isolated in the past; quite to the contrary, Americans had become British in the eighteenth century. What he did point out was that Parliament had no real role in America before. Local authority under the auspices of a Crown far removed had ruled in America. Order had been maintained.

Now it seemed that as Parliament tried to assert its right to rule, order had been attenuated, peace had become a thing of the past, and each new measure passed became an excuse for a new round of riots. "Will they be content in such a state of slavery?" Burke had asked in 1774. He had encouraged the ministry to "reflect how you are to govern a people, who think they ought to be free, and think they are not." Parliamentary scheming "yields no revenue; it yields nothing but discontent, disorder, disobedience, and such is the state of America, that after wading up to your eyes in blood, you could only end just where you begun."[73] They had ignored him, yet the remedy to his mind was simple. Leave America alone. A new generation of homegrown leaders was emerging. Leave them be to manage the tensions of society. "Deny them this participation of freedom," he warned, "and you break the sole bond which originally made, and must preserve, the unity of empire."[74] The bond, however, was broken already.

Others proposed plans of their own. As America reeled and as British plans foundered, a few provincials thought that the colonies should be integrated along the lines of Scotland and Ireland. Adam Smith, a Scot, advocated what he knew to work. In the *Wealth of Nations*, Smith argued that the best way to heal the rift was to follow the Scottish model, to allow Americans representation in Parliament. "Unless this or some other method is fallen upon, and there seems to be none more obvious than this, of preserving the importance and of gratifying the ambitions of the leading men of America," he warned, "it is not very probable that they will ever voluntarily submit to us."[75] Joseph Galloway proposed an Irish model as the solution, reviving talk of a Plan of Union that resembled the one Franklin had drawn up. Like the Irish parliament, an American Grand Council would "be an inferior and distinct branch of the British legislature."[76] The time for such possibilities, however, had passed. Americans used the language of England's seventeenth century to make sense of their incorporation into the state. And there was nothing unusual about doing so. But because of the vacuum of authority, the emasculation of local institutions, and the flurry of events, Americans resorted to the language of the seventeenth century because they found themselves trapped in the seventeenth century. A process of state formation and empire-building had developed into a crisis of sovereignty that would engender revolution.

Amid the onset of competition to restore authority in regions and communities in the north and south, as well as the east and west, it appeared that only the Crown had withstood disorder. But without local institutions that gave meaning to the king's sovereignty, with his ministers deemed bankrupt, with Americans beginning to exercise power through homegrown, provisional associations, the Crown had become something of a paper tiger. Not all Americans rejected the Crown, far from it. In fact, it is critical to understand that the Continental Congress was sending petitions to the king, arguing that all they were asking him to do was his appointed task, a task dictated by the nature of the social contract. In late 1774, the Congress asked "that Your Majesty, as the loving father of your whole people, connected by the same bonds of laws, loyalty, faith and blood, though dwelling in various countries, will not suffer the transcendent relation formed by these ties to be further violated." Reforging old bonds by any means could never "compensate for the calamities through which they must be gained."[77]

Increasingly, however, such sentiments began to ring hollow.[78] What the so-called "radicals" or patriots had done in trying to deal with the crises of the day is to develop a viable alternative, a model of sovereignty, one that responded to the crisis over national integration and one that also promised to channel the surging forces of popular ferment. Was the American Revolution about rule at home, keeping the lower sort down, or about home-rule, breaking from Britain? The issue is not how the question is posed. In fact, it is the wrong question. Revolution began as a crisis of sovereignty touched off a crisis for society. It would not conclude until viable authority could be reconstructed, authority that could contain the tensions and fissures in society and that could serve as a symbol for efficacy and legitimacy. These issues would define the world of this generation of Americans.

CHAPTER 5

The Devil Is in the People

As Royal Governor of Virginia, Lord Dunmore not only hoped to use actors in the West for his purposes. He planned on doing so in the East as well. In early November 1775, Dunmore issued a proclamation offering freedom for the slaves of so-called patriots who made their way to British troops or officials. "Peace and good Order of this Colony may be again restored," the famous proclamation stated, "which the ordinary Course of the civil Law is unable to effect." In it, Dunmore declared "all indent[ur]ed Servants, Negroes, or others (appertaining to Rebels) free, that are able and willing to bear Arms, they joining his Majesty's Troops, as soon as may be, for the more speedily reducing this Colony to a proper Sense of their Duty, to his Majesty's Crown and Dignity." He did not compose it seated in the governor's mansion in Williamsburg; rather he did so on a warship anchored near the Chesapeake. After he had tried to keep stores of gunpowder held in the magazine in Williamsburg out of the hands of militia directed by radical members of the Assembly, Virginians had forced him to flee.[1]

To a great extent, therefore, Dunmore's famous proclamation represented a last stab at reclaiming authority. He had tried the carrot in the West; perhaps the threat of the stick in the East would do the trick. Dunmore had good reason to play this game. By pandering to their base material interests, Dunmore hoped to force men such as Washington, who of course owned slaves and speculated in land, to put their allegiance behind British authority. The thought of slaves fleeing or even revolting would bring Virginians to their senses. Dunmore did not issue his proclamation with the blessing of the ministry in London. Intent on ensuring that rich holdings in the West Indies did not go the way of the mainland colonies guaranteed that the proclamation would not be far-reaching. Nonetheless, in the local contests for power, the ones staged between Dunmore and the Virginia arrivistes, the threat could be used to good effect.

Trying to force Virginia's planters and merchant elite by appealing to material concerns did not work. In fact, it backfired. What explains their decisions is the status of authority in their own communities at the time. They decided, in effect, that they could and should be the arbiters of order in their colony. That aspiration was

Figure 5.1 John Singleton Copley, *Head of a Negro*, ca. 1777–78. Detroit Institute of Arts, USA/ The Bridgeman Art Library.

compromised by fears that the British would liberate slaves. By consorting with the British, slaves threatened the hold of elites upon the colony. In so doing, even the most powerless of subjects in Virginia had agency, inducing even those who leaned loyalist, such as William Byrd III, to side with patriots.[2] By holding the specter of slave revolt and emancipation over the heads of planters the British encouraged whites in the South to forsake Britain.

African Americans would take advantage of the larger struggle over authority, pursuing their own courses of liberation, a dynamic central in transforming tangled contests over sovereignty into revolutionary crisis.[3] In fact, Dunmore's proclamation played out before a deeper backdrop of slaves taking their lives into their own hands. In 1772, Lord Mansfield, an English Justice, heard a case of a runaway slave from Virginia named James Somerset, who had fled from his master while both were in England. Under earlier English judicial decisions, Somerset should have been returned to his master. Mansfield, however, ruled that Somerset had status as a person while in England. He suggested, therefore, that there could be no imperial slave policy. A slave in Barbados or South Carolina could be a free person in the metropole. Attorneys for the West Indian planters' lobby, realizing the implications of Mansfield's ruling, mounted the slave-owner's defense. Potentially, if runaways could be freed in England, slavery could be barred in the colonies. Or so they feared, and the ruling initiated a flurry of pamphlets from New England to the Caribbean.[4] More critically, slaves understood the implications of the ruling. Sambo Freeman from

Boston had circulated a petition in which he made mention of "those sublime ideas of Freedom that Englishmen have." In the wake of the *Somerset* decision, Gabriel Jones and his wife had run away, as a newspaper notice recounted, to the coast to reach a ship for England "where they imagine they will be free." And a slave named Bachus from Georgia, his master charged, had done the same "to board a vessel for Great Britain from the knowledge he has of the late determination of the Somerset case." They believed that Britishness represented freedom.[5]

Dunmore did not come up with the idea of freeing the slaves from thin air; rather, he was reacting to events on the ground. Slaves petitioned for freedom in the North. They resorted to running away and the force of arms in the South. In Georgia, a group of rebelling slaves killed four whites. Desperate planters, fearing slave rebellions in 1774 and 1775, executed those they thought conspiring. As one slave put it, "the War was come to help the poor Negroes." As order was becoming increasingly uncertain in Virginia, some slaves began using the opportunity to revolt against their masters. Small-scale slave revolts that were occurring throughout Virginia in 1775, the very year British sovereignty was crumbling, put the idea in Dunmore's head.[6] Like "Dunmore's War" in the West, Dunmore's proclamation in the East stemmed from opportunism, as well as desperation. Both represented attempts to employ disorder for the purposes of frantically reconstructing order. Unsuccessful in winning over the colonists, he sailed off for England.

He proved successful, however, in arming slaves. Famously after his proclamation, young men ran from their masters to the British. Between 800 and 2,000 slaves took Dunmore up on his offer in the first few months, some of whom commanders organized into an "Ethiopian Regiment."[7] The regiment, of which some of its members wore sashes emblazoned with the words "freedom to slaves," fought with distinction, seeing its first action at the end of 1775. In general, when British armies moved throughout the American countryside, slaves ran away, and in 1776, slaves fleeing in the Carolinas would be formed into a regiment called the Black Pioneers.[8] The British, however, the masters of islands in the Caribbean dominated by the institution of slavery, would never style themselves liberators. In fact, slave freedom mattered to them only insofar as it could inform or be used for the broader war. In this case, the forces unleashed by the crisis of authority and ensuing revolutionary chaos—and large numbers of slaves searching for freedom epitomized this process— were rationalized in terms of a war between the patriots and the British.

In many ways, Dunmore's proclamation and the various responses to it reveal as much about the relationship between the War of Independence and the American Revolution as they do about "freedom." To be sure blacks were declaring independence by running away. But they were largely doing so within the context of what was taking shape as a broader struggle between two competing visions of legitimate authority. The war for independence, thus, was not the revolution. Nor was it a discrete phase of revolution. In fact, it represented the crystallization of competing programs—and nearly all-encompassing competing programs—for restoring order in a disordered world.

It would be unfair to say that the war was incidental. It structured revolution, offering viable forms of authority. And in many ways, it simplified the process of revolution. Other tensions, such as those erupting between master and slave, were consumed or comprehended within it. By way of comparison, in France no sooner had common men and women asserted their rights, often with the blessing of the bourgeois members of the Third Estate, than structures of authority collapsed and those same elites fretted over how to put an end to revolutionary violence. America's equivalent of the reforming bourgeoisie confronted a similar dilemma. But the war solved this dilemma for them, for a while at least. The war also complicated that process. What had been emerging as apparently clear-cut debates and conflicts over status and power in local contexts were now entangled in struggles between loyalist and patriot. In a world of competitors and vying notions of sovereignty, the idea of an "American" program versus a "British" one added two conspicuous actors to the mix. With time, some people would contest both, as neither could restore order. But in the heady early days of America's revolution, no actors knew this yet.

And this gets us to the final lesson from Dunmore's attempts to reconstitute sovereignty. When Dunmore failed in the East, his plans for the West foundered as well. It appeared that he alone stood poised to reassert sovereignty, but he too was swallowed up by disorder and uncertainty. Slaves may not have accomplished all they wanted by making their own declarations of independence, and they may have been forced to choose sides in a war between two programs for authority as they did so. But in the process, they were becoming actors, as were all men and women. With armies in the field, with American society turned upside down and the almost kaleidoscopic process of order to disorder again gripping more and more American communities, the first stirrings of what we could call self-sovereignty were becoming evident. Actors were not setting the agenda; but they would increasingly refuse to be manipulated by the likes of Dunmore, and by doing so, they were deepening uncertainty. The search for order would not be simple.

As Dunmore was making his plans for East and West, war began. In April 1775, as part of a broader plan to reinstitute authority, the British commander of North America and acting governor of Massachusetts, General Thomas Gage, under pressure from the ministry to do something, instructed a detachment of troops to proceed to the town of Concord. The British had learned that the locals had been stockpiling ammunition for the militia, preparing for the possibility of armed resistance. It was rumored that in another Boston satellite community on the road to Concord, the smaller town of Lexington, a number of leading "patriots," including Samuel Adams and John Hancock, were hiding out and meeting with local sympathizers. Under the command of Lt. Col. Francis Smith, 700 grenadiers and light infantry left their barracks in Boston at 10 p.m. on the night of April 18 for the Back Bay, where they boarded transports. Major John Pitcairn, who led the Second Marines Regiment, served as Smith's second-in-command.

The story that follows, one of the most famous in American history, demonstrates how great events hinge on contingent factors. As the British left their barracks by sea, Paul Revere—along with William Dawes and a number of others—spread the alarm to Middlesex villages and farms. Revere, both artisan and self-styled gentleman, mattered less as a messenger than as an organizer of a network of patriots. He and the riders never cried "The British are coming!" Revere considered himself British. And he only was able to raise an alarm because of a lunar anomaly. The moon on the night of April 18 had a southern declination, allowing his boat to be shrouded in shadows as he rowed across the bay. The British march bogged down no sooner than it had started. They could not commandeer enough transports to get the troops across the bay, necessitating a number of trips, and the first soldiers to land waded through a marsh to come ashore, then stood for hours until the others came across. They did not begin the march to Lexington until 2 a.m. When they arrived, apprehensive about a looming confrontation, they confronted nervous Americans, anxious to assert their right to provide authority for their local community on their own terms. Considering this a civil action, British officers ordered the militia to disarm. The locals refused. Although both sides were under orders not to fire, someone did so. No one knows who fired the first shot. The end result was eight dead militiamen and nine wounded. The troops found no patriot leaders.[9]

The British contingent then marched to Concord to fulfill its mission. Meanwhile, as word got out of what had happened at Lexington, the numbers of militia grew. A contingent of troops held a bridge to keep the militia at bay while homes and barns were searched for goods. They found a small amount of ammunition and dumped it into a stream, which the locals picked out later. The troops also chopped down a liberty pole. Tensions grew to a fever pitch, as rumors spread that the British were burning part of Concord, and the troops exchanged fire. The militia, outnumbering the bridge's defenders, got the best of the confrontation. One injured soldier, who lay on the bridge, was found by a local boy, who took a hatchet to his head. The British, then, feared the locals were scalping their dead. Although there was as much truth to this charge as to the one that the British were firing the town, these rumors produced further tension.[10]

A conflict had begun, one that would have dramatic implications for the revolutionary process. This, of course, was not on the minds of the British as they tried to beat back a retreat to Boston. As Smith's troops prepared to march the 17 miles back to Boston, locals lined the route. More than 3,600 men poured into the corridor between Concord and Boston, hiding behind walls, trees, barns, and hedges. As the British retraced their steps, they came under fire from militiamen using their knowledge of the countryside to harass the cold, hungry, and exhausted British at every turn. Flankers tried to search houses along the route for snipers, but to little avail. Most notably, they attacked and killed some revelers in a local tavern. When all was said and done, the New Englanders suffered 93 casualties. And 273 British died or were wounded, nearly 20% of their force.[11] What had started out as a routine search for weapons, an attempt to trumpet British pretensions of authority, a civil action in other words, had ended in a bloody forced march. When they finally made it back to the barracks, it was clear that the British now confronted something much greater than they could have imagined. Inside Boston, along with the troops, were those whose loyalties remained with the British. Outside the town, surrounding it, were growing numbers of men, members of militia from all over the countryside, who resolved that they would win back Boston from the murderous troops that had killed the men in Lexington and Concord.

The British regarded the people they confronted outside of Boston as an illtrained rabble. And in many respects British officials were right. Compared to a redcoat, the typical militiaman cut a very poor figure. But the martial spirit, valor, and proficiency of the assembled militiamen mattered less than what such associations meant. Like the committees of correspondence, like the Continental Congress, militias represented the first line of American pretensions to sovereignty. They gave institutional flesh to networks of communications and decision making. They did not represent the stuff of a nation per se, but they did give life to what had become an imagined community, one forged less by common interest than by the tumult of disorder.[12]

The most significant aspect of this legendary confrontation lay not in the fact that it signaled the beginning of the end of British rule in America. That had effectively ended already. In 1775, Burke made a plea for conciliation with the colonies, arguing that a more flexible definition of sovereignty was needed than the one offered by Coke. "The very idea of subordination of parts," he argued, "excludes this notion of simple and undivided unity." England, he continued "is the heart; but she is not the head and members too. Ireland has ever had from the beginning a separate, but not independent, legislature." Why not something similar for America, he suggested.[13] It was too late for such measures. Nor was the confrontation in Massachusetts the beginning of Americans acting through local institutions to create the stuff of resistance. They had done this since the days of the Stamp Act and had by this time constructed elaborate, intercolonial institutions to structure society. Rather, the series of events transformed the course of revolution—if not its essential nature, at least its direction. By and large, from this point forward, Americans and British would think of the revolution in terms of two broad categories: American and patriot, British and loyalist. A complex debate over the meaning of sovereignty became a much more simple conflict over who should be sovereign, at least for most people.

Choosing sides, in some contexts, could tame the disorder and violence of revolution. So, for instance, the sons of farmers, who were struggling to imagine a prosperous future, had an outlet for their anxieties. And the militia structure, in turn, strengthened the networks that provided a rationale for resistance and a legitimate claim to authority. In this way, the discontents unleashed by the crisis of sovereignty actually served the cause of order. Jeremiah Greenman, a 17-year old son of a Newport sailor, joined the other young men around Boston because he did not have a profession to pursue. Similarly, Ebeneazer Fox, 12 when he ran away to join the army, spoke to the difficulties his generation experienced and how they could be channeled into the patriot cause. "I, and other boys situated similarly to myself," he declared, "thought we had wrongs to be redressed; rights to be maintained." They were both personal and political: "We made direct application of the doctrines we daily heard, in relation to the oppression of the mother country, to our own circumstances; and thought that we were more oppressed than our fathers were." American freedom dovetailed with his own. "I thought that I was doing myself great injustice by remaining in bondage, when I ought to go free," he concluded, "and that the time was come, when I should liberate myself from the thralldom of others, and set up a government of my own."[14]

The same held true for those who supported the British model. The Boston poet and playwright Mercy Otis Warren, who also sat for Copley, lampooned loyalists as "Blockheads" and went so far as to call three characters in a farce "Simple," "Surly," and "Meagre." They were in her mind "a pack of strutting pedanticks" in

Figure 5.2 John Singleton Copley, *Mrs. James Warren (Mercy Otis)*, about 1763. Museum of Fine Arts, Boston.

search of the most lucrative post or royal commission, men who "embrac'd the shadow of grandeur, but the substance has fled."[15] She was creating a caricature. No doubt, so-called loyalists may have had a conservative cast of mind or enduring ties to England, such as Benjamin West. Some envied or hated patriots for personal reasons. Some remained loyal to settle old scores. Others may have an ethnic affinity, as in the case of Highland Scots, or a financial stake, as in the case of some Lowland Scots. In some regions, supporting the British cause promised order amid chaos and bloodshed. Northern Anglicans, generally through religious ties to England and social standing, tended to remain loyal. Patronage held others still. Many variables went into deciding how and why one remained loyal to the Crown. Or perhaps, as in some areas of New York, North Carolina, and Georgia, keeping faith and peace with ones neighbors meant being loyal.

Ultimately, between one-fifth and one-third of all Americans remained loyal to the Crown. Loyalists included the recently arrived and the descendants of the oldest American families. They came from every colony and every social position and occupation and lived on the frontier and in cities. Some Indians, such as many Mohawks, were loyalists, as were at least 20,000 African Americans. These people also believed the British program of sovereignty spoke to their ideas and their interests, and they remained loyal at great personal cost. Families, like Copley's, were torn in two by decisions of loyalty. Benjamin Franklin's was another. Franklin's son William, the royal governor of New Jersey, organized troops in support of the king. Most significantly, these men and women also considered themselves American.[16]

All of these reasons, however, were in some ways incidental. Loyalists saw in the British cause a way of making sense of a world that was changing, and changing catastrophically. Loyalists tended to see rebellion as something "unnatural." They also, as a rule, justified their adherence to principles of loyalty as they addressed local tensions and fears in a dynamic context. Calling rebellion unnatural, in other words, structured their beliefs and discontents.[17] This sensibility, in turn, strengthened the structures of British authority in America, as these people through their networks would come to play prominent roles in the conflict over sovereignty. Both they and the farmer's sons who joined the militia swarming around Boston were up to the same thing. They wanted to control the tensions and uncertainty that were defining American life. Now they had vehicles for doing so. Indeed, as much as ideas, the notion of a conflict between two sides competing to reshape the fabric of society gave meaning and direction to often unarticulated frustrations, fears, and uncertainty. For at its heart, revolution was about these three things and about overcoming them.

The chief way of making authority manifest, as the British knew, was through an army. The Americans now knew as much as well, though they came to this conclusion after a great deal of deliberation. A few weeks after the incident at Lexington, a second Continental Congress assembled. Moderates knew what lay on the horizon. John Dickinson urged caution. "We have not yet tasted deeply of that bitter Cup called the fortunes of War," he warned. Dickinson catalogued what would happen: end of trade, disease among troops, divisions between the colonists, slave insurrections, Indian attacks, "selfish Designs." Moderates also encouraged the Congress to send an olive branch to the king, a last desperate attempt to forestall the inevitabilities of war. The representatives acquiesced, but most understood the futility of such measures. The time for such petitions had passed; indeed, far from reading the petition, the king declared the American colonies in a state of rebellion, an unnatural act that could be rectified through violence. For their part, the members authorized communities to manufacture munitions. They also allowed Massachusetts to establish a formal government of its own.[18] The British were sovereign no more, and members had come to the resolution that the colonists needed an army. The structure of an army would provide an umbrella organization for the militia members who were coming and going as they pleased. But the army meant a great deal more. Not only had the colonists taken a fateful step of matching violence for violence and organizing themselves to do so, but more critically, the Continental Congress was also grasping the branch of sovereignty. Its members had given birth to the proverbial legitimate monopoly of power. Like the parliamentarians facing off against the royalists of old, they were creating the foundations of authority.

Choosing a Cromwell for this new model army did not prove a difficult choice. Although John Hancock made it no secret that he wanted the job, John Adams believed that it was critical at this juncture that a southerner take the position. He and the other delegates did not want this conflict to be considered a quarrel between New England and Britain. "This appointment," he wrote to his wife

Abigail, "will have a great Effect, in cementing and securing the Union of these Colonies." As Congress met to discuss the matter, George Washington strode into the session wearing a uniform. Snubbed by the British in winning a British officer's commission—Washington's provincial dilemma—he now had his revenge. He could become what he envisioned himself to be.[19]

The British hoped to put an end to this threat as quickly as possible. As an army took shape on the outskirts of Boston, the British tried to dislodge it. In three charges they tried to force what they regarded as a rabble with fowling pieces from Breed's Hill, right next to Bunker Hill. Twice they failed. The third time they prevailed at a very high cost after the Americans had run out of ammunition. The victory achieved nothing for the British. As the numbers of provincials swelled, the British had little alternative but return to Boston. Soon the Americans commanded positions from which they could train artillery on the city below. Realizing their predicament, the British had little alternative but to leave, sailing out of Boston, along with many of the loyalists who feared what would become of them, for Halifax, Nova Scotia. This was not surrender, or even a retreat, but a strategic withdrawal. The British would not make the same mistakes they had made in Lexington and Breed's Hill. They would now come prepared to fight and rout an army.

All of this did not mean that Americans thought of themselves as a people. Their aspirations, frankly, were at this point more geographic and strategic than cultural. Indeed, the strategic and geographic converged in one of the early measures passed by the Continental Congress. At the moment that Washington was taking command of the troops around Boston, turning them into a "continental" army, Congress tried to persuade the other men and women on the continent—meaning those in Canada—to join their cause. "Since the conclusion of the late war," Congress wrote, "we have been happy in considering you as fellow-subjects, and from the commencement of the present plan for subjugating the continent, we have viewed you as fellow-sufferers with us." Each found themselves in the same spot. "Being both devoted by the cruel edicts of a despotic administration, to common ruin," they continued, "we perceived the fate of the protestant and catholic colonies to be strongly linked together, and therefore invited you to join with us in resolving to be free, and in rejecting, with disdain, the fetters of slavery, however artfully polished."[20] Of course, colonists had little in common with former French subjects, all of whom were Catholic, in the province of Quebec. Yet in finding common cause, the members of Congress hoped to make a case for their own program of authority. If they faced resistance from Quebec to Georgia, it was believed, the British would realize that their idea of making America part of the nation on their terms was doomed to failure. With these aims in mind, two forces under the command of Benedict Arnold and an Irish-born veteran of the Seven Years' War named Richard Montgomery mounted an expedition to Canada to replicate what the British had done to the French in the Seven Years' War by taking Montreal and Quebec.

The expedition proved a disaster. Montgomery set off first and had some early successes, including the capture of Montreal. Colonel Benedict Arnold had a more difficult time. He set off with a large contingent, including a number of riflemen under the command of Daniel Morgan. It was hoped that these men from the wilds of Virginia and Pennsylvania would be able to use their long rifles to pick off British officers and so demoralize the enemy. These skills, it was hoped, could bring a swift end to this crisis. Arnold soon ran into problems. The bateaux that his force were using leaked and soon proved useless. His maps were faulty. He thought he would have to march 180 miles to Canada. It turned out to be over 350. He soon ran short of supplies, and the men were forced to eat their dogs and their leather shoes to survive. On November 13, his force numbering 675 men reached the walls of Quebec. Early December, Montgomery arrived with 300 men.[21]

Arnold and Montgomery faced a race against time. They could not initiate a siege because the British, as they knew, would arrive with reinforcements by the river once the winter ice melted. Moreover, the enlistments of many men on the expedition would be up at the end of December. To make matters worse, they were battling an enemy far deadlier than the British: smallpox. The virus *variola major* took more lives during the war than the British. In fact, from 1775 to 1782, smallpox ravaged areas in North America ranging from Massachusetts to Mexico, striking Philadelphia in 1774, Boston in 1775, and Virginia in 1776. It now hit the northern army. Compromised by hunger, fatigue, and stress, an army containing men who had no immunity to it, now crammed together, was a prime candidate for smallpox. The disease spread through the ranks with appalling efficiency. "The smallpox is all around us," a terrified soldier wrote in December 1775, "and there is great danger of its spreading in the army." Montgomery and Arnold knew that they had to attack before they lost their army.[22]

On the night of December 31 in a blizzard with a temperature well below zero, the decimated force attacked from the famed Plains of Abraham. Arnold went down at once, shot in the leg. Montgomery fell almost immediately with a bullet through the head. Daniel Morgan fought valiantly after Montgomery's fall, but the assault failed. The beaten, disease-ridden troops had to make their way down the Hudson River Valley to Fort Ticonderoga while the British were counterattacking. Fever overcame many. Many were abandoned along the way.[23] What the expedition did accomplish is tie up Britain's northern force. Although Sir Guy Carleton had few good troops to work with in the first year of the war, he was still intent on moving a sizeable force south toward Albany to secure forts and harass New England. The American offensive complicated his strategy, forcing him to scuttle such plans until the next campaigning season.[24]

The loss, however, provided the Americans with their first hero to be later immortalized in a famous painting. Although buried in Quebec, Montgomery was almost idolized in many American communities, achieving more in memory than he did in life. Eventually, his body would be interred with great fanfare in New York's St. Paul's chapel. He was not alone, as local committees staged lavish public funerals for fallen heroes, especially during the first year of the war. Rituals of remembrance had a great deal to do with the fact that Americans as yet did not understand the nature of the conflict in which they were engaged. Early on in the war, many romanticized what war meant, creating a virtual *rage militaire* in the colonies. Most also thought that the conflict would be short-lived. Although acts like creating an army represented the first hesitating steps of re-creating sovereignty, most still hoped against hope that the British would recognize that coercing the colonists to accept sovereignty on British terms would not work, and that the colonies could be integrated

Figure 5.3 John Trumbull, *The Death of General Montgomery in the Attack on Quebec, December 31, 1775*, 1786. Yale University Art Gallery.

into the nation on their own terms.[25] Funerals, however, pointed in other directions. These rituals involved more than remembrance; they also engendered occasions for shaping the nature of revolution. As struggles over authority were channeled into a conflict between two increasingly well-articulated programs of sovereignty, the notion that this was a struggle over home rule continued to grow in its appeal. Ironically, it would be the men like Montgomery, the relatively well-to-do gentlemen farmers of America, who stood most to gain from such rituals. Armed conflict, so long as it did not last too long and so long as it did not unleash popular forces it could not control, thus played into the struggle for rule at home.

In some ways, the Canadian escapade represented a first stab at foreign policy even before there was an "America" to speak of. And less than a year later, Congress dispatched a diplomatic mission north to try to win over Canadians to what by then was taking shape as an American cause. Benjamin Franklin accompanied Charles Carroll, his cousin Father John Carroll, who would later become the first Catholic bishop in the United States, and Samuel Chase to try to convince French-speaking Catholics that they had more in common with the people to the south than the British across the ocean. Congress exhorted Canada to "establish associations in your different parishes of the same nature with those, which have proved so salutary to the United Colonies; to elect deputies to form a provincial Assembly, and that said assembly be instructed to appoint delegates to represent them in this Congress."[26]

The mission failed. Although Franklin cited the poor credibility of the Continental Congress because of poor credit, more elementary issues dogged the delegation. Order may have gone missing in the colonies to the south; not so in the north. The fleet lay in Halifax, and a garrison government had ruled Quebec since the end of the Seven Years' War. And the nerve center for all British operations west of the Appalachian Mountains lay in the French-speaking settlement and fort town of Detroit. Most significantly, the people and the Catholic hierarchy had become supporters of the Crown. The bishop after the Quebec Act wrote, "Here we enjoy perfect peace under the government of one of the most amiable of men," adding that the Quebecois had "complete freedom" and "hardly notice that we are under a Protestant prince."[27]

In many ways, armed struggle tamed the forces of revolution. Local discontents found release in ritual and in participation in an ordered conflict. The actions of Massachusetts's militiamen on the hills surrounding Boston epitomized this dynamic. Soon after Washington took command of the siege of Boston, militiamen from all over the colonies began arriving, brandishing what they regarded as patriotic flags. These flags not only appealed to the cause they espoused but also reflected local custom. So New Englanders, for example, arrived with flags emblazoned with images of pine trees at the corner, an old symbol of New England. One flag with a pine in the middle also had the words "an appeal to heaven." The flag conveyed many meanings, which together summed up the ways these men and boys from Massachusetts understood their world. At the most basic level, appealing to heaven resonated in a society still awash in a sea of faith. Evangelical Protestantism ordered the ways that many New Englanders, especially those living on the margins of society, made sense of the crisis. Appealing to heaven was part of their culture and, more to the point, stood at the heart of their beliefs. God expected them to resist tyrants. "In every struggle Heaven has, as yet, given us strength equal to the day; its hand is not shortened, nor its arm weakened," wrote a patriot from Connecticut. "We fix on our Standards and Drums," he declared, "the Colony Arms, with the motto, 'qui transtulit sustinet,' round it in letters of gold, which we construe thus: 'God, who transplanted us hither, will support us.'"[28]

On another level, the motto echoed the words that John Locke had used in his *Second Treatise* to explain what individuals could do if the sovereign became a tyrant. In the state of society, after the social contract had been negotiated, individuals surrendered some rights to end the inconvenience of the state of nature. And Britons believed that this state characterized the political arrangement and stability of the nation. Americans had no such stability. On the one hand, by unfurling the flag, they were announcing that they now had reverted to a state of nature. A new social contract was needed, and their God-given rights allowed them to negotiate.[29] On the other hand, the use of a flag in the context of the creation of a continental army was making real the aspirational. These men were compacting with each other at this moment to remake society. To the militia members, those younger sons who hoped to recover a world that was being lost, the flag made perfect sense. It was as much an appeal to end the tumult of revolution as to begin a war of independence.

Revolution created such contradictions. And more Americans struggled to make sense of the dynamics of the broad process amid local tensions. In fact, each informed the other. The story of a group of vigilantes from Maine, who also took things into their own hands, is a case in point. At the same moment the men from all over southern New England rushed toward Boston, Samuel Thompson, the son of immigrants from Ulster, people who had lived through the Glorious Revolution when Protestant and Catholic communities had fought one another, used that past to address his present. Although people in Ireland did not see things this way in 1775, Thompson portrayed what was happening in Maine in stark seventeenth century British terms. When he got word of what had happened at Lexington and Concord, he decided that Britain had declared war on America and that the political pact had been dissolved, giving him license to beat and intimidate those deemed as almost Jacobites in their midst, local loyalists. Peering through his Old World lenses, Thompson believed that George III, as James's mythically had done a century earlier, had metaphorically thrown his royal seal into the river. He and his followers decided to launch a guerilla campaign against the British Navy, hoping to capture a supply vessel that trolled the coast called the *Canceaux*. They wore no uniform, except a sprig of spruce in their hats. As the captain of the vessel came ashore, Thompson captured him, demanding the surrender of the ship. The British would not negotiate, he was told. Reluctantly, as others in his town pleaded with him, Thompson released the captain. The ship returned a few months later, this time bombarding the defenseless town of Falmouth.[30] Thompson justified his actions in a state of nature through personal background, and local experiences and culture, as well as through ideals common to all in the British world. He drew his interpretation of the contest for sovereignty from older Irish Protestant mythology, contract theory, and like many people living in New England, evangelical Christianity.

Although the mixture of ideological ingredients differed from place to place, the dynamic was much the same. In North Carolina, for instance, local tensions, along with Old World traditions, helped determine how men and women responded to the crisis of British authority. Like Dunmore, Royal Governor Josiah Martin had to take to the seas as his authority crumbled. In January 1776, the exiled governor told his superiors in Britain that he hoped to raise enough men loyal to the king to restore Crown sovereignty, banking on former Regulators and recently arrived Highland migrants as his most ardent supporters. Many former Regulators indeed supported his bid. Since many coastal and backcountry elites, who had ignored the complaints of smaller farmers, cast their lost with the burgeoning patriot cause, Regulators saw an opportunity to discredit their enemies and so grasp levers of power.[31] Highlanders also had good reason to remain loyal. Seen by many of their neighbors as the lackeys of royal government for the fact that many highlanders had backed the Jacobite cause and seen by many as alien because most spoke Gaelic, the Highland migrants from the Cape Fear region also could follow the old dictum that "the enemy of my enemy is my friend." Most highlanders in the colonies, moreover, were recent arrivals, hardly attached to popular causes in the colonies, and many had received their land through grants from government under the Crown. Finally, many highlanders now fought for the British, including some living in the region who had served under the Crown during the Seven Years' War.[32]

Martin raised 1,400 men, only 520 armed, to march to the coast and rendezvous with him and the Royal Navy. The ministry augmented his force with five regiments that had been stationed in Ireland. The plan was to make use of these troops during the winter before sending them up north for more central operations.[33] Martin wished to see "no violence be done against the laws of humanity but that resistance shall make necessary, to that end that the people who have been deluded into rebellion may be made sensible...to reclaim them to a proper sense of their duty and obedience to lawful Government." At a place called Moore's Creek a rebel force under the command of James Moore met Martin's army led by General Donald MacDonald. MacDonald appealed to those "who have been under the unhappy necessity of submitting to the mandates of Congress and Committees—those lawless, usurped, and arbitrary tribunals." His mission was "to restore peace and tranquility to this distracted land—to open again the glorious streams of commerce—to partake of the blessings inseparable from a regular administration of justice, and be again reinstated in the favourable opinion of their Sovereign." Most in his command were highlanders, who brandished only broadswords. At a bridge over the creek, Moore's men pulled up the planking and greased the beams. On the other side, they set up an ambush, enticing the Scots to charge with their broadswords. The loyalists were massacred. After the battle, the rebels killed a few Tories in the woods and swamps, but most were taken prisoner. The battle proved decisive, for the time being, in the region. The rebels instituted rituals of their own to ensure the allegiance of those loyal to the Crown. Nearly all living around Cape Fear signed oaths of loyalty to a new order.[34]

These stories illustrate how nearly all had to make choices about where they stood in the midst of flux and fear. In this context, Americans read Thomas Paine's *Common Sense*. A stay-maker's apprentice who emigrated from England to the colonies in the midst of the crisis leading up to conflict, Paine is normally seen as "the spark that set off the Revolution." Given what he had to say in *Common Sense*, the most successful pamphlet written during the period, such a claim would seem to have some credibility. In the pamphlet, Paine argued that Americans had matured to become a people who no longer needed the link to Britain. "The laying of a country desolate with Fire and Sword, declaring War against the natural rights of all Mankind, and extirpating the Defenders thereof from the Face of the Earth," he contended, "is the Concern of every Man to whom Nature hath given the Power of feeling." The king had broken the social contract. He dared his readers to show "a single advantage that this continent can reap, by being connected with Great Britain."[35] Some, nonetheless, still clung to the idea of the Crown, afraid to be rid of it. Given the present economic condition of the colonies, and their future prospect, declaring independence made "common sense."

The pamphlet sold more than 100,000 copies, an astonishing number for the day. As the saying went, "*Common Sense* for eighteen pence." The message proved timely especially because Paine had hit upon a critical cultural shift in the broader Atlantic world that resonated with an America in crisis in particular. "Common Sense" appealed to a world of democratized actors. The term and the ideas that sustained it assumed that those reading the pamphlet possessed the capacity to exercise their moral sense, that they had a source of knowledge that trumped argument and even fact. Experience living in the world conferred it, and once conferred, understanding was self-evident. No evidence could surpass common sense. It did not need to be proven; it was. Common sense suggested equality. Because the faculty was universal, all were the equals of any man. The broad appeal of common sense also demonstrated that society had become democratized, that as more people could employ an innate sensibility, they should also enjoy the political rights that went along with that sensibility. A new political vision of participation went hand in hand with an invisible shift in how to evaluate the relationship between people and government. In doing so, Paine was mixing radical ideas from the Continent, which defined "common sense" as an anti-authoritarian concept, with the common sense ideal, Scottish in origin, which suggested all people possessed the sensibility. In the context of a crisis, in which men and women were becoming political actors, the invocation of these ideas proved revolutionary.[36]

Paine's message struck a popular chord. Yet it did not so much reveal a hidden truth as it spoke to an evident reality. Many Americans had, more or less, already committed themselves to an existence beyond the Crown. Indeed, by 1774 many Americans were reappraising their image of George III. A number of the colonists began to portray him as "the British Caesar," the leader who had turned Rome away from virtue and toward power, and more pointedly as the empire's Nero, the pernicious emperor who had fiddled while Rome burned. Typecasting the king as a Roman tyrant tapped into a sense of history that Americans shared with other Britons, one rooted in classical antecedents. Colonists had hoped, as late as the 1760s, that Britain had inherited the mantle of republican and virtuous Rome, as Benjamin West had suggested, and that the king could balance liberty and power. Now they feared that they were not living through the birth of a republic of virtue but its death. The corruption of Crown and Parliament spoke to their anxieties that liberty could not coexist with imperium. They had held onto the conceit that perhaps the British could succeed where Rome had failed. But by 1774, more and more Americans were convinced that they could not escape the imperatives of history.[37]

Any attachment to the Crown was based on nostalgia or hope, but not on reality. This applied even for those who claimed to be loyalists. Nicholas Creswell, imprisoned for his loyalist sympathies, observed at the time *Common Sense* was published that "Nothing but Independence will go down." The reason was simple: "The Devil is in the People."[38] The assistant rector of Trinity Church in New York City, Charles Inglis, declared, "I find no Common Sense in this pamphlet but much uncommon phrenzy." What Paine portended was a Hobbesian state of war. "Ruthless war" lay in the future. "Torrents of blood," he prophesied, "will be spilt."[39] For years, neither the Crown nor Parliament could make good on its pretensions. As Americans reeled from disorder, the need for efficacious government grew. Instead, those loyal witnessed impotence. Paine enjoyed the success that he did because he could articulate what already had happened, not what had to be done. *Common Sense* was less catalyst for what the colonies would become than a lens through which to view what they had become.

Fittingly, Americans declared independence. We usually fix on a number of points to understand the meaning of the Declaration of Independence. Of course, it articulates an animating vision of rights. Mixing Locke's three rights—"life, liberty, and property"—with an idea of happiness rooted in "the moral sense" that the Scot Francis Hutcheson had espoused and Paine had popularized, Thomas Jefferson, the chief author of the document, was suggesting an aspirational ideal for how societies had to function.[40] We could also view it as a legal document, announcing to all that

America was taking its place among the nations of the world. After all, it declared "these United Colonies are and of Right ought to be FREE AND INDEPENDENT STATES; that they are Absolved from all Allegiance to the British Crown" and now had the "full Power to levy War, conclude Peace, contract Alliances, establish Commerce, and to do all other Acts and Things which Independent States may of right do."[41] Certainly it had propagandistic value. After all, it listed grievance after grievance for which it held the king responsible, "a long train of abuses and usurpations" which seemed "design[ed] to reduce them under absolute Despotism." Maybe even it comprised part of the attempt of elites to keep the lower orders subservient under the guise of liberal-sounding principles.[42]

In fact, the Declaration of Independence represented less an aspiration than the moment that some Americans were voicing a well-formulated notion of authority, one that was already being actualized on the battlefield, in rituals, in flags, and in new forms of association. It did not so much create a nation as speak to the reality that in a vacuum of power a new program for authority was taking shape. In this regard, it was more responsive than aspirational. Up to this point, Americans had fought for the right to claim authority that most believed could only be accomplished under an adapted British notion of sovereignty. With the declaration and out of the tumult of revolution, citizens of the new states now fought for something more fundamental than authority. They were making their bid for sovereignty.

The form that this bid for sovereignty would take was another matter altogether. But the Declaration gestured toward the shape of some of things to come in both what it said and what it did not say. It did not say that "all men and women" were created equal. Using this silence to address tensions over gender, or male anxieties over women now becoming part of the political nation, raises difficulties. Was Jefferson using "men" to mean males or to mean all persons? No one knows for certain, however likely it appears that he was including women. But on the vexing issue of race the Declaration was clear. Take, for example, one of the grievances that did not make the final draft, the issue of the slave trade. In his first draft, Jefferson had argued that the colonists had to declare independence because the king and his ministry had encouraged the growth of the transatlantic slave trade, implying that southerners were duped into complicity. George III, the excised text read, "has waged cruel war against human nature itself, violating its most sacred rights of life & liberty in the persons of a distant people, who never offended him, captivating & carrying them into slavery in another hemisphere, or to incur miserable death in their transportation thither." The king "determined to keep open a market where MEN should be bought & sold, he has prostituted his negative for suppressing every legislative attempt to prohibit or to restrain this execrable commerce." Moreover, "he is now exciting those very people to rise in arms among us, and to purchase that liberty of which *he* has deprived them, by murdering the people upon whom *he* also obtruded them: thus paying off former crimes committed against the *liberties* of one people, with crimes which he urges them to commit against the *lives* of another."[43]

The charge, as the other members on the drafting committee—Benjamin Franklin and John Adams—understood, was laughable, too far-fetched to be of rhetorical value. The committee, therefore, struck it from the final draft of the Declaration. Nonetheless, even raising the thorny issue of slavery went to the heart of the reason of why places like South Carolina did not go the way of the Caribbean. Ever the Virginian, the slaveholder Jefferson blamed those further to the south. "The clause too reprobating the enslaving the inhabitants of Africa," he argued, "was struck out in complaisance to S. Carolina and Georgia, who had never attempted to restrain the importation of slaves, and who on the contrary still wished to continue it." Slaveholders could only sign onto any form of broader association so long as the numbers of slaves were diluted in that broader association. Because of the threat of slave insurrection, they could not have broken off alone. Only unity with a nonslave society North could save slave societies. For the North, the same equation held. "Our Northern brethren," Jefferson added, "also I believe felt a little tender under those censures; for tho' their people have very few slaves themselves yet they had been pretty considerable carriers of them to others."[44] The institution bound them together, as did resistance to Britain. Without the South, authority on their own terms was unthinkable. Unanimity in what was becoming a cause mattered more than the liberty of slaves. The exclusion of this grievance points to the ways in which Americans had come to no resolution over the issue of race. Yet that in and of itself was a resolution. In fact, Americans would learn to live together with contradictions. Quakers in Pennsylvania and men and women from Massachusetts may have condemned slavery and argued that it contradicted the vaunted principles elucidated in the Declaration. But they would consign these scruples to oblivion to keep slaveholders on their side. American liberty did not so much trump slavery as subsume it.

Another of the more outrageous grievances listed stated that the king had "Endeavored to bring on the inhabitants of our frontiers, the merciless Indian Savages, whose known rule of warfare, is an undistinguished destruction of all ages, sexes, and conditions." In fact, he had not.[45] Westerners, of course, bore the brunt of the attacks that the Declaration alleged. These were not wealthy planters or merchants but the lower sort, not the types of men and women that Jefferson, Franklin, and Adams were accustomed to giving much thought to. And in general, these men regarded Indians favorably, while the rabble of the frontier did not. Just as critically, arguing that the Crown had unleashed savages pointed to another issue Americans were grappling with. Castigating King George as an instigator of Indian attacks suggested that the British, who should have been protecting subjects, were acting like savages by killing their subjects. In the minds of many Americans, the Crown had ceased to have meaning because the king would not or could not perform his primary role, protecting subjects. Subjects existed where government existed. And government's first responsibility was not necessarily providing for rights to life, liberty, and the pursuit of happiness; rather, its first task was to protect. Without protection, there could be no society. Without society, there could be no rights, at least those that could be exercised. No rights implied no subjects. Without subjects, there could be no Crown. And no Crown meant no sovereignty.

The ambiguities of the Declaration aside, in the wake of its signing this concern of where ultimate sovereignty should be situated led to telling instances of iconoclasm and even symbolic regicide, as in many places former subjects destroyed images of the king. Just as tellingly, even though Americans had declared independence, such episodes still relied on distinctive British vanishing points. On July 9, when news of the passage of the Declaration reached New York, the document was read to citizens and soldiers at the Common. The jubilant crowd then marched to the Bowling Green where a statue of George III had stood for the past 6 years. The crowd pulled down the equestrian statue, modeled on Marcus Aurelius, the same historical figure Benjamin West had used to memorialize William III in his *Battle of the Boyne*. Many Americans, of course, had already recast the king as classical tyrant. These New Yorkers went further, beheading the statue and placing it on a pike. They sent the rest of the toppled statue to Connecticut, where it was melted down into 42,088 musket balls. The number was not arbitrarily chosen; it referred to the years 1642 and 1688, times when tyrannical monarchs were deposed, one of whom, of course, was to be eventually beheaded. Ironically, the patriots who hoped that "the emanations from the leaden George" would make "deep impressions in the bodies of some of his red-coated and Tory subjects" used the mythic dates surrounding the creation of the British state to contest symbolically the Crown's pretensions to rule British America. Americans, though declaring political independence, were still in many ways Britons. Only the crucible of revolution could efface such marks. The failure of British sovereignty, declared in the Declaration and personified by acts of iconoclasm against kingly images, had brought about what was now a more complicated civil war.[46]

Certainly, this state of affairs stemming from what many Americans regarded as a dereliction of sovereign duty defined the West. In fact, as had already been the case, the western crisis offered a more accelerated model of the dynamics animating the whole. As a war of independence began and Dunmore's plans for the West unraveled, much of the frontier descended into simmering violence. Rumors, always going hand-in-hand with revolutionary situations, flew in both settler and Indian communities. Young men from both camps used the vacuum of authority to settle old scores, to find land, and to assert autonomy for themselves. Doing so further attenuated authority in both communities. Some saw the state of disorder as a threat, some as an opportunity. This troubling state of affairs defined relations up and down the frontier, and it was only reinforced by the strategies of the British and Congress. The British, at this point, hoped still to pull the colonies back into the nation. Commanders understood that trying to encourage Indians, who already had ample reason to launch raids, to attack frontier settlements might inspire fear but would not help their cause. In fact, doing so was sure to play into the hands of propagandists who hoped to tar the British as unscrupulous.[47]

Moreover, commanders were focusing their attentions naturally on the East. Americans, for their part, did not give the West much thought. True, they hoped that riflemen from the West, like those who had marched to Canada, could help make quick work of the conflict. The great western rifleman coup, however, never materialized. Leaders also believed that the West would provide resources for the eastern conflict. But the same leaders more or less agreed, tacitly, that they did not want to inflame tensions with Indians by making use of frontier settlers. Congress asked settlers to treat Indians civilly. It also asked the Iroquois to remain neutral. In fact, although Iroquois delegations, which were meeting with officials from both sides, made all sorts of noise about helping one or the other, for the most part the Six

Nations settled for neutrality. Americans and Britons, as well as most of the leaders of various Indian nations hoped to keep the frontier quiet. So everyone colluded to leave well enough alone. Indians did attack settlements. Settlers did savage Indians. But they both did so without the formal backing of either of the chief protagonists in the War of Independence or of Indian leaders.[48]

But among Indians, as among all in America, revolution was producing or revealing all sorts of tensions as individuals were compelled to choose sides in the complex conflict. The Creeks, for instance, living in the Deep South, found themselves in an uncomfortable middle ground between many competing programs and categories: white vs. black; British vs. American; state vs. Congress; and Spanish vs. each of these affiliations. Negotiating these different programs transformed Creek society. As John Stuart put it, the location of the Creeks ensured that they had "always been courted by different interests." They tried to remain neutral, but the pressures of the period began to create fundamental fissures in Creek society. Those Creeks who were mestizo, that is with one Creek parent and one European parent, tended to embrace the market economy, European conceptions of property and slavery, and the opportunities presented by the tumult of revolution. They played British off of Spanish in the Floridas and on the edge of Georgia, captured slaves and sold them for profit to each group. Many of the enslaved from Georgia and South Carolina ended up in Havana, Pensacola, and New Orleans or working for the Scot Creeks. Alexander McGillivray, the son of a Scottish trader and a Creek woman, championed this perspective. Born in 1750, he spent 5 years with his mother's people before heading to Charleston for his education. He also worked in his father's slave-importing business and as a landowner. He sought to use what was happening to the borderland he lived on to further Creek interests, as well as his own. McGillivray emerged from the early years of revolutionary ferment as a wealthy man of influence among the Creeks. Others contested his rise. Hopothle-Mico, a great speaker and son of a traditional Creek elite, resented how wealth began to denote status among the Creeks. They acted like white people, he argued, "Because they have a great number of stolen Negroes." Although most Creek warriors fought with the British, their revolution revolved around the divisions of the group exacerbated by that same revolution and by the war.[49]

All over America men and women were struggling with similar tensions. They did not articulate an agenda of popular sovereignty, though we can see glimmers of it; rather, they were stepping in to fill the void of authority as no patron could or would emerge to restore order along lines that were even minimally acceptable to them. Popular sovereignty did not only flow undistilled from the minds of great American thinkers, as they reached back to the English seventeenth century for republican precedents. Nor did it simply ferment as a well-articulated idea embodying the collective will of something called the people.[50] It also emerged through the revolutionary process and its crisis of order. And at first, elites—be they so-called radicals or not—were convinced that they could channel such sentiments. But with time, they began to founder on such assumptions.

Take the case of state constitution writing, the apogee of radicalism in the early revolutionary years. In 1776, thirteen states began drafting constitutions. The reason was simple: societies needed blueprints for order. As John Adams put it, one the most important challenges the colonies faced was "to contrive some Method for the colonies to glide insensibly, from under the old Government, into a peaceable and contented submission to new ones." On May 4, 1776, Maryland cut its ties to the Crown. Virginia soon began work on a new government as the old arrangement was considered dissolved. Finally, on May 10, Congress advised each of the colonies to adopt new governments, based on the maxim that with the dissolution of Crown rule, the people were sovereign and they now had to take on the task of "revolutionizing all the Governments." Americans were not steering an unprecedented course. Republics dated back to classical antiquity. Yet how would they define replublican rule? How democratic did a republic have to be? Did popular sovereignty entail responsive and representative institutions?[51]

Some states embraced a more restrictive definition of republic. Maryland, in which a planter elite devised the terms of the constitution, comes to mind. Here the constitution reflected the attitudes of Maryland's wealthiest and best educated citizen, Charles Carroll. Carroll, chosen by the Congress to meet with French Canadians, was a Catholic who spoke fluent French and who had the benefit of a superb education on the Continent and in England. Moreover, he had amassed a massive fortune through inheritance, shrewd management, and marrying well. In many ways, Carroll had an almost Augustinian understanding of government. Man, he believed, was a fallen creature, and as such needed order to survive and to thrive. From one vantage point, order trumped liberty in this regard. Carroll, however, argued that they worked hand-in-hand, that only good order could sustain society and so guarantee true liberty. Only then could people flourish. Left to their own devices, people would descend into vice and luxury. Order maintained virtue. Maryland's constitution, which Carroll played a large role in crafting, reflected these sensibilities. A mixed government, similar to the one recently dissolved, would ensure that liberty and order prevailed together. Maryland, then, would have a senate, an upper house insulated from popular passions in which the virtuous could act as sentinels.[52]

Other states, however, seemed to take the injunction of popular sovereignty literally. Pennsylvanians, for instance, nearly elevated universal manhood suffrage as the centerpiece of deciding who could draft the constitution. No sooner had the war begun than Philadelphia became a hotbed of popular radicalism. Common people, of course, had little prior experience in politics at the colonial level. Politics was the province of the well-heeled and well-educated. The process of politicization, touched off by the revolution, changed this pattern, as those hitherto excluded from working the levers of power took a hand in ruling themselves. All those who paid taxes, versus property owners, could vote for delegates, a drastic change in assumptions about suffrage. In the colonial period—and persisting throughout the British Atlantic world—only people truly "independent" could vote. Only those who owned land and were beholden to no other men were permitted to have a voice in public affairs. Slaves, of course, did not qualify. Nor did women. But many white men had no right to participate in formal political life. With the revolution, they could. Now politicized, working men, who had been at the forefront of resistance, refused to step back into their assigned roles. The war especially had helped bring an end—or at least a pause—to old attitudes. In recognition of the sacrifices that young men were making in the conflict, all members of the militia could vote. This was, however, not an unfettered license to vote, or even an unfettered ideal of active citizenship. Only those who supported the patriot cause could participate. In this way, popular impulses were once again channeled.[53]

Nonetheless, each state debated the issue of who should draft a constitution and who should participate. Should the wealthy, the educated, those accustomed to rule decide on the rules that would govern society? Was virtue the virtue of the "independent"—those with property and a proper sense of detachment from the impulses of the many—or did it reside in the many or the all? Already some, such as John Adams, were clamoring for orderly processes and respect for order as the prerequisites for the end of tumult in the United States. Return those who could restore authority, he argued. Pennsylvanians did not heed such advice. They aimed for, as a newspaper put it, "a radical reformation."[54] In some ways, they produced a constitution almost primitivist in a Calvinist way. Many of what they regarded as accretions to an ancient Saxon constitution were smashed in the name of constitutional purity. They sent as delegates to draft the document farmers, shopkeepers, immigrants, artisans, militiamen, hardly the cream of Pennsylvania patriot society. Politicized by the world in which they lived, they produced a constitution that claimed sovereignty but made little room for substantive authority. The legislature would be unicameral—no House of Lords here or even upper house, which historically had become a tool of wealthy and well-connected interests. Pennsylvania would have no governor as such, but a weak president and council, which could not veto laws. Nearly all white men would have the right to vote. A few voices called for a restriction on the amount of property a single person could possess. But this failed to pass muster. Even in the tumult of resistance, as people began to imagine the possibilities of a new order, such ideas proved beyond the pale.[55]

Some of the constitutions—and Pennsylvania's in particular—elicited a great deal of criticism. It is easy to see critics as conservative-minded, wealthy, or timid. Yet they agreed not so much that things had gone too far, but prefiguring Edmund Burke on the French Revolution, they suggested that tossing aside conventional understandings of how society functioned too quickly would invite a further disintegration of society. Men like John Adams applauded the break with Britain but also feared a vacuum of power. In local communities, men and women came up with new rules, largely based on patriotic credentials, to maintain or restore order. The basis of order may have bothered some, but at least some semblance of authority was present in communities. Now one of the largest states of the united states had a constitution with a much attenuated notion of authority. The American case was not unusual. The French would later grapple with the same issues. And those who were behind a great deal of the colonial resistance to Parliament would have to negotiate the horns of such a dilemma. For America's arrivistes, parlaying popular discontent was one thing; living with it was another. And containing it proved the most vexing of all.[56]

Common people were playing uncommon roles, and in so doing, compelled their neighbors to decide where they stood. When Anglican missionary Jacob Bailey, a Harvard classmate of John Adams, refused to honor a special day of thanksgiving set aside by Maine's liberty men, locals countered that they would erect a liberty pole in front of his church and whip him there. They also killed some of his livestock. Bailey considered his tormentors no better than "savages." A worse fate awaited Thomas Brown. The recent arrival to Georgia tried to steer a middle course between patriotism and loyalism, but his neighbors pressed him to make a stand. Because of his refusal to sign onto the Association, a group of men beat him unconscious, tied him to a tree, then poured burning pitch over his feet. They set his feet on fire and partially scalped him. Brown survived, but after his torture, he swore to fight for the Crown. The violence of his neighbors compelled him to embrace loyalism.[57]

As the revolution progressed, Americans became politicized as never before.[58] We can find no better example of this than the active roles women continued to play in America's towns and cities. Revolution and war, of course, not only disrupted authority but also severed the very sinews of society. Who would tend to crops? How would farmers get goods to market? How would one purchase what was needed? The revolution, like the years of crisis leading up to it, kept much of America on a subsistence footing for a prolonged period of time. And in these circumstances, women grew accustomed to their important status and continued to act upon it. From Braintree, Abigail Adams wrote her husband John serving with the Continental Congress that "I miss my partner, and find myself unequal to the calls which fall upon me; I find it necessary to be the directress of our Husbandry and farming." She added good-naturedly "I hope in time to have the Reputation of being as good a Farmeress as my partner has of being a good Statesman."[59] To be sure, women played the role of "deputy husbands," stepping in to do the tasks traditionally conceived as men's work, especially for those husbands away fighting. They looked after farms and after businesses. They also helped supply the army with necessities.[60] A few fought on the battlefield. A young woman from Massachusetts, Deborah Sampson, even dressed as a young man to do so.[61] Some took the place of fallen husbands. But this was the least of what they were doing. Women became the guardians of proper order in a world in which many actors vied with one another to create competing notions of authority.[62]

Violence melted down distinctions, putting all on an equal footing. Most women experienced the agonies of war on the home front. And during this time, the war was the home front. The painter John Trumbull's sister Faith saw the carnage firsthand. After she watched the slaughter of Bunker Hill, she laid aside any ideas of the "pomp and circumstance of glorious war." She "became deranged" by what she had seen. On Staten Island, as the British readied to take New York in 1776, troops raped women, with the knowledge—and apparent blessing—of their superiors. "The fair nymphs of this isle are in a wonderful tribulation, as the fresh meat our men have got here has made them as riotous as satyrs," one said. Consequently, troops "ravished" the local women, "and they are so little accustomed to these vigorous methods," he added, "that they don't bear them with proper resignation." For Eliza Wilkinson of South Carolina, war meant suffering. "We have been humbled to the dust," she wrote after British and loyalist troops "plundered" her home. "The whole world," she lamented, "appeared to me as a theatre, where nothing was acted but cruelty, bloodshed, and oppression; where neither age nor sex escaped the horrors of injustice and violence; where lives and property of the innocent and inoffensive were in continual danger, and the lawless power ranged at large."[63]

Nonetheless, women were actors in this drama. They continued to boycott merchants who either did not display the proper patriotic virtue or who were price-gouging. Abigail Adams recounted an incident in 1778 illustrating as much. In that year, an "eminent, wealthy, stingy merchant"—also a bachelor, she added—refused to sell coffee at a reasonable price. In response, "a number of females, some say a hundred, some say more, assembled with a cart and trunks, marched down to the warehouse, and demanded the keys, which he refused to deliver." Incensed, they grabbed him by the scruff of the neck and tossed him in the cart. They then took the keys and helped themselves to the coffee. "A large concourse of men," Adams noted, "stood amazed, silent spectators of the whole transaction."[64] Resorting to social ostracism in local worlds where face-to-face interactions still had a privileged role in maintaining a sense of community allowed women to act as society's moral sentinels. They could also be judge, jury, and executioner. Some merchants who did not heed warnings were "carted" by women. Carting was an elaborate ritual, not unlike erecting a liberty tree or tarring and feathering. Usually a group of women marched on a merchant's place of residence or business, ordered him into a cart—or forced him in—before parading him around the town to endure public scorn and scrutiny. Sometimes he had to sit for a mock trial and execution, with women playing both of these roles. Other times he was tarred and feathered. And women executed this sentence as well.[65]

New Jersey offers an exception—certainly in terms of women's voting rights—that proves the broader revolutionary rule of politicization. The 1776 constitutional franchise clause for the state allowed single adult women—those not covered in law by husbands—to participate in state elections. This clause was debated and purposefully written. The politicization of all segments of the population, including that of women, was responsible. The clause recognized how revolution had melted down deferential forms and created new actors. As such, it represented a logical culmination of all that was happening within the state.[66]

Patriarchal assumptions still held sway. For instance, only women unbound by laws of coverture could vote. Moreover, women were most effective not on the battlefield, the courtroom, or the statehouse, but in the market and the streets, arguably preserves that men had taken over only with the advent of market relations. But it was in these places even more than the preserves of traditional male power that order and authority were most needed. In acts such as carting, women were not so much contesting gender norms or patriarchy as they were playing the constructive part that the broad webs of culture had in the past. In other words, by playing these roles in the streets, women were both sustaining and subverting deferential attitudes, which were teetering in any event, as they were creating new criteria for the reconstitution of order and authority.[67] In this way, what women did represented integral aspects of the kaleidoscopic process of revolution. Their actions, like that of other actors, were part of the fabric of the breakdown and re-creation of order.

Like the women of Paris who would memorably "escort" King Louis XVI to Paris in the midst of bread riots, these women were acting to restore what had been lost. Yet in so doing, they were becoming something more. In much the same way that men and women acting on their own had precipitated the crisis of sovereignty, they were also, through their actions in the revolutionary crucible to reconstruct authority, laying out the limits of the shape any prospective settlement had to take. To be sure, they were energized by the liberating ideals articulated by elites, and the things most of them did were channeled into a broader political cause. Men and women were becoming self-sovereign in the cauldron of revolution. Ideas, of course, played a role, and with the popular press men and women had unprecedented access to a world of print. But focusing on ideology can make one miss the process of politicization that was gripping America as the crisis of authority deepened, as men and women in communities and within their states tried to come up with new models of order, especially as the conflict with Great Britain was growing into a war. Through their acts of commission, and omission, they were establishing the contours of the shape that sovereignty would take. This, as much as anything else, would define the revolution's legacy.

Such dynamics did wonders for the "home front." They proved less than ideal for the army. Popular sovereignty was a two-edged sword. In some instances, it helped Americans reimagine the basis of authority in their communities, as people were laying out the limits of the contours any prospective settlement had to take. By playing prominent roles in the towns, villages, settlements, and cities, common men and women were not only complicating the question of sovereignty; they were also reconstituting authority. But popular sovereignty could retard the effectiveness of institutions that thrived on hierarchy. Washington, of course, hoped to create a European-style army. Nothing of the sort had happened. In a relatively informal society, one without orders or nobility, Americans had even failed at this during the Seven Years' War. Doing so during a revolution proved impossible.[68]

Young men fought in the early stages of the war for any number of the reasons: for a cause, for adventure, out of boredom, the *rage militaire*, because they could not imagine doing otherwise, to preserve a world that was slipping away, for honor and glory, and a few out of desperation in a failing economy. James Thacher, a surgeon, joined for a variety of reasons. "I find our country about to be involved in all the horrors of a civil war," he wrote in 1775. "A series of arbitrary and oppressive measures, on the part of the mother country, has long been advancing to that awful crisis, when an appeal to the power of the sword becomes inevitable," he argued. The social contract had been dissolved. "A contract abrogated by one party," he declared, "can no longer be binding on the other. If we are menaced with royal power and authority, we justify ourselves in defending our indefeasible rights against despotism and tyrannical oppression."[69] Amos Farnsworth fought for "the Great General of our Salvation." A minister he heard preaching had declared "May our land be purged from all its sins! May we be truly a holy people, and all our towns cities of righteousness!" Only then, he argued, "the Lord will be our refuge and strength, a very present help in trouble, and we shall have no reason to be afraid though thousands of enemies set themselves against us round about,—though all nature should be thrown into tumults and convulsions."[70] These were not professional soldiers, the sort the patriots were facing. Without a military culture, Washington hoped he could create one. But in the heady atmosphere of revolution, young men did not prove deferential, to the chagrin of Washington. And he and his officers, and the courts-martial many of them sat on, would struggle throughout the war with this issue.

This dilemma proved the least of his worries. Indeed, he should have focused first on his own abilities, especially his generalship. We are apt to think of Washington as a totemic figure, the man who would father America. In fact, his early experiences in the War of Independence differed little from his early experiences in the Seven Years' War. Only this time, they took place on a grander scale for all to see. After the siege of Boston and the evacuation of the British to Nova Scotia, Washington moved his army to New York, which, he recognized, represented perhaps the key for thwarting British ambitions for America. If the British foundered here, they might recognize the cost of trying to coerce America. New York lay in Lower Hudson Bay, the southern entry point to the most strategic corridor in eastern North America—the Hudson River Valley, which divided New England from the rest of coastal America. Hold it, and one nearly controlled America. Fail to hold it, and regions could fracture, allowing the British to pacify one after the other, an early-modern domino theory. If Washington could beat the British at their own game in this place, in pitched battle, he potentially held the keys to independence.

In March 1776, Sir William Howe, one of two brothers taking over for Thomas Gage as North American commander, left Halifax with a massive force. The sight, as the fleet entered New York harbor, impressed all who beheld it. Ambrose Serle, the Secretary to naval commander Lord Richard Howe, declared "So large a Fleet made a fine Appearance upon entering the Harbor, with the Sails crouded, Colors flying, Guns saluting, and the Soldiers both in the Ships and on the Shore continually shouting. The Rebels (as we perceived by the Glasses) flocked out of their lurking Holes to see a Picture, by no means agreeable to them." All told, "the whole Fleet consists of about 350 Sail. Such a Fleet was never seen together in America before."[71] As the navy bottled up the harbor, the army trained on Staten Island, preparing to deliver a deathblow to a force it had scant regard for. The Howes promised to pardon any rebels who submitted to lawful government. They sent a copy to Washington, but since it did not address him by his military title, he would not receive it.[72]

Not knowing where the British would strike, but understanding he had to hold New York, Washington divided his defenses. Half of his force dug in on Long Island near the East River. The other half fortified New York. Arguably, it was foolish enough to expect untrained American provincials to stand toe-to-toe with British regulars, hard seasoned fighters from England, Ireland, and Scotland. It also did not make much sense to pit what had been junior provincial officers against senior British officers who had campaigned against the best armies of Europe. These two considerations were damning in and of themselves, but by dividing his forces, Washington made a monumental blunder.[73]

As American troops prepared for a decisive battle on Long Island, the British commanders took their forces around the American lines through the Jamaica Pass. Performing this rudimentary maneuver did not outflank Washington's army; it surrounded his army. What was to be a battle devolved into a rout. "The Rebels," as Ambrose Serle reported, "abandoned every Spot as fast, I should say faster, than the King's Troops advanced upon them." Many "ran in the most broken disgraceful and precipitate manner at the very first Fire." The British "followed them with Spirit, and, as the Ground was pretty clear, cut them down in a terrible manner before any of them could get off from it." Washington's army could not stand up to

Howe's. "Some ran into the Woods," Serle explained, "some posted towards their own Quarters; others, rather more bold though not more brave, fired, as they ran or as they could find Cover, from Walls and Hedges; and many were killed and taken Prisoners."[74] As Americans fled from the British, they found themselves up to their knees in a muddy swamp, where the British picked them off one after another. By all logic, and by European military convention, Washington should have surrendered. Instead, he ordered the evacuation of his defeated troops across the East River to Manhattan at night. The British had, in effect, leveled what should have been a coup de grace. Yet by pulling his defeated army out, Washington would live to fight another day, but in so doing, his plans for grand victory and strategic superiority were scuttled.

So too, ironically, were British plans. Both sides could agree on little save this: they both wanted this conflict to end quickly. The British, after all, hoped that the rebellious colonists could be brought back into the fold, that British ideas of sovereignty would prevail. They had no desire to slaughter Americans, to prolong conflict, or to terrify.[75] From the start of hostilities, the British ruled out a war of destruction. The goal was political and civil, of restoring order and transatlantic unity. The ministry adopted force reluctantly and would continue to try to find political solutions to the problems at hand. The British must, a commander put it, "treat our enemies as if they might one day become our friends." As such, they would depend on those subjects who remained loyal to restore order. The ambivalence of what they were doing, and their ambivalence in doing it, was reflected in strategy. Commanders believed

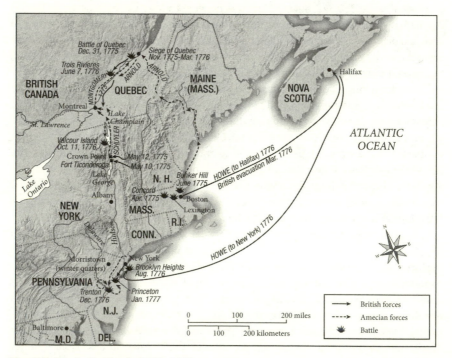

Map 5.1 War in the North, 1775–1777.

the rebellion in New England had to be isolated. They viewed the geographic bounds of that region as the Hudson River. Early on they envisioned a simple plan in which a force would march from Canada while one marched up from the New York area. Doing so took time and coordination, which the British lacked as they were coming off of a peacetime footing.[76]

Nevertheless, British commanders understood that because the Continental Congress had created an army—the one institution that epitomized sovereignty—the then-colonies had rejected British notions of sovereignty. That army, therefore, had to be crushed before authority could be restored. Overwhelming the Continental Army with a show of force and superior strategy and tactics should have done the trick. But when Washington failed to play his assigned role in this drama, the rules of the game changed. The British would race to land that deathblow to the army. The Continental Army would race to survive. Outside the army, Americans had precious few symbols of sovereignty. If the army was destroyed, so too would the American program of authority. The army, therefore, mattered more for what it represented than what it could achieve. Washington only reluctantly realized this point.

Washington's army fought, lost, and ran throughout all of 1776 and into 1777. The army retreated across Manhattan, tried to regroup and lost in Westchester, and crossed to New Jersey where the pattern held. But the British could not bring their quarry to bay. Throughout the year, the Continental Army, as a British officer reported, "lay in Ambush and Attacked our flank Corps." They moved in and out of "their lurking places," hit and ran, "but dare not stand our Charge, and fled."[77] The army, of course, would have a few notable victories as well. In late 1776 and early 1777, Americans under Washington—after crossing the Delaware on Christmas Eve—would surprise the British and their Hessian mercenaries in Trenton, defeating them in a skirmish, and would win a small victory at Princeton. Contrary to legend, the Hessians were not drunk in their barracks in Trenton when Washington surprised them, but rather exhausted from patrolling. Hardly the stuff of legend, the battles became the stuff of history books because the army managed to survive the first year at all. Washington would live to spend 1777 in New Jersey in much the same way he had spent 1776 in New Jersey. Yet the small victories allowed him to win back the New Jersey countryside from the British, and he used the anger raised by British and Hessian atrocities in New Jersey to good effect in dispatching parties to attack British foraging parties in early 1777. The victories and the subsequent war over supplies allowed the victories in Trenton and Princeton to have symbolic and practical significance. Nonetheless, New Jersey rightly earned the moniker the "crossroads of revolution" less for what was achieved by the army than for what was not lost.[78]

Meanwhile, grand strategy of the British was constrained by manpower, the nature of the force they confronted, and what they hoped to accomplish. The British had three simple goals in America early in the war, each of which, as their commanders believed, could be achieved by destroying Washington's force. Strategy revolved around demonstrating military superiority and winning territory, encouraging the people to stop supporting the rebels or better to support the Crown, and to force the American leadership to the negotiating table for a settlement to the crisis. Decisive victory over Washington covered each goal. Trenton and Princeton provided the first glimmers of some difficulties commanders faced in accomplishing these tasks. Any win by the rebels gave their cause hope, which stymied British attempts to win hearts and minds. Moreover, cost, manpower shortages, and logistical challenges limited mobility and the ability to engage in extensive campaigning. Finally, their lack of useful intelligence and difficulty of the terrain in America made destroying what was becoming an insurgency difficult.[79]

The British fielded an experienced force, but one that with time would require a concerted mobilization effort in Britain and Ireland to sustain. At first, Gage believed 20,000 men would be needed to put down what he regarded as a New England rebellion. Many more would be required. By the height of the war, more than 100,000 men from England, Ireland, Scotland, and Wales were fighting in America and elsewhere. Over the course of the war, more than 136,000 from regular British army units served. However impressive the numbers, those from the margins made up the bulk of the rank and file. About half would be regarded as laborers; most others had some trade. Few, in fact, were paupers or prisoners. Even these numbers would be insufficient, and Indian allies, runaway slaves, and at least 19,000 American loyalists swelled their ranks. Many of these came from Georgia and South Carolina, areas close ideologically to the loyal West Indies and thinly populated East and West Florida, which also remained loyal. Finally, large numbers of German mercenaries also served in America, reflecting the ties Britain had to the Continent. Some came from Hanover, as George III was the elector there. Others were hired out from Hesse-Cassel, Brunswick, and Hesse-Hanau. The British war effort relied a great deal on Britons from beyond the British Isles and foreigners.[80]

In 1776, the British attempted to build on the basic strategy they had devised at the outset of the war. The continued existence of an army meant that this conflict would not end quickly. In addition to trying to corner Washington's army, Howe and officials in London continued to try to accomplish what Washington could not, securing the Hudson River corridor to cut off New England from the rest of the colonies. And if the most radical region, or what officials regarded as the most radical region, could be isolated, then perhaps New Englanders and their neighbors would realize their folly. As Ambrose Serle wrote, "Though I am an utter Enemy to all Tyranny, I am persuaded that absolute Submission would be eventually the Interest of this People, because it would take the Power out of improper Hands, and prevent the Land from becoming an Aceldama, a Field of Blood, perhaps for ages." Another officer realized New England should be the focus of the British effort even after the first years of hostility. "As the principal strength of the Rebellion lies on the New England Provinces," he believed, "our whole force should be collected there, and all our efforts made against them." Other troops should "burn the towns & settlements. Such operations would divide and harass the Enemy, and prevent the whole force of the Country from assembling at one point." He admitted that "such a mode of Warfare might appear cruel, but it would be the most effectual towards a conclusion of the War, and in the end the most Economical."[81]

In prosecuting such a war, however, the British faced a dilemma. The longer they had armies in the field, the more difficult it would be to return Americans to the fold. To restore sovereignty, they understood, required force, the veritable sword of leviathan. But unsheathing that sword brought disease and hardship and violence to American communities, the very people whose hearts and minds had to be won. Strategic considerations, focused on taking and holding space not peoples and communities, proved the clearest way around this dilemma, but it did not resolve it. Losing New England would, they hoped, flush out Washington, requiring him to take a stand. The destruction of the army, after all, still comprised the core of the plan. A final aspect of British strategy was not as clearly articulated, but would also emerge as part of Britain's developing plan: taking the capital of Philadelphia.

British strategy was placed in the hands of two generals serving with the Howes, Henry Clinton and John Burgoyne, who had reiterated the idea of controlling the Hudson River corridor with a force marching south from Canada, which he would command, to the king and to Lord George Germain, the new American Secretary. Germain still reckoned that if New England were isolated, Americans could be persuaded to admit the supremacy of Parliament. Only then could American grievances be addressed. The ministry gave Howe permission to march on Philadelphia. Germain understood that Howe could not support Burgoyne's Canada mission with his full strength, but agreed with the plan for taking Philadelphia, so long as he would cooperate with Burgoyne. In 1777, General Howe left New York in Henry Clinton's hands to try to engage Washington's army near Philadelphia. Clinton did not plan simply to garrison a loyal New York City; instead, he was to move a force up from the city, where he would push up toward Albany and rendezvous with Burgoyne who would lead a force down from Canada through Lake Champlain.

Howe believed the destruction of Washington's army, and the symbolic gesture of taking the capital would bring an end to the war. Moreover, if former rebels agreed to submit to British authority and receive pardons, he could kill off the mania for independence in the Middle Colonies. He believed he could accomplish these tasks and still help Burgoyne. He had not, however, reckoned with the fact that he would face a mobile force that did not intend to fight. Howe left New York by sea in July, with his brother's fleet securing his communications and supply line, sailing around the Delaware capes up to the headwaters of the Chesapeake and landing at a place called Heads of Elk on August 25. Washington would move his army to harass Howe. He would not march north to face Burgoyne. "Now let all New England turn out and crush Burgoyne," he wrote, as he prepared to risk an engagement with Howe. On the way to Philadelphia, the two armies collided at Brandywine Creek. Howe used the same tactics he had used on Long Island, ordering the troops on his left to move around the American right and envelop the army. The results were similar. The Americans had not prepared for such a move and once again retreated. This time, however, Washington and his subordinates were able to allow for something more orderly than a rout. Confusion gripped the rear, as those running ran into reserves being brought up to fight. But Washington restored order.[82]

The Americans continued harassing the British even after such a decisive defeat, refusing to be outmaneuvered by Howe, who still hoped to destroy the army. At Paoli, Anthony Wayne led an ill-considered attack on the rear of Howe's column. In a humiliating defeat, the Americans lost more than 1,000 men, the British 500. Finally, after a number of smaller engagements, Washington moved his army off to the West to avoid further confrontation, and Howe's road to the capital lay wide open. Washington made the decision to cede the capital because he was out-numbered and his army had suffered a large number of casualties. His army simply needed a rest after battle and exhausting marches. On the morning of September 26, Lord Cornwallis, one of Howe's chief subordinates and the officer who was respon-sible for the outflanking maneuver at Brandywine, entered Philadelphia with 3,000 troops as a band played "God Save Great George Our King." Washington tried to attack what he regarded as a vulnerable British garrison at Germantown in October, but a heavy fog fouled his attempts to coordinate the strike. The experienced British had no such problems. Washington lost 1,000 more men. The British lost about 500, including Howe's dog, which Washington returned under a flag of truce two days after the battle. The British victories impressed the Philadelphians. They had made a successful amphibious landing miles away, defeated Washington's army a number of times, including in one major battle, taken the capital though masterful maneuver-ing, and repulsed a major counteroffensive.[83]

In terms of scope and scale, the Philadelphia campaign was the war's largest, and perhaps most significant. More men died and engaged the enemy directly that in any

Map 5.2 War in the North, 1777–1779.

other series of battles. The campaign revealed that American troops, Continentals and militia, could not stand up to British regulars. Yet it also demonstrated that Washington had learned critical strategic lessons over the first phases of the war. His strategy, he came to recognize, had to be one of survival and fighting for time. The capital could be lost, as well as the initiative. But his troops had to harass continually the British, avoid the deathblow, and make the contest drag on. The army survived even though it lost the battles and despite the fact that the British performed beautifully. What happened in and around Philadelphia, moreover, would be the last time that the British army, and just as crucially the navy, could concentrate their war efforts on regaining the colonies. What had been a rather simple, though difficult, task of putting down a rebellion would become much more complex in the wake of the victory in Philadelphia, as a colonial rebellion would grow into a world war.[84]

In 1777, despite the promising aspects of the campaign, the prospects for American success were not bright. The British had instituted a blockade, halting trade between the rebellious colonies and European states, which made supplying the army difficult. In fact, it put the economy "in irons." Early on in the conflict American farms had the capacity to feed the army; it relied on foreign support for the stuff of war, such as arms and uniforms. With the escalation of 1776, however, domestic trade was hampered, leading to rising grain prices, shortages, and severe want for the Continental Army. Without outlets for trade, famers ironically slowed production, exacerbating the problem the army faced and leading to inflation. These problems dogged Washington in these years.[85]

In these circumstances, the Americans had an army that was difficult to figure. Some British had little respect for their abilities. Wolfe had called American troops "the worst soldiers in the universe." By 1777, they had not risen in estimation. One commander argued that Washington's army would have to rely on immigrants because "the native American is a very effeminate thing, very unfit for and very impatient of war." Others, especially after Bunker Hill, thought otherwise. Gage wrote that they exhibited "a conduct and spirit against us, they never showed against the French, and everybody has judged them from their former appearance and behaviour."[86] By the time of the Philadelphia campaign though, the numbers of deserters were rising. Congress did not have the capacity, or the will, to supply the army with food or men. The *rage militaire*, which had swelled after Lexington and Concord and had valorized the militia, had long since subsided. Communities would not or could not muster the numbers of militia requested.[87] Indeed, only the truly desperate, those who could not survive or get by in America given the dislocations of revolution, were poised to join the Continental Army, "the strangest that ever was collected," as a British officer suggested.[88] As Cresswell found, recruiting parties could not turn up fit men. "They get some servants and convicts which are purchased from their Masters," he contended.[89]

Later ethnic chauvinists would take great pride in the fact that more than half of the army was comprised of immigrants and nearly one-third was Irish. If the Scots remained loyal, the Irish had an affinity for the rebels, regardless if they were Presbyterian, Anglican, or Catholic. Certainly some British commanders and American loyalists saw it this way. Joseph Galloway declared that "about one-half" of the Continental Army was "Irish." A British officer from Dublin claimed that "the chief strength of the Rebel Army at present consists of Natives of Europe, particularly Irishmen:—many of their Regiments are composed principally of these men." A Hessian captain concurred, calling the war "an Irish-Scotch Presbyterian Rebellion." Others pointed to large numbers of Catholics with even a sprinkling of Irish speakers. Many Irish had sound ideological reasons for supporting the Continental Army. Since most migrants were Presbyterian, they did not comprise part of the kingdom's established church and its ruling ascendancy, a group they regarded as tethered to the Crown through placemen and patronage. Those Catholics that came to the colonies, nearly all poor and working as indentured servants, harbored folk memories of being dispossessed by the English in Ireland. All of these left a kingdom energized by colonial nationalism. "Mere subsistence," however, drove most to enlist. The Irish represented the dregs of society. Although the Pennsylvania line was known as "the Line of Ireland" and the Irish served out of proportion to their numbers, they did not dominate the army as some suggested.[90]

Moreover, despite southern misgivings, a sizeable percentage of the army was comprised of blacks. Over the course of the war, about 400,000 men would serve at one time or another in the army. About 5,000 of these were African Americans, most as freemen but some as slaves. Some earned their freedom by serving, as did large contingents from Rhode Island and New York and a smaller, though not insignificant one, from Maryland. The master received a bounty or land, the army received a soldier, and slave earned his freedom—if he survived. Given the ways Washington considered black troops, it's a miracle any served at all. After taking over control of the army, he wanted all slaves and free blacks removed from the Continental Army. Because of manpower considerations and fearing that free blacks would enlist in the British service, Washington allowed freemen to enlist.[91] Washington, who did not want blacks in the army for the tensions they could occasion, had little choice but accept them as states would not fill their quotas.

Washington had other reasons to keep blacks out of the army, reasons that also demonstrated the volatile nature of the sorts of men who were fighting for him. Virginia planters needed a stable slave labor force to keep the peace on their plantations and to remain solvent as they fought for independence. They also needed the cooperation of poorer whites in the commonwealth, whom Washington hoped could be disciplined to fight the British. Throughout the war, these men made service with the Continental Army and with the militia contingent. As the war dragged on, the sacrifices of the common sort led them to challenge their betters. Problems arose as Washington and other planters continued to charge rents from their tenants. In some regions like Loudon County, resentments boiled over, leading soldiers from Virginia in 1776 to march on Leesburg to close county courts hearing cases of debt and to resist mustering. Here many families had signed short leases, too short for many of them to enjoy the right to vote in Virginia. They also complained that as common soldiers they were not paid as well as officers, leading some planters to fear what they called "the Spirit of Levelling." Common men resisted the draft and refused to serve from time to time if they found the terms of compensation unacceptable. Planters had to try to control such men as they worked shoulder to shoulder with them to resist British authority. Any alliance between a gentry-led army and a lower sort rank-and-file increasingly politicized by the ferment of revolution was grudging and negotiated.[92]

These were the sorts of men who had nowhere else to turn in these years of uncertainty. Joseph Plumb Martin, an enlistee from Connecticut, characterized the Continental Army as "a motley group." He found himself in an army of "Yankees, Irishmen, Buckskins and what not." His regiment "was made up of about one half New Englanders and the remainder were chiefly Pennsylvanians—two sets of people as opposite in manners and customs as light and darkness." He would have preferred to serve "with a tribe of western Indians as with any of the southern troops, especially of those which consisted mostly, as the Pennsylvanians did, of foreigners." He was amazed at what he saw in his years of service: "A caravan of wild beasts could bear no comparison with it. There was 'Tag, Rag and Bobtail'; 'some in rags and some in jags,' but none 'in velvet gowns.' Some with two eyes, some with one, and some, I believe, with none at all." Some serving, as he put it, "'beggared all description'...There was the Irish and Scotch brogue, murdered English, flat insipid Dutch and some lingoes which would puzzle a philosopher to tell whether they belonged to this world or some 'undiscovered country.'"[93] The composition of the army did not so much reflect the fortunes of the patriot cause for independence as the tenuousness of one program for reconstituting sovereignty.

Disorder vexed Washington. Adding to the motley mix he struggled to turn into a fighting force, were up to 400 women who lived in camp during the early winters. The British called such women "trulls" or "doxies"; the Americans knew them as camp followers. Trulls, desperate women coming from the lowest orders of society, often became "camp wives" to the British. Americans had a more ambivalent relationship with the women who traveled with the army. "The multitude of women in particular, especially those who are pregnant or have children, are a clog upon every movement," Washington complained. Common prostitutes, despite his orders to the contrary, had become "numerous." Prostitutes and women caught thieving were drummed out of camp. Yet, most women offered men the services necessary to make it through a winter, such as providing clothing, food, clean laundry, and nursing.[94] Most traveled with their husbands, the most famous of whom was Mary Hays, whom we remember as Molly Pitcher. "Molly Pitcher" was the name given to a woman who carried water to troops in the heat of the battle and who swabbed the cannon with water after it was fired. Hays's husband, Sgt. John Casper Hays, served with the artillery. Mary Hays, by reports, had no education, chain-smoked and "swore like a trooper." Also present from time to time in camp was a very different sort of woman. The wives of a number of officers, including Martha Washington, traveled to winter with their husbands. Washington, for the record, never complained of Martha's companionship.[95]

Because the army served as the most visible vehicle of American sovereignty, Americans had created the only sort of army they could expect to create, one born of the tumult of revolution. As Nicholas Cresswell sneered in 1776, this was an army of the uppity. An "Irish Tailor" he knew "metamorphised into a Captn. and an Irish Blacksmith his Lieutenant" once they joined the Continentals. Indeed, he found it amazing that Washington could enjoy any success at all. "That a Negro-driver should, with a ragged Banditti of undisciplined people, the scum and refuse of all nations on earth, so long keep a British General at bay" was "astonishing."[96]

The army was also a program for establishing order on a national level. It, therefore, served a socially prophylactic role by taking in the masterless men in what was threatening to become a masterless world. But signs were appearing that the disorder of revolution could not be contained. Deserting men were, in effect, voting with their feet. In leaving, they were moving to regions that were trapped in the flux of disorder to order. Their presence threatened to tip the balance at the local level. There were other concerns as well. Would women contest the fraying bonds of patriarchy, one of the last taboos standing? Would slaves rise up and kill their masters? These were questions not only of liberty, which undoubtedly they were; they were also questions about the nature of society. Some ideals of sovereignty, no doubt, were better than others, and a society animated by assumptions about freedom proved far more palatable than one ruled by a tyrant. But tyranny represented one answer to a crisis of sovereignty. More troublingly, as the French would learn during the period of the Terror, disorder and violence in a revolution could also become the organizing principles of society.

CHAPTER 6

⚜

Dark and Bloody Grounds

Violence, which lay at the heart of America's revolution, was a manifestation of the competition to remake sovereignty. The forms violence took were rooted in the distinctive tensions that defined different regions in America. In the West, bloodshed took on a racial tone yet still stemmed from the complex nature of the revolutionary process. The British and the Americans were not the only actors with interests in the West. The states were as well, none more so than Virginia. Because the untapped resources of the West meant future prosperity, power, and stability, revolutionary Virginia took over where royal Virginia left off. In fact, the state of disorder in the West presented an unprecedented opportunity to win the region for Virginia. And in 1778, one man hatched a plan that the governor at the time proved willing to act upon.[1]

George Rogers Clark, a Virginian who had moved to the West to try to make his fortune, approached Governor Patrick Henry with a bold idea. Clark proposed, on paper, to raise a force from the frontier under the auspices of the state of Virginia to attack Detroit, the nerve center of British operations in the West. From Detroit, the British lieutenant governor named Henry Hamilton was allegedly paying scalp bounties to Indians to harass settlements. Secretly, Clark planned on another sort of expedition. He hoped to make himself wealthy and powerful by winning the Illinois country for Virginia. Doing so would ensure that the region later called the "old northwest"—the future states of Illinois, Indiana, Ohio, Michigan, and Wisconsin—would become part of a greater Virginia. Henry supported the plan. To conquer Illinois would not require a great outlay of resources. Few British garrisoned the region, and the Indians were peaceful. It was hoped Clark could win over the former French subjects bloodlessly to the American cause with frontier militia. In fact, the expedition as it was planned looked a great deal like the earlier attempt on Canada. Only in this instance, Virginia stood to gain a great deal of land. In other words, Virginians were taking up Dunmore's mantle, attempting to use the disorder and vacuum of sovereignty in the West to claim the region as their own.

Map 6.1 Sites of War and Revolution on Frontier.

When he arrived at the settlements for what was supposed to be a march against the British, the men who had spent some time holed up in small stockades as rumors of Indian war swirled hoped that Clark would lead them against raiding Indians to put an end to the fear with which they were living. Clark explained that the force he was raising would do so by sacking Detroit, that is, after they tackled Illinois. Clark tried to persuade the men that capturing Illinois would end attacks in the West. The men knew better. And many of the same men who had campaigned with Dunmore refused to march with Clark. With his numbers depleted, Clark set off for Illinois. As expected, as he made his way from settlement to settlement, he faced no resistance. Then again, the British were not garrisoned here, and the Indians in the region had not been launching attacks. Clark then claimed the Illinois country for Virginia.

On hearing that Virginians had sent a party to Illinois, the British feared that they were trying to make a strategic link with the Spanish on the Mississippi. Nothing of the sort was happening. Nonetheless, Henry Hamilton, the lieutenant governor of

Detroit, set off with Indian allies to find Clark. The force encountered some of the troops Clark had left behind at Fort Sackville at a settlement called Vincennes. Once his forces had easily taken the fort, Hamilton decided to winter there, sending off his Indian allies until the springtime. When, in the dead of winter, Clark received word of Hamilton's arrival in the region, he took his rag-tag group, a group that was growing even thinner from desertion, to Fort Sackville, where he asked for Hamilton's surrender. After Hamilton's refusal, Clark and his men got their hands on a party of Indians and their French-speaking allies returning to the fort. In full view of all in the fort, Clark had a number executed and scalped. He then let the British contingent know that unless they gave up the fort, the same would happen to them. Recognizing the fury he was facing, Hamilton surrendered.

Hamilton was paraded through frontier settlements as a monster, what Clark called "the Famous Hair Buyer General."[2] Eventually he was sent to Williamsburg, where he languished in chains. His demonization, however, seemed to play an important role for Virginians. They could now claim the West through conquest. That is how Clark saw it in any event. Illinois was soon incorporated as a district of the "republic of Virginia." Clark never marched on Detroit. For one thing, he had accomplished what he had set out to do: Virginia could now claim sovereignty. But something more consequential was at work. While Dunmore had been able to manipulate people to his own ends, Clark failed. Earlier, those with western ambitions, such as Dunmore, had been able to use fear to mobilize settlers to march against Indians. Clark tried as well, but settlers proved more reluctant to follow. From this point forward, western men and women would refuse to be complicit in their own marginalization. To be sure, they did not have a program for a new ideal of sovereignty at this juncture. But they knew that the older formulas would not work.

This story speaks to the many directions the revolution was taking by the late 1770s. On the one hand, no one could have anticipated that frontiersmen would be standing on their own. Revolution created unanticipated results. On the other, frontiersmen slaughtering Indians proved all too predictable. The American colonial past was littered with similar incidents. War, it seemed, could not contain the frontier's past. The struggle for independence had channeled the forces that threatened to overwhelm. In some places, however, violence overawed affiliation with any of the sides competing to remake sovereignty. In the stalemated world of the frontier, in which neither the British nor the Americans could legitimate claims of authority, violence was becoming the only ordering principle.

In fact, the revolution in general was taking a decidedly violent turn by 1778. When the French opted to ally with the Americans and the struggle became an international war, the process of revolution continued to fuel and unleash social tensions. Yet the alliance—especially its indirect effects—had dramatic implications for the forces Americans were contending with. Violence began to define whole regions, exacerbating these tensions even further. The West represented a prominent example of this pattern. Hence, settlers and Indians in the almost primal state of nature that the American West was becoming—a world beyond sovereignty—would kill one another with frenzied, and in some cases genocidal, passion. Settlers killed Indians, and Indians killed settlers, as all struggled to comprehend chaos.

The frontier was not exceptional, as America seemed to be falling into the abyss. Disaffection was growing throughout the states, as it became increasingly difficult for any group to claim sovereign authority. As this happened, men and women were forced to act on their own. And in some cases, they were acting on self-sovereign sensibilities that had been emerging over the course of the war. The later years of the war would see this trend amplified. That said, America did not experience a "Terror," as the French would when their revolution devolved into a phase of state-sponsored and often arbitrary violence. The reasons why are complex. For one thing, the war in many regions still served as a rallying point, forestalling arbitrary and unsanctioned violence. Race also channeled violence, ensuring that it did not saturate all. And ironically and tragically, race would provide one of the few platforms for order throughout the whole United States, East and West.

Indeed, the story of Clark's adventure speaks to another reality that gripped many regions of the United States. All men and women were becoming self-sovereign actors. But common white people were becoming self-sovereign actors at the very moment they were terrified by, and in some cases terrorizing, other races. Racist impulses and popular sovereignty grew hand-in-hand as the revolution progressed. In fact, the moment that such sentiments were paired is when we can speak of an "American" revolution. In these years, a transnational, transhistorical dynamic of revolution was channeled through American fault lines. There were any number of major fault lines that chaos and violence could have been steered into, but race was the logical one. No other issue, given America's colonial past, could mobilize, excite, or generate fear like race. The state never had to sanction unfettered violence. Race and war maintained the limits of revolutionary violence even as they exacerbated tensions. This was the American paradox.

The fact that a revolution was taking place within the context of a war, or better a war was taking place within the context of revolution, continued to simplify and complicate the fundamental issues of sovereignty that all Americans were struggling with, as well as the ways in which those struggles were prosecuted. Take British strategy, for instance. It had been simple. Overwhelm with a show of might, hope to win the people back to the Crown, force leaders to negotiate, and contain rebellion against what was considered properly constituted authority by isolating New England. Unwilling to conceive of the crisis as a military problem, British commanders hoped to use the military to achieve civil ends. In practice, this meant destroying the symbol of American pretensions to sovereignty, the Continental Army. Doing so proved more vexing than it should have, by and large because the Americans could not be brought to bay. Frustration did not lead officials to rethink grand strategy but to focus on different means to achieve goals. Increasingly, they allowed commanders to use the military in ways to which it was more accustomed. One aspect of an emerging military strategy was to create diversions along the frontier for American commanders, creating havoc instead of order.

America would grow more violent in part because commanders were learning to view America in much the same way they would view a map of Europe in a military struggle against a European army. They would see where they could deploy their forces to divide what was increasingly regarded as an "enemy" and its territory.

Moreover, some commanders increasingly considered Americans as traitors, almost like Jacobites, who should be treated like those leaving the king's protection and imperiling the state. In mid-1777, Burgoyne set off from Quebec with both of these considerations on his mind. Traveling with a wagon train loaded with champagne and the finer things in life, including his mistress, the wife of one of his officers, Burgoyne's force consisted of British regulars, German mercenaries from Brunswick, American Tories, and Iroquois scouts. Among his commanders was Simon Fraser, now a general, the same man who years earlier had featured in West's famous painting.

The Americans did enjoy a few advantages. No doubt, as Burgoyne started south, the American northern army—led by a Dutch patroon named Philip Schuyler, a man detested by the militia from New England—was struggling with desertion. The men hoped instead that Congress would give his chief rival, Horatio Gates, command of the army. To hold the army together as Burgoyne made his march, Congress did so. Burgoyne also did not ingratiate himself with the locals. He issued proclamations condemning the "unnatural rebellion," and promising that he would unleash Indians upon isolated settlements unless the people swore loyalty to the Crown. He promised "the vengeance of the State against the willful outcasts."[3]

The Americans, who rejected British sovereignty, began to interpret the promised vengeance in troubling ways. They began to see the British as savages. The story of Jane McCrea, more than any other, cemented in some American minds the equation between Indian savagery and British strategy. Jane McCrea, as the tale goes,

Figure 6.1 John Vanderlyn, *The Death of Jane McCrea*, 1804. Wadsworth Atheneum Museum of Art.

hoped to travel to meet her fiancé who was serving as a junior officer with Burgoyne as the army was marching south. In fact, she stayed with a family friend, a cousin of Gen. Simon Fraser. In the midst of the confusion gripping the region, McCrea was shot and scalped by Indians allied with the British. Fraser and Burgoyne, though appalled at what had happened, realized that they needed their Indian allies and could not execute the Indian alleged to have killed McCrea. The search for a middle ground destroyed the faith of all. Indians feared that Burgoyne was deserting them and their cause. Whites in the region saw the killing and the failure to exact vengeance as little better than savagery. Reports of what had happened to Jane McCrea spread far and wide throughout America and even became a topic that Edmund Burke raised in Parliament. Horatio Gates sent a letter to Burgoyne and to Congress, condemning how he "should hire the Savages of America to scalp Europeans and the descendants of Europeans."[4]

In the midst of the uncertainty of the period, the killing, and its lurid reporting, became one means of making sense of what was happening. As one writer put it, "there is very little difference between the regulars and indians." The scalping of McCrea became one of the iconic images of the war, memorialized in printing and in myth. She came to represent an America defined by virtue and beauty but surrounded by barbarity and violence. That she had been engaged to a loyalist or that no one could really tell how she had come to die did not matter. Her death offered a justification for further violence and simplified how Americans in the Hudson River Valley, and throughout America, were coming to understand the conflict.[5]

Ultimately, geography stymied Burgoyne. Traveling down Lake Champlain was easy. The stretch from the lake to the Hudson River was not. His army's pace stalled, as sappers had to construct roads and bridges to get the large detachment to the river. Heat and sickness not only sapped the spirit of the men, they also delayed the march and ate up precious supplies. Men deserted. "The general is trying by all means to prevent desertion and has given permission to the Savages not only to shoot the deserters they meet but even to scalp them," a German officer reported.[6] On August 11, a foraging party of Brunswickers, none of whom spoke English, traveled to Bennington to seek supplies. A force twice its size surrounded the Germans and destroyed the party. When he learned that Clinton had not kept up his end of the bargain and did not set off from New York, Burgoyne realized the difficulty of his situation and the vulnerability of his army. Soon his Indian scouts began abandoning him.

The end came soon enough. Burgoyne hoped to push on to Albany and winter there. As he moved on, he faced the brunt of the northern American army. Led by Benedict Arnold and a Polish engineer Thaddeus Kosciuszko, the Americans constructed fortifications at a place along the Hudson called Bemis Heights. From this perch Arnold and Daniel Morgan and his Virginia riflemen attacked the British with ferocity. British soldiers who had fought in Europe during the Seven Years' War had never experienced heavier fire. Meanwhile, the numbers of Americans swelled to 11,000, as militia from nearby turned out emboldened by the news of the victory at Bennington and enraged by lurid tales such as McCrea's scalping. Arnold, who clearly understood the strategic importance of the Hudson River, began probing Burgoyne's army for weaknesses, and on October 7, Burgoyne's army was routed by

Figure 6.2 John Trumbull, *Surrender of General Burgoyne*, 1821. Architect of the Capitol.

an Arnold-led American force. Among the casualties was General Fraser, killed by an American rifleman named Timothy Murphy. On October 9, Burgoyne's army had reached Saratoga. Gates followed him. On October 12, Burgoyne asked for terms, creating another enduring image of the war.[7]

The American victory did not immediately transform the face of the war. In fact, in the immediate aftermath of the battle, the Continental Army nearly disintegrated. By the end of 1777, both sides were stalemated, not in the sense that they were evenly matched after rounds of fighting, but in the sense that despite asymmetries of power neither could accomplish what it had set out to achieve. Washington now only hoped to survive. But prospects did not look promising. By the winter of 1777/78, he lay holed up in Valley Forge. The British, not that far away in Philadelphia, which they had captured in September, had also settled down for the winter. While Lord Cornwallis, led by English and Hessian grenadiers, entered the city, most of the inhabitants departed. Only one-quarter remained. For many of those who stayed, especially the wealthy, times were good. A Hessian commander commented on the balls held every week, as well as the "comedies here, which are performed by English officers."[8] Ending this rebellion would, alas, take another campaigning season. They had taken the city, as they would take other ones, but they had not finished off the army, had not isolated New England, had not won over hearts and minds, and had encouraged no one to come to the negotiating table. The efficacy of their program of sovereignty did not look much more appealing than the one represented by the Continental Army.

While the British attended balls with Philadelphia's loyalists, the Americans under Washington's command endured a winter at Valley Forge. Those in the region during that winter spoke of "piercing cold," "bitter cold," "amazing cold," "exceeding cold," and "intensely cold" weather. The few days of thawing brought "mud and mire." All suffered.⁹ These were indeed "the times that try men's souls." Thomas Paine, of course, had written these words, as the story goes, as Washington's army was foundering earlier on. "The American Crisis," as the piece was called, spoke of an America at a crossroads. "The summer soldier and the sunshine patriot will," he argued, "in this crisis, shrink from the service of his country; but he that stands it *now*, deserves the love and thanks of man and woman." The task was not easy: "Tyranny, like hell, is not easily conquered; yet we have this consolation with us, that the harder the conflict, the more glorious the triumph."¹⁰

More was at stake than Paine had fully realized. A particular vision of sovereignty that was taking shape, that offered some sense of unity, and that was tied to the fortunes of a freezing army was at stake. The crisis that Paine alluded to extended well beyond independence, whatever that entailed, and ideas such as freedom, however they would have been defined. Armies and the causes they represented kept the tensions that threatened to overwhelm in check. And in this way aspirations for sovereignty were far better than no sovereignty at all. If the army faltered, the most significant and promising symbol of order in a disordered world was gone. Submission meant the state of war: "a ravaged country—a depopulated city—habitations without safety, and slavery without hope—our homes turned into barracks and bawdy-houses for Hessians—and a future race to provide for, whose fathers we shall doubt of." Paine chided Americans to "Look on this picture and weep over it! and if there remains one thoughtless wretch who believes it not, let him suffer it unlamented."¹¹

Yet in the long run, the victory at Saratoga changed the course of the war, representing a crucial step in reconstituting authority. With the victory at Saratoga, the French entered the fray as allies to the Americans. The path to alliance had been fraught with difficulties. As soon as they signed the Declaration of Independence, members of Congress commissioned John Adams to draw up the outlines of a prospective treaty. Adams hoped to construct commercial relationships with other nations and to avoid the pitfalls of entangling alliances. Reflecting the language and thrust of the Declaration, Adams feared the corruptions of Old World diplomatic relations, the Hobbesian world of all against all. He knew that Americans were entering a world of predation, in which monarchical nation-states held colonies for their own benefit. Adams believed the possibilities of trade with America would play into European self-interest. Congress then sent diplomatic teams to the Continent to conclude relationships with France, Spain, the Netherlands, and Russia.

France, as Britain's longtime enemy intent on revenge, was the logical choice for such an alliance. The French, led by Louis XVI's foreign minister Charles Gravier, Comte de Vergennes, wanted to use the colonial rebellion in America to humiliate the British and hoped for some sort of alliance once Americans demonstrated their ability to stand up to British arms. He also harbored reasonable fears. If the colonists and Britain reconciled, they could unite to challenge French interests in the Caribbean. In the meantime, Vergennes dispatched secret agents to discern American strengths and weaknesses. He also sent secret aid, including weapons, uniforms, and ammunition. Franklin led the delegation in France and used his charm and duplicity to further American aims. He had a difficult task. Less than a generation before, British Americans had celebrated the mythic victory over a Catholic enemy, who threatened them from the north. The war with Britain had softened such sensibilities but not suspicions.

Saratoga changed the landscape of diplomacy. When news of the victory reached Paris in December, Franklin entered serious negotiations with the French. They still fretted over an alliance between the British and their colonists; Franklin assured them that an alliance between France and the United States would serve as a guarantee against such an eventuality. Vergennes agreed, believing that France's now reconstructed navy could threaten Britain and ensure that reconciliation did not take place between it and the colonies. In the wake of Saratoga, and through Franklin's shrewd use of connections and ability to improvise and teach himself the finer points of diplomacy, the French signed a Treaty of Amity and Commerce with the Americans, as well as a Treaty of Alliance. The treaties bound the two nations together in a war with Britain. They also offered the prospect of much-needed financing for the war, as well as freeing the American economy from the iron grip of the blockade. The French government recognized the new republic, itself a critical step on the road to sovereignty laid out by the Declaration, and promised to help Americans more fully realize their pretensions to sovereignty.[12]

The decision of the French turned a civil conflict over authority into an international war about sovereignties. Much more was now at stake. With France as a belligerent, the British stood to lose much more than the mainland colonies or an army. Their whole colonial enterprise—stretching from India to the Caribbean— was in jeopardy. On the one hand, from the British perspective winning in America could not be achieved at the expense of global maritime empire. Caution was in order. On the other, more than winning American hearts and minds was at stake. The struggle in America took on greater urgency because of the global dimensions of the war they now had to prosecute, and the British could no longer fight it as they had.[13]

The transition from colonial rebellion and British civil war to global war would stretch British resources and imagination, forcing them to create new strategies for winning back the colonies and for holding onto to the rest of empire. It would tax the army and the navy. And it would re-center the war effort on the Caribbean. After France entered the war, the British had fewer than 2,000 able-bodied troops in the Leeward Islands and on Jamaica. The French had 9,000 on their holdings. "The war," one commentator noted, "has and ever must be determined in the West Indies."[14] To defend what they had, they confronted the possibility of global overreach.

The internationalization of the war changed American fortunes in less dramatic, but no less significant, ways. With the new alliance, a number of idealistic Europeans—romantic figures of noble birth—volunteered to serve with the Continental Army. The most famous foreigner to do so, of course, was the Marquis de Lafayette. The young French aristocrat was a devoted republican with little military experience when he offered his services without pay to the American cause. Seeing Lafayette as a surrogate son, Washington kept him by his side and taught him the finer points of command. His most important contributions came in the field of diplomacy. Although he led American troops from time to time, Lafayette also played a crucial role in acting as liaison between the French command and the Continental Army.[15]

The most significant foreigner to help transform the army came from Prussia. In 1777, Friedrich Wilhelm von Steuben arrived at Valley Forge. Part charlatan, part genius, Steuben had served as a captain on the general staff of the Prussian army during the Seven Years' War. At war's end, out of work, he christened himself a Baron and made his way to Paris, where he was introduced to Benjamin Franklin. Franklin then alerted Washington that a Prussian general and nobleman wanted to volunteer his services to the Continental Army. Washington charged Steuben to make an army out of a rabble. He instituted drills at Valley Forge, simplifying Prussian drilling techniques that Americans soon mastered. He made new rules for sanitation and for laying out camps. And he devised a system so that trained drillmasters could in turn train new troops. Steuben enjoyed immediate results. After the alliance with France was finalized, Washington invited French officers to a grand review of the army to honor the alliance. The intricate series of drills and maneuvers went off without a hitch. What Steuben taught was critical for an eighteenth-century army. Drilling providing a point of discipline, so that under fire troops could act without thinking. Complex maneuvers, done exactly, were necessary to move troops around a battlefield.[16]

The Continental Army was also improving as it adapted to the forces it was confronting. Because of the constraints they faced in using conventional eighteenth-century tactics against rebels in America, the British began favoring speed and mobility over massed firepower. Quick strikes on the flanks with bayonet charges proved the most effective means to counter a mobile army of the insurgent, which enjoyed the advantages of difficult terrain. The British infantry was well trained now for such warfare, especially elite units such as light infantry and grenadiers, which saw the lion's share of action in combat. With British changes, Americans learned to protect their flanks, find escape routes, and mass their firepower to counterbalance British tactics. Such adaptability depended on the sort of drill and discipline instilled by Steuben.[17]

The work paid off in one of the principal engagements of the war. After occupying Philadelphia for nearly a year, the new commander of British forces Henry Clinton pulled the army and 3,000 loyalists out to head back to New York. He did not want to evacuate the city, but the new nature of global war dictated he do so. The British needed troops to defend the Floridas from attack, as well as the Caribbean. And most of Howe's forces were slated to leave from New York for an offensive against St. Lucia in the Leeward Islands. Clinton decided to march from Philadelphia and not sail directly to New York because the navy was overtaxed. He had to ensure fleeing loyalists were able to leave and he did not want to cut the throats of the 5,000 horses in his command.[18] It was a hot June. Marching through New Jersey, a number of men died of heatstroke. Washington ordered Anthony Wayne to shadow Clinton's army. On June 25, Clinton reached Monmouth Courthouse, as Charles Lee was given command of a vanguard that would attack Clinton's rear. The fighting began on June 28. Although 5,000 Americans engaged 2,000 British troops initially, the Americans retreated. Either Lee had been spooked, even though officers like Wayne were encouraging him to attack, or the inexperienced Lafayette, who commanded the left, had retreated when he should have attacked, exposing Wayne at the center.[19]

With the temperature reaching 100 degrees, Washington assumed command. He put together an American line, and after the initial debacle, Americans acted with purpose and with discipline. Americans faced the famed Black Watch in a bayonet charge. And the fabled highlander regiment left the field. It was here that a soldier named Joseph Plumb Martin may have witnessed Mary Hays's finest hour. As a Molly Pitcher cooled her husband's cannon with water from her bucket, a cannonball passed between her legs "without doing any other damage than carrying away all the lower part of her petticoat." Hays looked down and then said "it was lucky it did not pass a little higher, for in that case it might have carried away something else."[20] After the battle, the British reached Sandy Hook and took transports to the safety of New York. Soon after, Washington was bold enough to strike on the doorstep of British-held New York. Under the command of Henry "Light-Horse Harry" Lee, the Continentals took more than 150 British and Hessian prisoners at Paulus Hook, a British fort directly across the Hudson from Manhattan and key strategic point for securing New York City.[21]

The complex backdrop to the story of the Battle of Monmouth demonstrates how the new nature of war transformed the scope of war for the British and also for Americans. International war now extended the bounds of conflict to the oceans. For the British, this meant concentrating resources not on American coasts but in the Caribbean as a deterrent against the French. As Lord Shelburne argued, Britain had more compelling interests than the mainland colonies. For him, Jamaica was "first in point of importance to this country, after Ireland, of any of her numerous dependencies."[22] Earlier, the navy's main role revolved around supporting the army and in intimidating wayward American subjects, as it did in 1775 when it shelled the Maine coast after the locals had taken a British schooner. Moreover, the navy was undermanned and on a wartime footing. As with the army, it would take time and resources to prepare it for war. Commanders blockaded the colonies, but with only 10 warships available in the Caribbean continuing to do so proved impossible. Although Britain ruled the waves, the rebels smuggled goods and weapons in from European and Caribbean ports with impunity.[23]

By 1779, from a peacetime footing, the British would build a navy as great as the one that had defeated the French in the Seven Years' War. However, they would fail throughout the war to win ascendancy at sea because by 1779, they faced both France and Spain, and a year after that, the Dutch also. This turn of events was to some extent caused by Britain's confused foreign relations. Ministry after ministry demonstrated limited vision and competence in making sense of Britain's role in the world of power politics by myopically focusing on how things had been done in the past and with an eye mainly trained on what France was doing. From the heights of 1763, successive governments had been unable to negotiate a changing diplomatic landscape. The rise of new powers in eastern and Central Europe and a new system of alliance marginalized Britain within the Continent's power structure. Ironically, a fixation on France and America, coupled with indifference and inattention to European changes—themselves products of preoccupation on empire—led to the epic mismanagement and shortsightedness that allowed France, Spain, and the Dutch to enter the war and that now overstretched Britain.[24]

In 1779 and 1780, the British paid for diplomatic short-sightedness. After the treaties were signed between the United States and France, Vergennes pressured the Spanish to join the alliance. Spanish officials, however, proved reluctant to support the Americans, fearing a growing republic on its borders in America. So the secret alliance signed on April 12 did not include the United States but bound Spain to fight with France against Britain, with the hope that the Spanish could take back Gibraltar from the British, who had taken it earlier in the eighteenth century. Congress tried to garner aid from Spain during the war, sending John Jay to Madrid in 1781. The Spaniards snubbed Jay, even when he promised that Americans would forego navigation of the Mississippi to allay Spanish fears over American territorial growth. Although they sent arms, ammunition, blankets, and shoes to Americans via the port of New Orleans and Havana, large-scale formal aid was not forthcoming. At the same time, friction was increasing between the British and the Dutch. They had given aid to Americans, and as a result, British ships stopped Dutch traders and searched them. In 1780, the British imposed a blockade on Dutch shipping, and with that the States-General allied themselves with France and Spain. Dealing with the Dutch, John Adams likened to swimming in a "school of sharks." Nonetheless, two years later, the Dutch recognized American independence and bankers from Amsterdam made a large loan to Congress.[25]

The British now faced the second and third largest navies in the world in Spain and France. The French promised to threaten the East India Company, and in 1779 the British dispatched 6 ships of the line to India amidst rumors that a French fleet was sailing there. The ministry feared the French wanted to succeed the Dutch as the chief power in the Indian Ocean. The Spanish sent ships to the Caribbean to support an attempt to take West Florida and secure New Orleans. In April 1779, they began siege operations of the British fortifications at Pensacola, leading to its capitulation less than a month later. Ultimately, under the leadership of the governor of Louisiana, Bernardo de Galvez, Spanish forces defeated the British in Natchez, Baton Rouge, and Mobile, diverting British manpower from the colonies further to the north. As well as worrying over the Caribbean, and Jamaica especially once Spain was involved, Britain stood to lose the key Mediterranean points of Gibraltar and Minorca. Neither could withstand a long siege, both lay close to Spain, and both were critical for the trade in the East. Ships would have to defend them. If the British pursued an offensive course, they could attack Spanish holdings in the Pacific, such as the Philippines or even the Central American isthmus. Either approach, meant they had to patrol most of the oceans of the earth, and when the Dutch joined in the war against them, they had to keep the shipping lines in the North Sea to Baltic ports open as well.[26]

The changing scope of war offered more opportunities for the Americans to harass the British on the seas. Early on, before Britain confronted a world war and so could focus resources on suppressing a colonial rebellion, such missions were impossible. In 1775 and 1776, American naval ambitions, if we could even use such a term, were modest. As soon as word of hostilities reached American coastal communities, merchantmen and fishermen restyled themselves privateers. The most

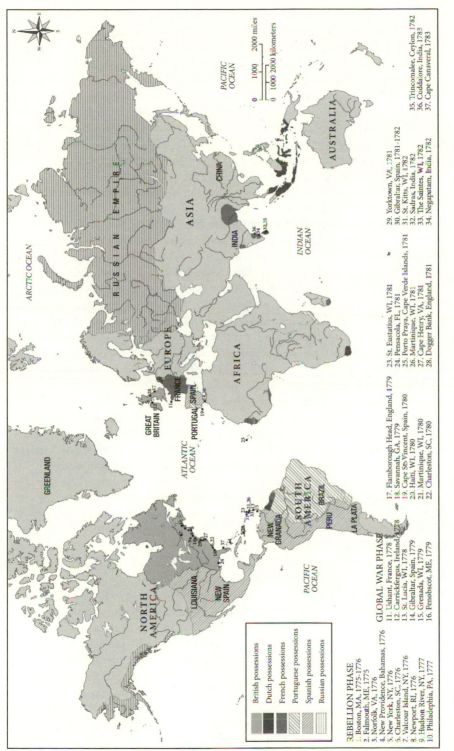

Map 6.2 War and Naval Encounters on Global Scale, 1775–1783 (adapted from map of naval operations on www.hmsrichmand.org)

REBELLION PHASE
1. Boston, MA, 1775–1776
2. Falmouth, ME, 1775
3. Norfolk, VA, 1776
4. New Providence, Bahamas, 1776
5. New York, NY, 1776
6. Charleston, SC, 1776
7. Valcour Island, NY, 1776
8. Newport, RI, 1776
9. Hudson River, NY, 1777
10. Philadelphia, PA, 1777

GLOBAL WAR PHASE
11. Ushant, France, 1778
12. Carrickfergus, Ireland, 1778
13. St. Lucia, WI, 1778
14. Gibraltar, Spain, 1779
15. Grenada, WI, 1779
16. Penobscot, ME, 1779

17. Flamborough Head, England, 1779
18. Savannah, GA, 1779
19. Cape St. Vincent, Spain, 1780
20. Haiti, WI, 1780
21. Martinique, WI, 1780
22. Charleston, SC, 1780
23. St. Eustatius, WI, 1781
24. Pensacola, FL, 1781
25. Porto Praya, Cape Verde Islands, 1781
26. Martinique, WI, 1781
27. Cape Henry, VA, 1781
28. Dogger Bank, England, 1781

29. Yorktown, VA, 1781
30. Gibraltar, Spain, 1781–1782
31. St. Kitts, WI, 1782
32. Sadras, India, 1782
33. The Saintes, WI, 1782
34. Negapatam, India, 1782
35. Trincomalee, Ceylon, 1782
36. Cuddalore, India, 1783
37. Cape Canaveral, 1783

famous of these was Jeremiah O'Brien, a son of liberty from Machias in the Maine district. O'Brien and his followers captured two merchant vessels and a British Navy schooner dispatched to Machias to collect food and firewood for the besieged British troops in Boston. Early on, Congress was reluctant to create a navy. An army could be justified for defensive purposes. A navy, however, suggested an offensive strategy, and as Americans understood, the creation of a navy would cross a line of sovereignty that could not be easily uncrossed. Eventually, as the colonists began creating state constitutions, Congress changed its strategy by authorizing the outfitting and purchase of frigates so that an American Navy and Marines could ensure that Britain did not dominate the American coastline.[27]

The "Continental Navy," as it was called, lived up to its oxymoronic name early in the war. Aside from a raid on the Bahamas in 1776 for gunpowder for the Continental Army, its greatest successes occurred close to land, but often times far from North America. Congress had heady plans of raiding the British from Newfoundland to the Caribbean and from contesting British naval power from the American coast to Africa. These plans never panned out. American seamen, as Washington deadpanned, did not rise above the level of "rascally privateersmen." The navy enjoyed modest success, raiding British ships off of Bermuda and Jamaica, as well as in Hudson's Bay. Seamen also endured dismal failures, as they did off the coast of Charleston and Penobscot Bay in Maine. For the most part, however, the navy adopted a defensive strategy, clearing British ships out of Long Island Sound and supporting the army. The most famous American victory in American waters involved the man regarded as the father of the American Navy, the Irish-born John Barry. Returning from France to the United States in 1781, Barry's ship the *Alliance* was overtaken by two vessels of the Royal Navy. Barry had other troubles as well. He had just put down a mutiny aboard, hanging the ringleaders by their thumbs from the yardarms as the boson flogged them. Off the coast of Sandy Hook, Barry restored order on board as he outmaneuvered the enemy ships, taking both.[28]

The navy's greatest triumphs came in British home waters, especially after the war became internationalized. With British fleets dispersed around the world and keeping an eye on Spanish and French ships in many ports, Americans resolved to use their meager naval resources to take the war home to Britain and to capture British shipping. The British fleet in home waters was focused on the Channel, as fear of invasion from France was quite real. The French plan was to keep the British bottled up there.[29] With the greatest challenges faced since the time of the Spanish Armada, the Americans did not command attention and the British did not have the resources to stop them. The sea raider Gustavus Conyngham took more than 30 prizes as he raided British shipping in European waters, largely cooperating with the French. American commanders like John Paul Jones, who was born in Scotland, knew as well as anyone the shipping lanes between the British Isles and the Americas. And he used his knowledge to attack shipping with dramatic results. Congress authorized such forays knowing full well that Americans could never best the Royal Navy in the open sea. Indeed Americans acted more like the English privateers of old like Sir Francis Drake when they preyed on Spanish shipping leaving the Spanish Main. Aboard his converted East Indiaman named *Bonhomme Richard* in honor of Benjamin Franklin, John Paul Jones raided communities in

England, Scotland, and Ireland on the Irish Sea. And for the inhabitants of places like England and Ireland, the minor naval engagements off their coasts must have come as quite a shock. Jones, for instance, took the *HMS Drake*—an irony lost on no one—at Carrickfergus in Ireland. Later, he took the *Serapis*, a powerful 44-gun frigate, returning from the Baltic with a convoy of naval stores off the coast of Yorkshire after exchanging broadsides and boarding her. In the three-hour engagement, half of the crew of each ship were killed or wounded. This was the closest the Americans came to a mythic victory.[30]

Nonetheless, the limited and time-tested strategy served a symbolic role every bit as important as maintaining an army in the field. Perhaps more so. Admittedly, navies, as much as armies, epitomize sovereignty. They also demonstrate sustained commitment and capital investment, the sort only a state can sustain. Jones's forays to the British Isles had anticipated and unanticipated consequences. As he put it later, the raid on Carrickfergus "caused great harm to Great Britain and she found it necessary not only to fortify her ports but also to arm the Volunteers of Ireland." The Volunteers at first were raised because of fears of French invasion and American plundering, especially as so many troops normally garrisoned in Ireland were serving in the American war. Over time, however, the Volunteer movement would grow to support the American cause and challenge the British to roll back Parliament's claim to sovereignty over Ireland.[31] The small naval victories, most significantly, did not matter because of the prizes secured or strategic payoffs. They mattered because rebels do not have navies. Nations do.

What was happening to the British on land and at sea also made them reconsider what was at stake in America. A leader in the Admiralty argued that "the object of war being now changed, and the contest in America being a secondary consideration, our principal object must be distressing France and defending...His Majesty's possessions." With this in mind, the ministry once again made overtures for peace in America, but along lines that would have been inconceivable even a year earlier. Commissioners under the authority of Lord Carlisle urged Congress to consider breaking the alliance with France and restoring peace with Britain if the British granted the Americans full legislative independence. Parliamentary authority would no longer be the sine qua non of British sovereignty, and the British would not tax the Americans for revenue. The Crown would bind them to Britain as subjects. Most significantly, perhaps, the commissioners treated with Congress as a legitimate body. The thinking was not novel; in 1782, the British would grant the Irish legislative independence, though at the time of the Commission Irish patriots complained that Americans would enjoy far more liberal rights than they could.[32] The new realities of war dictated that the British would rather recognize the near-independence of the northern colonies than risk losing the West Indies to the French. Perhaps such a plan would have worked in 1776. With the French allied to the American cause and republican ideas encouraging Americans to conceive of themselves as citizens, however, anything short of complete independence seemed like defeat.

While the international scope of war transformed where it could be fought and the scope and scale of battle, prosecuting war still served as a means to order society in the midst of chaos. The war continued to mute or channel some revolutionary violence. The dynamic was especially evident not too far from Saratoga. Much of the Hudson River Valley in the years just before and during the early years of revolution was wracked by growing tension between poorer men and women and great proprietors who dominated the region. This was an unusual place, one of the few regions where tenants outnumbered freeholders, a holdover from older and distinctive Dutch notions of landownership. Regardless of the precedents, the years of upheaval that led to revolution also allowed those who lived in the most remote regions of the areas between New York, Massachusetts, and New Hampshire to give vent to their frustrations, particularly land tenure and rents, as well as unresponsive colonial governments and absentee landlords. These people did not decry the market. In fact, they railed against the lack of markets in the region. Yet, they did not embrace free market ideals; rather, they lambasted their betters for failing to uphold traditional obligations, especially going easy on rents in the face of economic crises. The ideas espoused and championed by Bostonians and New Yorkers caught in similar straits resonated in these circumstances. The ideas did not awaken slumbering people; rather, they gave grievances an edge and an avenue of articulation.[33]

The war offered an opportunity for liberation. It afforded the means, to be sure, to contest the privileged position of great proprietors in the region, as well as the marginalization of the poorer sort. The whole region around the Hudson River was alive with tension. Beginning in 1766 with the Stamp Act riots, tenants began refusing to pay their rents. Complaining of short leases and rising rents during difficult economic times, those from the Van Cortlandt Manor marched to the landlord's townhouse in New York City threatening to pull it down unless the proprietor gave them "a grant forever of his Lands." The same summer, the Livingston Manor and Van Rensselaer proprietorship exploded. As one witness put it in 1766, alluding to seventeenth-century English history, "Seventeen hundred of the Levellers with fire arms are collected.... All the jails [are] broke open through all the countries."[34] Like Bostonians, these people were Janus-faced. They looked backward to better times when their betters remembered their responsibilities. They also looked forward to the possibility of undoing a system that marginalized the vulnerable.

Embracing the rhetoric of the day, the men that would found Vermont resisted the rapaciousness of New York grandees to claim authority in the region. During the 1760s, poorer men and women streamed into the regions west of the Hudson River on what they thought were valid land grants offered by the governor of New Hampshire. New Yorkers contested these claims, and used their authority to evict settlers. Meeting in Bennington at Stephen Fay's Tavern, a group of men led by a firebrand and opportunist named Ethan Allen formed themselves into the Green Mountain Boys. In the vacuum of power that gripped much of the Upper Hudson River Valley, ordinary men and women assumed the mantle of authority, and like their neighbors in Boston, they created the institutions that defined local sovereignty. They tried those who refused to recognize the courts they created, doing so in the most colorful ways. Wayward citizens, for instance, were hoisted in a chair eye-level to a stuffed catamount that was nailed to the eaves of a tavern roof. The ritual, like all rituals, combined common revolutionary discourse with local flavor. The end result was a community tied to the forms of authority created by common people, and those forms reflected the ways local tensions merged with broader patterns.[35]

Such rituals did not so much foment violence as forestall it. The Green Mountain Boys, of course, could have terrorized the countryside to effect their plans. But they chose to yoke their cause, which the process of revolution brought to the surface, with the burgeoning struggle for independence. With armies roaming through the countryside, the magnetic pull of the American program, which jibed with many of the demands of locals in places like Vermont, promised order. Violence was ritualized. It was also projected onto the British. So when Burgoyne marched down from Lake Champlain, he was not only confronting a run-of-the-mill militia, but one that was politicized and whose violent energies were directed toward the British. The merger of local demands exacerbated by revolution and now articulated through revolutionary ideology ensured that violence was focused and not diffused.[36]

As the war progressed and grew even more violent, this trend was even more pronounced, gripping other places that were divided along such fault lines. Maine is a good example. Here the poorer sort styled themselves the region's "liberty men." These people believed they had a right to land that was unimproved along the frontier. Hardly proletarians, they wanted to become freeholders and dreaded working for wages or living as tenants. The proprietors they resisted hoped to sustain a world based on hierarchical control and a market economy in which land was held by the few. The great proprietors became not only bogeys or enemies of the poor but also Tories. As they left the region with the end of British authority, the poorer sort streamed in, hoping now that they could claim abandoned land on their own terms. As one settler put it, "the Proprietors are all Turnd Torrey and the Proprietors' Claim is Good for Nothing."[37] The simplicity of drawing a line in society between patriot and loyalist also provided a simple template to comprehend local disputes and durable tensions that were in essence quite complex. This is the form much state-sanctioned violence took in America. Because Congress represented an aspirational state and British forces an actual state, most projected their struggle to create or maintain authority in local contexts onto these programs, allowing violence to stay within predictable and controllable bounds.

The centers of rebellion before the revolution provide a case in point. During the war, many cities became less rebellious.[38] The reason is simple. At one point or another, troops occupied them. Although a standing army in their midst galled inhabitants, troops cowed them as well. Loyalists, of course, scurried out of Boston when the Continental Army occupied it in 1775. After New York was occupied less than a year later by the British, an exodus of patriots resulted. Throughout the whole war, New York remained relatively quiet. As soon as General Howe occupied the city, Tories from the surrounding area streamed in, wearing red badges in their hats. Soon, the city became a center for loyalists and British troops, what one commander called "the Gibraltar of North America." In November 1776, residents marched to City Hall where they signed a "declaration of dependence," one that affirmed "loyalty to our Sovereign, against the strong tide of oppression and tyranny, which had almost overwhelmed this land." New Yorkers raised loyal militia units, such as the King's Orange Rangers, the Loyal American Regiment, the British Legion, and the Volunteers of Ireland. In fact, it was the Volunteers that led some of the first St. Patrick's Day Parades, which during the war served as recruiting drives for the British Army. By 1779, the city's population swelled to 30,000. These numbers included Lord Dunmore and other major and minor royal government functionaries, as well as slaves and freedmen from the surrounding areas of Westchester, Long Island, and New Jersey. The wealthy soon forgot the years of republican austerity, of nonimportation and boycott, and reveled in foxhunting, golf, and cricket. The city remained remarkably calm for its size.[39]

New Yorkers labored under an oppressive sense of order. Of course, local patriots protested and rioted. But these were hardly violent episodes and proved episodic. If anything, New York was too calm. The city was ruled by martial law, as British commanders held and made use of dictatorial powers. They confiscated property without permission, occupied churches and homes without apology, and employed press gangs. Residents had to deal with drunken assaults by soldiers without recourse to the law. To make matters worse, two fires, one in 1776 and the other in 1778, destroyed one-third of the city's housing stock, forcing the poorest to live in what they called "Canvas Town," an area of the city dotted by makeshift tents. While the rich enjoyed all sorts of diversions, the poor suffered. Moreover, the calm of the city was juxtaposed with the disorder of the countryside. Tory units pillaged surrounding areas, the most infamous of which was organized by none other than the son of Benjamin Franklin, the former Royal Governor of New Jersey William Franklin. New York was, therefore, a Gibraltar in more ways than one. It had arisen as a loyal fortress, but an isolated one in a sea of disorder.[40]

Philadelphians, too, dealt with the same issue for more than 9 months in 1777, less than a year after Pennsylvania's radical constitution was drafted. As they entered the city, soldiers plundered and abused the populace. Officers and men occupied houses, and the poor suffered from inflated prices and shortages. After the initial period, however, calm came to the city, albeit the sort that came with garrison government. Joseph Galloway, now a prominent loyalist, served as "Superintendant General of the Police in the City and its Environs and Superintendant of Imports and Exports to and from Philadelphia." As the lofty titles suggest, the British wanted life to go on. People could come and go to the villages immediately around the city. British force created such order. Soon, it became a center for loyalists, who were coming in from the countryside as partisan bands and outlaws attacked the vulnerable in outlying areas. Nonetheless, trade continued in the city, and the wealthy enjoyed a season with balls held weekly. The troops settled in for a winter of drinking, gambling, dueling, and womanizing.[41] Charleston would suffer a similar fate later in the war. And the rule held: the cities in which armies decamped remained peaceful. The nature of that peace may not have agreed with many, but it proved that peace came only with effective authority.

The period after occupation proved a different story. The British left desolation in their train. As a French officer discovered, once the British left Philadelphia, they spared little in their wake. "The nearer you approach Philadelphia," he cautioned, "the more you discover the traces of war. The ruins of houses destroyed, or burned, are the monument the English have left behind."[42] Tumult came to Philadelphia after the occupation as the competition for authority took grip of the city once more. As the war continued, Philadelphians struggled with rising prices for food. The committees running the city insisted on price controls, but the efficacy of such a measure depended on the cooperation of some leading merchants. Some refused, and the legislature balked at passing such measures. The Committee of Trade, led by middle-class radicals, disbanded over the impasse, refusing to try to coerce the merchants. Militiamen had no such qualms. They seized 4 merchants and carried them over to the house of James Wilson, a leading defender of the merchants' position, with a drum beating the Rogue's March. Wilson and his friends barricaded the house, as the militiamen fired on his home and tried to batter down the doors. Five men died in the melee that would become known as the Fort Wilson Riot. Most Philadelphians decried what happened as a step toward "mobocracy." Nonetheless, these militiamen were instituting new terms for a new order. They not only contested the form that authority was taking in the city. They were creating a new form. The agitators eventually were pardoned, merchants were warned by the government to cooperate, and the state assembly distributed flour to the poor.[43]

Boston here is the exception that proves this rule. After the British left for Nova Scotia, they would not occupy Boston again. It would be dominated by those who had been Sons of Liberty, such as Samuel Adams, James Bowdoin, and John Hancock. Both Bowdoin and Adams would help write the state constitution of Massachusetts. They would also serve as governors of the state, as would John Hancock. Boston became a "well ordered town" soon after the British evacuated. The people struggled throughout the war with shortages. They sent loved ones off to the army. They endured brutally cold winters without adequate fuel. Nonetheless, Bostonians used the institutions created to contest British sovereignty as the very stuff of order throughout the war. Government regulated markets, saw to the inoculation of the citizens against smallpox, cared for the poor, warned out strangers, swept chimneys to prevent fires, and supported education for children. A body called the Committee of Correspondence, Inspection, and Safety enforced price controls, in much the same way that it did to support the Continental Association.[44]

In 1774, Bostonians may have tried to enflame tensions to accomplish their ends. By 1777, however, such tactics served no purpose, and leaders had little stake in popular riots. In fact, they labeled those who dissented as "loyalists." In March of that year, for instance, the town's selectmen reported to the Committee of Correspondence, Inspection, and Safety on those "whose Principles are known to be *unfriendly* to our present Contest with Britons, & some, who would sacrifice the public Interest to satisfy their Lust & Appetites." Those tarred as loyalists were "daily using every Means in their Power, not only to frustrate the good Intention of the Act of this State to prevent Monopoly & Oppression, but to lessen & depreciate the Value of the Money established by the Continental Congress, & the several United States in America." These were deemed "public Enemies." The selectmen called on the Committee to ferret out such people and publish their names in newspapers. Unless stopped, they would "unavoidably reduce the People of this State if not the *united* States to the utmost Misery and Distress."[45]

The ironies that revolution generated stemmed as much from the collapse of sovereignty as the subsequent interplay of disorder and order. In one context, one group clamored for revolutionary violence and chaos. In another, they became pillars of certainty and order. This complex dynamic gripped cities, towns, and villages all over America. Such ebb and flow between certainty and ambiguity defined America in these years.

Dynamism, of course, leads to variation. In some places, the tug-of-war between order and chaos, which was exacerbated by warfare, led to peace. In other regions, the same dynamic led to social dissolution. This dynamic explains why New Jersey was such a violent place. Troops marching throughout the state caused harm enough. One officer argued that "the Jersies [should be] laid waste as much as possible." He believed "the most effectual means of reducing the Country to subjection, is to burn and destroy every thing the Army can get at."[46] To some extent, his belief was realized. Nathanael Greene wrote, "the ravages in the Jersies exceeds all description." He catalogued a grim list of "Men slaughtered, Women ravisht, and Houses plundered, little Girls not ten Years old ravisht and Daughters ravisht in presence of Husbands and Sons."[47] Armies, however, exacerbated tensions already present, and in some cases, allowed men and women to vent hatreds. From the time of the Seven Years' War, wealthier men and women in the colony styled themselves a provincial gentry. As much as elites in other colonies, they adopted British fashions and sensibilities with a view to refining New Jersey. After the war, they tried to assert their newly claimed status, creating tensions in places such as Newark. Yeomen resisted, and with the crisis over sovereignty, they embraced the patriot movement to contest their status. To complicate matters, the mid-century witnessed evictions of squatters, who fought back by tearing down fences and ruining crops of large proprietors. With the crisis of sovereignty, the colony cracked in two and teetered on the brink of violence. Finally in 1769 and 1770, agrarian violence wracked New Jersey.[48]

The revolution in New Jersey devolved into a violent civil war between these factions. Wealthier Anglicans, those who emulated British ways, used the chaos of war to victimize their neighbors. The yeomen-led patriots did the same. A runaway slave from New Jersey epitomized what the state became over the course of the war. Owned by a cruel Quaker, Titus toiled as a slave in Monmouth County. When he received word of Dunmore's proclamation, he ran away and served with the Ethiopian Regiment, surviving battles in Virginia, as well as smallpox. In 1778, he fought with the British at Monmouth. He then stayed in the region, using his knowledge of the area to lead a band of guerilla fighters in New Jersey. Col. Tye, as he came to be known, and the Black Brigade terrified the area. Operating out of Refugeetown in Sandy Hook, Tye and his band engaged in malicious fighting, a war of reprisals in which loyalists killed patriots and patriots killed loyalists. Tye, who by reports led "a motley crew at Sandy Hook," operated with a unit "of about 20 blacks and whites" whose main task was to sustain violence and terror. In 1780, he died of gangrene after being wounded in an engagement at Toms River.[49]

Some communities, such as the southern backcountry, devolved into crucibles of unspeakable violence, pitting neighbor against neighbor. To understand this dynamic entails exploring the meanings of "loyalism" as well as the complex relationship between loyalists and evolving British strategy. After Burgoyne's debacle, British policymakers went back to the proverbial drawing board. Grand military strategy had failed to achieve a military victory, and the Continental Army still existed. The ministry, though, had numbers on its side in America but had failed to make use of this advantage. With the expansion of warfare to a global scale, reliance on loyal American subjects came to define the limits and possibilities of British strategic thinking. With troops dispersing around the globe, loyal manpower—white and black, Indian and settler—proved critical for British plans. Only 30% of Americans were what we could call ardent patriots, those committed to the American cause of sovereignty. More or less 20%, if given the chance, preferred the British program, though this percentage could and did fluctuate. Loyalists, lambasted by their patriot neighbors, either believed in the sovereignty of the Crown or acquiesced to the sovereignty of Parliament. But in some ways, political loyalties proved incidental. In essence, they abhorred what had happened to hitherto orderly communities and ideals of social relations as the crisis of authority had progressed. The rest of Americans lay somewhere between these two extremes.[50]

A group of loyalist exiles in London—or rather groups from various colonies—for years had been lobbying the ministry, arguing that relying on loyalist elements in the colonies would restore order. The loyalists in London, usually wealthier men, well-connected by personal history and trading ties to the metropole, had a well-articulated sense of what being British American meant. They debated the finer points of the crisis and filled each other in on the latest news in coffeehouses, which catered to loyalists from each colony. They even lived in the same sections of London. Rebuild authority around the people who supported the Crown, they suggested. Do so, the émigrés argued, by establishing military control of certain regions before turning over authority to local loyalists. In this way, whole regions could be secured with minimal British manpower, and with time, the revolt against established authority must end. Loyalists in London who styled themselves experts on all things American assured the ministry that they were the types of people who could be depended on to sustain sovereignty. The loyalists, often intimidated by patriot mobs, could win the day if given a chance, and the South was the ideal place to start.[51]

Leave aside for a moment the desperation and willful ignorance involved in believing that this series of measures could work; frankly, the ministry was doing what it could as its army and navy were overtaxed. The new strategy that the London loyalists helped devise represented one aspect—but a key one nonetheless—of a broader plan in which forces would be dispersed to critical points for a broader defense of the western end of the Atlantic. Because the scope and scale of thinking grew to global proportions, it was crucial to secure Nova Scotia as a northern anchor and the Floridas and Georgia as a southern anchor. The colonies could then be isolated. Key port regions like New York and Rhode Island should also be secured, along with the Highlands of New York, a choke point on the Hudson River. Securing these places could disrupt Washington's ability to move and communicate. Forces, then, could be sent to areas that had to be held or that the French, and later the Spanish threatened. The Caribbean was especially vulnerable in this regard, and troops stationed in the northern colonies were quite often dispatched to defend or take islands in the West Indies, as had been the case with the withdrawal of Philadelphia. The navy was to shuttle the troops while it shadowed the French and Spanish out of their ports in the Mediterranean, the Eastern Atlantic, the Caribbean, India, and of course protected the home islands. British troops could land in the South, which had a deeper loyalist base, secure territory and so isolate and squeeze rebellion. Loyalists could then occupy the mainland colonies once pacified.[52]

On paper, it looked like the southern aspect of the plan stood a chance. The South was filled with men and women disaffected from the patriot cause, who in some manner professed hope that British troops would relieve them of their suffering. Many of the South's loyalists, even if they had grievances with British authority, found themselves trapped between the insistence and intimidation of patriot neighbors and their loyalty to the Crown. However, the southern backcountry's loyalists were a different breed altogether. In the backcountry, motives were a bit murkier. Like London's loyalists, they had good reason to support the Crown, and they shared ideological commitment and worried about their futures in communities filled with the patriotically inclined. They also supported king and country because they hated their neighbors. An advertisement for raising loyalist troops in the South suggested as much. "All active young men," it read, "fit for Light Horsemen, and willing to serve his Majesty King George, for the space of two years, or during the present rebellion" were urged to join. They would be doing more however than "testifying their loyalty to the best of Kings, and manifesting their abhorrence and aversion to this unnatural and unprovoked rebellion." They would "have now a fair and honourable opportunity of revenging themselves on the authors of the many cruelties and horrid murders committed on their relations, friends, and fellow subjects."[53] The British would pin their hopes on these seeming loyalists. In doing so, they courted disaster.

In the backcountry regions of North and South Carolina, the 1760s and early 1770s had witnessed riots and protests and even combat between westerners and easterners. In South Carolina, those in backcountry regions who had hoped to transform wildernesses into settled societies found themselves trapped between squatting banditti who wanted no laws and eastern officials who did not want westerners to have local autonomy. In North Carolina, similar groups of people decried the ways in which easterners ignored their concerns, focusing their hostility on the construction of a lavish palace for the governor going up in New Bern. Regulators in both colonies took it on themselves to police their own communities, to see to it that order along their lines prevailed. The revolution exacerbated these tensions, leading them to explode. For the most part, those elite easterners who remained in North Carolina through the early years of the war supported the cause of independence. Those who had been Regulators in the colony had made up a great number of the loyalist force that lost at Moore's Creek. Others tried to remain neutral throughout the conflict. In other words, they found little to attract them to the patriot cause.[54] And why should they? The two programs for authority, after all, attracted all sorts of people for all sorts of reasons. Revolutionary dynamics and the languages that gave articulation to tensions in society were mediated—all over America—by local concerns. The same held true for Boston and Philadelphia, as well as the frontier for that matter.

In the South, a history of deep-seated hostility and the revolutionary competition to remake sovereignty combined to sustain appalling violence. No sooner had war started than patriot and loyalist patrols traveled through the countryside harassing and terrorizing one another. For each side, the revolution, in fact, offered an opportunity to settle old scores and to refashion society along lines to its liking. Competing interests saw perfidy in each other's motives. In one grisly episode, a loyalist band came across the house of a local patriot. In it they found his pregnant wife. They stabbed her with bayonets, cut open her breasts, and in her own blood wrote on the wall "thou shalt never give birth to a rebel."[55] Such incidents invited reprisal. And so much of the South, in the absence of authority and with a balance

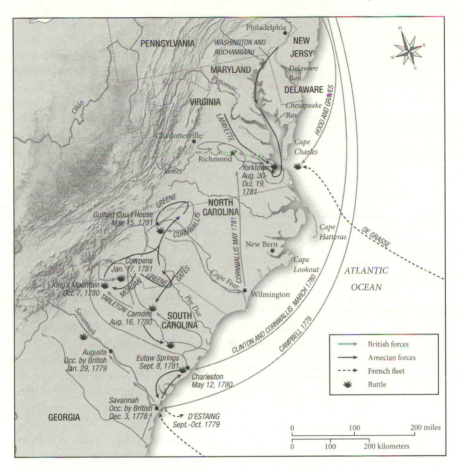

Map 6.3 War in the South, 1778–1781.

of power and terror between the two sides, simmered in a civil-war-like setting. In the revolutionary crucible, therefore, this society had cracked along its most salient fault line, and episodic violence was becoming endemic violence. To be sure, the hatreds were funneled into the cause of the war. But in this instance, the war was almost incidental. The more principled loyalists also had all sorts of motives for rallying to the Crown, from base material concerns to psychological makeup. But their support for the British cause did not entail the sort of unfettered violence that was engulfing communities in the South. It was on these sorts of people that the British strategy hinged.

Predictably, the arrival of large numbers of British troops to initiate the southern strategy did not ease tensions but heightened them. On St. Stephen's Day, 1779, Henry Clinton and General Charles Cornwallis sailed from New York for Charleston. After a tempest-tossed journey of 4 weeks, the transports landed at Tybee Island, where the crews and troops dried out. They then slogged their way to the outskirts of Charleston, whose inhabitants were preparing for a siege. The city's defenses were in a sorry state, and its commander, Benjamin Lincoln of Massachusetts, had no experience defending a siege. Lincoln commanded a mixture of militia and continentals, along with the Pulaski Legion, named after its leader, the Polish nobleman Casimir Pulaski. On April 1, the British began siege operations. Day by day, sappers dug their way closer to Charleston's defenses. As they did so, the city came into artillery range. The British fired cannon and mortar. Americans fired back whatever they could, loading their cannon with axe-heads, pistol barrels, broken glass, anything hard and sharp they found. While the Americans inflicted grievous damage, the relentlessness of the siege drove some Americans to madness. Clinton wanted to take the city with as little damage as possible. He knew that to win the South, he needed to win hearts and minds. He considered it "Absurd, impolitic, and inhuman to burn a town you mean to occupy." Finally, on May 12, Charleston surrendered, but not before 4 deserters were brought into the town. Two whites, a mulatto, and a black were hanged from a beam by the city's main gate. They hung there all day.[56] With the taking of Savannah and Charleston, loyalists from the surrounding areas swelled the numbers in the cities, which became for these beleaguered people the New Yorks of the South.

After securing the city, the British headed west, planning to pacify South Carolina by building a base of loyalist support before turning to North Carolina. As the army marched and rallied and buoyed the cowering loyalists, order would be restored. The British issued proclamations offering pardon for any rebels who relented and who would take oaths of allegiance.[57] Clinton then left the army in command of Cornwallis as he headed back to New York. In short order, they hoped to move north toward Virginia, where the process would pick up momentum. Winning the South, in this way, would make rebellion untenable, forcing the rebels to the bargaining table. The plans were complicated by the arrival of American armies. However, the British had at their disposal thousands of American loyalists all too eager to fight for the Crown. The civil war now had formal sanction. And the violence escalated.

Throughout 1780 and 1781, South Carolina devolved into a world of skirmishes, raids, and appalling violence and humiliation. The daughters of a loyalist named Flora MacDonald, for instance, were imprisoned by patriots who "put their swords into their bosoms, split down their silk dresses and, taking them out into the yard, stripped them of all their clothing."[58] William Gipson, whose home was destroyed by Tories, joined a small guerilla band of Whigs, as he put it. In the summer of 1779, he and his men captured "the notorious Hugh McPherson, a Tory." They tried and executed McPherson. Another Tory named Campbell "was condemned to be spickketed, that is, he was placed with one foot upon a sharp pin drove in a block, and was turned round... until the pin run through his foot." As cruel as the torture may have been, Gipson "viewed the punishment of those two men with no little satisfaction, as they were supposed to belong to the identical band who inhumanly inflicted corporal punishment upon his helpless parent."[59]

At Camden in August, the British defeated the patriot forces and local militia under the command of the man who had helped defeat the British at Saratoga. Horatio Gates may have beaten Burgoyne, but he met his match in Cornwallis. He bumbled his way into a fight at Camden, and it turned into a rout, with the North Carolina militia throwing down their weapons and running.[60] Gates's command was taken over by Nathanael Greene, who proved as brilliant as Gates was mediocre. Daniel Morgan led another American army. In general, the rule of warfare that had defined the American cause up to this point held in the South as well. The Americans, especially under Greene, lost and ran to live another day. The British pursued and tried to corner the Americans, only to be frustrated, winning the battles but losing the war.[61] The further west they moved, the further into America's heart of darkness the British traveled. Resistance grew as they drew closer to the mountains. What should have been an easy march, one that pacified the country, became slow and tedious and bloody. Each time the British hoped to leave the region, more resistance emerged, forcing them to tarry in South Carolina far longer than they had anticipated. Atrocities mounted, and in 1781 they were still trapped in the southern quagmire. As a British officer conceded, "we seem throughout this war to have adhered to the injudicious plan of dividing our Army into numerous detachments, and carrying on operations in several Colonies at once." Because of such a strategy, "we are not formidable in any one place, and actually raise more troops for the Enemy than they could possibly draw together in one, or even two Armies." He concluded that "we have been induced to act thus by the vain and ill grounded hope of finding numerous bodies of Loyalists to join and co-operate with us; but we should have learnt by experience how little assistance is to be expected from them."[62]

Two men who have passed into myth epitomized the ferocity of warfare in the region: Banastre Tarleton and Francis Marion. Tarleton, the Oxford-educated son of an English slave trader, infamously played upon violent tensions in the region, encouraging acts of violence to terrorize and intimidate a patriot populace. Allegedly, as he led a band of cavalry through South Carolina he ignored pleas for surrender and was behind the massacre of scores of Americans at Waxhaw. Order would come by the use of the sword not by providing a rallying point for the timid. His tactics also involved visiting bloodshed on local communities. In what was becoming a guerilla war, he understood that to kill the proverbial fish means drying up its pond. Marion was that fish. Violence was met with violence, and the "swamp fox," as the name suggests, used the disaffection of his neighbors and their knowledge of the land to harass British forces and to terrorize local loyalists. Marion had a great deal of experience in terrorizing. A veteran of the Seven Years' War, he had participated in brutal raids of Cherokee villages. He was also a slave owner. Moses Hall, a Whig from South Carolina, recalled how and why warfare became so cruel when Whigs and Tarleton's Tories engaged one another. Hall and his men had captured some men from Tarleton's command. Without warning, his compatriots brandished broadswords "and the prisoners were immediately hewed to pieces." The event horrified Hall, that is until the next day when he came upon the body of a 16-year-old boy who had been "run through" with a bayonet and left for dead by Tarleton.[63]

Bloodshed in the southern backcountry reached a climax at a place called King's Mountain in October 1780. Here on the western border between North and South Carolina, American patriots and loyalist Americans fought a battle in which retribution defined the day. No quarter was given and none expected. The only non-American in the fight, a Scottish commander of loyalist militia named Patrick Ferguson, was killed. The rest of the combatants were Americans. In this civil war battle, the patriot Americans won. After the battle, patriots urinated on the corpses of their loyalist brethren and slaughtered prisoners. Other prisoners were tried by the victors for treason, and some were executed. The battle pitted neighbor against neighbor, and each side fought with a ferocity fueled of old hatreds, in this instance the prewar struggle involving Regulation. In general, the majority of South Carolina Regulators became patriots. Their prewar enemies remained their enemies at King's Mountain.[64]

Ferguson's fate epitomized the tangled nature of the battle and of much of the South. After the battle, the body of Ferguson was stripped and urinated on. As one witness put it, "on examining the dead body...it appeared that almost fifty rifles must have been leveled at him, at the same time." Both of his arms were broken.[65] Ferguson had traveled to King's Mountain with two mistresses. One, named Virginia Sal, was killed in the battle. The other, Virginia Paul, betrayed Ferguson during the battle. She fingered him to patriot leaders as the loyalist commander. Ferguson was dumped in a grave with Virginia Sal. Virginia Paul rode off with the patriots.[66] Although by this point the War of Independence had been subsumed into an international conflict, the rules of civilized warfare did not apply in the South. This was an American version of the Terror. What was happening in much of the South in these years illustrates how if local patterns of conflict were simple, the revolutionary cause could subsume local tensions, channeling them and curtailing violence. But in the southern backcountry, terrifying violence reared its head where no prospective state actor could monopolize violence. The British did not learn this lesson. "We should have acted as if every man in America was an Enemy," an officer lamented.[67]

If no state actor could assert control in America, then how and why did much of America in these years escape from becoming a Hobbesian nightmare, a world of all against all? There are a number of reasons. For starters, Americans had a long tradition of self-governance. So when the British left Boston, locals could fall back on older traditions of government. They may not have held the highest positions, such as governor, but they had served as selectmen and had voted for deputies for generations. Moreover, as they created institutions to protest British state formation in America, they were also cobbling together the stuff of government. Differences of opinion, then, could be managed with provisional institutions that had a great deal of legitimacy. In the minds of people, these were one of the few tokens of sovereignty. Violence could be channeled into these bodies.[68]

The most intriguing answer to the question of "why no Terror in America" lies in America's fault lines. The salient divisions in society could provide the basis for violence, as was the case in the backcountry and on the frontier. But in other regions, throughout much of the rest of the South for instance, the issues that divided society could ensure that bloodshed did not saturate all. In the low country and the Chesapeake, the threat of slave revolts and runaways animated the search for order. Race and fears of slave agency became defining characteristics of the revolutionary process, motivated white society, and constrained disorder. Slaves ran to British lines conscious of Dunmore's proclamation and others like it promulgated by officers such as Clinton. Certainly, Thomas Jefferson saw things this way. In 1781, as British troops marched through Virginia, Jefferson estimated that 30,000 slaves had run away. And he feared that more would follow suit. If they did, not only would slave owners stand to lose a massive capital investment but the worst fears of southerners could be realized: a massive slave rebellion. The specter of this sort of violence stirred southerners like no other.

There was some truth to Jefferson's claims. Slaves indeed did run away. The most famous slave to do so was named Thomas Peters. Peters was born at Yoruba in what is present-day Nigeria. Captured by slave raiders, he was transported to Louisiana by a French slave trader. Eventually, he was sold to a Scottish planter who had settled in North Carolina near the mouth of the Cape Fear River. In 1776, when British warships came to the region culminating in the Battle of Moore's Creek, Peters ran away for British lines. He then fought in the war for the British as a "Black Pioneer." By doing so, he earned his freedom. If Peters's experience was the rule, then perhaps as many as one-half of those who could run away and fight—young unattached men—did so. Few blacks, with good reason, fought for the patriots. The vast majority who went to war sided with the British.[69]

In fact, Jefferson got his numbers wrong. For a start, many of those tallied as runaways were, in fact, the slaves of loyalists who were fleeing. The British never offered to free these slaves. In fact, it was not in British interests to use fear of slave insurrection as a central tenet of their strategy. The wealthiest holdings the British had, of course, were the sugar islands in the Caribbean. On this score, the British did all they could to buoy the slave systems there, even selling some runaways from regions in revolt to the West Indies. Americans did as well, in this case selling captured slaves of loyalist planters, to raise money for the war effort. Another strategy revolved around confiscating and re-enslaving those who ran away. If a former master could not be found, slaves could be put to work doing menial labor. It would appear at first glance that the revolution offered an unprecedented opportunity for liberation for slaves; in fact, the revolution proved a nightmare. Most of those who were able to overcome these nearly insurmountable obstacles, negotiate the chaos of period and place, and make their way to British lines usually died of disease, especially smallpox. Most British commanders, after all, did not bother to inoculate freed slaves. Moreover, some turned away slaves seeking asylum. For example, Simon Fraser, a commander bearing the same name as the Fraser in West's painting, ordered all his officers and enlisted men "that got Niggres to Desmess them amidlity." When slave numbers overwhelmed the British, commanders sent them off.[70]

All told a total of 20,000 slaves ran away from their masters—12,000 in the southern states—during the war. And of these only 2,000 or so would live to see their freedom.[71] Peters, therefore, proved the exception, not the rule. Why, then, did Jefferson exaggerate? For one thing, Jefferson was in grave peril and Virginia was in a state of disarray. In 1781, British forces were rampaging through the commonwealth, burning tobacco and freeing slaves. Jefferson and the assembly fled Richmond, which he assumed would become a target for the British, for the quiet of Charlottesville. Learning of his departure, Cornwallis ordered Tarleton and his white-coated cavalry to capture Jefferson. In early June, Tarleton led a lightning quick raid to take the governor at Monticello. Only the warning of a patriot named Jack Jouett allowed Jefferson to escape.[72] In the midst of the chaos of invasion, playing upon fears of slave insurrection, then, could focus attention on Virginia's plight.

More to the point, the answer to the question of Jefferson's numbers goes to the heart of the ways in which planters like him tried to ensure that disorder did not engulf their communities. The requests that followed inflated numbers usually asked for some help. And nothing mobilized institutions and people like the specter of slave rebellion. Local committees did not only function as provisional governments; they also sanctioned slave patrols to ensure that slaves did not rise up against their masters. Planters also increased the levels of punitive discipline against their slaves to overawe them. Committees, as did one in North Carolina, gave orders to shoot any slaves who assembled in groups off of their plantations. In fact, South Carolinians balked at raising militia units because most whites preferred to stay at home "to prevent Insurrections among the Negroes."[73] Local committees of correspondence stated numbers sure to rally state governments. In one instance, South Carolina militia crossed into Georgia following reports of a maroon colony on Tybee Island. In general, while slave patrols worked to ensure that slaves did not run off, state officials exaggerated to receive help from Congress. South Carolinian Henry Laurens, for instance, regaled Congress with the numbers of slaves he and his neighbors expected to lose unless Congress acted to thwart the movement of British troops. Laurens catalogued how British warships trolled the coast seizing slaves. He also made the case that retaining control of the South was a key for winning the war, for both the British and the Americans. "The recovery of South Carolina and Georgia," he argued in 1778, "is a project of the first magnitude to Great Britain in her present circumstances." The British would succeed "unless in the meantime an ample aid shall be supplied by their Northern neighbors." Until then, the British would plunder "an abundance of provisions," including "many thousand of negroes." Congress dispatched an army. In other words, fears of slaves could move mountains in revolutionary America.[74]

Fears were not only articulated by elites. If any dynamic could motivate all whites, it was this. Over the course of the eighteenth century ordinary whites in places like Virginia had risen in status in absolute terms. More significantly, whites had risen in status relative to the slaves around them. Ordinary white farmers, most of whom in the years before and during the revolution did not own slaves, depended on the existence of a debased laboring majority to secure a relatively privileged place in society. All white southerners, therefore, had a stake in a form of order that depended on the existence of slavery.[75]

Excesses were often reined in by the peculiar fault lines along which society was cracking from revolution. Divisions could heighten violence, as had happened in the southern backcountry; they could forestall and channel it as well. Race played the most critical role in this regard. In regions of the South, race and the anxieties associated with it ensured that some form of order prevailed. In other words, social control flourished even in the crucible of revolution. The dynamic worked out differently in different parts of America, such as, for instance, in the West. Here race did not forestall violence. Bloodshed, in fact, permeated the region. But that bloodshed was channeled against Indians. And Indian violence was focused on white settlers. Here the War of Independence proved both incidental and instrumental to more fundamental concerns and more elemental hatreds.

Western patterns of violence were determined not only by old hatreds, which fully emerged at the time of Seven Years' War. They were also fashioned by the enduring failure of any single group or patron to bring an end to fear and uncertainty—to restore sovereignty—and shifting British strategy. In the wake of the Clark fiasco and as the effort to put down rebellion in the East stalled, the British decided that the region west of the Appalachians Mountains had utility to the broader war effort. The attempt of Virginians to claim the West mattered less to the British than the possibilities of the rebels creating a strategic link with the Mississippi. With the French joining the war effort, officials feared that the Americans could use the West's river system in much the same way the French had intended to. If the Americans dominated the Ohio country, they could control Illinois. If they controlled Illinois, they had a durable link to New Orleans, one of the most important North American ports and a potential depot for French aid. Officials also worried that Americans would seek to create a linkage with the Spanish who held the west bank of the Mississippi River. Reports circulated of American armies leaving Fort Pitt and heading down the Ohio to the Mississippi. Building settlements here and linking with New Orleans would give the Americans entry into the Caribbean. Worryingly, British officials noted that some settlers had approached the Spanish for help against Indians. Settlers did this because neither the British nor the Americans had taken effective control of the West. Nonetheless, these perceived threats, as well as the opportunity to create a diversion in the West, led the British to reformulate strategy.[76]

Early on, of course, American and British commanders tacitly agreed that Indians should not be encouraged to join the fight. Both understood how Indian–white violence, racialized in nature, would enflame the West and could complicate their aims for the East. The British now took the opposite tack. Fear and terror, they reckoned, could be used to good effect. About this time, British commanders were now instructed to make use of Indian grievances to prosecute the broader war. War, they suggested, must now involve more than armies. It involved society. This modern notion of warfare made sense given the fact that young Native Americans had been sporadically attacking frontier settlements throughout the war years, or at least threatening to do so. Uncertainty, more or less, defined the early years of the War of Independence, as no single patron would or could establish order in the region. But as they were embarking on new strategies in the East, in the West the British were less interested in creating order than in fostering greater levels of disorder to further their aims. Commanders dispatched ranger units to coordinate attacks with Indians. The "green coats" were well skilled at guerilla warfare, often having learned the brutal "American way of war" during the Seven Years' War. They also began sponsoring Indian raids, equipping young disgruntled men, offering scalp bounties in some cases.[77] Indians were more than willing allies in accomplishing these aims. In fact, interests converged in creating a violent West.

The effects of the convergence were felt immediately. Raids picked up in Kentucky, the western borders of the Carolinas, northern and western Pennsylvania, and upstate New York. Iroquois hammered American settlements, paying back men and women for years of landgrabs. The most infamous raids were led by British rangers and the Mohawk Joseph Brant. Brant consciously adopted the loyalist cause and had traveled to London to demonstrate the loyalty of the Mohawks. The former

Figure 6.3 George Romney, *Joseph Brant*, 1776. National Gallery of Canada.

brother-in-law of William Johnson, Brant was an inspiring leader, a tactical genius, and a strategic thinker, who embraced the British cause and launched devastating raids from New York to the borders of Virginia and all points in between. Brant was responsible for an especially brutal attack on Cherry Valley in 1778. Ranging up and down the upper Susquehanna Valley with the British commander Richard Butler, Brant led a force that killed women and children in a series of raids in retaliation for the forays of militia into Iroquois settlements. Unsurprisingly, terror gripped the vast frontier.[78]

Americans did not sit still. If the British could use the West to divert American energies from the East, the Americans could follow suit. If Indians could be a British hammer in attacking, American commanders reckoned, they could also prove a burden if vanquished. Congress advocated a change in policy for strategic and political reasons. After all, the war would eventually end, and when it did, questions such as who had controlled the West would determine who would win the West. Men like Washington, veterans of western campaigns and speculative ventures, fully understood the significance of countering British moves along the frontier.

In implementing a new policy, Americans encountered significant obstacles. They faced an uphill battle in taking the fight to the British on the frontier because they had more or less lost any leverage they had in the West up to this point. Congress did not even have the resources to sustain western garrisons in any real fashion. The troops stationed at Fort Pitt, for instance, had not been paid in years, dressed in rags, and had little food or drink, save whiskey. The troops proved useless in defending the West. These sorts could not stop squatters or land jobbers from settling where they wanted, men and women who used the uncertainty of the period to claim land.

Moreover, nearly all Indians with a few notable exceptions sided with the British when push came to shove. Many Delawares, whom Americans tried to keep well affected to the neutral course, also fought for the British. Early on in the war, American commissioners were able to keep Delawares neutral. As the war progressed, however, they could not supply the goods necessary to keep young men from becoming restless. "The Delaware Chiefs, with upwards of thirty warriors, are come to aid me upon an expedition," Fort Pitt's commander wrote in 1780. "But, as I have neither bread nor meat to give them," he conceded, "they will soon discover that it is not in my power to act offensively. They appear much dejected on account of the total want of goods, which they were promised in exchange for their peltry." American inability to supply them proved the tipping point for many Delawares. Already incensed at landgrabs in the West and appalled by violent settlers, siding with the British, who had goods and agents skilled in Indian diplomatic protocol, made common sense.[79]

The new American western strategy, a strategy really by default, was first made manifest in Iroquoia. As the British began to shift their policy, they relied on Iroquois, especially the Mohawk, who had a history of cooperation with the British. In fact, the nephew and son of Sir William Johnson, kept the old networks alive and now used their influence to encourage raids on the borders of New York. Washington had little choice but to counter the attacks. In fact, Washington hoped that by marching forces through the West, he could create a humanitarian disaster that the British would have to address, one that would relieve pressure in the East. "It is the desire of Congress," he wrote in 1779, "that some offensive expedition should be carried on against the Indians." He, therefore, organized an expedition "to chastise and intimidate the hostile nations, to countenance and encourage the friendly ones, and to relieve our frontiers from the depredations to which they would otherwise be exposed." To this end, he "proposed to carry the war into the heart of the country of the Six Nations, to cut off their settlements, destroy their next year's crops, and do them every other mischief, which time and circumstances will permit." Washington instructed John Sullivan, a general from New Hampshire, to invade the land of the Six Nations as one part of a three-pronged offensive to end the threat from Indian attacks once and for all. In particular, Sullivan was charged with creating as much havoc as he could.[80]

If this was his aim, Sullivan succeeded admirably. Sullivan departed for Iroquoia with 2,000 troops from the East. At the same time, David Brodhead assembled a force at Fort Pitt that would march north through Pennsylvania. Brodhead could not amass the forces he needed. Sullivan had no such troubles. In part, he was able to accomplish much of what he set out do because he had the support of warriors from the Oneida nation, one of the Six Nations, but the only one that sided with the Americans because of the influence of pro-American missionaries who had worked with the Oneida for some time. Using Oneida scouts to make their way to Iroquois villages, Sullivan and his men killed Indians, burned villages, and destroyed crops. By September 1779, Sullivan's loss of men was "trifling." However, as Washington observed in a letter to Lafayette, "he had advanced to and destroyed fourteen Towns, large and most flourishing Crops of Corn." Sullivan "was proceeding in his plan of chastisement" and would convince the Iroquois "that their cruelties are not to pass with impunity; and, secondly, that they have been instigated to arms and acts of Barbarism by a nation, which is unable to protect them."[81] Long before Napoleon and Sherman, this amounted to total war, aimed at combatant and noncombatant alike, as well as that society's ability to wage war.

The march through Iroquoia, as the Americans expected, created a humanitarian crisis. Starving men and women tromped to the British fort at Niagara for shelter, protection, and food. Refugees overwhelmed the ability of the British to look after them. But they would with time provide a potent fighting force for the British in the future. Later next year, Iroquois from other nations would have their revenge, laying waste to Oneida country and American settlements around New York and the upper Susquehanna Valley. The region would witness a number of Cherry Valley-like massacres, meted out by each side. The league that had pre-dated the arrival of Columbus and had made the Iroquois one of the power brokers of early America and the most powerful group of Indians inhabiting the eastern woodlands collapsed.[82]

The Americans and the British could unleash unspeakable violence. What they could not do was win the West. In fact, violence did not bring order but greater uncertainty, in turn generating even more violence and making for a vicious revolutionary cycle. In the East, the competing programs for sovereignty contained or at least channeled bloodshed. In the West, such was not the case. The Cherokees wartime experience offers the best example of the dissolving power of bloodshed in the West. For Cherokees, violence called all authority into question. Throughout the 1760s, in response to pressures from settlers, speculators, and officials, Cherokee elders had ceded a great deal of land. The trend continued into the 1770s, as leaders granted a chunk of the Kentucky country to a trader from North Carolina named Richard Henderson. The thinking that went into these deals was simple: cede land judiciously to keep a buffer between settlers and Cherokees, most now living west of the Mountains. The plan, however, incensed young men, who saw their hunting lands lost to white settlers.[83]

As pressures were ratcheted up in the region with the War of Independence, young men staged a coup against their elders. They declared "that their Nation was under very great apprehensions and uneasiness and complained much of the encroachments of the Virginians and Inhabitants of North Carolina." Cherokees "were almost surrounded by the White People, that they had but a small spot of ground left for them to stand upon and that it seemed to be the Intention of the White People to destroy them from being a people." The British offered to help, suggesting that Virginians encroached on Cherokee lands "contrary to the Kings Orders, [and] that affairs were in such a situation at this time that they seemed to trample on his Authority." British agents pointed out, however, that Cherokees had brokered "private Bargains for their Lands contrary to all the Talks that they had received." The younger men countered that they "had no hand in making these Bargains but blamed some of their Old Men who... were too old to hunt and who by their Poverty had been induced to sell their Land."[84] Promising to take the message of resistance to other nations, and forming pan-Indian alliances, one such young leader named Dragging Canoe promised to make places like Kentucky "dark and bloody grounds." These men refused to listen to their leaders, declaring their independence to prosecute the war. Disorder, therefore, was spreading to all communities. Unsurprisingly, warriors like Dragging Canoe found ready allies in the British.

They also found allies in the Ohio country. Shawnees had already been raiding in the Ohio Valley. Now they had the formal blessing of the British to do so, as well as the cooperation of the Cherokees. Dragging Canoe made his way to Shawnee settlements to make a plea for a confederation. Emissaries moved from village to village carrying war belts, that is, dark-colored wampum, with their faces blackened. Dragging Canoe and the Shawnees discussed how to "secure the friendship of all nations" and how to conceive of "their interests as one." Young men cowed their elders, who looked on "dejected and silent." Forts came first, then settlements of "the Long Knife," leading all to believe that "there was an intention to extirpate them." It would, the young men declared, be "better to die like men than to diminish away by inches."[85] Although a formal structure never got off the ground—Shawnees were also wracked by intergenerational tensions—coordinated raids followed. Delawares also cast their lot with confederates.[86]

For years, the Ohio Valley, a land beyond sovereignty, had seethed in uncertainty. Now it boiled over in violence. Kentucky bore the brunt, and from 1779 until the war ended settlers holed up in stinking blockhouses and makeshift forts. Situated near rivers and in the midst of settlement regions, these were designed as neighborhood safe houses, places to stay for a few days until danger passed, in other words well-designed for the early years of uncertainty. These were not constructed as fortresses that could withstand sieges and months of privation. Once coordinated raids started, settlers could not leave to sow or reap crops. Water supplies were fouled, children were captured, and cattle were killed. Fear lingered for months.[87]

In these circumstances, settlers clamored for help. None came. Americans could not relieve the pressure. In fact, events like Sullivan's march intensified pressures. Although Washington made noises of dispatching forces from Fort Pitt and other frontier garrisons, troops never left their stations. They had a difficult enough time sustaining themselves, never mind protecting exposed settlements that were being hammered by Ranger-led attacks. Virginians still claimed regions like Kentucky. But no substantive forces came from these quarters either. All sorts of patrons claimed sovereignty, but the people stood alone. The problem was one of sovereignty, and since this was the case, disaffection grew. Increasingly, men and women refused to support any side in the war. Some flirted with loyalism, including a number of men and women who could not stand another season in this wild West without protection. Their number included none other than Daniel Boone, who was captured by Shawnees during the violent years of the war and who seems to have given information to British officials about settlements in Kentucky. Although he would run away and rejoin his community, the taint of loyalism dogged him for some time.[88]

The distinctive dynamics gripping the West made for possibly the most gruesome episode of the war. Early in 1782, without the blessing of any government, men from the frontiers of Pennsylvania and Virginia set off to destroy the Indians responsible for raids the previous summer. They found what they conceived to be a guilty party at Moravian mission villages on the Muskingum River, a tributary of the Ohio.

At these settlements, the Moravians and the Indians "had built a pretty Town and made good improvements and lived for some years past quite in the style of Christian white people." Here, they farmed like other settlers in the Ohio Valley and had thrived in these years of violence.[89] Although the Delawares there proclaimed their innocence and neutrality, the frontiersmen concluded that they had to be lying. After all, as they reasoned, the Indians possessed goods, such as kettles and clothing, that only whites could use. They, therefore, must have taken these items on raids. The frontiersmen gathered the Delawares from small villages along the Muskingum, assembling them in the mission town of Gnadenhütten, German for the "huts of Grace."

Their professed Christianity could not save them. After holding a "trial," the volunteers and their elected officers condemned each and every Delaware to death. Throughout the evening, the Indians sang psalms and comforted one another. In the morning, troops escorted them into a cabin by pairs. The Delawares did not resist. The frontiersmen then smashed the heads of the condemned with wooden mallets, scalping each of them. In all, they killed 96 Delawares, men, women, and children.[90] The killings alarmed eastern officials.[91] The incident also shocked the British. One officer could not believe what had happened. The frontiersmen had "destroyed the poor innocent Moravian Indians, their near Neighbours, who never went to War against them, or any other People." Most damningly, "under the Cloak of Friendship they murdered them in Cold Blood, and reduced their Bones to Ashes that the Murder might not be discovered."[92] An American commander questioned the men involved, but he found "no man can give any account…nor will they give Evidence against themselves."[93] However inexplicable, in the West this type of slaughter was becoming the norm.

Killings unsanctioned by any government continued. The following spring, the same militia unit responsible for the Gnadenhütten massacre reassembled under a newly elected leader, William Crawford, and marched to destroy other Delawares at Upper Sandusky. "We Want Revenge Appon the Savages for the Enjurys the Dun unto our Brother Soldiers," a petition from frontier inhabitants read, "to proqure as meney scalps from our Enemy and make Sutch Discuverys as can be maid."[94] Spies, moving ahead of the force, ran into Indians on the fourth of June. For 5 hours, the force exchanged fire with Indians and a small number of British rangers. Throughout the night, the Indians received reinforcements, encircling the militia, and the fight continued the next day. Many of these Indians, like the victims of Gnadenhütten, were Delawares, but unlike the Christian martyrs, were neither peaceful nor neutral. The men from the frontier regions beat a retreat. The Indians pursued them, killing and scalping stragglers. About 40 died, but most made their escape.[95]

Colonel Crawford and a small party did not. Delawares captured them and marched them back to Sandusky. At the village, a trader greeted Crawford, informing him "that the Indians were very much enraged against the prisoners." A Delaware leader ordered the faces of the men painted black, marking them for execution. Boys and women tomahawked and scalped a number of the prisoners.[96] The dead were the fortunate ones. Delawares stripped Crawford of his clothes, sat him down by a fire, and beat him. "They then tied a rope to the foot of a post about fifteen feet high, bound the Colonel's hands behind his back and fastened the rope to the ligature between his wrists." Men shot powder into his body "from his feet as far up as his neck," cut off his ears, and thrust burning sticks into his body "so that whichever way he ran round the post they met him with burning faggots and poles." While women threw hot coals on the ground, Crawford begged to be killed. The tortures continued like this for 2 hours when "at last being spent, he lay down on his belly: they then scalped him." A woman grabbed a board, placed hot ashes and coals on it, and "laid them on the back and head after he had been scalped." The Delawares then burned him alive.[97] As he "roasted," he declared "some great blows would be struck against this country."[98]

States existed, settlers reckoned, to protect. If they could not protect people, society could not exist. If society could not exist, they owed no allegiance. In other words, in a world without sovereignty men and women were becoming self-sovereign. Although pleas for protection continued, with time they became less desperate and more calculating. Communities began sending out their own militia, who acted more in their name than in the name of Congress or Virginia or Pennsylvania. The results in this atmosphere of racialized violence proved predictable. Settlers slaughtered Indians. Commanders out West began to recognize that a shift was occurring. If these people could kill Indians, they could also threaten officials who did not subscribe to the racist vision that seemed to energize frontier settlements. To give just one example, the commander of Fort Pitt pretended to support the massacre at Gnadenhütten although the violence appalled him. To stand against the people in this world without authority meant courting ruin. People had been growing increasingly assertive, even suggesting that American troops "had an attachment to Indians in general." They also threatened they would scalp an officer. Common people were associating to oppose the payment of taxes and to serve in militias. Some were even intent on killing "every Man that was blacker than a White man." So said a man who had bludgeoned a Delaware. The commander wisely refused "to express any sentiment for or against those deeds."[99] Disaffection, therefore, did not imply powerlessness. Quite to the contrary, it meant that a people were coming of age. In the West, this maturity, which took place in the crucible of revolution, merged notions of popular sovereignty with race.

The dreadful things that happened at Gnadenhütten and the raids in Kentucky, per capita the bloodiest region during the war, proved exaggerated instances of what was happening throughout America. Indeed, we see the revolution writ small here, as well as its most troubling aspects. Race, for instance, while precipitating new levels of bloodshed, also channeled violence. Speculators, jobbers, and squatters may have hated one another, and even during the war years tensions festered. But raids put all whites on the same uneasy footing, ensuring that tensions in the vacuum of authority that defined the West did not become generalized and determining that violence would know limits, however appalling those limits might have been.

To some extent, the same held true for Indians. Men and women who had no innate propensity for bonding together—an American myth—found common cause. Cherokees and Shawnees, longtime rivals, could launch raids together. And racially heightened violence, in most cases in response to raids by race-addled settlers and militia, prompted counterviolence. Bloodshed, therefore, stayed within racially circumscribed bounds. But the Indian experience also differed from the white experience in a fundamental way. For whites, violence united, obviating other cleavages such as class or status. For Indians, bloodshed dissolved relationships, breaking societies down along their most conspicuous fault lines, be it nation or generation. The unity of the Six Nations was a thing of the past. Bloody struggle defined the Cherokee experience as well.

In many regions in America, especially in the South and in the West, self-sovereignty and race went hand-in-hand, revealing the ways that revolution functioned in America. This revolution, of course, had a transnational and transhistorical character. Sovereignty collapsed, competition ensued, and then order would eventually be restored. The shape and character of the distinct phases, however, cohered to the historical characteristics of the society in which the revolution took place, the fault lines that divided the regions of that society, and the ways in which disorder and order were experienced in local communities. In other words, the distinctive quality of the revolution represented a variation on a common theme, creating in this case the nature of a distinctive "American" revolution. In France, for instance, during the Terror the state attempted to monopolize violence; but in reality it brought order to the violence that was threatening to overwhelm the streets. A similar dynamic gripped America. The fact that revolutionary tensions were channeled into the programs of a failed state and an aspiring state ordered violence, not allowing Americans to claim themselves as self-sovereign outside of the competing visions of sovereignty on offer. Only where these programs failed to restore authority at all—in the West—did the sort of revolutionary violence that would dominate the streets of Paris and places like the Vendée hold sway.

This American phase of terror represented an American counterpoint to a common revolutionary process. During revolution, America's societies fractured along their fault lines. America had many tensions and regions, but the fractures created by race would channel the tensions arising from the other divisions, especially class, as would the war itself. Americans were reaping this whirlwind because of the nature of their society and its history. The question none could contemplate as violence engulfed region after region was how the furies of revolution could be contained, and at what price, when war came to an end. This issue represents the most vexing question that revolution raised.

PART III

The End

Founders

In 1786, some years after the War of Independence had ended, a painter named John Trumbull, whose sister Faith had been so deeply affected by the bloodshed at Bunker Hill, began work on what would become an American icon. He called the painting *The Declaration of Independence*. Completing it, as well as subsequent copies of the painting, would consume much of his life. Trumbull worked metaphorically and literally on a large canvas. In the painting, Trumbull portrayed nearly all of the signers, spending years traveling far and wide collecting portraits of the signing founders. The painting, then, amounts to a series of portraits. Trumbull had 36 signers sit for him. He copied 9 from existing images, one from a description, and one from memory.[1] The faces of most of the men who would sign the Declaration look with pride and determination toward the center of the composition, to the committee that composed the document. Between John Adams and Benjamin Franklin stands the person most responsible for the document, Thomas Jefferson, who is handing the now completed draft to the president of the Continental Congress, John Hancock.

Trumbull, whose father had been governor of Connecticut, was an American wunderkind, who enjoyed a college education and patronage from an early age. Although he had wanted to apprentice "under the Instruction of Mr. Copley" in Boston, his father refused, considering it below his station and instead insisting his son attend Harvard. While there, he visited Copley, who proved an inspiration. Trumbull was impressed both by the quality of Copley's work and his lavish lifestyle. "I remember his dress and appearance—an elegant looking man, dressed in a fine maroon cloth, with gilt buttons," he gushed. "This was," he added, "dazzling to my unpracticed eye!"[2] When the war broke out, Trumbull left Cambridge for the glory of the battlefield, where his talents won the attention of George Washington. Trumbull had sketched the British defenses around Boston so well that Washington placed the young painter on his staff. Trumbull, however, did not imagine himself as soldier or scholar. After serving with some distinction and after earning a field commission as a colonel, he did what Copley had done just a few years earlier and headed

Figure III.1 John Trumbull, *The Declaration of Independence*, 1818. Architect of the Capitol.

to London to hone his craft, where Benjamin West befriended him. West helped the young man find his way about the city. He also taught him a fair amount about the finer points of painting. The government imprisoned Trumbull for treason during the war as a supporter of the American cause. But with the help of the loyal West and Edmund Burke, both of whom put up £100 for his bond, he was released. He then traveled to the Continent. His time in London and on the Continent made Trumbull the painter that he became.[3]

Although Trumbull returned to America, painting portraits of those who could afford to pay, he wanted to do more with his talent. After the war, at West's encouragement he traveled again to London and produced a series of pieces that commemorated the war, including a painting of Gen. Richard Montgomery's famous fall near Quebec. *The Declaration of Independence* was to be a centerpiece of that history series. It remains his most famous image.

When regarding the painting, viewers are apt to focus on the date it commemorates. In point of fact, it would be wiser to focus on the dates during which the original and subsequent copies were painted. Trumbull began conceiving it a decade after the signing of the Declaration and less than a year before delegates would meet in the same room to draft the Constitution. He continued at the theme for years thereafter, even after Jefferson would become president. By this time, as far as Trumbull was concerned, principled debate, not violence, lay at the heart of a staid revolution. If the painting lacks the dramatic appeal of his war series, the statement of meaning it makes is no less grandiose or daring. Trumbull presents history that spoke to America's present as he interpreted it, not quite as it happened on an epic scale. He knew that viewers should not take the piece literally. Nonetheless, deeper truths could emerge from idealized representations. This drama does not take place on the battlefield but indoors. Spectacle and thought matter more than action.

These men of virtue and moderation, these founders, animate the piece, the sacred space of the spectacle, and by extension the nation. Notice the use of light. Although the back of the room, where the British colors hang, is dark, the curtains closed, and doors shut, Trumbull bathes each of the founders in light. His was a painting of "distinguished men, who were present at that illustrious scene," which is likened to a birth.[4] Some are more distinguished than others. The men of the central group are the light-bearers and have a more important role to play in the piece. In some ways, Trumbull melts down social distinctions in the painting. All those in the room are dressed in republican simplicity. Space within the room does not divide spectator from actor. All belong in the room. Abigail Adams judged Trumbull's work in this regard as well conceived. He had, through his work, suggested "that it is not rank nor titles, but character alone, which interests posterity."[5] Here then is a new sort of philosophical history, though not the sort Joshua Reynolds had in mind. Through what the founders have crafted, however, some draw more light than others. Trumbull here plays with illusion. Hierarchy of status would seem to have no place in the piece; nonetheless, status, rooted in merit and ability, still defines the central action of the painting, the handing over of a draft of a declaration. In this room, we find no faces of women or of color. Those he portrays are an elite in a nation in which older notions of deference and hierarchy were supposed to have vanished.

This scene, Trumbull insisted, represented the event that made the nation what it was. For virtue and self-sacrifice, citizens needed to look no further than the founders who pledged their lives, fortunes, and sacred honor to the cause. This was a revolution as much about principle as action. As he wrote in 1789, he wished to commemorate "the great events of our country's revolution ... to preserve and diffuse the memory of the noblest series of actions which have ever presented themselves in the history of man." He hoped to inspire and "to give to the present and future sons of oppression and misfortune, such glorious lessons of their rights." Such an audience needed to look to "those who have been the great actors in those illustrious scenes."[6] In portraying the founders, then, he was crafting a vision of what the American Revolution meant not in 1776 but in the years thereafter. Trumbull presents, then, the viewer with a mythic image, one rooted as much in fact as illusion.

Fittingly, Jefferson stands at the center. Jefferson not only authored the Declaration but also inspired Trumbull to paint *The Declaration of Independence*. After the war, Trumbull and Jefferson became friends. And while Jefferson was serving the new nation in France, he suggested the idea of such a painting to Trumbull and even sketched a layout of the room in Philadelphia in which the scene took place. Jefferson also summed up the role of the founders for Trumbull, who offers a story of nation-building with Jefferson as the architect. Finally, the placement of Jefferson represented the very real tensions afflicting the United States when Trumbull was composing the piece. The painting hinges on the man who epitomized many of the Revolution's contradictions for Americans. A father of American democracy, who insisted "all men" were created equal, lived like an aristocrat and owned slaves. Whether Trumbull placed Jefferson at the center of his painting for this reason, out of friendship, or a sense of "historical accuracy" is immaterial. In the America of 1826 when a large-scale version of the piece was placed in the Capitol's rotunda, all knew the contradictions that Jefferson epitomized. No one could escape them, though try as they may. Trumbull painted a myth that Americans accepted as reality, no matter what they thought of that reality. By 1826, they had become trapped in the room that Trumbull portrays.

CHAPTER 7

In the Chair of Independency

The way the war ended revealed how the course of revolution was transforming America. Uncertainty, violence, vacillation, fluidity, and circumstance played prominent roles in the war's final phase, a story that began with one mythic figure, soon to be a symbol of treachery, and ended with another, who with time would come to symbolize the virtue of the founders. Throughout the summer of 1781, the British had moved north to Virginia, where they were wreaking havoc. On the surface, it appeared that the strategy of converting patriots into loyalists, which had run into difficulties in the Carolinas, was better suited for Virginia. Indeed, the British had won over one of the most prominent patriots. Benedict Arnold considered himself underappreciated. He had proven himself one of the Continental Army's ablest field commanders. Although he had born grievous wounds for the cause, Congress had passed him over for promotion, but for good reason. After the British had evacuated Philadelphia, Washington made Arnold governor of the city. Arnold used his position to line his pockets and discredit his enemies, and Washington and Congress had reprimanded him for his venality, corruption, and abuse of power.

Why Arnold turned coat, literally, is complex. His pride was clearly wounded. Moreover, he married into a prominent Tory family while he was stationed in Philadelphia. He also worried that the American cause was foundering, particularly after the alliance with France. He did, after all, have an insider's view of the army and Congress. Neither cut an impressive figure. Most likely the confluence of these factors determined his decision to join the British. Named military commander of West Point, a strategic point on the Hudson River, Arnold contacted Clinton to hand over the post. The plan backfired. Major John André, the British officer charged with turning over the plans of West Point from Arnold to Clinton, was caught and later hanged. Arnold then fled to the British in New York City.[1]

Clinton turned to Arnold to disturb Virginia. Commanding 1,600 greencoats and a number of ships, he led forays that drove the commonwealth to the brink of panic. He raided ports, destroying warships and capturing commercial vessels. He also burned 2,000,000 pounds of tobacco. Here Lafayette earned his stripes. Washington sent him to Virginia to harass the harassers, and he and his 900 men stood between Arnold and the destruction of Richmond.[2] Meanwhile Cornwallis with the main army arrived. On the face of it, the British seemed to be in a commanding position in Virginia.

Things were not as they seemed. In fact, Cornwallis had languished in the South. Nathanael Greene, by hitting, running, and refusing to be brought to bay, had whittled down Cornwallis's army. As a popular song at the time set to the tune of "Yankee Doodle Dandy" went:

> Cornwallis led a country dance,
> The like was never seen, sir
> Much retrograde and much advance,
> And all with General Greene, sir.[3]

The Americans, meanwhile, had secured a number of victories in the South, including the battles of Guilford Courthouse and King's Mountain. These did not so much cripple the British as reveal the illusory hope that they had placed in their plans for the South. It was clear the southern strategy had failed; in fact, the British plan only exacerbated tensions in the region, further eroding order. When he arrived in Virginia, Lafayette's small force, joined by Anthony Wayne's Pennsylvania line, was sufficient to force Cornwallis to suspend operations. By October, his army was nearing Yorktown on the Middle Peninsula of Virginia's tidewater region. Only miles from Jamestown, Cornwallis waited for ships to remove his troops to New York. He also awaited word on Clinton's army from New York that he hoped was protecting his exposed position. Although he had to contend with Wayne and Lafayette, he did not plan on having to confront another army from the North, perhaps one led by Washington. Nor could he account for the French, whom he believed were sitting in Rhode Island, waiting for a good opportunity to join the fight.

Washington at last had the moment he was waiting for. He scrapped his ideas for confronting Clinton and taking New York and instead made hasty plans with the French army to march down to Yorktown to initiate a siege. He also pleaded for French naval support to trap the British on the peninsula. Under normal circumstances, what he hoped for would not have been forthcoming. Yet at that moment the British navy was defending Gibraltar and preparing for a Spanish offensive in the Caribbean. The Spaniards had already taken West Florida. Jamaica could be next. The main fleet, while Cornwallis waited to be evacuated, had left to defend the Caribbean, the most important New World holdings the British possessed.[4]

Admiral François-Joseph de Grasse, the commander of the French fleet, had a window of time before he had to sail to the Caribbean to support the Spanish and seized the opportunity, deploying a line of ships in the Chesapeake Bay. The British could not hope for immediate evacuation. Moreover, French naval guns could be trained on their exposed positions. On cue, Washington arrived with American and French troops under the command of Jean-Baptiste Donatien de Vimeur, le compte de Rochambeau, an expert in siege operations. As Washington put it after planning with the French, "What may be in the Womb of fate is very uncertain," but he added, "we anticipate the Reduction of Ld Cornwallis with his Army."[5]

Cornwallis found his force of 7,000 with their backs to a sea dominated by the French fleet and surrounded by 17,000 American and French troops. Washington's soldiers dug in, and siege operations began. As Joseph Plumb Martin observed, "General Washington had struck a few blows with a pickaxe," so "that it might be said 'General Washington with this own hands first broke ground at the siege of Yorktown.'"[6] French and American troops first cleared the forward redoubts that the British held. Then day by day, instructed by French engineers, sappers dug a long trench parallel to the British position in the town where they could set their artillery. Within a week, they moved even closer, inflicting terrible damage on the British. A surgeon with Washington's army reported how cannonballs were "clearly visible in the form of a black ball in the day but in the night, they appear like fiery meteors with blazing tails, most beautifully brilliant, ascending majestically from the mortar to a certain altitude, and gradually descending to the spot where they are destined to execute their work of destruction."[7] Cornwallis knew it was only a matter of time before his command would be destroyed if a British fleet did not appear to relieve his position and Clinton's army did not arrive to lift the siege. A Hessian trapped in Yorktown beheld something akin to the apocalypse. "The besiegers have fired bombshells incessantly," he declared, "so that the entire assault resembles a bombardment. The greater part of the town lies in ashes." The besieged resorted to desperate measures. "All the artillery and baggage horses, for which there has no forage, were killed and dragged into the York River," he wrote. "Several days after their death these poor animals came back in heaps with the tide, nearly up to the sunken ships," he added. "It seemed as if they wanted to cry out against their murder after their death."[8] Cornwallis wisely surrendered.

On October 19, 1781, Washington expected to receive Cornwallis's sword. Cornwallis, however, did not appear, claiming to be taken ill. He asked one of his

Figure 7.1 John Trumbull, *Surrender of Cornwallis at Yorktown*, 1820. Architect of the Capitol.

aides, Brigadier General Charles O'Hara, to hand the sword over to his near equal, Comte Rochambeau. Appalled at the affront to Washington's honor, Rochambeau refused to accept Cornwallis's sword. This victory belonged to the long-suffering Americans. He directed O'Hara to give the sword to Washington. Washington would not take it. He ordered his subordinate, General Benjamin Lincoln, to accept it. Washington would not be outdone when it came to recognizing status.[9]

As the farce ended, a British military band may have played one of its own, a tune called "The World Turned Upside Down." If a band did not play it, or more likely beat out the tune on drums draped in black, it should have. On one level, the song celebrated what was called "the feast of fools," when common people stepped outside of their accustomed roles for a day and assumed the positions of author-ity in society. On such days, when assumed roles were inverted, jesters served as mayors, and harlots as ladies, or as the song went, "if ponies rode men and if grass ate the cows." "The World Turned Upside Down" was also the title of an English bal-lad published during the 1640s when Puritans were attempting to remake English society. The song protested the attempts of reformers such as Oliver Cromwell to strip away older rituals, such as the celebration of Christmas, as popish supersti-tions, suggesting that refashioning traditions could turn the world on its shoulder.[10] "The World Turned Upside Down" also had radical connotations and was associated with groups that had sprung up in England during its crisis of sovereignty in the seventeenth century. Groups like the Levellers, who hoped to level all social distinc-tions, were conspiring to turn the world they knew upside down.[11] The song, then, was a fitting end to the war in so many ways. It epitomized what had happened to American society over the course of the war. Common folk, indeed, had assumed positions of authority and taken up unaccustomed roles in the vacuum of sover-eignty. More to the point, Americans found themselves in a moment very much like that Englishmen and women had confronted in the seventeenth century, when men and women struggled to refashion sovereignty in a disordered society.

In an even more famous gesture, Washington later would metaphorically turn over his sword to Congress after the peace treaty with Britain was signed. With a trembling voice, he told Congress he would "retire from the great theatre of Action" before handing over his commission. In so doing, he was playing the part of—and was recognized as—Cincinnatus.[12] Like the Roman hero, who had left his plow to take up the sword, with the end of war Washington would refuse to be ensnared by the corrupting allure of power but would retire with honor to work on his farm. The image of the honorable Cincinnatus contrasted with the British Caesar that Washington had just defeated. By portraying Washington in this light, Americans were hoping they could escape their recent past, that unambiguous virtue could sus-tain a republic born from a war against a corrupt empire. Perhaps liberty could be theirs and they could avoid the anxious pitfalls that gripped all Britons in the 1760s who had fretted over balancing *libertas* and *imperium*.[13]

Understandably, this ritual of handing over the commission symbolizes Washington the founder, the man who through dint of his talent, honor, and ambition shaped the world around him. But in many ways, what happened at the surrender at Yorktown, when Washington struggled to maintain his status amid destruction and in a world askew from revolution and violence, reveals more of what was happening

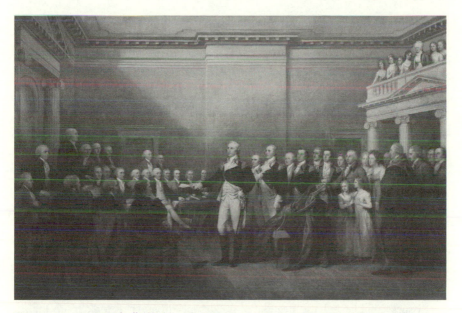

Figure 7.2 John Trumbull, *Washington Resigning his Commission*, 1824. Architect of the Capitol.

in America after hostilities with Britain had ended. In America, men and women had become actors while a new basis for authority had not emerged. States wrestled with debt and basic questions about the structure of governance. With peace, loomed questions about the disposition of the West. At least one-fifth of the population still remained loyal to the king. Merchants and workers in cities did not know what would become of trade. Planters faced difficult questions—both ideological and practical— about their labor force. And a disgruntled army had not disbanded. The year and a half between peace and a treaty revealed that Americans were engaged in disputes over foundational principles and economic and social interests.[14]

In other words, the war had ended, but not revolution. A form of sovereignty had been restored, but it did not provide order, certainty, and peace. It certainly seemed incapable of imprisoning the furies of revolution or turning the world right once more. Moreover, the shape that sovereignty would take had not been resolved. The British no longer ruled America. This was the only certainty of the period. Who or what would assume that mantle in America was anyone's guess. How and if that sovereignty would be manifest represented the period's great unresolved question.

The period after the war heard many voices of many actors struggling with many questions in a context marked by disorder. At the heart of it, all Americans confronted the issue of what political sovereignty meant in a world of self-sovereign people. Now an American government and its states confronted a problem the British had: imposing meaningful authority on such a diverse, large, and fractious set of societies that had been wracked by violence for a long period. In other words, they faced the prospect of completing revolution.

With the surrender of yet another army to the Americans, the war had not ended even though Lord North exclaimed on hearing the news "Oh God! It is all over."[15] Disaster at Yorktown had followed on the heels of losses in India, the Caribbean, and Florida. The British now faced the humiliating prospect of having to devote yet more resources to putting down a colonial rebellion while embroiled in a worldwide conflict with traditional foes France and Spain. British troops still fought in India against French-allied forces. They were defending Gibraltar and Minorca against Spanish assaults. And a French fleet still threatened the West Indies.[16] Meanwhile, Americans kept diplomatic teams in both Paris and Madrid, seeking loans, as they did in Amsterdam. In the face of such complex challenges, the ministry ordered operations in America ceased for the time being and asked the Americans to dispatch a diplomatic team to discuss terms for peace. John Adams, Benjamin Franklin, and John Jay, who had been already working for Congress in European capitals, led the mission to come up with a settlement. The treaty with France stipulated that the Americans would not sign a treaty with Britain so long as France was engaged in the war. France had similar obligations to Spain. Nonetheless, the Americans heading to France to negotiate with the British hoped to come to terms and then present such terms to their allies.[17]

Issues complicated the negotiations. For one thing, they took more than a year. For another, the commissioners did not always get along. Adams could not stand Franklin, and no one much liked Jay. More critically, neither France nor Spain wanted to see a powerful republic rising in America. "Independence" was a novel

Figure 7.3 Benjamin West, Unfinished painting of the *Treaty of Paris*, 1783. Winterthur Museum.

and troubling concept to diplomats schooled in older ways. Old powers had not treated rebels as equals. Spaniards still recalled their own experiences with civil war in the Netherlands a century earlier against republican forces. As colonizers them-selves, the thought of a war of independence freeing American colonies was not a prospect they relished. French officials, still teetering from debt after the global crisis of the Seven Years' War, feared the specter of republican ideologues in their own country. Calls of corruption now could be heard, especially in the wake of the American example. Even the Holy Roman Emperor, Joseph II, let his unease with American independence be known. All these interests and insecurities had to be managed within reigning alignments in Europe, making the case of independence a close-run thing.[18]

Moreover, the merry-go-round of British ministries did not stop with the end of hostilities, making it difficult for the British to come up with a consistent stance on what would become of America. Some balked at even considering granting Americans independence, most conspicuously King George III who could not even bring himself to use the word "independence" in instructing his negotiators. He used "separation" instead.[19] Almost fittingly, Benjamin West started but did not finish a painting of the treaty negotiators. The British commissioner, because of vanity or because of the sting of the loss of the colonies, refused to sit for West. The difficult and unclear nature of what was happening spoke to the anxieties of both sides.[20] Moreover, the uncertainty of who would or could form a government made prin-cipled stands difficult to sustain. Eventually, the Earl of Shelburne, the same man who had helped fashion the Proclamation Line, emerged from the political wilder-ness after Lord North's resignation, the untimely death of Lord Rockingham, and the resignation of a political rival. Although the king loathed the man because of his vanity, the stars were aligning for Shelburne, who was one of the few with enough of a political following on which to build a ministry. Fortunately for Shelburne, 1782 had been as bright for Britain's global war as 1781 was dark. In that year, the British had defeated the French, Dutch, and Spanish in campaigns in Asia, the Caribbean, and Gibraltar.[21]

Shelburne did not stand watch long, only 8 months, but his term came at a crit-ical time when the British had to decide if they would make independence a part of any settlement. They did, due in large part to Shelburne. Shelburne reasoned that lenient terms would entice Americans back into the British empire. Shelburne hoped Americans and Britons could be held together in some sort of "federal union," an arrangement Henry Laurens likened to "Platonic love," an ideal that Shelburne had "mumbled but could not define." He hoped that free trade would continue to con-tain the states into a British cultural and mercantile orbit.[22] They would, he believed, remain dependent on British manufactured goods, which would dull the zeal for independence. Shelburne hated the idea of independence, considering it "a dread-ful blow to the greatness of this country." He feared "the sun might be said to have set." At the same time, he played a key role in reforming the Irish constitutional relationship with Britain, also with an eye to luring Americans back into the fold.[23] Shelburne's calculations were not rooted in fears of American strength but in his desire to bring pressure to bear on France, Spain, and the Netherlands into making peace. His rationale allowed the two sides to come to terms. In this way, a Petty once again sketched the contours of empire, but in this case as one contracted. After his contribution and the failure of his ministry, Shelburne would be fobbed off with a peerage of higher status. He would not play a role in British politics again.[24]

Almost fittingly, John Singleton Copley was painting a portrait of Elkanah Watson, a prominent New England merchant and patriot, the evening after George III conceded the colonies to be independent states. In the background of the work, Copley had painted a ship with a British ensign. He changed it to American stars and stripes. As Watson recounted, Copley "with a bold hand, a master's touch, and I believe an American heart, attached to the ship the stars and stripes. This was, I imagine, the first American flag hoisted in old England."[25]

With independence accepted as nonnegotiable, the American diplomats in Paris negotiated with the British taking little heed of the concerns of their allies. And they won more than could have been expected. The treaty began with the premise, as Americans insisted, that the king now had recognized independence. The land north of the Floridas as far west as the Mississippi River and below the present border between the United States and Canada belonged to the Americans. For joining the war, Spain regained the Floridas, which they had lost in the Seven Years' War. The newly recognized sovereign state did not have complete authority over its own territory. The British would not compromise on some issues. They wanted to

Figure 7.4 John Singleton Copley, *Elkanah Watson*, 1782. Princeton University Art Museum.

protect the assets of loyalists who had fled because of fear and intimidation. They were loath to forgive prewar debts, especially those of Virginia planters. Until the Americans paid what they owed, the British would not leave their frontier outposts. Nonetheless, neither side wanted to recommence hostilities. Americans then had little choice but accept the fact that the British would not relinquish their forts on lands they handed over to the Americans.[26]

The war had taken its toll. In May 1783, about a year and a half after hostilities had ended, no one knew for certain the shape of things to come. A formal peace treaty had not been concluded, though commissioners from Britain and America were working on one. British troops still manned forts and occupied some cities such as New York. Violent episodes still occurred. In October 1782, for example, loyalists from southern New Jersey killed a number of patriots asleep on a beach

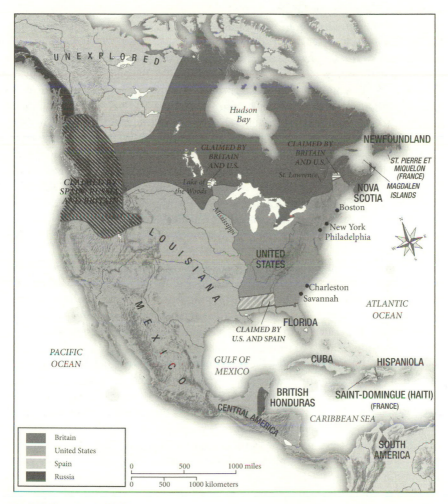

Map 7.1 America in 1783.

after they had captured a British vessel that had run aground near Barnegat on Long Beach Island. Frontier violence also continued.

Nevertheless, the Americans had some things in their favor as they struggled to restore order. For one thing, the military and loyalists, each of whom could have been the most viable candidates in contesting either the liberating aspects of revolution or American independence, did not preach counterrevolution. The reasons why hinged on contingent factors and broader processes. Averting a military counterrevolution was not a foregone conclusion in the early 1780s. American troops, though many had left to go home, also waited for a formal declaration of peace. And as they waited, hoping to be paid for their troubles, they grew angry. American soldiers had grumbled during the war. Now their officers joined them. These men believed they had made substantial sacrifices for the American cause. Many had vacillated. Many had flirted with or embraced loyalism. Not these. The officers who served in the army argued that they, more than most, had personified virtue. And they kept an often unruly rank and file in check.

To celebrate their roles and status, officers had banded together to create the Order of Cincinnati. After the war, they hoped, as the mythical Cincinnatus had, to trade in their swords for plowshares. They would, it was assumed, assume positions of leadership in the new society that they had helped create through virtuous sacrifice. On May 13, 1783, a number of "the officers of the American Army" swore to "associate, constitute and combine themselves into one SOCIETY OF FRIENDS, to endure as long as they shall endure, or any of their eldest male posterity." In doing so, they hoped "TO PRESERVE INVIOLATE THOSE EXALTED RIGHTS AND LIBERTIES OF HUMAN NATURE, FOR WHICH THEY HAVE FOUGHT AND BLED," and "TO PROMOTE AND CHERISH, BETWEEN THE RESPECTIVE STATES, THAT UNION AND NATIONAL HONOR SO ESSENTIALLY NECESSARY TO THEIR HAPPINESS, AND THE FUTURE DIGNITY OF THE AMERICAN EMPIRE."[27] In the days after warfare had ceased, Americans had created all sorts of societies, many of which were to be used to push for a revolution settlement to their liking. The officers were engaged in the same sort of struggle.

No one more enthusiastically supported the idea than George Washington. Washington too felt aggrieved. He had spent some of the best years of his life in service. He had won the war with inferior troops, mass desertions, mutinies, little pay, few supplies, and fleeting moral support. The Order of the Cincinnati, for him, represented a brotherhood of sacrifice, so much so that he agreed to become its first president.[28]

Some of his officers, however, went further than Washington was willing to go—Horatio Gates for one. Gates, the hero of Saratoga and the goat of Camden, led a group of young, tight-knit officers upset with their lot and the state of the union. The officers, now holed up in a barracks in Newburgh, about 50 miles north of occupied Manhattan, were beginning to believe that only they could restore order. After all, they embraced the conceit that only they possessed the requisite virtue for the job. In December 1782, they had sent a petition to Congress. When their requests were not heeded, they began plotting.[29] Some proposed mutiny; others may have been planning a coup d'état.

Along with the Superintendent of Finance Robert Morris and his able assistant Gouverneur Morris, one of Washington's chief aides named Alexander Hamilton hoped to use the army's grievances as leverage to press for a government that was more efficacious. Hamilton epitomized the self-made man. Born the illegitimate son of a Scottish merchant, Hamilton had left the West Indies of his childhood for the mainland colonies in the years before the War of Independence. Seen as a brilliant young man, he attached himself to patronage networks in New York. He trained himself as a lawyer and attended King's College in the city. When the war broke out, he supported the patriot cause and caught the attention of Washington, who kept him at his side throughout much of the conflict. Now he hoped to use his dissatisfaction and that of his fellow officers to push for order.

Hamilton and some of his fellow officers believed that the civilian government in charge was not up to the difficult task it faced. The Congress had not been able to impose order on society. The failure to pay the army was a symbol of the government's impotence. In March 1783, rumors floated that the officers in Newburgh were planning a coup, one that they argued was necessary for the success of revolution and the gaining of independence. Joseph Jones, a congressman from Virginia, wrote Washington that "reports are freely circulated here, that there are dangerous combinations in the army; and within a few days past it has been said, that they are about to declare that they will not disband until their demands are complied with." He regarded their designs as "ambitious."

Nearly 8 years to the day that the British had evacuated Boston, Washington arrived at Newburgh to address his officers and the rumor. He pleaded with the men with whom he had served to be patient with Congress. He understood their frustrations, but it was critical that they not take the step some were proposing. Washington believed that with due time their voices would be heard, that they would take their appointed places in the new society. But they must wait and act with honor. Their actions, he told them, could drench a precarious nation in renewed violence, agreeing with their goals but not with their methods of achieving them. The war, Washington knew, "has placed her in the chair of independency," but peace did not bring expected blessings. Did they find "a country willing to redress your wrongs, cherish your worth and reward your services, a country courting your return to private life, with tears of gratitude and smiles of admiration, longing to divide with you that independency which your gallantry has given and those riches which your wounds have preserved?" Or did they live in "a country that tramples upon your rights, disdains your cries and insults your distress?"[30] Washington's sacrifices had not been recognized either. What especially galled Washington was that he did not receive the deference he had expected. In many ways, he was out of step with what had happened in America in the years of the war. He supposed that his status as commander entitled him to respect. It did not. Even the officers, who expected the same deference from civilians, would not accord it to Washington.

Stunned, he delivered perhaps his most dramatic gesture. After addressing the troops by speaking to their frustrations, Washington reached into his pocket for the letter from Jones that he planned to read to his officers. He then opened the letter and fumbled for something in his pocket. He produced a pair of reading glasses. Gasps must have been audible. To win their support Washington appealed to their sympathy. This man who personified the masculine virtues of self-control and resolve revealed his vulnerabilities, and in putting on the glasses he was taking off a mask. He said that he "had grown gray in their service, and now found himself growing blind." He had not only sacrificed his health, reputation, and fortune for the cause, but also his eyesight. The performance helped forestall a coup. It did so because he appealed not to practicalities but to that sense of sacrifice that also was the wellspring of the officers' grievances.

In loyalism, the United States confronted an even graver threat to securing order. Throughout the French Revolution, "aristocrats" proved an ever-present threat to revolutionary principles, and the specter of aristocracy underscored the unending uncertainty that defined the nation for some time. The closest America came to such a group had left. Indeed, about 80,000 loyal Americans departed the United States, many with the British withdrawal. This number included 15,000 slaves and former slaves, as well as Indians, such as Mohawks. Benjamin West captured the diversity of the loyal exodus in the background of his portrait of J. E. Wilmot, a man who tried to ensure that loyalists were fairly compensated.[31] Although Americans were obligated under the terms of the Treaty of Paris to make some reparations to loyalists, including giving them a year to purchase property confiscated by other Americans during the war, most states ignored such claims. The trauma suffered by many Americans during the war, during which much suffering was meted out by Americans on Americans, would not allow it. As British Americans, those who remained loyal to the Crown had choices. Some would return to America, but they would be reintegrated with time, even in Boston. Few in number, they did not pose a threat to the fledgling state. For most, emigration seemed a better option.

Figure 7.5 Benjamin West, *Portrait of Wilmot, Loyalist Commissioner*, 1812. Yale Center for British Art.

The writing of the treaty had been on the wall for some time, and as rumors of a permanent peace reached America, loyalists prepared to leave. In 1782, some began streaming out of Savannah, a center of loyalism after the British occupied the city. These refugees headed to other loyalist centers, such as Charleston, Jamaica, or East Florida, yet another stronghold. Their sojourn was heart-rending. As one put it, "the distress and misery brought on His Majesty's Loyal Subjects here, you cannot conceive." Regarded as "traitors" by neighbors, they had little choice but to leave their homes. However, with the signing of the treaty and the British evacuation of Charleston and the surrender of East Florida to the Spanish, these people had to move once more. "The war never occasioned half the distress," wrote a migrant leaving East Florida named Elizabeth Johnson, "which this peace has to the unfortunate Loyalists." The Bahamas became the choice destination. Generally, those loyalists from the South headed to England if they could afford it, or to the British Caribbean if they could not.[32]

From the North, most would move to what remained of British North America, including Quebec. In early 1783, New York loyalists sent agents to Nova Scotia to find a settlement. None other than Brook Watson, the same Watson immortalized by Copley, served as commissary-general of the association overseeing the evacuation to Nova Scotia and supplying migrants with provisions for the journey.[33] In all, at least 38,000 resettled in what remained of British North America after the Treaty of Paris was signed. With the potential influx of large numbers of refugees, British officials had carved the new province of New Brunswick from Nova Scotia. Eventually Upper Canada would be hived off from Quebec, as the creation of new provinces doubled the number of patronage and government positions available. Loyalist Americans, then, formed a majority of men and women living just north of an uncertainly drawn border. No doubt, the existence of two Americas in close proximity, one loyal and one republican, made for a tense border in North America, a problem that would lead to war a generation later. But in the immediate aftermath of the War of Independence, Canada provided a safety valve for potential dissent.[34] Eventually, some would venture to Africa and India, making their diaspora global in scale.[35]

Nearly 40,000 loyalists left New York alone. Since Washington had lost the city in 1776, it had remained a British bastion throughout the war. Now in 1783, the army of occupation and those loyal to the Crown made ready to sail, and November 25 was set for evacuation day. With the exception of Mrs. May bloodying the nose of a redcoat who tried to erect a royal ensign in the city, the evacuation proved uneventful. As the British left, Washington entered. Along with the governor of New York, he was feted in one tavern after another. As he reached the Bowling Green, at the exact spot where men and women had torn down the statue of George III in 1776, the crowd saw that a British soldier had left a parting gift: a union jack affixed to a greased pole. A young sailor with cleats scampered up and pulled it down, to the rapturous applause of those assembled. Although the king had been torn from his perch in 1776, it would take 7 more years to ensure that the British would not be sovereign in New York. A few days later, Washington met with his officers in Fraunces Tavern not far from the Bowling Green, and there bid them adieu before taking a barge across the Hudson to Paulus Hook. New York was now American.[36]

Among those leaving the newly liberated United States was Thomas Peters. He too sailed to Nova Scotia, having boarded a ship on New York's South Street. Like the other loyalists, Peters hoped to find peace in Nova Scotia. Instead, he clung to life on the margins, as did other black refugees. Here they faced cold winters and the sometimes racist attitudes of their loyalist neighbors, many of whom, after all, had fled southern colonies and some of whom had owned slaves. But Peters's extraordinary story did not end here. He helped create a network of abolitionists and freed slaves that spanned the ocean, and he traveled to London to lobby for the plight of freed slaves. Here Peters argued that freedmen should be given the chance to return to Africa. Some thought that only repatriation, as it was called, could bring an end to slavery in America, as removing blacks, or so it was thought, would avert racial conflict and ease the process. In other words, the cost of freedom would be born on the backs of blacks. Peters, however, saw things a bit differently. Repatriation for him represented a dream. He had, after all, been taken captive in Africa. It was home to him. Through his efforts, the British government would found the colony and later nation of Sierra Leone. Peters was one of the first to be repatriated. So ended an extraordinary American odyssey.[37]

In many ways, the flight of the loyalists and the end of the war produced ideal conditions for a return to order. The War of Independence simplified revolution. It had channeled tensions. The legacy of the war would also narrow the possibilities of debate. With the supporters of the Crown gone—for the moment at least—loyalism as an animating ideology, never mind as the basis of sovereignty, died. Debate over what sovereignty would look like, its very foundations, and the nature of the civil society that sustained it would take place within the discourse of patriotism. In America in 1783, to champion any viable position meant referring to the War of Independence and what that war now meant in defining one as American. Conflict did not end. Rather, conflict stayed within certain bounds, constraining the terms of negotiation. Americans would descend into debates that looked a great deal like seventeenth-century England's struggles, with those who were in power—the so-called Court party—vying for control of the reins of power with those outside the government, the Country party.[38] In fact, the memory of shared violence and the flight of the counterrevolutionaries did not leave many options to those out of power or to the disaffected. Legitimacy stemmed from sacrifice in the war, uniting even those opposed to one another. Because of the broad consensus that set the limits of legitimate debate, it appeared that revolutionary uncertainty was bound to end soon.

Nothing could have been further from the truth. The competition to remake the basis of authority still continued. As the Philadelphia physician Benjamin Rush observed, "There is nothing more common, than to confound the terms of American Revolution with those of the late America war." One was not the other. "The American war is over," he reasoned, "but this is far from being the case with the American revolution." Rush believed that revolution had not yet achieved its ends.[39] Yet more to the point, it had not completed its course. Uncertainty still reigned. In fact, America in 1783 looked a great deal like British North America in 1763. Eerily, Americans would have to struggle with many of the same tensions that British officials had to negotiate after the Seven Years' War. National euphoria over winning a war against a now mythic foe was tempered by realities that made authority difficult to construct. Debt proved an intractable issue, as did conceptions of the form that sovereignty should take, and where it should be vested. Moreover, the West—and how to govern it—presented thorny problems of its own. The not-so-new problems were complicated by two other issues: unlike the British in 1763, Americans had no workable blueprints of power; and in addition, they had to contain the disorder and uncertainty of revolution, something that did not challenge British rule in America in 1763.

In other words, Americans faced daunting tasks in reestablishing authority as they asserted sovereignty. None loomed larger than debt. During the war, Congress churned out reams of Continental scrip. By April 1781, $150 Continental had dropped to $1 in specie. By the end of the year, the scrip had depreciated to 500 to 1. This obligation was written off to the tune of $226,000,000. Benjamin Franklin justified the write-off of the currency as it served as a de facto tax on all Americans for funding the war. The currency conundrum reflected the impotence of the government to prop up the nation's finances. The government funded debt with more debt, relying, for instance on loans from the French and the Dutch to service debt and keep the government functioning. In 1781, Congress gave the job of bringing financial stability to Robert Morris. As head of the Department of Finance, Morris wanted to consolidate all the nation's debt to rationalize its finances. By his reckoning, the central government had accrued debts of more than $27,000,000, which had to be repaid. The United States owed this amount to the states and to soldiers, as IOUs and as bonds. In addition, at the end of the war, Congress owed millions to France and other nations. Morris wanted to fund the debt with taxes on lands and polls and through an excise. He also hoped the states would allow Congress to erect a tariff on imported goods, as well as create a Bank of North America to loan money to the government on a short-term basis. Most critically, Morris argued that the national government had to assume as much debt as possible in order to make the government solvent. Chaos would follow any other plan.

His plans came to naught. Congress needed the states to cooperate by sending tax revenues to the national government, which they would not do. The states also struggled with debt. Virginia owed £4,250,000 and Massachusetts owed £1,500,000. Fifty to ninety percent of state revenues went to servicing debt. As the states refused to answer Morris's call, the national government balked at paying back interest to international creditors. In addition, as each of the states confronted the specter of spiraling debt as well, they, in turn, transformed obligations into state notes. These notes were also losing value. Currency finance, as it was called, repaid debt with further obligations. Many from the states believed that—as sovereign entities—they were supposed to assume the debt of the Congress, not the other way around.

And each state handled debt differently, making a coherent policy impossible. In Massachusetts, for instance, citizens were obligated to pay high taxes in specie. Debtors had little relief with such a deflationary policy. Virginians offered soldiers land to the West, land that some in Congress claimed it should not be entitled to. Rhode Island stood on the side of debtors, demanding that creditors accept the state currency at face value even though it had depreciated. If the states assumed the national debt in piece-meal, helter-skelter fashion, finances would be in a further shambles. How or if the united or disunited states would manage the debt crisis, no one knew for certain. But it was becoming clear that older approaches, such as state-sponsored currency finance, were not up to the task. Congress negotiated with the Dutch to finance the many layers of debt, but in reality each government of the newly liberated nation was facing bankruptcy.[40] Inflation only heightened worries.

The postwar recession looked more like a great depression. The war had disrupted nearly every sector of the economy. Production slowed in every state. Naval operations halted fishing. The fur trade stagnated. Troops marching through countryside and pillaging destroyed farming. And men going off to fight hampered the labor supply. Some domestic industries were stimulated by the war. Clothing and munitions had to be made, and armies had to be fed. But at war's end, these gains were offset by contraction. Trade had withered, as old networks fell apart. Americans hoped to reprise the lucrative trade with the sugar islands of the Caribbean, but the British boxed Americans out of these former markets. Despite howls of protest from planters on the sugar islands, the government would not relent. The most significant prewar trade Americans had was effectively dead. The trade with Britain itself, of course, stalled in the years immediately after the war had been won. That changed quickly as British merchants were anxious to reestablish trade with America. Such trade may have enriched some merchants and relieved pent-up demand but did not stimulate the economy, which by some estimates fell 46% between the beginning of the war and 1790. The American economy was still a colonial enterprise. But the united states were no longer colonies.[41]

As demands for consumer goods grew again after the war ended, no one could figure a way to fulfill these demands, that is, if people even had money. Feeling the severe pinch, creditors tried to collect from men and women, using the power of the states to do so. Debtors' prison and foreclosure seemed distinct possibilities for some. For their part, common men and women clamored for tax relief, claiming their sacrifice and God-given rights as justification. They did not fight alone. Those who styled themselves entrepreneurs wanted a looser money supply. Paper money would help risk-takers and debtors. Creditors, who opposed such schemes, saw debtors as deserving their fate and even heretical. Some saw those protesting tax measures as levellers, and their demands demonstrated the implications of the "excesses of democracy" that threatened any sort of search for order. Both sides argued that the other had made a fetish of luxurious living. Each group used the press, the pulpit, and political institutions to make their claims heard. In some regions, these fights reached a fevered pitch and dominated local political debate.[42] To make matters worse as far as elites were concerned, returning soldiers had difficulty finding work. They too soon joined the chorus seeking relief.

The end of the war saw old economic tensions reemerge in new guises. In Maine, which had been wracked by conflict between great proprietors and people who hoped to achieve competency, the war had collapsed these disputes within the discourse of republicanism. The common folk styled themselves "liberty men," who were fighting for their status and American rights. During the war, they had cast the land magnates as Tories. After the war, many of these same magnates, who had in fact supported the American cause, attempted to claim the land they had held under British rule and to marginalize those who hoped the war would change landholding patterns. A similar dynamic gripped Massachusetts. The wealthy believed that the end of the war would usher in a period of peace that would insure they could collect debts and assume positions of authority once more. With debt now a common problem, the old tensions took on a new urgency. In fact, debt became an even larger issue for some. For those who owed prewar money to British creditors, peace did not bring relief. Some creditors, who would not accept Continental scrip as money, found agents in the states to prosecute debtors. State and local courts complied.[43]

As in the past, land in the West tempted those who struggled with debt. As speculators lined up to claim lands, some officials hoped the West would become a land bank to pay back soldiers for their service and so ease fiscal pressure. But who owned the West? The federal government did not. States used colonial charters from the seventeenth century, as well as "conquests" made during the war to stake their claims to the West. The war, in fact, unleashed unbridled competition for areas over the mountains. Virginia claimed Kentucky and the regions north and west of the Ohio River to the boundary with Canada and the Mississippi River through conquest and charter right. Illinois, taken by Clark, was included in these claims. Pennsylvanians wanted a part on the Great Lakes and now claimed Pittsburgh. New Yorkers had their eyes on lands west of New Hampshire. Connecticut officials argued that their claims to the west could leapfrog New York and Pennsylvania. The region around Lake Erie in the Ohio country, they argued, belonged to them. And they would not relinquish what they believed to be their rights to northeastern Pennsylvania. Massachusetts similarly vied for a section of Ohio. North Carolinians wanted to create a new state of their own on their western border, named Franklin. Landlocked states such as Maryland and New Jersey added to the mess by doing what they could to stymie the overlapping landgrabs of the other states. Colonies had nearly gone to war with each other over boundaries earlier in the eighteenth century. With the stakes now higher because of debt, similar conflict seemed a distinct possibility.[44]

To complicate matters, the British had not relinquished their forts in the West. Indians threatened violence if they attempted to turn forts over to the Americans. Moreover, the weakness of the new republic—and its dim prospects for a bright future—convinced the British that they had to stay for the security of the border. They promised to stay in them so long as the complaints of loyalists and creditors went unheeded. This meant that to grasp the West, state officials had to pay off loyalists first, not a particularly viable political option in the wake of the war and in the midst of a financial crisis. In the West, sovereignty was still uncertain even as pressures grew in the East to exploit the vast region.[45]

Governments had no viable means to adjudicate such disputes. Americans now faced the daunting task of recasting authority within institutions that had evolved from colonial precursors and had been created either to bring an old order down, such as committees and conventions, or to fight a continental war, such as Congress. The frame of government—the Articles of Confederation—had been drawn up during the war to more or less legally endorse what the Congress had been doing to prosecute the war and to maintain order in difficult circumstances. Although representatives of the Congress did not ratify the Articles until the war was nearly over, they had emerged as a formal projection of authority from what had been a quasi-sovereign institution. Simply put, the men of Congress did not know what form sovereignty should take, nor did they debate the meanings of federalism, or how power should be allocated. The states were, after all, "states," that is, through history and practice they had developed during the colonial period as autonomous units, yoked to the center but not to each other. "Each state," the Articles stated, "retains its sovereignty, freedom, and independence, and every power, jurisdiction, and right, which is not by this Confederation expressly delegated to the United States, in Congress assembled." Confederation was, therefore, an expedient, and the government that emerged from it was provisional in the practical sense of the word. Congress struggled throughout with confusion and external pressures. Although all had lived with its limitations through the war years, few had taken the trouble to discuss the implications of a confederated sovereignty. The exigencies of war, or the forces that created a confederation, did not encourage Americans to articulate where the ultimate powers of government should lie. Moreover, the weakness of government powers, in general, may have been all that stood between the states and internecine warfare. In this regard, impotence had its advantages.[46]

The Articles vested just enough sovereign power in the states to ensure that they could not function as sovereign entities. The right to tax, for instance, was reserved to the states, and each had its own method of determining taxes. If Massachusetts had to pay taxes on land, which were inflated relative to the rest of America, its citizens would pay an exorbitant amount of tax. If population determined taxation, then states like Virginia were bound to pay a larger amount. Moreover, if a state had taken care of its debt, its citizens proved none too happy about helping finance the debt of another state. The executive lacked any real power. Each state delegation had one vote, and majorities were needed to pass simple measures. More far-reaching decisions required a super-majority, and any amendment to the Articles required unanimity. Tiny Rhode Island, therefore, had the same power as the other states and could scuttle any plan. By the end of the war, as the Articles took effect, Congress had ceased to be a significant voice in governance. The "United States" were—not was— vested with authority, but given the nature of the many pressures they faced, had little reasonable hope of addressing the problems of the period. Fittingly, as Barbary pirates initiated a campaign assaulting American shipping and capturing seamen in far-off seas after the War of Independence, no force could stop them.[47]

The pressures and problems Americans faced in the 1780s stemmed from the process of prosecuting a war. Armies had moved through town and country. Soldiers had to return home. Trade had stagnated. And debts—personal and public—had grown. Institutions created to prosecute the war now had to be adapted to peacetime rule in a still uncertain environment. Other issues that had haunted the colonies had not been resolved by war. Old disputes, specifically over land, had not vanished, either between groups or between states. But Americans also had to address tensions that proved more difficult to comprehend. Over the course of the war, and even before as British authority came tumbling down, men and women had assumed self-sovereign roles. As a South Carolina physician and historian David Ramsey put it, the war years had transformed Americans "from subjects to citizens." Ramsay saw the difference as "immense." "Subjects," he argued, "look up to the master, but citizens are so far equal, that none have hereditary rights superior to others."[48] As social constraints came down along with established order, all faced new barriers but new opportunities. These pressures from below energized people and complemented the ideological content of the revolution. The languages of seventeenth-century England that Americans used to make sense of their plight—languages themselves constructed in a period of profound social and political instability—allowed many Americans to imagine their status in new ways. For the first time, many who had lived on society's margins saw new possibilities for liberation. And they had acted upon it. But the cacophony of voices, especially in the difficult postwar years, was not conducive to order.

In fact, voices turned the old order upside down. With the destruction of royal and local authority, men and women began to imagine their status in society less in terms of vertical relationships and more in terms of horizontal relationships. In other words, they did not so much look up and down at others around them in a status-conscious way to figure their position in society; instead, they increasingly looked to others in similar positions to reckon how they should conceive of themselves.[49] With the stresses to older understandings of status and authority, some women thought of themselves as members of a group. Slaves began to speak of their plight in the context of all other African Americans. Dragging Canoe certainly voiced a similar sensibility when it came to Indians. Two things were at work. First, popular sovereignty did not amount to an idea that fell from on high or had to be grasped from the past. It reflected what was happening on the ground as men and women made sense of their lives in the crucible of revolution. Second, as older deferential ideas melted down, and as Americans struggled with disorder for a long period, they began to think of their interests and those who shared such interests. Ideas that questioned deferential attitudes and called for a common notion of virtue also gave men and women a means to articulate their new sense of status and belonging.[50]

And with good reason many showed no signs of returning to their older roles. Indeed, in the years immediately after the war, some women began questioning what role women should have in the republic, arguing that women could not be considered intrinsically inferior to men.[51] The Quaker Susanna Wright wrote:

> Reason rules, in every one, the same
> No Right, has Man, his Equal to controul
> Since, all agree, There is no Sex in soul

Women, Wright suggested, were equal to men in the eyes of God; they also equaled men in rational capacities. Women could claim the mantle of the revolution. They had struggled and they had sacrificed. Many had taken up hitherto restricted roles, serving as deputy husbands as men were off fighting. They had, given the fact that the war thrust many Americans back on a subsistence footing, wielded substantial power. As the war ended, their valued roles still entitled them to a special status.

A few began to press for their rights as women. Prominent women, who had served the American cause in the war, argued that, if taught, women could reject vanity and luxury. The revolutionary experience had served as a classroom of virtue. Such an education had to continue if women were to achieve substantive results from their years of sacrifice. Throughout the new nation, boarding schools and academies opened for the education of young women. The curriculum, which differed little from what young men learned, catered to the wealthier sort who now had the leisure time to attend such schools. And they were deemed critical to the republican experiment. As the physician Benjamin Rush put it, "The equal share that every citizen has in the liberty and possible share he may have in the government of our country makes it necessary that our ladies should be qualified to a certain degree." Indeed, within a short period after the war, women were generally regarded as the protectors of republican virtue. For Rush, women had to be charged with "instructing their sons in the principles of liberty and government." They had the responsibility for raising the next generation that would be untainted by monarchical ideas and the trappings of aristocratic privilege. Later, women would play similar roles as the midwives to capitalist values in the home; but in the aftermath of the war, they were to serve as republican mothers. Speakers went to great lengths to extol the distinctive and essential characteristics of women. Only they, not men, could ensure that education in the home kept the republican flame alive. Women, therefore, had a more critical role to play in the life of American society.

Instead of being thrust back into familiar and often invisible roles, the revolution placed women on a pedestal. And women were complicit with this. Guarding the republic could consign women to roles outside the domains men dominated, especially those of public life. Even the most vocal proponents of women's education did not imagine that the position of men in the economy, in society, or in public life would be altered. They did not seek to expand the economic choices of women or their political roles. The novelist, playwright, and education advocate Susanna Rowson urged America's men to "Teach us to prize the power of intellect," but in so doing, each would gain "an affectionate and faithful wife." Moreover, few women championed the enlightened views of Wright, Rowson, or Rush. After the war, most women returned to the lives they had known before. For women in towns and farms, there was work to be done, and marriage and family remained the center of their lives as they had been before. For the wealthy, homespun gave way to the latest fashions, as they imported clothes from abroad as their mothers had in the 1750s.

For blacks, there would be little ambiguity. What happened at Yorktown is a case in point. As the British marched north toward Virginia in 1781, runaway slaves swelled their ranks, including the 3,000 African Americans among the besieged at Yorktown. Here, the British put these men to work on the earthworks around their position, and blacks did much of the labor to prepare for a siege. The British, however, did not repay such loyalty. When they surrendered, the British reneged on their earlier promises. Just days before capitulation, Cornwallis sent away a large number of blacks, many suffering from smallpox, to fend for themselves. Most of the newly freed were abandoned in Virginia. Most wandered in the maelstrom of war and found their way back to whence they had come. Joseph Plumb Martin "saw in the woods herds of Negroes which Lord Cornwallis (after he had inveigled them from their proprietors) in love and pity to them, had turned adrift." From the British they received "smallpox for their bounty and starvation and death for their wages."[52] Yorktown meant more suffering and uncertainty. "One could not go ten steps," a witness recounted, "without meeting the wounded and dying, destitute negroes abandoned to their fate, and corpse after corpse on every hand."[53] A Hessian commander realized the injustice of refusing to stand by the former slaves. "We drove back to the

Figure 7.6 John Singleton Copley, *Death of Major Peirson*, 1782–1784. Tate Gallery, London.

enemy all of our black friends whom we had taken along to despoil the countryside," he wrote with shame. "We had used them to good advantage and set them free," as he put it, "and now, with fear and trembling they had to face the reward of their cruel masters."[54] One of the first Americans to enter the besieged town reported "an immense number of Negroes have died in the most miserable manner at York."[55] The heady days of the Ethiopian Regiment had long since gone.

A painting from the period is a case in point. In 1784, John Singleton Copley completed *The Death of Major Peirson*, which commemorated a battle fought between the British and the French in the Channel Islands after the War of Independence became a world war for Britain with the French alliance. Copley based the scene on one drawn earlier by his half-brother, Henry Pelham, who as a boy had posed with the squirrel. Pelham had made an engraving of the Boston Massacre, one that Paul Revere allegedly pilfered and made famous. The composition of the painting gestured to West's *Death of General Wolfe*, not only in subject but also in the tripartite division of the piece. The painting is an allegory for revolution. To the right, with the boy looking directly at the viewer, flee those terrified and uprooted by the state of war. If refugees and loyalists animate the right, military strength and order define the left. For only authority will reform the center. Here the hero dies, but not in vain. In the painting, Copley conspicuously placed what is popularly believed to be a member of the Royal Ethiopians. In doing so, Copley suggests that the soldier avenged the death of his beloved major. Hierarchies, Copley suggests, may have been inverted by the state of war, but the idea of loyalty restored order. In fact, no such soldier ever fought in the battle. A servant of one of the British officers may have been present,

Figure 7.7 Henry Pelham, *Boston Massacre*, 1770. Courtesy, American Antiquarian Society.

but he did not serve with the Royal Ethiopians and he did not shoot the Frenchman who killed Peirson.[56] The inclusion of the soldier in the image is telling in two ways. First, Copley's hope of the "loyal servant" fighting for empire and hierarchy was dead and little more than a nostalgic touch. Second, and more critically, although promised freedom since the days of Lord Dunmore, few former slaves would ever enjoy it. The image made for better propaganda than truth did. The British did not distinguish themselves in liberating slaves, even if they did an immensely better job than the Americans did.

War may have offered opportunities for some individuals to assert their rights to freedom, but it also strengthened the institution of slavery. Although those at Yorktown, of course, comprised a tiny fraction of all slaves and most had stayed right where they had been, the war had compromised planter power. In the upper South, the tumult of war had further disrupted an already poor plantation economy. But war did not end slavery; if anything, the war strengthened it, as planters pruned the system. Planters retooled, focusing even more intensely on wheat production. Although many slaves had run away during the war, the number of slaves actually increased during the war years through natural increase. Virginia, for example, had a little over 200,000 slaves at the beginning of the war and 236,000 at the end of it. If anything, planters had a surplus of labor. This fact, in part, explains why some slaves were manumitted after the war. Maryland's character changed in a funda-mental way through the number of slaves who gained their freedom after the war. Some were granted their freedom, some toiled as "term slaves," that is they would work for a while until they were granted their freedom, and others purchased it. Realities gave some the incentive to make good on the revolutionary ideal of liberty. So a number of blacks gained their freedom, but at the same time, many more were still slaves. Virginia's character did not change. Planters fiddled with the system, but with an eye to sustaining it. The slave system survived the war in the upper South.[57]

In the lower South, the situation proved even direr for slaves. Before the war, planters had relied on the state, and their ability to manipulate it, to maintain con-trol of their societies. Even though provisional and transitional government under committees had allowed them to patrol city and countryside to stem the possibilities of slave insurrection, their grip on the South appeared tenuous and their labor force in shambles. The number of slaves in Georgia, for instance, dropped from 15,000 to 5,000. Those who still lived in Georgia or the Carolinas found themselves in des-perate straits after the British left. Slaves who had run away roamed the country-side as bandits or had joined maroon colonies. Some tried to flee North. Planters faced a dual challenge of reestablishing control after the civil war conditions and of redeploying their labor force to save the economy. Although the indigo trade was destroyed by the war, never to return, in addition to rice, planters in South Carolina and Georgia turned to cotton as their new staple crop, for which they would need a reliable labor force. Elites, who offered no halfway measures of freedom and as a rule did not manumit, could not envision a world without slavery. Determined that these would still operate as slave societies, planters would think about turning else-where for their slaves, as they would try to use the power of the state, both local and national, to bring order to their societies.[58]

The postwar period, in fact, promised a strengthening of the slave system for most as it ushered in freedom for some. In the context of a failing economy, in which a reliable labor force proved more critical than ever and with debt a nagging prob-lem, human capital proved one of the few commodities planters could rely on. The story of Thomas Peters is dramatic but atypical. All may have dreamed of freedom; some may have grasped at it; but for most, nothing good came of the war. Since few blacks fought for the American cause—with good reason—the vast majority could not cite revolutionary sacrifice as a rationale for freedom.

Nonetheless, in the North, because of the war, slavery would come to an end. Some states did away with it immediately. From its inception, for instance, the state of Vermont outlawed slavery. Massachusetts did so immediately through court order. Others like New York, New Jersey, and Pennsylvania passed laws for gradual emancipation. The states in the North where slavery was most entrenched—say, New York—allowed for a slower process.[59] Bonded labor in general fell out of favor after the war. The ideology of rights had something to do with it. More critically, the successive dislocations of the Seven Years' War, the crisis leading to revolution, and the war had torn at the foundations of the bonded labor system. With surplus labor after the war, masters had little incentive to reinstitute artisanal cultural norms. Slavery was part and parcel of this labor regime. Those places where slavery mattered least— such as Vermont with only a small handful of African Americans—outlawed the system immediately. In cities like New York, freedmen transitioned to wage labor.[60] Slavery did not lie at the heart of the political or economic system in the northern states, and with the shocks of war, it mattered even less. Where it mattered most, it survived and even thrived.

Slavery, of course, contradicted many of the stated aims of the revolution's rhetoric. The appeal for emancipation in the North was led by those who championed the liberating discourse of the revolution. While earlier abolitionists relied on religious grounds to argue for emancipation, after the war, republicanism formed the basis of such arguments. Yet, these same sorts of arguments could be used to keep blacks in fetters. Some, in other words, found a way of getting around the ideas that all people were created equal. To make room for such an idea, planters began to reject older patriarchal assumptions of authority and deference that had buttressed the institution of slavery in the colonial period but were now discredited by the discourse and process of revolution.[61] Southerners, unsurprisingly, proved adept at finding new justifications for slavery, none more so than Thomas Jefferson. Most famously, Jefferson contended that blacks did not have the wherewithal to enjoy their freedom. He did not argue like others that environmental pressures had made them so, that life on the plantation had infantilized blacks. "Their inferiority," he insisted, "is not the effect merely of their condition in life."[62] He argued that they did not possess the reasoning capabilities to enjoy all their rights. "Comparing them by their faculties of memory, reason, and imagination, it appears to me, that in memory they are equal to the whites; in reason much inferior," he declared, adding that "in imagination they are dull, tasteless, and anomalous."[63]

In making this startling claim, he did not argue that blacks were subhuman. He regarded blacks as innately equal, in terms of their dignity as humans. According to the reigning ideas of the day on such questions, ideas at the heart of the Scottish Enlightenment, all possessed a "common" or "moral" sense that made humans human. This sense allowed people to be sociable and for society to flourish. It found joy in the joy of others, and empathy for another's pain. All people possessed it, though hard usage could dull it.[64] But the rub Jefferson faced was imagining blacks as his equals in practice. Blacks, he believed, could not fend for themselves and become independent or make decisions for themselves regarding their futures because of their reasoning capacities. Locke believed that what made people political animals was their reasoning abilities. Children and women were human, but could not sign onto the social compact because of reason. Jefferson argued the same held true for blacks. If they could not reason, though equal to whites as humans, they could not participate as equals in society.[65]

In this vein, Jefferson was hardly an enigma. Like all in the North and South, he used ideas to speak to the revolutionary realities he faced. His world saw blacks as inferiors. His world also needed labor. Because his world also was turned upside down—and as governor of Virginia he witnessed it firsthand—by war and the competition to remake sovereignty, the specter of black freedom was chilling to him, certainly when it was not managed. Of course, the notion that Jefferson had drafted the Declaration of Independence and considered blacks as less capable than whites appears contradictory. Reconciling these contradictions, however, in the context of postwar America and its many tensions, did not prove difficult. The world that Jefferson lived in gave him the ideas to do so.

But regarding blacks as intrinsically inferior in this way did create something revolutionary. By placing Lockean ideas about rationality within a Scottish Enlightenment framework in the way he did, Jefferson was doing something that placed him ahead of his time. No longer would the status of blacks be justified by custom in an unthinking way. Nor would older scriptural claims about the cursed nature of Africans keep them in chains, nor for that matter Western European prejudices. By their fatally flawed conceptions of human difference, men such as Jefferson argued that innate capacity made slaves what they were. The logic Jefferson used allowed white men to participate politically as citizens but not blacks. Even when he thought of the prospects of emancipation, he had to make room for this logic. So unsurprisingly he advocated schemes for the "repatriation" of blacks to Africa. "They should," Jefferson suggested, "be colonized to such place as the circumstances of the time should render most proper." Planters had the responsibility of "sending them out with arms, implements of household and of the handicraft arts, seeds, pairs of the useful domestic animals." Former slaves could then become "a free and independent people." His half-baked scheme, however, recognized the necessity of labor. Repatriation depended on dispatching "vessels at the same time to other parts of the world for an equal number of white inhabitants; to induce whom to migrate hither."[66] If blacks did not live in America, Americans would not have to live among a people equal in dignity but unequal in reasoning capabilities. They should, if free, inhabit separate worlds. If together, a dependent relationship was necessary for a people who could not exercise their independence.

Jefferson did not see Indians in this light, although they were not, in his estimation, the equals of whites. Yet this had to do with nurture not nature. Jefferson believed that they possessed capabilities every bit the equal of whites. "To form a just estimate of their genius and mental powers," he argued, "great allowance [had] to be made for those circumstances of their situation which call for a display of particular talents only." Taking environment into account, he found that "they are formed in mind as well as in body, on the same module with the 'Homo sapiens Europaeus.'" They were intelligent. In fact, they proved even better orators. He cited the example of the famous oration of Logan, whose kin had been killed on the eve of Lord Dunmore's War: "Who is there to mourn for Logan? Not one." Indian differences stemmed from culture not race. As Jefferson put it, "the causes of this are to be found, not in a difference of nature, but of circumstance."[67] If they accepted white cultural norms, then they could act in an independent fashion.

Blacks and Indians inhabited different worlds in postwar America, literally and figuratively. Blacks lived among whites. The barriers between the groups, therefore, were legal in nature. If these groups had enjoyed equality in practice, then laws—if they were just—had to take this equality into account. If unequal, as Jefferson and many southerners believed, then unequal laws could prevail. Indians, like Logan, had either died or lived in the West. Jefferson could imagine them as equals, since their equality in the context of postwar America did not have costs for men like him who lived in the East. The barriers between Indians and whites had been geographic. With the end of the war, it seemed these barriers might remain. As long as they steered clear of one another, conflict could be muted. Jefferson suggested as much in his infamous *Notes on the State of Virginia* in which he compared blacks and Indians to whites. No doubt, he was doing so to refute French conceits about the innate superiority of the Old World over the New. Even the animals in Europe, or so the story went, grew larger than those of America. The document was making an argument of how America measured up to Old World standards. As the indigenous people of the New World, Indians had to hold their own. Africans, as people of the Old World, did not. In fact, casting them as inferiors served Jefferson's purpose in writing *Notes on the State of Virginia*. That said, the tract was less a prescription of what to do than a recognition of what was happening in America in the 1780s. Slaves had to be imagined as drudges. Peace and prosperity in the South demanded it. Indians could be imagined as the equals of whites, so long as they embraced civilized ways. Or they had to move. Westerners, in theory, could live with this.

In other words, the constraints that context provided laid out the limits of equality that Americans could imagine. Such was certainly the case for Indians, whose experiences in the war had been nothing short of catastrophic. The Six Nations had fractured, as Iroquois killed Iroquois, such as when Oneidas led Sullivan to Iroquois villages and when the British and Mohawks attacked the Oneida in 1780. So awful had this pattern of retaliation become that only two Iroquois towns had gone untouched throughout the war.[68] Many moved to Canada with Joseph Brant. Others settled in the shadow of the forts the British continued to occupy on the frontiers. The victorious Americans saw the Iroquois as enemies and considered the land they had lived on as American by rights of conquest. In 1784 at Fort Stanwix, commissioners met with delegates from the vanquished nations, but refused to recognize their status as members of a nation. Because they were a conquered people, there was no pretense of Iroquois supremacy over other groups. The covenant chain had ceased to exist. The Six Nations, through negotiations some of which were held at gunpoint, ceded vast territories in New York and Pennsylvania, as well as any claims to Ohio. Most found the treaty unacceptable, but had little recourse to dispute it. Like the earlier Treaty of Fort Stanwix, Indians would lose land; unlike the 1768 treaty, the Iroquois bore the brunt.

To make the cession complete American purchased land from their Oneida allies, transfers also disputed within the Nation. For those of the vanquished who hoped to remain where they had lived, such as the Seneca, the United States set aside a reservation in what is now Tonawanda, New York. Here Iroquois faced again the pressures that had destroyed Native Americans since they first encountered Europeans. The Seneca lived on marginal lands, lands no Euro-American wanted. They struggled with disease, dependency, poverty, and alcoholism. What had been an independent nation became a dependent.[69]

In Ohio, violence continued after the war. We now know that the British encouraged raids along the frontier.[70] Nevertheless, Indians realized that they were competing to hold onto their worlds. During the war, most had sided with the British with good reason. And by the end of the war, most of the Ohio Indians were fighting alongside the British, leading raids into Kentucky. Like most of the Iroquois, they had chosen the wrong side. After the Treaty of Paris, American officials tried to coerce Delawares and Shawnees to come to the bargaining table. Groups met at Fort McIntosh in 1785 and Fort Finney a year later to formalize peace. These, too, the American regarded as conquered peoples, no matter their vacillation during the war. Officials found unsanctioned leaders—anyone really the Americans could claim as reputable—to negotiate treaties. Like the Iroquois, they traded land for peace. These Indians, in theory, like the Seneca, were to live on sovereign American territory only because the Ohio country was not yet settled, and Indian presence was tolerated but little more.[71] Nonetheless, few recognized the validity of such treaties, and raids picked up in ferocity immediately after the war. With a feeble presence in the West, the American government could do little. The Ohio Valley, therefore, remained in a state of war after the war.

The Cherokees experience appeared eerily the same. The divisions that had haunted other groups broke the Cherokees in two. Young men had cast their lot with the British in a bid to maintain control of their lands in the face of chaotic violence, as state militias from Virginia, the Carolinas, and Georgia had attacked Cherokee towns, each trying to win a chunk of it for their settlers. The older chiefs used the attacks as an opportunity to reassert control and sued for peace, while the younger men left to create a new Cherokee society. And Americans continued the war against them, burning their chief settlement Chota in 1780. "The miseries of those people," an American commander found, "seem to exceed description; here are men, women & children almost naked; I see very little to cover either sex but some old bear skins, and we are told that the bulk of the nation are in the same naked situation." To compound the dire situation "their crops this year have been worse than ever was known, so that their corn & potatoes, it is supposed will be all done before April; and many are already out, particularly widows and fatherless children, who have no men nearly connected to them."[72] In 1785, Cherokees came to terms at a place called Hopewell. The arrangement of peace for land held here as well. Those groups in the region that had sided with the Americans, such as the Catawbas, also lost their land. The new government promised to set aside 225 square miles for the Catawbas. That area shrank to 62 and eventually 12 square miles.[73]

Further south still, the Creeks also fractured along lines that had been revealed by the ferment of revolution. The divisions were complex. Alexander McGillivray, who accepted many white cultural norms including Euro-American concepts of property and chattel slavery, contested American and Georgia claims to Creek territory while he declared himself head of the Creeks. Like Brant, he tried to remain loyal to the Crown even after the British had ceded his land to the Americans. After the British abandoned the Creeks, he turned to the Spanish, offering the services of the Creeks to contest the new American government and the state governments. He even encouraged Creek warriors to attack American settlements if doing so furthered his financial and political aims. As he put it, he wanted to "civilize" the Creeks, to make them in his own image. Others, who resisted white cultural norms, such as Hopothle-Mico, whom McGillivray condemned as "a roving beggar, going wherever he thinks he can get presents," tended to take a more accommodationist stance, agreeing to land cessions to Georgia for the prospects of peace and the possibility to live unmolested by settlers. In his eyes, McGillivray was a "boy and a usurper." Revolution, as in other regions, made for unpredictable outcomes. Eventually, McGillivray would sign a treaty with the United States in New York, agreeing to cession and for Creeks to turn over any runaway slaves in return for guarantees against white encroachment. Yet the divisions persisted as mestizos became wealthier and more like their

Figure 7.8 John Trumbull, *Sketch of Hopothle Mico*, 1790. The New York Public Library.

white slave-owning neighbors. For the Creeks, the legacy of revolution would pave the way for civil war in the first decades of the nineteenth century.[74]

The West, therefore, seethed after the war had ended. This state of affairs did not bode well for settlers who were streaming westward. In fact, they faced a world eerily similar to those who headed West after the Seven Years' War. They tried their best to stay a step ahead of speculators and their agents and to steer clear of belligerent Indians, as competition seemed to increase between the well-heeled and the squatter in places like Kentucky. With peace between Britain and the United States, adventurers tried to claim land and to warn the poor off. Indian attacks, however, which were growing in frequency and ferocity with the movement of Euro-Americans west, placed wealthier and poorer whites in the same camp. Together, they began to formulate a new vision of what the West should look like.[75] Easterners, they argued, ignored their pleas, since governments did not protect them and treaties did not end violence. They wanted armies to march. The British still manned forts and were encouraging Indians to keep things disorderly. The Spanish, who held land west of the Mississippi, were not allowing traffic down the river. The continuing state of uncertainty and violence made Kentucky a distinctive place, one in which speculator and squatter signed a tacit alliance.

The Kentucky experience points to the fact that at times elites found common cause with their social inferiors. The stakes were too high not to. Poorer folks in the West promised to keep the West in the violent abyss. Normally, under such circumstances, wealthy settlers would have warned them off the land or threatened them with armies. But with the specter of Indian violence, even in such civilized places as Lexington, concerns proved more elemental. Self-preservation and a common sense of grievance did not rectify tensions; these concerns merely allowed all to overlook the tensions. In areas where a common enemy did not emerge, different patterns prevailed.

With the end of war, small town life in the East did not return to normal. Would-be farmers returned to find towns that they had known, such as Concord, changed by the war. Concord, too, suffered as many towns did after the war. The economy languished in the 1780s. Transients came and went. The end of the war ushered in a heady period of hope, only to be dashed by postwar realities. Yet, on the face of it, things looked the same. The same sort of well-born wealthy men assumed positions of leadership. Their devotion to republican principles and virtue, not status alone, guaranteed their rights to assume positions of rule. Virtue, indeed, belonged especially to these, who had the leisure and inclinations to practice virtuous habits, as they claimed to be dependent on no man. Nor did those who returned to farms find life unchanged. The wars years had politicized common men, and they would not defer to their betters as they had before. Common people had deep suspicions of outside authority, especially as the government in Boston issued its broad tax plan. But their independence also begot mobility, which acted as a safety valve for tensions that could boil over. In places like Concord, there was not enough land for all, encouraging those with few prospects to leave, either west or north to join the swelling numbers looking to make a living there or to cities. Indeed, more than half of the militia men who had turned out to face the British in 1775 had left Concord for other regions within a few years of the war's end. Vagrants were warned out of towns, as officials tried to keep the forces that could lead once again to disorder at bay. Without the prospects of movement, such towns may well have exploded.[76]

Cities, too, stirred with disorder. With the end of the war, veterans returned, some in rags, some as beggars. The postwar recession hit Boston so hard that some worried the city would never recover, and veterans had a difficult time finding employment. Although Continental soldiers had been promised upon enlistment 100 acres of land in the West, such promises panned out for few.[77] New York similarly reeled from the end of the Caribbean trade. At the same time, because the renewal of trade with Britain struck budding industries, work was hard to come by. Nonetheless, refugees from the countryside, many away from the city after years of exile, poured into New York. The almshouses in the city, constructed to hold no more than 400, filled beyond capacity, as did the jails that held debtors.[78] Cities, then, were swelling with masterless and politicized men.

These men, who had sacrificed, some for years, for the cause, claimed the revolution as theirs. "Every private soldier in an army thinks his particular services as essential to carry on the war he is engaged in, as the services of the most influential general, and why not?" declared Joseph Plumb Martin. "Alexander never could have conquered the world without private soldiers," he concluded.[79] In the ideas of the revolution, particularly its notions of rights, the common sort found justifications for their grievances. But the process of revolution, an elemental struggle in which all had to fend for themselves, also emboldened them. Authorities in some cities were able to keep pressures under wraps. They had, after all, been the same people who had staffed Committees of Correspondence and, therefore, had revolutionary bona fides. And in some cities that had not been occupied throughout the war by the British, such as Boston, there was a precedent for rules of order. Yet in some places, returning soldiers threatened to tip the balance. Veterans had participated in mutinies during the war, some of which, such as the Mutiny of the Pennsylvania Line, threw the army into a panic. During the later stages of the war, especially after soldiers had gone unpaid for some time, they let their voices be heard. In 1783, for instance, privates marched on Congress in Philadelphia to collect back pay.

While it may have been easier to marginalize people on the basis of gender and race, it was less so on the basis of class. White men, after all, had filled the ranks of the Continental Army and had served in militias. Primogeniture and entail, the bundle of laws that allowed elites to pass privilege onto the next generation, were done away with in law in places like Virginia. Here elites had been able to amass huge estates and pass them on intact to the eldest son. Such laws withered away with time in other states where they did not have such wide-reaching implications. To have supported their maintenance would not only have flown in the face of republican ideology, as Jefferson who championed the abolition of entail in 1776 understood, it also would have imperiled the newly won peace.[80] The young, poorer sort, those who suffered most through such laws, would not have stood for it. Resistance would have been too great, in other words.

After the war, radicals exiled from Britain and Ireland began trickling into America, adding to any prospective resistance "from below." Most radicals would reach America after 1792; however, the movement began as the war ended. With war's end, migration from the British Isles resumed, and tens of thousands of men and women journeyed to places like Philadelphia for the same reasons their forbears had sailed before the war: for opportunity and freedom. But times had changed in the Old World. These émigrés were politicized and saw America as a republican city upon a hill. In Ireland, largely through the example of American revolutionaries, men and women were pressing for fundamental reform and for the end of subservience to the British Parliament, the measure Shelburne would support to curry favor with Americans. The Irish Volunteers, the group that John Paul Jones had noted, was one such pressure group. Agitation would lead to parliamentary independence for Ireland in 1782. Nonetheless, with Catholics still subject to penal laws, some Protestants and Catholics were banding together to form associations to press for radical change, including a fundamental consideration of the relationship between Ireland and Britain. People styling themselves Defenders defied wealthy landlords to protect the rights of poor, Catholic farmers. The most radical group eventually to emerge, the United Irishmen, would raise the possibility that Irishmen and women might be willing to fight a war of independence for a republican Ireland.[81] The governments in Britain and Ireland drove the group underground, and in the midst of repression, some left to America.

Once in places like New York and Philadelphia, they showed no hesitation in participating in politics, lending their voices to the push for radical change by arguing that the revolutionary work of transforming American society was not over. One example serves as a case in point. After the Catholic printer Mathew Carey wrote what was regarded as a seditious pamphlet in support of the end of penal legislation in Ireland, he fled to France. There he was befriended by Benjamin Franklin and Lafayette. Bearing letters of introduction from Lafayette and Robert Morris, Carey eventually sailed to Philadelphia, where he established himself as a leading publisher. In America, he considered himself "an adopted son." He claimed that the Irish had played "a very great (perhaps I might say the major) part" in the fight for independence, entitling him and other migrants to consider America a new home. As he put it in 1786,

> From old Hibernia's troubled isle,
> Where oft the Graces deign'd to smile,
> An injur'd, humble VOLUNTEER,
> I follow FREEDOM'S fortunes here,
> To guard her rights, espouse her cause,
> Assert her claims, and guard her laws.

That cause was his, whether the fight be in Ireland or Americas. And in Philadelphia, the fight continued. He was no outsider. Nor was he alone.[82]

Similar radicals from Britain also migrated to America. In January 1783, only days before Britain signed preliminary articles of peace with France and Spain, John Miller arrived in Baltimore. A London printer, Miller had supported the causes of John Wilkes and the American patriots in the press. For his efforts, the government imprisoned him five times, leading to his decision to sail to America for asylum. Like the Irish, English and Scottish radicals saw the Atlantic as a highway and what was happening in America as a fitting conclusion to what had started in Britain in the seventeenth century, tying radicals together in a transatlantic community. They also considered America a home for those who struggled for liberty in the Old World against the forces of tyranny. The Scottish political exile James Thomson Callendar, a devotee of Jonathan Swift, saw America's cause as Scotland's as well, even if most of his countrymen were cautious in their patriotism.[83] Eventually, these exiled radicals would include such prominent Britons as Joseph Priestley, who left in the midst of crackdown against radicals in England and Scotland. As a rule, these people condemned "elites" and claimed that common men and women in America and Ireland, and even some in Britain, were true republicans, and as such were entitled to a full share of their rights. Try as groups like the Cincinnati might, so long as men and women invoked the war, there was only so much they could do to stifle the voices of ordinary people. Émigrés channeled these voices, and in many cases amplified them. The war had emboldened and entitled many to push for a liberating revolution settlement.[84]

Liberation, in other words, occurred where and for whom it could. Without substantial pressure from women to press for a full share of their rights, men did not pursue such a course while recognizing the role women had played in the revolution. In the North, where the cost of slavery outweighed the benefits, the institution more or less withered away. With shoals of willing workers inhabiting cities, the North would not face a labor question. The South was a different matter altogether. White men fared better than most, but they too only enjoyed the proverbial half a loaf. Nonetheless, they would not take second-class status lying down. Elites could claim the revolution and its virtue as theirs. But the specter of masterless men, though less frightening than the prospect of masterless slaves, proved frightening enough.

During the war and before it, as authority crumbled, women, poorer men, slaves, and Indians participated in the same story of liberation as elites. They too struggled and competed, largely by channeling discontents into a war of independence against Britain. The narrative of events was their narrative as well. With the end of the war, however, this changed. They now lived lives partially separate from that political narrative. Poorer men still formed part of the broader tale—sacrifice they could point to had made it so—and their struggle to imprint the revolution settlement with their hopes and aspirations would help drive the master narrative. Elites, too, such as Washington, were also prey to events and to the nature of a society now politicized. Their society, too, had crumbled. They, however, had stood the most to lose by the end of deference and traditional bonds. And they had the power and rhetorical ability to act. With the help or acquiescence of common white men, they had, in part, begun to reinscribe those bonds for women and to reimpose them for blacks and to relegate Indians to geographic margins. Doing so for lower class white men or even the middling sort would prove much more challenging and complex.

The first portent of what was to come emerged in western Massachusetts. Before the war, western Massachusetts had been relatively peaceful. When royal authority had come tumbling down, local magnates—the so-called "River Gods"—tried to maintain control of the region. As British sovereignty teetered, so too did the River Gods, and as in other settlements, common men and women assumed positions of control behind the veneer of committees and conventions. With the war, many young men went off to fight, and loyalists fled. The economy was in tatters but was no longer rooted in subsistence. And when soldiers returned, they transformed the world they had known. Deference as a strategy had become a thing of the past, hence so did the rule of the River Gods. The old elite tried to reassert control in a new republican guise, as did new people. Yet, like most other regions, debt and economic stagnation gripped the region, people came and went, and vagrants were warned out.[85]

Upheaval defined the period. Merchants and magistrates from the East also passed on some of the highest taxes levied in the new United States, claiming they had self-interest and virtue on their side. They also felt pressure from British factors who were competing with them to sell goods to the West. With the credit crunch, the self-styled leaders of the state put pressure on those in western communities who owed money to them, who in turn passed on demands to those struggling to make ends meet. Easterners were also consumed with the idea of helping the confederated government buttress its claims to sovereignty. Given the tensions people from western Massachusetts faced, especially as local authority for the first time was called into question, such a choice made sense. So too did the attempt of easterners to suppress paper currencies. Hard currency brought stability and sustained their control over economy and society. These attempts, however, did not go unchallenged, as upper, middling, and poorer sorts vied for control of the local courts.

Here it seemed the violence and uncertainty of revolution would not end. In fact, disorder reemerged.[86] In late 1786, in the midst of similar upheavals through the state, a group of 2,000 aggrieved farmers rose up to challenge those trying to reconstitute authority in the region. In popular memory, a militia captain named Daniel Shays led a group of what officials in the East called "rebels" aroused by the state of affairs. In fact, Shays emerged as one of a number of local leaders who tried to channel the anger around them. A piece written for a child's alphabet lesson coupled Shays with veteran militia officers Nathan Smith and Job Shattuck, who also led "the people." It went:

> R stands for Rebels who mobs dare to raise,
> S stands for Satan, Smith, Shattuck, and Shays.

The "Regulator" armies, which were trying to reinstitute control in a chaotic world, took over local courts that had been prosecuting debtors. When they threatened an arsenal in Springfield, the easterners reacted. After pleas to Congress fell on deaf ears, merchants fearing that what were decentralized risings would coalesce into a movement raised funds to outfit an army led by Benjamin Lincoln to suppress what they called a "rebellion."[87]

In another light, Smith, Shattuck, and Shays were offering their own version of sovereignty. They formed an army of their own, as well as courts, suggesting that older revolutionary conventions could play quasi-sovereign roles once more. The Regulators offered an alternative vision of authority, one that, given the context, must have seemed appealing and alarming. Poorer people and local elites feared not only economic marginalization but also an aristocracy, seated in the East, ruling over them.[88] Like the forces arrayed against them, these men were still caught in a vortex of violence and uncertainty. They would not stomach the program of those arrayed against them, nor would they recognize any government foisted upon them. What happened, in fact, represented less a rebellion against established authority than a fight against the pretense of some to claim their vision of society as the one that would sustain the reestablishment of legitimate authority. The so-called "friends of order" had many on their side, and unsurprisingly state officials were able to muster enough men to suppress the Shaysites. Yet the Regulating vision was not dead. All throughout America similar negotiations were taking place, most less dramatic, but none less critical to bringing about a revolution settlement.

What would be known as Shays' Rebellion was part and parcel of the process of revolution. After the war, societies were still caught in the thrall of competition and disorder of revolution. On the one hand, people hoped that a new order would emerge from these years of crisis. These were heady days. On the other hand, as Benjamin Rush worried, Americans were on the verge of "degenerating into savages or devouring each other like beasts of prey." In the state of nature—not society—individuals devolved.[89] Sovereignty had not been refashioned, certainly in the sense of sustaining meaningful and broadly accepted authority. French observers, writing to readers at home about the wonders of the revolution, also pointed out the dangers—dangers that, of course, would engulf France only a decade later. If "excessive jealousy distract their governments; and clashing interests, subject to no strong controul, break the federal union," they prophesied, "the consequence will be, that the fairest experiment ever tried in human affairs will miscarry; and that a REVOLUTION which had revived the hopes of good men and promised an opening to better times, will become a discouragement to all future efforts in favour of liberty." It could, they cautioned, "prove only an opening to a new scene of human degeneracy and misery."[90] To be sure, through negotiations and tacit consensus, some of the limits of any respective settlement, especially those revolving around exclusion from the body politic, were emerging. But too many questions remained unanswered, and as long as this was the case, violence could return.

Although the 1780s marked a period of intense uncertainty and anxiety over what shape sovereignty would take, the outlines of American civil society appeared clearer than they had before. The ethos of the new nation, given the realities of revolution and the discourses that Americans made use of to make sense of violence and uncertainty, was now firmly democratic. Meanwhile, the demands of some would be marginalized for the very same reasons. In other words, the broad parameters of a prospective settlement were beginning to take shape. But some also began to realize that to ensure the war was successful, the revolution would have to end. A newspaper of the period put it best:

> O America! arouse! awake from your lethargy! bravely assert the cause of federal unanimity! and save your sinking country! Let it not be said, that those men who heroically extirpated tyranny from America, should suffer civil discord to undo all that they have achieved; or to effect more than all the powers of Britain, aided by her blood-thirsty mercenaries, were able to accomplish.[91]

CHAPTER 8

Some Way or Other We Must Be a Great and Mighty Empire

In 1787, Benjamin Franklin little resembled the man he had been. The young man who had at one time swum across the Delaware for exercise had become old, bedeviled by recurring bouts with the gout and kidney stones. To dull the pain, Franklin had taken to dosing himself with laudanum, an opiate used in the eighteenth century. Yet when representatives from nearly all of the states were planning on meeting in Philadelphia in the summer of that year to examine and amend the Articles of Confederation, Franklin decided that he would preside over the Pennsylvania delegation. James Madison, the young Virginian who had been planning for such an occasion for some time, hoped that Washington and Franklin would participate in the Philadelphia convention. Because of the general prestige they enjoyed, their presence would give the proceedings an air of legitimacy. As a writer in a Massachusetts newspaper put it, a "union of the abilities of so distinguished a body of men, among whom will be a FRANKLIN and a WASHINGTON, cannot but produce the most salutary measures."[1]

The man who had done so much to make America British in the mid-eighteenth century, to declare independence from Britain, and to win an alliance with France during the war years, did little at what would be remembered as the Constitutional Convention. Although he arrived at the daily proceedings in a sedan chair carriage born aloft by four porters—so as to ease the bumpiness of the ride—he sat silent through most of the deliberations. One of the few proposals he made—one to abolish slavery—was virtually ignored. Delegates politely listened to what he had to say, but they understood that his ideas were out of bounds. He had some reservations concerning what he regarded as an antidemocratic sentiment of some delegates, and he chafed over the ways in which this sensibility was finding its way into deliberations. On this point, Franklin garnered attention. He worked diligently as president of his delegation. He served on subcommittees when asked. But, like Washington, he was now a figurehead, one whose presence mattered more than meaningful participation. One of Franklin's proposals, Madison recalled, "was treated with great respect but rather for the author of it than from the conviction of its expediency or practicability." Franklin

Figure 8.1 Benjamin West, *Benjamin Franklin Drawing Electricity from the Sky*, ca. 1816. Philadelphia Museum of Art.

had hoped to make the final statement at the convention, a plea to pass what he considered an imperfect but nonetheless visionary document. "I agree to this Constitution, with all its faults, if they are such," he declared, "because I think a general Government necessary for us, and there is no form of Government but what may be a blessing to the people if well administered."[2] Yet even his hope to have the last word was dashed, as others spoke after him.[3] As the debates over ratification raged in America's states including Pennsylvania, Franklin died.[4]

We think of the Constitutional Convention as James Madison's shining moment. This genius for thinking about political possibilities in unconventional ways, and for making the shrewd, timely argument to support his contentions, developed the plan that would more or less emerge as the backbone of the Constitution. He relieved the fears of delegates over the size of the country and the ability of any constitution to provide order for it. He had made the case that factions could help provide stability and that men, though not completely devilish, could hardly be considered angels. He had entered the convention arguing that only a strong federal government with the power to tax could bring order to chaos, and he had left the convention victorious. And most critically, he suggested that sovereignty did not reside in the states, which idea had stood at the center of the confederation government, but with the people. In other words, we see the Constitution as the "founders'" document, one they devised and handed down as if from on high.

But in many ways, Franklin's experience better sums up the nature of the contributions of the founders in the 1780s and early 1790s. They played critical roles to be sure, but they reacted to events as much as they crafted history, responding to realities on the ground as much as refashioning American destiny. The so-called founders, like all others, confronted and tried to manage the many tensions of the period. They too had to trim their sails, doing and saying what context allowed. They did not so much bring revolution to an end as try to manage or channel forces, much like anyone else. As much as actors, they were reactors, trying their best to contain the tumult of revolution but also abiding by the new rules inscribed by those furies. They too had to contend with the forces that threatened to overwhelm and that had ultimately conspired to press delegates to meet in Philadelphia behind closed doors. Those same forces that had melted down British sovereignty also had made the people self-sovereign. The idea of "We, the People" emerged from the crucible of revolution, not as an invention of the founders or as a fiction. It arose from below and had become animating fact.

From the mid-1780s until the mid-1790s, Americans were involved in a series of negotiations to bring revolution to a close. They argued and fought, threatened unending violence and promised enduring peace, all to try to refashion sovereignty in their own image. Men and women energized and constrained by what had happened to their local worlds used the languages and sensibilities of the day to cobble together a collective order. Some had more formative voices than others, say, like James Madison. But men and women of lesser means, as well as those of other races, participated as well. Their presence too contributed to what would be wrought. The anxiety that gripped the states in the early 1780s, and haunted them in many guises, stemmed from these debates, as well as the enduring competition to remake society. By the time that Franklin lay dying, these negotiations were coming to a close, and rough, hard-fought consensus was emerging over what American sovereignty would be and what sort of order would spring from it.

And what was emerging did not please everyone. The Constitution, of course, did not end slavery. Nor did it liberate women or consider the plight of Indians. It tried to insulate political processes from the hands and passions of the sort of men who had sacrificed in the War for Independence. But the Constitution only proved one part of a broader settlement that was taking place in the 1780s and 1790s. In these years, Americans would struggle over the meaning and future of the West. They would also argue over the future of economic development and financial policy. They would debate the meanings of citizenship and participation, as well as who comprised the political nation. They would struggle with gender. They would also fight over race. They did so in print, in taverns, in fields, in cities, through ceremonies, in oaths, in bedrooms, and on battlefields.

By 1800, the broad outlines of a revolution settlement had emerged. Americans are not accustomed to use the term "revolution settlement." They usually see the Constitution as the end of the story of revolution. But seeing things this way obscures the many voices at work in these years, including those that would be muted, as well as the trade-offs and contradictions that went into containing the upheaval of the period. More than politics was at stake, more than the sorts of debates that take place in the rooms of great public buildings. And more than the founders mattered. So much was contested and debated that most Americans could claim something. A loss in one arena could be offset by gains in another. The achievement of a revolution settlement was premised upon such cultural cross bracing, ensuring that each debate, struggle, and fight did not become a zero-sum game. Checks and balances did not only pertain to the functions of government in the Constitution; they applied to society as well.

This dynamic helps explain why Americans would achieve stability in short order, why they would not be convulsed by chaos and overwhelmed by recurring violence. The only groups that found no solace were blacks and Indians. But enough whites did, especially in the marginalization of those of other races, to accept the settlement in its many guises. The genius of the settlement was not the ways in which Madison played with political theory; genius, rather, lay in the ways that tensions did not dissolve the union. Tensions, in fact, sustained it.

The Constitution was not simply America's Thermidor, that is to say it did not represent merely a conservative reaction to the liberating ideology of revolution, such as the movement that would grip France during its revolution; rather, it represented the most visible culmination of some of the negotiations that went into bringing revolution to an end. These negotiations were regional, as well as ideological. They turned on the identity of groups, as well as the individual, and involved fear and vision, as well as attempts to tame what some regarded as excess and for others to press for greater rights.[5] The give and take of the convention, and the famous compromises, reflected the critical significance of such issues. Forging a constitution meant understanding what had emerged from the crucible of revolution. These possibilities and constraints that were not threatening to vanish were the legacies of the period. The brilliance of the so-called founders lay in recognizing realties and trying to come up with a settlement that reflected the limits imposed by them.[6]

The story, usually told, revolves around mythic heroes. James Madison stands above all in this regard, as the slight man's ideas loomed over the proceedings. For weeks after a convention to revisit and revise the Articles had been scheduled, Madison prepared for the event, to fashion a state "of such a vigor in the general government as will be able to restore health to any diseased part of the federal body."[7] He thought he knew what needed to be done, and most of the Virginia delegation saw things as he did. Although Patrick Henry wanted no part of the convention, the only Virginian who had qualms and who attended was the planter from Fairfax, George Mason. Madison reached Philadelphia before nearly all other delegates, and he quickly went to work planning meetings with like-minded men from other large states who saw a more efficacious central government as the only way out of the chaos, uncertainty, and anxiety that defined the 1780s. In doing so, Madison hoped to set the agenda for the convention, angling to have his ideas become the bases of debate. As the delegates

Figure 8.2 Gilbert Stuart, *James Madison*, 1804. The Colonial Williamsburg Foundation.

assembled, an Irish-born planter and slave owner from South Carolina named Pierce Butler proposed that the deliberations be secret. The doors would be shut and the windows shuttered, despite the summer heat. The delegates also decided not to leak what was going on in their deliberations.[8]

Madison and his allies achieved what they wanted to. What historians would remember as the Virginia Plan amounted to James Madison's vision for an orderly settlement to the chaos of revolution. The central government would be sovereign and much more powerful than the states. Critically, it would have the power to tax. Madison believed that the vexing problems of the decade could be overcome if the state proved powerful enough to act. Sovereignty had to be meaningful, in other words. To ensure that balance between power and liberty did not tip too much to one end, Madison also proposed that representation in a bicameral legislature should be based proportionally upon population, which ensured—not altogether coincidentally—that the most populous states, such as Virginia, would have the lion's share of power in both houses of the national legislature. But Madison did not advocate direct democracy and did not have faith in the virtue of the people. Madison hoped that having two houses would temper popular impulses.

In thinking this way, however, Madison was not exceptional. Most delegates agreed that unmediated democracy or unicameral legislatures, such as Pennsylvania's, ensured that chaos would not end. Instead of one tyrant, the new

United States would be confronting millions of men and women emboldened by their experiences in war and revolution. A number of the big state representatives did not so much fear government as have a healthy respect for what it could accomplish. They feared disorder. Roger Sherman of Connecticut believed "the people immediately should have as little to do as may be about the Government. They want information and are constantly liable to be misled." He was not alone. "The evils we experience flow from the excess of democracy," contended Elbridge Gerry, who based his case on the idea that "the people do not want virtue, but are dupes of pretend patriots."[9]

Gouverneur Morris, a one-legged delegate from Pennsylvania, believed that although liberty was a hallmark of the revolution, it would never have any real meaning without meaningful sovereignty. And an unfettered people proved the greatest obstacles to order. Morris did not style himself an elitist tyrant—he had an avowed hatred for slavery on ideological grounds, for instance—but he had little faith in common people exercising authority unmediated by national institutions.[10] Other men, such as Robert Morris, made the same sorts of arguments in trying to figure a way out the economic and financial maze the United States found themselves trapped in. The national government had to tax to ensure that the United States could borrow if need be from European banks and governments. Morris did not fear debt. Indeed, he argued it could prove beneficial, sharpening and refining the powers of government, as well as guaranteeing that influential people were invested in the nation. He instead feared a people who did not accept the obligations imposed by debt. Only a strong sovereign state, he believed, could end the financial chaos of the period. And Madison's plan looked promising on this score.[11]

The Virginia Plan yoked taxation to representation. As Madison suggested, larger states would not overestimate their populations to gain greater representation because doing so would make them responsible to pay higher taxes. Smaller states would not underestimate their population to defray taxes because doing so would penalize them in the legislature. "It is of great importance," he believed, "that the States should feel as little bias as possible to swell or to reduce the amount of their numbers." The remedy was to link the two. In that way "the States will have opposite interests which will control and balance each other and produce the requisite impartiality."[12] Madison believed varied interests could be balanced using this simple formulation. Land would not be taxed, a move, according to advocates of Madison's plan, critical for the success of any fledgling central state. Taxes on land handicapped the wealthy. And if they did not see their interests reflected in the new government, they would not support it. If they did not support it, chaos would not end. As critics understood, the power to tax also contained the power to destroy. Some feared what a powerful national state could do to personal liberties. Some voiced concern over the tone of debates or of comments that disparaged the wisdom of the people, as well as the categories in which some were placing competing camps in the Unites States. Samuel Adams argued such stratagems were "used for the mean purpose of deceiving, and entrapping others whom they call the Vulgar; but in this 'enlightened' Age one should think there was no such Vulgar to be amused, and ensnared."[13]

But truth be told, a general consensus emerged rather quickly in Philadelphia. The consensus took shape around one idea: only a strong national government could rescue the nation from revolution. Delegates from the small states, of course, countered Madison's plan with one of their own. William Patterson of New Jersey proposed a plan that he hoped would receive an airing similar to Madison's. The so-called New Jersey Plan was advocated by smaller states that bristled at losing their voices in a bicameral legislature elected by proportional representation and thereby dominated by larger state interests.

Patterson understood the issue revolved around sovereignty. He wanted the states to remain sovereign units. Patterson did not, however, claim this position because he hoped to increase the liberty of the people. He, like the Morrises, did not champion radical democracy. Rather, he argued that the interests of his state were better guaranteed if an equal number of representatives from sovereign states met in a national legislature. Although Patterson even conceded the point that the power of taxation, the key instrument of sovereignty, should be in the hands of the national government, he wanted the authority of sovereignty to rest with the states. "If the sovereignty of the States is to be maintained," he charged, "the Representatives must be drawn immediately from the States, not from the people: and we have no power to vary the idea of equal sovereignty."[14] While critics pointed out the contradictions of this position, the small states held out, hoping to maximize their power in the convention. Delegates divided over the issue of where ultimate sovereignty should reside, but most agreed that some form of sovereignty symbolized in the power to tax had to be exercised in the United States.

Of course, each delegation looked after its own interests. Madison's plan favored Virginia, while Patterson's counterproposal favored New Jersey. Enough delegates from other states saw their own interests represented in either plan and picked their sides accordingly. All states followed this rule on every major issue that came up, letting others know what the sine qua non for unity amounted to. Georgians wanted a strong government to defend them from Indian attacks and to strengthen the border against Spanish threat. They also had other interests even more vital to their general welfare. Southerners would not hear of doing away with slavery. Yet even on this score, delegations followed their best interests. Virginians had no qualms about doing away with the slave trade. As more and more planters became farmers by turning from tobacco to wheat, Virginians had a surplus of labor.[15] The continuation of the transatlantic slave trade was not of vital interest. In South Carolina, it was. Early on, their delegation insisted that South Carolinians would not compromise their way of life or their economic interests in uniting with the other states, suggesting they would give no ground on the slave trade. "South Carolina and Georgia cannot do without slaves," a delegate from South Carolina asserted. "As to Virginia she will gain by stopping importations. The slaves will rise in value, and she has more than she wants." More critically, those from regions with a black majority threatened the idea of union to safeguard slavery. John Rutledge, also from South Carolina, warned northerners that the issue was not the viability of slavery in the United States. "The true question at present," he countered, "is whether the Southern

States shall or shall not be parties to the Union."[16] The brinksmanship worked. For all such posturing, interests on fundamentals or essentials were converging. Even with the unveiling of the New Jersey Plan delegates were arriving at a consensus.

Throughout the summer, the founders hammered out a document that reflected the consensus that was emerging, as well as those issues that could not be compromised. The final document encapsulated this process of negotiation. We normally conceive of the convention as a dramatic story revolving around a "Great Compromise." Virginians pushed for their plans. Small states followed a different course. The wise Roger Sherman from Connecticut then intervened, laying out the idea of allowing the states to retain their sovereign status while also recognizing the demands of larger states. Representation in the lower house would be based on population while all states would be equally represented in the upper house. The story of the compromise is myth as much as reality. Franklin proposed something along these lines, but he was ignored. The same happened when Sherman aired the idea. Only when delegates had to get down to brass tacks, to flesh out in document form what they were beginning to agree upon, did the so-called "Connecticut Plan" gain general currency. At first, Madison would have nothing to do with it. He believed that small states were holding the larger ones hostage and that the logic of the system proposed was ludicrous. "The Convention was either reduced to the alternative of either departing from justice in order to conciliate the smaller States, and the minority of people of the U.S.," he found, "or of displeasing these by justly gratifying the larger States and the majority of the people."[17] He wanted a unified sovereignty, not a divided one. But he was mistaking unified sovereignty for efficacious sovereignty. The idea of a strong national government had not been compromised. William Patterson agreed that the federal government needed more power. Few voices in Philadelphia argued otherwise. In fact, the emerging consensus rested on the notion that state power and unity were needed not so much to curtail democracy as to ensure revolution ended.

Soon other details began to take shape. Dividing power functionally did not engender debate. Colonial governments had done so since their inception, and Americans were quite comfortable with a legislature separated from an executive, even one that had an adversarial relationship to the other. Delegates did wrangle over how the president would be elected. Most agreed that the people should not directly elect him. Would he be elected by the states? Again, the idea of situating sovereignty proved an obstacle. So delegates fudged the issue, much in the same way they did for the congress. An electoral college elected by the states would select the president. How this body would work, no one had a clue. Because order was the order of the day, however, most accepted the idea that the election of the executive should be insulated as much as possible from popular impulses.

Franklin, for one, claimed to believe in the wisdom of a people who had recently sacrificed so much for independence. "It seems to have been imagined by some," he suggested, "that the returning to the mass of the people was degrading the magistrate." In republics, he believed, "the rulers are the servants, and the people their superiors."[18] Although others nodded in agreement with Franklin in principle, with the exception of a few outliers like George Mason, none suggested that Franklin's point should lead the convention to reconsider the tenor of the document that was taking shape. Order and liberty, the delegates believed, were not at odds. Perhaps they had been, when these very same men were taking over the reins of authority in America as British sovereignty had collapsed. But experience during the difficult years of revolution had taught them that order was needed to make liberty possible. This formulation, as much as any other, formed the basis of consensus in Philadelphia. Even small states that wanted the articles to be overhauled and not scrapped agreed on this. The delegates, to be sure, placed more emphasis on ensuring that elites would have to buy into the state than in recognizing the wisdom of the people to govern themselves. Nonetheless, what would be seen as antidemocratic maneuvering, in their eyes, proved critical for shoring up sovereignty and sustaining order.

The Constitution, then, reflected the tenor of American society. However unsettling and troubling some of its particulars were, it emerged as a compromise document that distilled what the lowest common denominator for union had to be. It was a revolutionary document in the sense that it arose from the many experiences of Americans during the troubling years of disorder. It also demonstrated the limits of freedom within the United States, constraints from the colonial seventeenth century and the provincial eighteenth century that the tumult of revolution did not erase. Through recent and distant history, Americans had overlapping and countervailing interests, and no one would leave Philadelphia completely satisfied or accept the document with unvarnished enthusiasm. All could find something to hate in it. But nearly everyone received something critical in it, particularly a return to order that reflected in some measure the ways American communities had changed in the crucible of revolution. Nearly everyone, that is. The negotiations to reconstitute meaningful sovereignty were born on the backs of some groups. In some ways, the Constitution did not remedy the deficiencies of an old prerevolutionary world; it codified them.

African Americans had status as "persons" in the Constitution, but they did not enjoy liberty or political rights. The Constitution infamously referred to them as "all other persons." Most delegates did not want to use the words "slaves" or "slavery" in the Constitution, though a few delegates from the North argued for the use of the terms so there would be no confusion over what had transpired in Philadelphia. In general, delegates considered blacks to be persons; some also saw them as property. This contradiction underwrote the consensus that blacks would not have political rights. Nor would they have freedom. Although southern delegates would not negotiate on this point, in all fairness, they were not pushed on the issue. Some, such a Gouverneur Morris, made heated speeches about the evils of slavery, but such rhetoric amounted to sound and fury signifying little. Northerners washed their hands of troubling contradictions. Slaves were persons but not free persons. Whether blacks were political persons or free persons would be left up to the states. Union, in other words, trumped freedom.[19]

However unjust these calculations of exclusion might have been, most Americans had few qualms about them. Luther Martin of Maryland decried the slave trade as "inconsistent with the principles of the revolution." It was "dishonorable to the American character to have such a feature in the Constitution." Rutledge shot back that "Religion and humanity had nothing to do with this question. Interest alone is the governing principle with nations." If northerners would "consult their interest, they will not oppose the increase of Slaves which will increase the commodities of which they will become the carriers."[20] Northerners could salve their consciences with the idea that the slave trade would come to an end. Famously, southerners insisted, especially those from South Carolina, that the trade could not be meddled with. Northerners, as well as Virginians, wanted it to end. So they compromised. In exchange for guaranteeing that specific tariff policy would not be written into the document ensuring federal control and flexibility over regulating commerce, southerners received a temporary stay on the end of the slave trade. As Luther Martin found, "the Eastern States notwithstanding their aversion to slavery, were very willing to indulge the Southern States" in this regard. New England and the South had struck a deal. And those northerners who had great moral reservations about slavery and the slave trade such as Gouverneur Morris and James Wilson remained silent while the bargain was struck.[21]

The trade would stay in place for about a generation. In that time span, of course, South Carolinians could and would import unprecedented numbers of Africans, while Virginians would only have to wait until the trade ended to become to main supplier of slaves to other parts of the South. And northerners could claim some sort of moral victory, however shallow that victory seemed. Northern delegates claimed that this evil had to be stopped, but not so much that they would jeopardize the order and unity that the Constitution promised. South Carolinians may have been willing to go the proverbial wall for the peculiar institution, but no one else was willing to do the same to end it—at least not in 1787. Indeed, South Carolina was still much more of a Caribbean society. Whites in the state needed the security of a larger confederation to protect them from the perils of slave insurrection. While planters in Barbados and Jamaica opted to remain part of the British empire, southerners, especially where there was a black majority, needed similar security within the American confederation. They would also barter the long-term trade for the security of unity. Because of this moral decision, a transatlantic trade would give way to a transcontinental middle passage.[22]

The famous 3/5 "compromise" obscures this reality. In fact, it did not represent a compromise—or a supposition that a slave was 3/5 of a person—as much as a guarantee of the survival of the institution of slavery. The tension between freedom and unfreedom could not be evaded or meaningfully compromised. At the convention, the contradiction was canonized. The formula for counting "all other persons" as 3/5 of a free white person for the purposes of representation and taxation, which was not new, was employed by the confederation government and revived in Philadelphia without a great deal of fanfare or debate. Some northerners detested the idea that slaves would still be part of the calculation to figure taxation and representation. They pointed out the absurdity of the South's position in arguing for the ratio. Gouverneur Morris condemned the logic: "The inhabitant of Georgia and S.C. who goes to the Coast of Africa, and in defiance of the most sacred laws of humanity tears away his fellow creatures from their dearest connections & damns them to the most cruel bondages, shall have more votes in a Government instituted for protection of the rights of mankind, than the Citizen of Pennsylvania or New Jersey who views with a laudable horror, so nefarious a practice."[23] Yet he and others signed onto an agreement that posited that slaves were total persons, but unfree persons. The 3/5 ratio reflected this diabolical calculation, one that Americans, North and South could not wish away. Although morally opposed to slavery, Rufus King of Massachusetts conceded that most states "agreed to consider Slaves in the apportionment of taxation; and taxation and Representation ought to go together." Such was the cost of compromise and union.[24]

Little would change for blacks in the South. Where the institution defined economy, social relations, and cultural inheritance, laws would continue to separate the races, as they had since the colonial period. African Americans threw their frustrations and energies into religious life. Their quest for freedom and equal dignity as men and women would continue through their churches and through family and community, as they asserted their status as humans not chattel.[25] Situating the institution of slavery firmly within the Constitution but allowing states the autonomy of undoing the practice if they wished established as fundamental law what had been. The viability of slavery was essential to union and therefore order, and American slavery underwrote American freedom insofar as it paved the way for American order. Without slavery, the United States could not have been. Euphemistic language and the rhetoric of compromise employed in addressing slaves and slavery obscured this deeper reality.

The Constitution was designed—willy-nilly—as a pro-slavery document that created a slaveholder's union by protecting slave property and ensuring that slave states could maintain their power. Arguably, by creating a strong confederated union, the Constitution created the idea of a southern state cause. While the issue of slavery made union necessary, it also represented the most salient difference between one "region" and the other. Deal making and compromise to maintain unity, therefore, created sections self-consciously divided over slavery. Ironically, by curtailing the slave trade in the future, the Constitution encouraged the importation of thousands of Africans in the short-term and the expansion of slavery at least south of the Ohio River in the long term. Indeed, by rooting southern representation in slave population, a contest between northerners and southerners for western states was in the offing. The infamous three-fifths clause also ensured that one certain form of property would be a basis for apportioning representation, further entrenching the institution. Finally, by allowing it, the national government under the Constitution would offer de facto protection for the institution. What had been before the custom of the country, had become, literally, the law of the land. That the deal was not explicitly mentioned made it all the more powerful. The tacit acceptance of the institution, and its legal protections, also made the national government stronger by ensuring that no single region would predominate.[26]

On a deeper level, the Constitution did not create the conditions of political personhood but reflected what Americans thought. Most Americans could admit human equality. Indeed, some influential delegates were steeped in these sorts of ideas. The case of James Wilson from Pennsylvania, the American wartime official in the middle of the "Fort Wilson" riot in Philadelphia, is a good example. Wilson had emigrated from Scotland just after the Seven Years' War. He had studied at a number of the major universities in Scotland and became a devotee of the ideas of political economy and social development that Scots were crafting at the time. Neither Adam Smith's ideas about markets nor Francis Hutcheson's beliefs in a common sense that united all humans were foreign to Wilson when he sat in convention. One idea he held to particularly, like Jefferson, was the notion that all people shared a common sensibility for sociability that made them persons. "All men wherever placed have equal rights and are equally entitled to confidence," he believed, and "the cultivation & improvement of the human mind was the most noble object" of society and government. Yet essential human equality did not make for equality of condition or status. He conceded that there was a "variety and inequality of man...with regard to virtue, talents, taste, and acquirements," despite the fact "all men in society, previous to civil government are equal." In America, after the institution of "civil government" such was not the case. Just as talents and tastes would change with time and proper influences, so the end of the slave trade would bring in a "gradual change."[27] To deprive a man of his freedom or his political voice could be rationalized on grounds that he did not yet have the capacity to enjoy his rights. These contradictions Americans, or at least enough Americans, could live with.

For some groups, political equality proved a bridge too far. For women, who had no place in the Constitution, it was not really considered. The Constitution did not even recognize them as "all other persons." Older forms of authority may have crumbled but not the status of women despite the fact that their fellow citizens recognized their valor and sacrifice, giving them cultural cachet. Their visibility grew, but not politically. With the tumult of revolution, and the disruption to a market economy, women had important roles to play. For some, this culminated in voting in state elections in New Jersey. But after the revolution, women were disappearing from the public realm and were increasingly regarded as child-rearers charged with the task of shaping and forming sons for the rigors of being republican citizens. In New Jersey, female political activity subsided as soon as the war ended, though officials vying for office still campaigned for women's votes. The participation of women, however, never led to the emergence of women's issues.[28] For a republic to survive, or so the argument went, citizens had to be schooled in virtue and vigilance, and since this could only take place in the family, the republican mother and wife was the ideal person to attend to this task. As one young woman put it, a woman had to "inspire her brothers, her husband, and her sons, with such a love of virtue...that future heroes and statesmen...shall exhaltingly declare, it is to my mother I owe this elevation."

Benjamin Rush similarly argued that the education he advocated would prepare women "in instructing their sons in the principles of liberty and government."[29]

This amounted to a reversal of gender roles without a change in gender status. In colonial Virginia, fathers had borne the responsibility for creating independent-minded sons by fostering competition. Virtue, after all, was a male attribute, the quality of being a man.[30] Now, however, women assumed the role of creating independent sons. Ironically, it became the woman's role to create the preconditions for republic's chief safeguard: virtue. Meanwhile, women were relegated to the realm of dependence and domesticity. Women saw no material change in their status, even losing the vote, along with the indigent, aliens, and blacks in New Jersey in 1807. Although they had status in civil society, such a position did not translate into political rights. Although persons, they did not comprise part of the political nation.[31]

The discourse or cult of republican motherhood recognized the fact that women had pushed against the patriarchal bonds of traditional culture while maintaining patriarchal structures and assumptions. Far from decrying this redefinition of citizenship, women accepted or in some case even welcomed it, viewing republican child-rearing as a special vocation.[32] Seeming contradictions defined the lot of women in these years. On the one hand, to cite just one example, women were still bound or covered by laws of coverture to the legal status of their husbands. Yet, they could and did use the idea of coverture to assert their rights to support in the wake of separation and to avoid paying debts incurred while married. Women used what could be regarded as a badge of second-class status strategically. Similarly, their indirect effect on culture and education, and even politics, grew substantially after the war even as their political roles were circumscribed.[33] Women were regarded—white, middle-class women, that is—as political actors even if they could not vote, and they influenced how debates were framed in the new republic. In fact, because some men esteemed women as models of disinterested patriotism, women gained enough status to become social reformers and authors in the new republic as they grew to become the inculcators of virtue. Finally, the war and its cultural aftermath ensured that the idea of virtue shifted from an emphasis on the martial to one rooted in the maternal.[34]

Abigail Adams famously and teasingly told her husband John to "remember the ladies" as he debated what form sovereignty would take in America during the war. "Do not put such unlimited power into the hands of the Husbands," she pleaded. "Remember all men would be tyrants if they could." John replied, almost patronizingly, "As to your extraordinary Code of Laws, I cannot but laugh." His response reflected the tone men used to describe the status of women in society. Women were citizens without formal political rights. Although some pressure came from some quarters to rectify this situation, the pressure was not great. Abigail Adams had done some extraordinary things during the war years. She engaged in business, advocated women's education, and even contested the idea that women should be legally covered by their husbands. Flying in the face of the patriarchal conventions of the day, Adams insisted that women could own property and dispose of it as they saw fit. She argued, like Elizabeth Murray, that young women should have some opportunities in the world of commerce and invested in real estate in Vermont. However, she was complicated. She relished fashion and embraced the domestic sphere; in part, she drew up her own will to protect the property of the family. Moreover, she was not asking for women's suffrage or requesting a change in gender norms.[35]

Nor were other women. Perhaps the best example of the gendered paradox of revolution comes from the life of Judith Sargent Murray. An accomplished writer, Murray became an advocate of "liberal education" for women. "*The idea of the incapability* of women, is," she argued, "in this *enlightened age*, totally *inadmissible*." Like many of the prominent men in America, she too was a devotee of Scottish Enlightenment thinking. Education heightened an innate moral sense. And she agreed with Locke that all persons were blank slates that could be written upon. Yet she never called for suffrage, and she suggested that citizenship for women stemmed from their relationship to the men in their lives. She hoped to elevate the status of women like her in literary circles. Status-conscious to a fault, she did not think that her prescriptions applied to all women, but only the virtuous, embracing the idea of hierarchy and fearing untrammeled democracy. Order meant more than equality.[36] Therefore, in reckoning with the status of women, delegates took a path of little resistance. Republican motherhood and maternal virtue made such a path possible. It appealed to the revolutionary sacrifice of women; it also ensured patriarchy would not be called into question.

Because whole groups were deemed to be dependents or unable by nature or nurture to assume a full measure of their rights, the idea of "We, the People" meant less than it should have. Patrick Henry, in fact, shuddered at the term, though not because blacks or women were excluded from the political nation. Rather, it untethered rights from their chief protector: the states. This does not mean, however, that popular sovereignty amounted to window dressing. Nor was it only a clever way of evading the thorny problems raised by instituting "imperium in imperio," that is, a sovereign state within a sovereign state—an idea that contradicted orthodox political theory.[37] As Wilson argued, "there can be no subordinate sovereignty." Sovereignty "resides in the people; they have not parted with it; they have only dispensed such portions of power as were conceived necessary for the public welfare. This Constitution stands upon this broad principle."[38]

The ambiguous idea of popular sovereignty did allow delegates to deal with the ambiguities of sovereignty that was divided between states and a national government. James Wilson put it beautifully in 1791 when he would be appointed professor of law at the College of Philadelphia. In a series of lectures, he compared the search for sovereignty to the search for the headwaters of the Nile. Many had proposed ideas for its source, but only with revolution could its true origins be discovered. It began, he argued, in a number of small springs. "The dread and redoubtable sovereign," he argued, "when traced to its ultimate and genuine source, has been found … in the free and independent man." This idea, he continued, "so simple and natural, and yet so neglected and despised, may be appreciated as the first and fundamental principle in the science of government."[39] The idea, however, acknowledged what had happened to America in the crucible of revolution. Common men could not be ignored or fobbed off. They had been the ones taking to the streets in the years without sovereignty. They had fought for the American cause. Participation in a war, which had democratized society, ensured they would not go back to a society that was stratified along deferential lines defined by the rule of the—in theory—disinterested few.[40] This was not even a remote possibility. Popular sovereignty was not an invention but a fact, one that had been fashioned in the tumult of revolution. Institutions may have been put in place to serve mediating roles, but authority still stemmed from the only place it could have: those men who had sacrificed and taken over the levers of authority after British sovereignty had crumbled. The Constitution did not determine who could and could not vote; it left that ambiguous issue to the states. But delegates certainly expected common men to participate. The insulation from popular impulses that they created in the Constitution's governing structure speaks to this reality. They created a state, therefore, where authority was rooted in common men whose voices would be muted. If the poorer sort enacted democracy through local action, and the middling sort in state legislatures, the virtuous would have the national government as a check on the "excesses of democracy." In this way, it would balance the tensions inherent in society.[41] Such was the price of order.

The ratification debates demonstrated that the Constitution did not undo or even relieve tensions. Rather, it depended on them, suggesting how revolutionary experience, popular sovereignty, local circumstance, and regional tensions intersected in tangled ways and defined how Americans interpreted the political roles they played and aspired to as they struggled to re-create order. It may have been America's most purely democratic moment. It also represented one of its most corrupt. The delegates, who did not want the document they had agreed upon to be debated in the confederation congress, did not even follow the rules prescribed for amending the Articles to put the Constitution into effect. They did not want it sent to state legislatures, some of which were apt to reject it or stall debate, or decided through a public referendum. They chose a more clever strategy. Delegates opted to send the document to state conventions, most uninstructed, specially elected for the task. If nine state conventions agreed, the Constitution would go into effect.[42]

Most states split on the Constitution. Debates in North Carolina appeared eerily similar to the fights over regulation, those struggles between rich and poor and east and west that shook the colony. Predictably—much as during colonial times—New Yorkers split into regions, upstate vs. the city, though some from the city supported the Articles because unregulated interstate trade tended to help New York mercantile interests. For these very reasons, many from Connecticut hated the Articles. South Carolinians were transfixed with little beyond the viability of slavery and importance of union to secure their interests. Debate never strayed far beyond how the Constitution ensured the viability of the slave system. In Pennsylvania the old divisions over class and visions of the economy arose once more, channeled through revolutionary discourse. Here too East battled West, as those on the margins in the trade-starved city of Philadelphia found themselves at odds with farmers in similar circumstances further to the west. Some New Englanders also wanted a stronger government to confront the economic problems of the day, and those who worked in the shipping industry especially, as well as artisans, threw their support behind a government that had more efficacy. Yet, they were heirs to a democratic ethos and had grown accustomed to political roles. And Virginians debated over what it meant to be a Virginian and an American, whether liberty could be protected under the aegis of an American people or through the power of the state. New Jersey, overrun by armies, wracked by civil war, and held ransom to New York trade restrictions, was only one of three states, along with land-locked and little Delaware and anxious and isolated Georgia, that saw little opposition to the Constitution. Each of these states saw the merits of a large and vital government.[43]

Elsewhere debates became ferocious. They took place in the ratifying conventions, of course, but they also were played out in taverns, coffeehouses, and the streets. In Pennsylvania, delegates tried to push through the Constitution as quickly as possible, hoping to use what they took to be the popular support it enjoyed in Philadelphia to overwhelm opponents. Partisans wrote opinion pieces in the newspapers, and although those who opposed the Constitution were free to publish what they thought, most newspapers operated in cities, which tended to lean pro-Constitution. The anti-Constitution side did not receive a fair airing, and the pro side, intent on ramming it through, did not try to persuade. Rancor defined the convention, and as one newspaper argued Pennsylvania was "peopled by...the most unprincipled, wicked, rascally, and quarrelsome scoundrels upon the face of the globe."[44]

Debates in Massachusetts and Connecticut were equally fraught. Merchants, the clergy, lawyers, and physicians supported the Constitution and were quick to discredit their opponents in the press. Westerners from Shays's region and the northern section of Connecticut tended to oppose the Constitution. Most others fell somewhere between the two. Most common people, hoping to be able to criticize certain aspects of the Constitution and then report back on what they thought, were apt to accept the document so long as they had their fair say; many of the same did not trust the propertied and educated men who supported ratification. For the same reasons, some made calls for a Bill of Rights to be included in the document. Massachusetts voted for ratification by 19 votes, but the ill-feeling lived on. In the wake of ratification, those on the losing side in the district of Maine, a region peopled by those who sympathized with Shays, went so far as to burn a copy of the document on the Fourth of July, 1788.[45]

In Virginia, titans for each cause battled one another in a lengthy debate. Many, such as George Mason and Edmund Randolph, hoped that the ratifying conventions could change the Constitution before it went into effect, that continued negotiations could shape the final document, but in this, they were disappointed. Pro-Constitution delegates insisted that the document be accepted or rejected on, as Mason said, a "take this or nothing" basis. Those calling themselves "Federalists" fought for a ratification process that accepted the document "as it now stands." George Washington used his influence to press for ratification, as did James Madison. Patrick Henry stole the proverbial show, sometimes speaking for hours at a time against the document. But the debate came down to whether amendments could be added to the document before ratification or only recommended after ratification, and whether Virginia could stand outside the union.[46]

The last debate became perhaps the most fevered. When New York took up the question of the Constitution, Virginia and New Hampshire were about to ratify; if New Yorkers rejected it, they would stand alone. Nonetheless, debate turned nasty, in part since it was dominated by two men with great rhetorical abilities and large personalities: Alexander Hamilton and George Clinton, the state's governor. Clinton hated the Constitution because the present arrangement that allowed him to balance the state's books included, along with confiscated loyalist property, the levies on imports from other states. Each side used all means fair and foul, including bribery, to compete for votes to the ratifying convention.[47] Each of the sides received a vigorous airing. And here Hamilton, Madison, and John Jay produced a series of letters to push for ratification that would become known as the "Federalist Papers." In them, they discussed the merits of the Constitution and, most critically, why the contradictions that animated it, such as divided sovereignty between people and states, comprised its strengths. The tensions, as Madison wrote, that could threaten to overwhelm the fledgling republic could, when harnessed by the state, become a strength. "Whilst all authority in it will be derived from and dependent on the society," he argued, "the society itself will be broken into so many parts, interests and classes of citizens, that the rights of individuals, or of the minority, will be in little danger from interested combinations of the majority." The writers admitted that tensions existed; only a fool would argue otherwise. But with the strengthened state providing the basis for a return to order, American society could now thrive and be enlivened by the forces that had been at the heart of revolution. The relationship of federal to state power reflected this dynamic, "by so contriving the interior structure of the government as that its several constituent parts may, by their mutual relations, be the means of keeping each other in their proper places," as Madison put it.[48]

In the *Federalist Papers*, Hamilton and Madison also addressed the pressing issue of a need for sovereign power, as the United States now inhabited a world of sovereign nation-states. Finances would have to be straightened out, and America would need an army because territory had to be defended. Americans, they argued, had a chance to build a state that could look after American commercial interests and territorial integrity, a state with the capacity to one day stand side-by-side the powers of Europe. In 1788, such a vision seemed far-fetched; people in the United States had more elemental concerns. Yet, as Hamilton suggested, postwar independence meant that such considerations could not be avoided.[49]

Ultimately, Clinton's allies pressed for an acceptance of the document "UPON CONDITION" that another federal convention was called to propose amendments. Such attempts had failed in other states where those opposed were outmaneuvered, intimidated, or outnumbered. In New York, they were outwaited. The press of other states ratifying made it clear that New York would be an outlier in the union unless delegates ratified. Hamilton and his allies continued to press for ratification and were willing to concede that they would do so "in full confidence" that amendments could be debated in Congress later. They did not want to go this far, but they did so to have the state ratify.[50]

The Constitution, though ratified, still engendered often-bitter divisions. Indeed, many Americans were divided within themselves. William Manning of Billerica, Massachusetts, for instance, condemned the "the unreasonable desires of the Few to tyrannize over and enslave the Many." Manning had seen his town transformed in the years before the war. Population surged, and speculators were making profits off the land. He had inherited a fine farm, ran a tavern, and engaged in all sorts of trade. But he did not consider himself one of the Few. Instead, he styled himself a man of the many, an ardent champion for the rights of common men. After the war, Manning grew ambivalent about his desire for liberty and for order. He supported some of the aims of the western Regulators; he also supported the government's decision to suppress Shays and his followers. He hated the Massachusetts taxing strategy; he also suggested that in these trying times, people had a responsibility to obey that government. He wrote tracts attacking the corrupting power of the Few; he also participated in market transactions. He championed the cause of farmers and artisans; but he did nothing to support the cause of blacks or of women. Similarly, he decried many aspects of the Constitution; but he ended up supporting it.[51]

Manning was one of a number of people whom opponents called "anti-Federalists." In general, a heterogeneous group of men and women opposed the Constitution. Each group had its own reasons for doing so. Planters feared debt and the attenuation of their power within their states. Backcountry farmers feared a government too distant from their immediate needs. The middling sort in the middle colonies feared an aristocracy usurping their rights to govern within their own states. Each group, then, still was unsettled on what the Constitution would mean for the exercise of sovereignty. In general, anti-Federalists harbored a number of well-articulated concerns. In the press, they argued that the Constitution needed a bill of rights. The taxing powers of the new government also gave them pause. What many found especially vexing was the worry that the Constitution would prop up an aristocracy. In a similar vein, they fretted about the nationalizing tendencies of the document, that power would become too consolidated. Anti-federalists came from many sections of the country, and they were as diverse in their beliefs and motivations as loyalists had been. They predominated on the fringes of New England, where great proprietors were trying to seize control of land and power, and Rhode Island, which had benefited from government under the Articles. They came from the Hudson River Valley of New York, which saw a great deal of struggle between tenants and patrons, and sections of North Carolina wracked by civil war. Wealthy planters in Virginia worried about their hold over their society and what the Constitution would mean for debt. Western Pennsylvanians feared for local control of their communities amid avaricious eastern speculators.[52]

Older radicals also held onto older ideas. These men pitted liberty against order, seeing the two in a zero-sum relationship. Almost all Americans coming out of the revolution favored the ideals of liberty. But for those who supported the Constitution, liberty and order were not necessarily at odds. Perhaps they had been in 1774. Not so in 1787. Some older radicals, to be sure, contested the idea of a strong central government, at least initially. John Lamb, a one-time Son of Liberty from New York, championed the anti-constitutionalist cause. Lamb headed up the Federal Republican Committee, which tried to establish networks to organize resistance to the Constitution. Although he reached out to some of the radicals from the 1760s and 1770s, a network never coalesced. With time, nearly all of the old radicals came to accept the new reality emerging. Both Samuel Adams and John Hancock, who had cut their teeth as radicals in the early 1770s, feared what was happening in Philadelphia and at first argued they would not stand for the antidemocratic ethos of the Constitution, but Hancock warmed up to it when he was promised support for his gubernatorial reelection campaign.[53] Patrick Henry, who famously "smelled a rat," contended that the nation's problems were not as dire as some suggested. The document, he argued, "squints toward monarchy." He did not believe that any government over so vast an area could comprehend a complex common good. Only a tyrant could. "If we admit this consolidated government," he declared, "it will be because we like a great splendid one. Some way or other we must be a great and mighty empire." The ambiguity of "We the People" could not safeguard liberty like the more tangible "we the States."[54] Nonetheless, most reluctantly accepted the idea that in America in 1787 all had to be friends of order to be friends of liberty. They may have stood on the margins decrying what was happening or the means to achieve order, but they accepted this formulation.[55] Most had mixed feelings. Some hated it, but they recognized unity and order as critical goals.[56]

The same sentiments held true for the most influential anti-Federalists. George Mason refused to sign the Constitution as the convention came to a close. Madison noted that he had left the federal convention "in an exceeding ill humour" and "with a fixed disposition to prevent the adoption of the plan if possible."[57] His refusal, however, did not stem from a principled support of the rights of common men and women. Rather, he and others did not believe that the Constitution was up to the task of reconstituting effective sovereignty, that it could not balance the competing forces within society because of its scope and scale. Yet when push came to shove, many anti-Federalists agreed with their political enemies that liberty could not be sustained without order. They agreed on the ends of sovereignty. They had just disagreed about the means of achieving it. In fact, some prominent anti-Federalists, like the writer Mercy Otis Warren, argued that the main reason to oppose the Constitution was that it could not uphold order and deference in a society run amok. Small republics, she believed, were necessary to balance the desires of the many with the privileges of the few and to resurrect patriarchal social controls. America after the war was like a "restless, vigorous, luxurious youth, prematurely emancipated from the authority of the parent, but without the experience necessary to direct him to act with dignity or discretion." People like Warren or Mason may have opposed the Constitution, but after ratification—and because of their fears of a politicized citizenry—they opted to work within the new system.[58]

Even if Federalists hated what they called "the mob," they had to concede that sovereignty hinged on legitimacy. In this vein, Federalists came around to the idea of a bill of rights. Conciliation on this score made the Constitution palatable to those who opposed it. Proposing a bill of rights appealed to many different groups on many different fronts. The rights enumerated, such as freedom of the press, of religion, of rights to trial by jury and due process, stated what was already present in the common law. Nonetheless, these proposed amendments eased fears. Patrick Henry had argued that a bill of rights was the price for his submission to the Constitution. Baptists in his state also wanted a bill of rights to guarantee their right to worship as they saw fit. Once the amendments were passed, Rhode Island and North Carolina ratified the Constitution, ending the constitutional debate. Men and women may have disagreed and fought over many issues. Most now would do so within the system.[59]

At the end of the revolutionary period, Americans were reaching a consensus based on ambiguity. Through debates over ratification emerged a novel way of sustaining authority in a society that was democratized. Heated contests over the terms of political debate, such as those that characterized the process of ratification, helped transform American political culture to reflect what had happened to American society. By the late 1780s, language, debate, and society had become thoroughly democratized. Yet within this context, most Americans understood that some authority was needed in America.[60] They struggled over its form and shape in a fluid context, each group arguing for a concept of authority that would speak to its aspirations and interests. And in a nation made up of states that aspired to sovereign status, comprised of different ethnic groups, divided into regions with distinctive traditions, each transformed in distinctive ways by years of violence and disorder, the search for unity presented profound problems. The war with Britain and the crisis leading up to it may have made most Americans leery of state power; the years of revolution made them understand that a vacuum of power was as dangerous as too much. The vague nature of sovereignty in the Constitution allowed Americans to address these complex concerns and realities. Power in the new system appeared and disappeared like a Cheshire cat. Checks and balances kept power within bounds. Although once the Bill of Rights passed one could make the claim that national authority protected the rights of individuals and minorities, or how the new government, in fact, limited authority, the new government was built for authority, to address the upheaval caused by revolution. Perhaps the greatest achievement of the so-called founders was in making Americans believe that power did not exist.[61]

The idea of federalism, of dividing sovereignty, reflected how framers tried to articulate a vision to address reality as they saw it. Dividing power, in some ways, was easy for Americans. They had lived throughout the colonial period with multiple—and messy—layers of authority, since town, colony, and imperial center each demanded its due. Federalists turned these traditions and the necessities of the period into virtues. Divided authority did not only connote a sharing of power; it also suggested a multiplicity of power. As Hamilton put it in "Federalist No. 9," only a "Confederate Republic," not a large or small one, but both a large and small one, could provide a basis of order. "The proposed Constitution," he argued, "so far from implying an abolition of the State Governments, makes them constituent parts of the national sovereignty." Such an arrangement "leaves in their possession certain exclusive and very important portions of sovereign power. This corresponds, in every rational import of the terms, with the idea of a Foederal Government." These ideas subtly shifted debates from where ultimate authority should be located—the question of sovereignty—to how it should be apportioned and divided—an issue of jurisdiction.[62]

Such consensus did not happen by accident; nor did it happen by design. The founders—both Federalist and anti-Federalist—shared a commitment to the idea of unanimity. At issue was culture. Throughout the ratification debates they used the metaphors of architecture to discuss the document. What mattered was the way the whole design functioned, not the individual parts. This argument that the whole was greater than the sum of the parts reflected an aesthetic belief in the art and craft of the whole piece, sensibilities that they shared with other men of letters in the Atlantic world. This sensibility also allowed them to live with what would appear to be irreconcilable differences. In fact, they believed that the differences could be a virtue. By resorting to a cultural commitment to unanimity, the framers could justify unsavory bargains struck to bring revolution to a close while recognizing the restraints on what they could accomplish given the realities of American society.[63]

Tensions could be crosscutting. One's political grievances, say, those of women, could be offset by the cultural currency one had gained as a member of a group that had sacrificed during the revolution. Or the economic marginalization of common men was balanced by the political roles they could play, however limited they were. Common white men could also cling to the rights they had secured and that they were not among the marginalized; they could celebrate the idea that citizenship was based on the ability to enjoy rights, an idea that encompassed them while excluding others.[64] The cross trussing, therefore, that animated American society in the waning years of revolutionary ferment was cultural, economic, and political. In fact, the stuff of the political, what was written on paper, reflected what the cultural allowed.

The founders, then, did not so much create American sovereignty as canonize it. The preamble reflects this. Indeed, the most overlooked section of the Constitution is the most significant. As well as enshrining popular sovereignty, it laid out the conditions for a return to sovereignty. Governments had to exist to rescue men from the state of war, to defend the citizenry, and to promote the benefits of society. Without meaningful sovereignty, arts and learning could not thrive. Without government, as Americans had learned, society could not survive. The negotiations that took place in the 1780s hinged upon this idea. Americans disagreed—vehemently at times—on issues great and small, peripheral and fundamental. But a broad consensus had emerged about the necessity of sovereignty and the shape it would take, given America's colonial and revolutionary history. The vague nature of American sovereignty that emerged, a reflection of the state of war and the complexities of uniting diverse regions and traditions, allowed people to see what they wanted to see in the Constitution.

Creating legitimacy did not prove as difficult as it appeared it would in 1787 when the delegates met in Philadelphia behind closed doors.

The West, a different matter altogether, threatened the national settlement that was emerging. For a start, it did not seem that the West was part of the eastern agenda. Indians received only a passing mention in the Constitution. Simply put, when it came to determining representation, Indians were to be "excluded." Indians lived on sovereign American territory; but they were not citizens. They considered themselves as members of semi-sovereign Indian nations, nations that the United States Congress had treated with. Moreover, they lived on the cultural margins of the new order emerging. If they lived in a savage or barbarous state, they could not become virtuous, which went hand-in-hand with civility. This age-old formula, which had underwritten the Britishness Benjamin West had memorialized, found new life in the United States during the revolution. To be independent, and to be considered an active citizen, one had to live a settled lifestyle. Most Indians lived in the West and did not recognize the new American state. So participation was an abstraction. And delegates wanted to leave well enough alone.[65]

Western settlers, wealthy and poor, following the news of what was happening in Philadelphia, generally feared eastern intentions. Westerners still struggled with the continuation of revolutionary violence. Sovereignty had not been made manifest in the West. They too were conflicted about the Constitution, embracing a democratic political culture, yet wanting above all a government that could protect them. For these men and women, self-preservation trumped other rights. "Our posterity," settlers from Pittsburgh believed, "depends on our speedy adoption of some mode of government more efficient than that which we now possess." They complained of the British manning American forts, the Spanish stopping trade down the Mississippi, and Indian attacks.[66] Nonetheless, poor settlers tended to see eastern avarice at work in the document. While wealthier settlers and speculators saw interests that were antithetical to western prosperity, architects of the Constitution like Hamilton did not want to see a United States oriented to the West but envisioned America's future as one driven by eastern cities and Atlantic commerce. The West, according to such thinking, could only entangle the new nation in disputes.

Those a bit more leery of centralized power and Hamilton's vision of America's future, such as Thomas Jefferson, thought that they had solved the western conundrum that had baffled the British. The West, it was hoped, would become a land reservoir for the nation.[67] The one triumph of the Articles of Confederation had been in rationalizing the West. The Confederation Congress had gotten Virginia and other states claiming land in the West to relinquish such claims. Virginians did not do so out of a sense of altruism. Indeed, the bargains struck ensured that their citizens would have first rights to many key regions in the West. Virginians, for instance, demanded that the claims of older companies had to be considered null and void, demanding reserves set aside for their veterans to settle upon. The West would not belong to Virginia but to Virginians— under the authority of the United States in Congress assembled. Connecticut won similar concessions.

Yet officials still had to craft a system of integrating the West into the established system of states. How would the West be considered in the new nation? Would it be regarded as an outward province, a place where citizens had fewer rights than those in the center? Jefferson rejected such an idea. He argued that the West eventually had to be divided into new states that could join the confederation with exactly the same standing as the older, established states, rejecting a conventional model of empire, one in which a powerful center ruled over dependent and subservient peripheries. Once territories had reached a certain population they would be allowed join, so long as their constitutions reflected a proper republican sensibility.[68] The so-called Northwest Ordinance of 1787 laid the groundwork for fleshing out new sovereign entities, determining the orderly manner in which land would be distributed and sold. To do so, it divided the West into perfectly proportioned sections. It also stated that schools and universities would be established to civilize these rude parts. If the West were to become part of the United States, it had to become a place where a virtuous, civilized citizenry flourished. Jefferson also concluded that slavery could not be permitted to take hold in the region hoping it could begin without the corrupting influences of that institution.

Private companies and individuals, it was hoped, would win the West under these arrangements, and with time, would transform the region. The state had little role to play. The West, then, could serve its purpose as land bank efficiently and economically. To make matters even simpler, officials had treaties in hand, however fraudulent, that ceded much of the territory they hoped would be settled initially. So some officials paid little attention to the West. Some saw it much like John Jay as a region that could literally be fobbed off to pursue eastern interests. Others took a more laissez-faire approach. They knew it had to made part of the nation, but did little more than put the political mechanisms in place to enable this to happen. In the meantime, as settlers went west, they would fill the coffers of Congress. An unmanaged West could help bring order to the East.

At least one prominent group of Americans, who shared Hamilton's enthusiasm for the Constitution and Jefferson's hope that the West could be integrated seamlessly and easily, saw things similarly. In 1785, a group of investors from New England created the Ohio Company. They too were appalled at what was happening to America in the wake of the War of Independence. Seeing anything but virtue in their towns and cities, they hoped to settle the West and plant a colony that would be defined by the principles of virtue and independence and that would serve as a shining beacon for the rest of America. These descendants of Puritans did not go west on a godly errand to reform the world. But they went to create a more perfect republican society, and they wanted only the most virtuous to come along with them. If they practiced what they preached, liberty would flourish and order would prevail. They would treat Indians kindly and keep ragged "Virginians" away, the sort who enflamed tensions. Investors used connections with government officials to use Continental scrip at face value to purchase land near the Muskingum River. In 1788, about 500 men and women ventured to the new settlement named Marietta, where they constructed some cabins, and in its shadow, an army detachment constructed a fort. They would try to keep tensions with Indians at a minimum, but if belligerent Indians caused problems for the settlers, soldiers could be sent to chastise them.[69]

Other groups came as well. A group of New Jerseyites ventured to the Miami River. Further to the east, French immigrants established a new settlement called Gallipolis. Connecticut men and women made plans to establish settlements on the Connecticut western reserve near Lake Erie. And Virginians continued to stream in. The disorder and violence still gripping places like Kentucky served as a deterrent for some. But it also beckoned many. Chaos ensured that the poorer sort could stay a step ahead of speculators and officials. With luck, they could make improvements on some land and try to claim it as their own.

The heady plans of the New Englanders never panned out. In fact, the place devolved into violence a few years after they arrived. In 1791, Indians began launching sustained raids throughout the Ohio Valley. Supported by the British—unknown but suspected by Americans at the time—Delawares and Shawnees attacked settlements from Pittsburgh to as far west as the Illinois territory. These Indians rejected the treaties that had been made in their name. American armies traveled west to chastise what they called "disaffected" Indians, but to no avail. Untrained, they were no match for better-prepared Indians. Kentuckians had long hated Indians and had come to see them as inherently inferior, regarding them as beasts and monsters. This sensibility, too, was an aspect of revolutionary violence. New Englanders did not feel the same way. But they now believed that for order to prevail in the West, Indians and whites could not live together.

This vision, ranging from racist ideas to a belief in Indian removal, defined the western program for reestablishing authority. Without protection along these lines, settlers argued, the revolution would not end. And along these lines, some men and women began looking for a sovereign state that could protect them. What was happening in the Ohio country was similar to what was happening in other frontier regions. In general, westerners believed they stood on society's margins. Vermonters, whose natural entrepôt was Montreal in British Canada, began contacting the British to see if an arrangement could be made to make the region part of Canada. Easterners, men such as Ethan Allen claimed, took no heed of Vermont and because of that it would languish. They also flirted with Shaysites. North Carolinians living in the west of the state hoped to secede and create the new state of Franklin. They needed representatives who would look after their interests. Certainly easterners had no inclination to do so. A few Kentuckians in especially exposed regions contacted Spanish officials with a view to seceding from the United States. If the eastern government could not protect them and their trade interests, at least the Spaniards who controlled the Mississippi could. The earliest threats of secession, therefore, did not come from the South but from the West.

These movements would reach their heights in western Pennsylvania. Harder hit by the recession and foreclosures than other regions, also reeling from Indian attacks, and preyed upon by wealthy speculators from the east, western Pennsylvania emerged as the epicenter of western discontent.[70] And inhabitants there had a potent symbol of that discontent in whiskey. With little trade down the rivers and no ability to send goods efficiently over the mountains, settlers distilled their surplus grain. Whiskey became a form of currency in the cash-strapped west. And its production—and consumption—epitomized the plight westerners found themselves in.

In 1791, as New Englanders in Ohio struggled with Indian raids, the new government passed an excise on distilled spirits. Alexander Hamilton urged Washington to support the measure, which would, he hoped, raise money but not disaffect the wealthiest citizens, those whose support for the new nation he deemed critical. Small producers would bear a disproportionate burden, but as Hamilton argued, such was the price of order. Westerners, however, refused to bear that cost. Many, after all, had served during the war. Most had dealt with years of instability and violence. They would not countenance sovereignty being foisted on them that did not provide a basis for order that spoke to their interests.

The story of what is called the "Whiskey Rebellion" started when insurgents refused to pay the excise. They tarred and feathered men sent to collect the hated tax, as well as those suspected of aiding and abetting them. They fired on federal troops, and attacked the home of the man in charge of collection. In fact, they went further. They created their own constitutions for regulating their own communities, suggesting that if the state would not act in a sovereign fashion, they would. They also styled themselves Regulators, much like the people from western Massachusetts had just a few years earlier, in that they were using traditional means to make a stand for more responsive government.[71] They created their own symbols of nationhood by reviving older revolutionary practices, such as erecting liberty poles, and decorating them with western slogans. They even formed western committees of correspondence to create bonds with other disaffected regions. Insurgents marched as members of armies, swarming around Pittsburgh to encourage the citizens there to join them. Men from other regions did find common cause with them. The whiskey men had the support of western Virginians, Kentuckians, and even some Ohioans, demonstrating that these people stood as the leading edge of western disaffection.[72]

Therefore, the very name used to describe what was happening in the West—a "rebellion"—obscures what was really at work. In fact, the rising in the West represented a final chapter of America's revolution. Westerners were laying out for all to see what they regarded as the legitimate limits of any settlement. Some called for a new western declaration of independence, one that would christen a new western nation. Concerns over secession, therefore, became quite real. In the West at least, because the revolution had not ended, sovereignty was still in dispute. Easterners had to address the concerns of protection and trade for revolution to end. If not, the West would be lost.

Easterners finally responded in two ways. With Alexander Hamilton's prodding, Washington dispatched an army to deal with the insurrection. The new government, much stronger than the one that had failed miserably under the Articles to put down a rising in western Massachusetts, had to demonstrate its abilities. "Domestic tranquility" demanded as much. As Washington's Secretary of the Treasury, Hamilton urged the President to dispatch "a competent force of Militia" to suppress the rebels. "The very existence of Government," he

Figure 8.3 *Washington and the Whiskey Rebellion*, 1795, attributed to Frederick Kemmelmeyer. The Metropolitan Museum of Art.

declared, "demands this course." If an army did not march, Hamilton warned Washington, "the spirit of disobedience will naturally extend and the authority of the Government will be prostrate."[73] When the army reached the West, the insurgents ran for the hills. But an important point was made. This government would and could act to suppress those who dared to flout its authority.

About the same time, Washington sent another army west. This one would not chastise Indians but conquer them. Led by Anthony Wayne, the well-trained and well-supplied "legion of the United States" defeated a Native American confederation at a place called Fallen Timbers. The victory was anything but mythic, but in this instance troops stood up manfully to well-skilled Indian fighters. The two armies of 1794, then, demonstrated the reach of the new national government's authority and ambitions. The armies also revealed the limits of what the new nation would and would not countenance. The government could act with vigor. But it could not trample on the concerns of citizens who could claim through revolutionary sacrifice the mantle of the revolution. The state would protect westerners but not fall prostrate before them.

Once the threat of secession evaporated with the marching of the two armies, order came to the West. The Treaty of Greenville drawn up in 1795 and ending hostilities in the West inscribed a line that would separate whites from Indians. But unlike the line drawn up by the British in 1763, the new line would protect settlers from Indians. The West would also be garrisoned by troops at key sites of trade and portage, such as Chicago, that would protect the interests of the state and its citizens. The line, then, was primed to move. The government also addressed other western grievances. In 1795, officials signed agreements with the Spanish government for the use of the Mississippi, as well as a new treaty with the British that turned over British forts on American sovereign territory to the United States. The United States was now sovereign in the West. Indians, on the wrong side of a line that would move, paid the price of the new order.

Indians, of course, lived in a constitutional limbo. In fact, their status reflected realties that had emerged through the crucible of revolution. The case of Indians, therefore, resembled the plight of blacks. The revolution settlement that was taking shape through negotiations, both peaceful and belligerent, ensured the two groups would not or could not enjoy their rights. Their liberties, after all, were the cost of order. And most Americans gave their blessing to these arrangements. Holding racist ideas, most Americans could and did countenance the institution of slavery and the exclusion of blacks from the political process. Easterners held more favorable attitudes toward Indians than their western brethren, but the ideologies they held that yoked the concepts of virtue and civility allowed them to write Indians out of the national equation. Doing so allowed a national settlement, one tying East and West, North and South, to come into being. The birth of the nation was assured through such negotiations. Common whites did not gain much politically, but they held onto what they had at the expense of Indians and blacks.[74]

A number of interlocking contradictions, then, sustained consensus, many of which hinged on the idea of citizenship, who was in and who was out. While power had multiple layers and could function almost imperceptibly at times, the ideals of citizenship that emerged in America after revolution seemed to provide for democratic self-actualization. During the war, Americans had rooted their ideas about participation in the body politic in natural rights theory, and Locke had served their purposes well. After the war, citizenship proved a highly contested category, one tangled because of available political theory, the fact of political mobilization that defined the war years, and the need to restore order. Federalists hoped to limit the ideal to a "national character" that they argued had emerged through the experience of revolution. Something essentially American had been created and should define the limits of political participation. Americans, through their revolution, had earned rights. Anti-Federalists held fast to a more expansive definition, one still rooted in universal ideals of rights that posited all were endowed with rights, but one that still reflected the constraints of a world shaped by the American peculiarities of revolutionary mobilization. Although universal in theory, political rights would not be enjoyed by blacks and Indians; indeed, their exclusion sustained the inclusion of others. Ultimately, therefore, an ideal of citizenship based on a limited vision of universal rights prevailed. It would do so within a structure that apportioned power between the central government and the states.[75]

The state made all of this possible. Hamilton's negotiations with Vermonters offer a vivid example. Neither the end of the war nor the bargains struck between the national government and many of the states had alleviated Vermont's concerns. Although claiming to be independent and not technically part of the union, Vermonters were still trapped by the rapaciousness of New York speculators and the claims of that state; indeed, many of the issues that had dogged the region and fueled revolutionary violence had gone unresolved or had grown even worse. Population surged in Vermont, as men and women fleeing debt elsewhere arrived to the northern frontier, and courts struggled to keep up with debt cases. It seemed the place was primed for crippling upheaval, leading Hamilton to fret that if Vermont's pleas for autonomy were not heeded, its citizens would either conspire with the British or the Shaysites. He proposed a bargain: statehood and admission to the union in exchange for an end to radical intrigue. In 1791, Vermonters opted for stability over a redress of more fundamental grievances. As in much of the rest of America, the poorer sort would have to strike out to make a go of it. An ample frontier, acting as safety valve, made such a deal possible. A responsive state would not redress any and all grievances, but enough to provide order.[76]

Only a powerful state could bring revolution to an end. Sovereignty may have been divided between the nation-state and the states within it. Its ultimate basis in "the People" may have been confusing, and some would say dissembling. Its efficacy may have been shrouded within a culture that was steadfastly attached to liberty. But as it demonstrated on its farthest territorial reaches, the sword of this leviathan could be used to bring order. The state, then, both emerged from the process of revolution and brought that process to an end. It celebrated the revolutionary experience of certain groups, while keeping them from holding all the levers of power. It excluded others along lines that most Americans could live with. The government would be deceptively strong, yet Americans would not trumpet the powerful abilities of its state. This contradiction, too, represented an aspect of the negotiations that went into forging a revolution settlement. This tacit arrangement, in other words, ended the revolution. Americans got the state they deserved, one that was out of mind so long as it was out of sight.[77]

Condemning or praising the settlement that the founders canonized—or focusing attention on the apparent contradictions that stemmed from the settlement—misses the point. The founders—elite and common, black and white, male and female—did not so much deal in paradox, as they struggled to understand what their worlds could offer given the realities of the revolutionary process that they hoped to bring to an end. What happened in the East and West, the North and South, was the logical conclusion to all that went on during America's revolution. The negotiations of the period knit together the kaleidoscopic revolutionary processes of any number of Americas in one settlement. Some won something. None won all they hoped to. Others lost all. And the state guaranteed these outcomes as it brought revolution to a close.

CHAPTER 9

✦

Puzzled and Prospering Beyond Example in the History of Man

America's Revolution had ended by 1802. In that year, Thomas Paine paid a visit to his old friend Thomas Jefferson in the White House in the new capital of Washington, DC. Two years earlier, Jefferson had been elected president, initiating a long period of rule by him and like-minded Virginians. Paine and Jefferson had thought alike. Each, in fact, believed in the innate moral worth of individuals and in the social sense that drew people to work together, an idea that allowed them to imagine societies based on freedom and on limited government.[1] Both styled themselves proponents of the "rights of man" and had played prominent roles in America's struggle against Britain, as they would later in the French Revolution. In 1802, Paine landed in Baltimore, after, as he said, the president had invited him to come to America. He did not encounter a grateful nation. He was lampooned as a "loathsome reptile," an atheist and agitator. One critic described him as "a lying, drunken, brutal infidel, who rejoices in the opportunity of basking and wallowing in the confusion, devastation, bloodshed, rapine, and murder, in which his soul delights."[2]

On one level, Paine was unwelcome in the United States because of his irreligious views. The author of *Common Sense*, who in part made his arguments by relying on scripture, had in subsequent writings revealed himself to be a deist. Americans were in the midst of an awakening, a development that, like its colonial-era precursor, brought Americans closer to Christ through vital piety. The era of the Revolution, in fact, seemed to punctuate a longer period of broad evangelical religiosity that straddled the ocean. Although a republican and democratic ethos colored the ways Americans understood the role of God in society in the wake of revolution, the forms of piety resembled earlier American patterns of belief.[3] In a society once more "awash in a sea of faith," the author of the deistic *Age of Reason* was out of step with many citizens of the United States.

Paine was harbinger of chaos. A newspaper reported that "so perfectly blasted is the reputation of Thomas Paine that, even in Paris, he can associate only with the lowest and vilest of the rabble." His role was now finished. "True it is," the paper continued, "that in a revolutionary state of things he has always found employment, and has been sometimes honoured with the attention of distinguished men.

Figure 9.1 William Sharp, *Thomas Paine, after George Romney Engraving*, 1793. Frick Art Reference Library.

His talents were suited to pull down, to overturn, and destroy."[4] Benjamin Rush refused to have anything to do with him. His old ally Samuel Adams denounced his return to America. They were not alone. When he landed, he could find no room, except a tavern run by "an honest hibernian." Soon he made his way to Washington, where he found few friends. The political atmosphere in the city was caustic, as Jefferson's opponents, the Federalists, were using the press to harangue the president. Nonetheless, despite advice to the contrary, Jefferson invited Paine to the executive mansion for dinner a number of times. As another guest put it, Jefferson, as was his habit, once greeted his old compatriot in slippered feet, so conscious was he of outward manifestations of aristocratic privilege and power. With time, however, the pressure on Jefferson mounted to ignore Paine, especially as he attacked no less a personage than Washington in the press. The dinners continued, but Paine was no longer extended a public welcome. Soon they had a falling out. Paine sent an aggrieved letter to Jefferson, questioning his "sort of shyness, as if you stood in fear of federal observation." By 1802, Jefferson could not have afforded to be seen with a radical like Paine. Either Tom Paine had changed, or America had.[5]

The answer to this question goes to the heart of when the American Revolution came to an end. Conventional wisdom suggests 1787. Cleverer writers point to 1865, when fundamental tensions were reconciled on Civil War battlefields. Those studying the process of re-creating sovereignty would be wise to choose 1795 when it seems American sovereignty had become manifest. One could argue for other dates, such as 1815, when Americans would complete a second war of independence against Britain—the ending of the War of 1812—an event that would secure sovereign status. From a continental perspective, the War of 1812, too, amounted to a civil war, one pitting loyalist Americans in Canada against republican Americans in the United States. The end of the conflict brought resolution in the form of a secure border.[6] Or 1821 when the trade-offs negotiated at the time of revolution that allowed North and South to remain in a single union were more or less laid bare for what they were with the Missouri Compromise. Ultimately, the date picked depends upon one's definition of revolution and how its legacy is regarded.

Whatever date chosen, one thing is clear: the question of how matters more than the question of when. The story of Paine's visit says more about how the revolution ended and how Americans had changed because of it. It reveals contradictions that had not been rectified, looming questions that still had not been answered, but in a nation in which sovereignty was secure. By 1802, America had become a contradiction wrapped up in a sovereign state. And already by this date, Americans had selectively created stories to manage such incongruities. They were an exceptional and exceptionally revolutionary people, whose revolution had ended through the power of a state robed in anti-statist rhetoric.[7]

Paine's visit to the White House explains a great deal about how both he and Jefferson had changed. More significantly, it offers a glimpse of how Americans had to conceive of themselves in the wake of revolution, as well as the more pointed question of whether the revolution was "lost." The visit also speaks to the ways political culture shifted from the radical fringes to the center and to the nature of American democracy. By the time Jefferson was elected, the civic culture was steeped in democratic ideals and discourse, but it rested on a revolution settlement that contained undemocratic elements. Such was the cost of bringing revolution to a close. A democratic ethos not only failed to jibe with reality; it also rested on a set of myths that sought to obscure this disjunction. America had to be democratic given the nature of its revolution. And a powerful state, rhetoric of impotence aside, held the bundle of paradoxes together.

By the time Paine paid his visit to the White House, an uneasy, and ultimately unjust, consensus on a number of issues had emerged. Americans had created new ideas of how the economy would function. They had a new understanding of how a state should function. They had drawn the limits of their political discourse. Each of these agreements involved inherent contradictions. But each had to be crafted to create a stable society. Stability did not imply perfection or even unanimity. America was still balkanized by all sorts of factions, riddled with differences over race and class. Regional variations and differing ideas of political economy also threatened to fracture the union. But by 1802, they had struck a workable balance between competing tensions. And they were already crafting a vision of who they were and what they had to be, rooted in mythic ideals and moments, to comprehend animating contradictions. In other words, they began to fasten on vanishing points to define themselves. Ultimately, the idea of the American Revolution was born as America's revolution ended.

By the late 1780s, the economy was reorienting itself. The nearly-great depression or contraction of the early 1780s that began to relent only to reemerge in 1785 was coming to an end in the last years of the decade. With the passage of time, international commerce began to pick up again, as levels of trade with Britain in the 1790s, although not reaching prewar levels, were continuing to rebound. Eventually, the United States would become a critical trading partner with Britain, so much so that America would comprise part of an "informal" British empire. The United States would be its own sovereign entity, but it would play the role the colonies once played in the British economy.[8] Trade with other European countries picked up as well. The disruption of revolution forced American merchants to look to new markets like Germany, the Netherlands, and Scandinavia. They also opened up trade to China. Most scandalously, one of the greatest commodities traded was slaves from Africa. All in all, exports by the 1790s began to exceed— barely—prewar levels.[9]

The development of new trade opportunities also stemmed from contingencies and the possibilities that Americans encountered in a wider world. As Americans struggled to find a niche in a competitive world economic environment after the treaty with Britain was signed, they did so during a period of tumult and warfare in Europe. Tensions between France and Britain provided openings for American merchants to pursue trade in the East, and at the beginning of the nineteenth century, Americans were poised to supplant Britons as the trading power in Asia and to become the leaders of the colonial carrying trade. The Tea Party, in other words, did not end America's fascination with the Orient or with its goods, and an age of upheaval in Europe offered the means to acquire these goods in new ways. Industrial might, financial structures, or central planning did not drive the impetus to trade; circumstances did, in the process creating capital for further international and domestic investment. Circumstances also encouraged Americans to champion the virtues of a free trade ideology, which at this time benefited merchants.[10]

The war had transformed the basis of the economy, as Americans began trading more heavily with each other. Food raised in the North was shipped to the South, as well as some manufactured products. And the West was now able to send its products down the Mississippi to the rest of the world. Although recovery was slow, with a rising population, indigenous industry created by wartime necessity, the movement of people to the West, and the integration of North and South, internal trade became just as important as trade outside American borders. Arguably, Americans had been wealthier in 1774 than they were in 1790, especially in the South. The terrible disruption of the war years and the flight of loyalists had eroded wealth. Nonetheless, the economy was coming back from the dead. Moreover, to prosecute a war, and to pay for its debt, had forced Americans to develop more sophisticated notions of banking and finance, changes that would sustain the new economy that was emerging.[11]

As internal and international commerce returned, older colonial patterns of political economy were shifting in fundamental ways, a change tied to neither planning nor happenstance but emerging from critical negotiations. To bring order to America required a broad agreement on how the new nation's economic aspirations would be structured, understood, and developed. And in the 1780s, Americans had many different ideas about the nature of the new nation's economy and the way it would be tied into the world economy. Famously, some argued that the United States had to remain an agrarian nation, one that provided markets for its own citizens.

Most Americans, or so the thinking went, should work the land. The planter John Taylor of Caroline was not alone in idealizing farming. "Hereafter I mean to till a soil, which promises to crown my labour with some success," he wrote Jefferson. "Mother earth offers to her children subsistence & repose," he declared, adding "it was foolish to leave the bosom which nourished me, for the sake of exposing my own, to the unfraternal shafts of all the wicked passions."[12] America enjoyed a competitive advantage when it came to agriculture. Unlike European nations, America had land; what it did not have was labor. Migrants tended to head to places where farmland was cheap and available, not to cities. Although they were growing because of increased demand during the war and the return of veterans, American cities remained small compared to their European counterparts. And they were geared for commerce, not manufacturing.

Some turned such a reality into a virtue—literally. One reading of Thomas Jefferson reveals an idealist who believed that America had to remain an agricultural nation to remain virtuous. He hated what he saw in much of Europe, where cities teemed with the indigent. He saw London as dystopia, a crime-ridden metropolis in a nation whose political economy was based in manufacturing. America had no Londons. Nor should it, he reasoned. Industry, he argued, destroyed men's republican souls, turning them into dependent drones. People seeking work in Europe's industrial capitals soon became wage laborers, and as they did so, they were beholden to the wealthy and so descended into vice. Jefferson did not want this to happen to the United States. By keeping American development at an agricultural stage, the country would encourage each of its citizens to remain an independent farmer, under no one's thumb. Popular sovereignty could only thrive under such conditions. If Americans maintained their independence, they would maintain their virtue. And the revolution had created a people, not an elite, who were virtuous. They would then serve as sentinels of the republic guarding it against vice, corruption, and tyranny. Jefferson understood that America possessed the land to make this vision a reality.[13]

Others held a different set of beliefs about political economy. Thinkers in Scotland, for instance, like Adam Smith, argued that development into an industrial, commercial economy was inevitable. Societies, they argued, moved through discrete stages of development. Britons, centuries ago, had toiled as hunters and gatherers, from which they graduated to the pastoral stage, in which the wealth of society and individual status were tied into cattle. Eventually, Britons moved toward agriculture, and for some time, that stage of development defined the manners and mores of the people, before advancing to a commercial and industrial stage. In *Wealth of Nations*, Smith argued that "according to the natural course of things," the "greater part of the capital of every society is, first, directed to agriculture, afterwards to manufactures, and last of all to foreign commerce." At this level, and only at this level, could culture and the arts flourish. Cities with opportunity would arise, and wealth would accrue.[14] Binding this vision together was not an indifferent "invisible hand," but the sum total of a people's sociability, through which the best, not the worst of people, would come to the fore. Because inevitability defined the process of development, government's task was to stand out of the way and let it transpire.

Alexander Hamilton wanted to turn this inevitability into America's virtue. "When all the different kinds of industry obtain in a community," he believed, "each individual can find his proper element, and call into activity the whole vigor of his nature."[15] He saw cities arising in the east. He hoped to build model towns that would serve as engines for American development. Patterson, New Jersey, a town drawn up on the Passaic Falls, served as his laboratory where government would incubate industry. Here all sorts of goods, ranging from women's shoes to paper, would be manufactured.[16] Far from a dystopia, Britain shone as Hamilton's beacon. Throughout 1791, Hamilton prepared a comprehensive plan of how government could foster industry. Entitled the "Report on the Subject of Manufactures," the plan argued that American industry depended on the "incitement and patronage of government" to give people confidence to invest and to allow American industries to compete internationally. Banks represented a key part of the plan because they leveraged what little capital there was. Funded debt also encouraged the growth of capital by enticing foreign investors. He was wary of an economy dependent on agriculture, arguing that mixed was wisest. If the government chose to fund certain manufacturing sectors, and these developed with time and tending, then the rising tide would lift all boats. The government could do so through the shrewd use of bounties and tariffs.[17] By his lights, "the spirit of enterprise" could be encouraged or discouraged by government and society. "It must," as he put it, "be less in a nation of cultivators, than in a nation of cultivators and merchants; less in a nation of cultivators and merchants, than in a nation of cultivators, artificers, and merchants."[18]

Not only did he hope that Philadelphia and New York would become Londons in the West, he thought it was just a matter of time. He too believed virtue would thrive in America, but not the virtue of the yeoman famer, which, for Hamilton, was a pipe dream, one that flew in the face of historical development. Rather, he prophesied a day when American arts would astound the world and when the nation would become an international republic of letters. Breaking away from Britain had allowed colonial dependence to be a thing of the past. Freed from its shackles, the United States could now seek its destiny as a powerful nation among nations. Hamilton considered himself a realist, much like thinkers on the European continent. By paving the way for development across the time, the government could prepare the United States to participate in the European world of power politics. The nation just needed like-minded men of virtue to light the way.[19]

Hamilton's America depended on sophisticated market mechanisms. Hamilton did not believe like Adam Smith that markets would regulate themselves. Government's main task was to foster this sort of development, to serve as a midwife to history. The creation of modern financial structures, policies fostering industrial incubation, and a uniform and viable currency formed key parts of the plan of how America would develop over time. He also wanted the national government to consolidate and fund all state and national IOUs, then to issue stock to pay off the debt. As long as investors bought the stock, debt could be an asset, preserving the confidence of friends of government and binding the wealthy to the nation. Debts could be paid back by a more modern system of taxes, one designed to ensure that the virtuous—those needed to lead the United States—bought in. The new nation could, he believed, be put on a sure financial footing, making the United States a wise place in which to invest, while political harmony was established. One, he believed, fostered the other.[20]

In theory, no common ground could exist between the two positions. And much of the conflict in the 1790s between Jefferson, Hamilton, and their followers stemmed from the incompatibility of a yeoman's republic suspicious of Britain, on the one hand, and pro-British industrial development and a system that would turn the United States into a European-style state, on the other hand. The sound and fury of difference, however, obscures an emerging consensus or common ground that Americans were brokering and that, in the process, created the ideological bases for American capitalism. Jefferson and Madison came to terms with the Hamiltonian vision by embracing the idea that America could grow across space to forestall development over time. The vision they embraced—on paper, at least—was idyllic. If a traveler were to head west to the Rockies, then look around, "he would observe in the earliest stage of association living under no law but that of nature." If he glanced across space and time to the east, he would "next find those on our frontiers in the pastoral state." Further still, he would "then succeed our own semi-barbarous citizens, the pioneers of the advance of civilization." Finally, he "would reach his, as yet most improved state in our seaport towns." Such a journey through space, Jefferson suggested, "in fact, is equivalent to a survey, in time, of the progress of man from the infancy of creation to the present time."[21]

In responding to what his context had to offer and what it could not permit, Jefferson used the Atlantic-wide discourses at his disposal and imagined combining the two visions. In general, such was the role of the founders in this period. They recognized the constraints and possibilities of the world around them and used the languages available in that world to rationalize its limits. In essence, the United States would grow to the northwest and southwest and in so doing provide more land for agriculture. The west would then become the safety valve of society. Cities, Jefferson and his followers conceded, would grow, but they would do so as outlets for trade. Migrants would enter eastern cities to learn trades that would support the international trade of the products produced in North, South, and West. America would have American—not European—cities, and in this scheme they could help provide the basis for virtue. Hamilton and the so-called Federalists got their cities and their financial structures. America would need banks, a stable currency, and a useful level of debt to promote a Jeffersonian vision of commercial development. Jefferson democratized such institutions, getting rid of much of Hamilton's fiscal program. He trusted people to make wise choices. Nonetheless, society would develop in much the way Hamilton had hoped and prophesied. In some ways, it would function more efficiently than if a government was capitalizing development. Ironically, Jefferson's deregulation of the Hamiltonian vision permitted the growth of individual and state investment. Competition, not privilege, underscored economic development.[22] And the cities, while serving as trade entrepôts, could also incubate industry, especially if cheap labor flowed in from Europe. The vision, of course, would be achieved through what historians would refer to as the "second American Revolution" that was the Civil War. Then the sinews of modern American capitalism would be created. But the ideology that would sustain and justify American capitalist development emerged from the first revolution.[23]

Each group, neither of which received what it wanted, compromised to maintain order and a sense of unity. Jefferson had to acknowledge that his rural republic could not be sustained without what he and his followers would regard as aristocratic elements, especially financial structures. Americans would move to the West, but they would do so as agents of an economy geared toward international trade. Hamilton would not turn American cities into sites of industry like those in northern England. New York would not be Liverpool. He and his fellow travelers would have to abandon the idea that America would be exclusively oriented toward the Atlantic. Moreover, the not-so invisible hand of state governments, along with the national government, would harness the energies of a virtuous citizenry to propel the economy.[24] His dream of a republic led by a virtuous elite manipulating the levers of government proved as illusory as Jefferson's republican vision. But in giving up aspects of these distinctive programs, Americans created something greater than the sum of its parts. By reconciling ideas of development premised upon space and land, they crafted a system that no single vision alone could sustain but that would come with time to define American capitalist development.

This negotiated settlement reflected the constraints of a world shaped by revolution. The founders did not so much design a blueprint for a capitalist engine as create the possible. The world all Americans were forging was peopled by slave and free labor, eastern merchants, and western farmers, some shackled and some liberated by the contests over sovereignty. Jefferson's ideal reflected these American realities most clearly. Hamilton's spoke to another sort of reality, the world of nations. Neither was possible on its own.

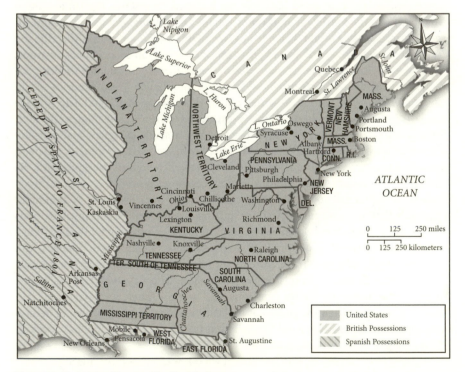

Map 9.1 The United States after Revolution.

The same dynamics, in part, explain why Washington, DC, would be the nation's capital. Southerners wanted a capital close to home and one that resembled what they regarded as the southern agrarian ideal. Northerners favored a capital in New York or Philadelphia, either place which would become a European-style capital that combined the functions of government with the energy of culture and commerce. Some feared the impasse, which reflected deeper divisions over the economic future of the United States, would fracture the new nation. In 1790, Congress came up with a workable solution. For the passage of the federalist plan to assume state debt, the seat of government was moved to the Potomac. The new nation now had an undemocratic financial mechanism that the state needed for stability; it also had a setting for a capital that reflected the ideal of a republic formed from popular sovereignty. In such a way, unity was maintained.[25]

The consensus that defined American political economy, above all, depended on a geographic sense of unity made manifest in the first decades of the nineteenth century. To hold seemingly distinctive visions together entailed tying the regions of the United States together. A policy of aggressive internal improvements yoked together a nation, disunited by regional interests. In this hybrid scheme, East and West relied upon one another. Eastern cities could not exist as centers of culture without western hinterlands. South and North were also knit together, as one provided an outlet for agricultural products and the other with time would do the same for industrially manufactured products. The national state fostered development when it acted and when it relinquished its role as incubator to the states. The state, both national and at the state-level, would act as an arbiter, but one that would foster this oxymoronic system. Officials of all political stripes would allow a financial structure to emerge that would sustain the arrangement over political economy. And they would create systems of transportation and communication to maintain its viability. The federal state working at different levels proved the bridge that would tie the two visions together, to magnify the size and scope of hinterlands and tie them to industrial and mercantile centers. The consensus that was struck also provided the basis for a return to a new order.[26]

Through negotiations that took place in Congress, courts, and newspapers, cities were poised to grow in unimaginable ways with the extension of hinterlands. The dynamic would make New York as an idea imaginable. Here again the federated state enabled development. The state of New York created the Erie Canal, which in turn encouraged the growth of inland cities, such as Cleveland, that served as entrepôts tying the hinterland to the cities of international trade. A road system constructed by the federal government yoked east to west. In fact, 2% of the sale of federal lands was to go toward constructing a national road. States allocated monies to county governments to construct the capillaries of the system. Through a system of roads and canals or "artificial rivers, " the Ohio country became a part of New York City's back-country. Soon canals sprouted up throughout Ohio, as the state government saw the wisdom in connecting Ohio to eastern markets. Meanwhile, as goods arrived from the canal to the Hudson River to the city, New York grew into the empire state. Cincinnati—on a natural river system—would grow into a center for internal trade, as corn, hogs, and whiskey produced in its vast hinterland were shipped down the Ohio to the Mississippi. As one settler put it, the Ohio was "the American Nile."

Understandably, because of this path of development, gaining control of the port of New Orleans proved vital to the maintenance of American stability.[27] In this vein, the Louisiana Purchase would represent a boon not only for land but also for its port. Without outlets of trade, consensus could crumble. It is no mistake that many regarded the state of Ohio in the early nineteenth century as the epitome of the American dream. Here the various visions intersected, literally and figuratively. It proved the one place where the hitherto conflicting ideas of American development found a common ground.

In compromising, the hopes of both visions were realized and many of their key aspects vindicated. The nation acquired multiple safety valves: the west for land, the east for growing cities. Cities, hitherto only tolerable to Jefferson's republican vision, would play a key role in development, with time, producing the goods that would clothe slaves and stock farms while serving at outlets for trade. As vast hinterlands were harnessed through internal improvements, they would grow and become magnets for men and women from other countries. Historically, migrants chose the most dynamic regions of America to venture to. Now they would have the choice of western farms, eastern cities, and the centers and projects connecting one to the other. Although the East and cities became with time places considered un-American because of the migration of people from abroad, cities proved critical for the survival of the fiction that America remained an agrarian republic.[28]

The South comprised a key part of the capitalist engine. With the agreement over a no-tariff policy in the Constitution to bring an eventual end to the slave trade, southerners traded the viability of their trade for the future security of their labor force. On paper, that is. The labor force, if anything, became more efficient and plantations became factories in the field. Capitalist mind-sets emerged not only because planters had to think more creatively about their labor force once the African slave trade came to an end but also because more efficient use of resources tied plantations more effectively into the emerging American capitalist network. Slave labor also functioned as an insurance policy for southern planters. With the movement west, development of cotton, and the end of the transatlantic slave trade, the price of slaves soared. The internal slave trade eclipsed the transatlantic one, and made the labor force a most precious commodity.[29] This dynamic explains, in part, how and why slave masters styled themselves paternalists, why they considered themselves caring men who sought to evangelize their slaves. They treated property as persons when doing so was sound business.[30]

What was grown in the South went north, and through cities, to the rest of the world. Meanwhile, northern factories would produce the goods that clothed the slave labor force of the South. Internal improvement did not align east and west at the expense of north and south; rather, it amplified the ties between east and west while not diminishing those between north and south. The South, far from a premodern almost feudal holdover from the past, became a cog in the machine created by the merger of Jeffersonian and Hamiltonian visions. Contradictions created a new national synthesis of political economy that could not have been imagined before revolution and could not be even comprehended by Adam Smith's "invisible hand."

Americans, therefore, were poised to create a modern capitalist society that looked and functioned in a premodern way. The labor force in the South seemed a stark anachronism. The agrarian vision that sustained the West with its ideological roots in Renaissance and English seventeenth-century political theory appeared out of line with the East. Only the industrialization of the North looked modern. Americans could continue to believe that they were a nation of yeomen, independent farmers, but this illusion rested on the trading prowess and growing industrial confidence of America. Northerners could tell themselves they were free; but slavery literally underwrote this conceit. The illusion strained at times, especially when outlets of trade were cut off, such as in the years of the Napoleonic Wars. Recession also could reveal the ill-clothed nature of the American empire. But it was poised to function. Efficiency in the West was sustained by farmers aggressively looking for land, in the North by wage labor and migration, and in the South by a slave system that was locked in place by political agreements. The state, therefore, had a critical role to play in buttressing this arrangement by yoking the sections together to reconcile what appeared to be distinctive visions but in fact complemented each other. The state, in this way, brought America into being.

Nothing short of oppression underscored the system. Wage laborers, of course, toiled—as Jefferson rightly feared—under appalling conditions. The history of Irish immigrants living in places like the Five Points section in New York or digging the canals that bound the system together demonstrates this much. But many had it much worse. African Americans, of course, would be debarred from citizenship by laws. But they were not the only victims. Lines would separate Indians, who also witnessed the canonization of colonial patterns, patterns now hardened by the creation of the new nation. The tragic twist was that the lines created by treaties, under this logic, could and would move, especially since lines were based on accommodating white settlement and proved critical for the reconciliation of different visions of political economy and for stability among a people who considered themselves self-sovereign. Jefferson rationalized his beliefs in the inevitability of the surrender of Indian lands by suggesting Indians would take up agriculture. He also knew that traders would ply Indians with alcohol and European goods, creating dependence, after which they would sell their lands. To Jefferson, this process seemed inevitable.[31]

In other words, inequality, now inscribed in laws and lines, determined the viability of the settlement. Blacks had to toil on plantations to keep southern planters content with the union. Slave labor, increasingly made compatible with capitalist ideology, also ensured that American raw products could be competitive in a world market, especially because international trade, as free as possible, represented a key aspect of the reconciliation of political economy. Notions of free trade, then, depended on unfreedom. Indians faced the stark choice of civilizing or moving. The system demanded as much. And, of course, the state in creating the conditions for this arrangement sustained such inequality in much the same way it paved the way for western expansion. Without the canonization of colonial patterns of inequality, it could not exist.

The state also ensured that lower-class whites bought into the system, not only in the sense that whiteness conferred status, but by offering opportunity. More

Figure 9.2 Samuel Jennings, *Liberty Teaching the Arts and Sciences*, 1792. The Library Company of Philadelphia.

critically, the arrangements over laws barring blacks from citizenship and lines push-ing Indians ever westward, with the safety valves of city, frontier, and internal works projects, allowed the poorer sort to stay a half step ahead of speculators and the wealthy. They would enjoy their political rights, especially as new states entered the union mandating universal manhood suffrage. Such arrangements allowed them to accept a national settlement that also consigned them to the margins of society. They possessed the greatest amount of rights of any common people in the world. They also had less security.

Ironically, only the "empire of liberty" could christen this arrangement. As a rule, revolutions by nature are expansionist, and bringing them to an end—or trying to—usually goes hand in hand with foreign adventures. So Cromwell extended his English revolution out to Scotland and Ireland. Napoleon would look to Egypt. Each used the discourse of the day to justify expansion, the language that their compatriots had employed to make sense of the collapse of authority and its reconstitution. Each of these, it should be noted, created amazing dislocations for the peoples in ques-tions. Although Cromwell and Napoleon ultimately failed in their goals, Americans succeeded as they expanded through space and time. The cities would develop, as would plantations, and the republic would spread. It did so through the negotiations that brought revolution to an end, as well as through the state. This complex process made the United States stable.

For these reasons, as Adams understood, Jefferson served as America's Cromwell. He also might have added its Bonaparte. Jefferson, too, used the languages of his revolution—seventeenth-century English and eighteenth-century British political theory—to rationalize expansion. His adventures, however, would not take place overseas but in the American West. His "empire of liberty," couched in the language of what he regarded as a libertarian revolution, was much the same as Cromwell's commonwealth and Napoleon's empire, differing only in incidentals. But it succeeded where the others did not because of the state and the distinctive vision of political economy that emerged as part of the revolution settlement. In particular, slavery, as an adaptable institution, was well-suited for expansion within an "empire of liberty." And African Americans would now experience the horrors of a second middle passage.[32]

The idea of an "empire of liberty" perfectly captured, as it answered, the anxieties that had transfixed Americans throughout the years of crisis and revolution. Americans still believed *libertas* and *imperium* to be in tension with one another and feared what the nation could become as they had no choice but try to balance the two. The phrase spoke to the conceit that they could evade historical processes, that they could stall the inexorable march of time and transition from one form of government to another and hold the two defining forces in perpetual balance. And they were right on this score. Because the empire was dynamically focused west, the pressures of the east could be dissipated. The balance between the categories of *imperium* and *libertas*, rooted in the movement of time, could be displaced across space. America could succeed where Britain and even Rome failed.[33]

Although the implications of these aspects of the revolution settlement lay on the horizon, by the time Jefferson was elected president in 1800 they were already becoming discernible. And no one captured the nature of that settlement better than Jefferson. In his famous inaugural address of 1801, he defined the limits and nature of the revolution. This address, which had something for everyone, did not prove remarkable for the daring vision it laid out but for the ways it captured the cross-trussing nature of the tensions that remained. Far from heralding a revolution, it was consigning one to memory. The "voice of a nation," it averred, "announc[ing] according to the rules of the Constitution, all will, of course, arrange themselves under the will of the law, and unite in the common efforts for the common good." With the election, "a wise and frugal Government, which shall restrain men from injuring one another, shall leave them otherwise free to regulate their own pursuits of industry and improvement, and shall not take from the mouth of labor the bread it has earned." The new social compact enjoyed widespread legitimacy. Disorder had ended.

His inaugural speech also spoke to the final piece of the settlement puzzle: the boundaries of legitimate discourse. Of course, the address is remembered to this day for Jefferson's famous line "every difference of opinion is not a difference of principle. We have called by different names brethren of the same principle. We are all Republicans, we are all Federalists." Although subsequent history would prove him prophetic with the withering away of Federalism, the line did not refer to parties; rather, it laid out limits. Jefferson was reflecting on the limits of political debate in the new nation in the wake of revolution, or the ideas and assumptions that would prove beyond the pale for an enduring revolution settlement, the sorts of ideas that could animate dormant tensions. In some ways, of course, the question of the terms of debate was solved by the departure and absorption of loyalists; without them, the United States could not be dismembered by counterrevolutionary forces. But in the wake of revolution, the most significant threat to stability came from the other end of the spectrum, from those who would argue that the revolution had not gone far enough. And Jefferson was addressing this threat.

Yet another irony of the revolution settlement stemmed from how Jefferson inspired the very groups in society that he needed to silence for order to come to America. By the time he was elected, Americans had reached consensus over the limits of legitimate political discourse. It was not an easy process but was a complex story, one informed by revolution elsewhere, especially France. In 1789, the global crisis of empire and sovereignty set off by the fallout of the Seven Years' War finally engulfed France in revolutionary ferment. Men and women in American towns, cities, and villages, energized by events in France, voiced their enthusiasm for the aims of French revolutionaries and also challenged more conservative understandings of America's revolutionary legacy. For some, the idea of revolutionary France occasioned fear and worry. This appeared a revolution, to be sure, but not an American type of revolution. French society was falling apart, but along very different fault lines from America. And the unsettling violence Americans witnessed across an ocean along lines of status and class, as well as religion and region, either brought back memories of the Furies or caused concern that they could return.[34] Federalists, in particular, worried that events in France could "bring about a state of what the Jacobins term *sovereign insurrection* and *permanent revolution*."[35] This idea of sovereignty in the wake of the tumult of revolution in America represented the unthinkable.

In 1789 and 1790, others, however, experienced nothing short of jubilation, and some prophesied that an American moment of liberty was setting the world on fire, toppling old regimes and old structures. As one American put it, the French Revolution could "date its *conception*" from "the late glorious struggle for Liberty" in America.[36] The ideal of a muscular popular sovereignty represented a realization of revolutionary principles. Ardent proponents of the French Revolution in the United States did not fear state power; indeed, they welcomed the thought of a state that most purely and directly represented the will of the people and made that will manifest through the deployment of power.[37] Americans gave voice to Francophilia by calling each other "citizen," and by studying French. The hero from bygone days Thomas Paine wrote *The Rights of Man*, stirring the pot of revolution and encouraging those excluded from power with the idea that they were entitled to it. And 50,000 to 100,000 copies circulated in America.[38]

In these heady, early days of revolution, associations espousing radical principles in America sprouted up. As one historian puts it, anti-Federalists were defeated, dismayed, and disarmed by the victories of the Federalists at the constitutional convention, the ratification debates, and the earliest elections.[39] They moved their politics out of doors, forming associations to champion their vision of what America should become. The French Revolution proved a catalyst in this regard, as men and women followed the French example of associating, much as they—or more likely their parents—had done in the 1760s and 1770s. In fact, revolution in France turned anti-Federalists into Democratic-Republicans or simply Republicans. Originally, Democratic-Republican societies linked political life to status, interests, and occupation. They existed to promote knowledge and self-improvement, to help immigrants, and to encourage virtue. As the term Democratic-Republican suggests, they sought to make the new republic as democratic as possible. As the Democratic Society of the City of New York announced, its members met to "support and perpetuate the EQUAL RIGHTS OF MAN."[40] In 1793, such associations began forming throughout the new nation. The Democratic Society of Pennsylvania, organized in Philadelphia by Benjamin Franklins' grandson—the editor of a newspaper Benjamin Franklin Bache—became the center of a network of associations stretching from the eastern seaboard to Kentucky.[41]

The societies were made up of a mix of people. Farmers, merchants, and entrepreneurs joined them, as did artisans and mechanics. Members of such associations created their own rules of order, governance, and their own agendas, as a rule arguing that vigilance was required to ensure that rights won in revolution would not be surrendered or violated. Although led by middle-class radicals, these societies gave voice to workingmen who believed that through sacrifice they had earned a place at the political table, as well as those who believed that they, not Federalist elites, should govern the nation. Most of the societies followed this vigilant line. They would not trust those in power, especially Federalists, to ensure that the bargains struck to bring revolution to a close were upheld. The specter of the French Revolution, with the implicit threat of urban violence, gave these sentiments a more persuasive and menacing edge. Officials may have hated the societies; they could not ignore them. While Federalists despised the associations and the thought of what was happening in France, elite republicans like Jefferson, who depended on the societies for support, also feared them.[42]

Men and women from abroad enlivened these societies, especially as more and more radicals began arriving from Britain and Ireland in the early 1790s. And these immigrants had decided political opinions. With the crackdown on radicalism in the wake of revolution in France, what had been a trickle became a torrent. Radical Irish émigrés, in particular, members of a secret revolutionary organization called the United Irishmen, saw the United States as a republican sanctuary. Once in America, they threatened to overturn the consensual balance being struck because, as outsiders, they pointed to the contradictions implicit in the revolution settlement. They chided successive administrations for undermining the liberating aspect of revolution. They decried the hollow nature of popular sovereignty, and they did not blink when they drew attention to the fundamental contradiction of slavery and freedom coexisting in the new republic. Émigrés, such as Mathew Carey, played prominent roles in editing newspapers, while also energizing Democratic-Republican societies throughout the United States, especially in the media center of Philadelphia. Many, particularly and most dangerously the "men of no property" of the lower sort, had embraced Jacobin principles. Some even went so far as to use the United States as a base from which to plot a French invasion of Ireland.[43]

English radicals, like Joseph Gales from Sheffield, who had agitated for change as members of radical corresponding societies in the Old World, likewise, questioned the revolution settlement. Like the newspaperman Gales, who eventually settled in North Carolina, the radicals from Britain championed the rights of the poor and challenged conventional ideas about property. They also raised questions about the status of women and made much of the ways the pedestal of republican motherhood would disempower women. English and Irish émigrés also challenged laboring Americans to continue pushing for their rights, to question the emerging capitalist arrangements that marginalized them, as well as meanings of the transition to wage labor. Finally, they bristled at the gap between American political discourse based on republicanism and the reality they saw around them. And with these contradictions in mind, émigrés threw themselves—unapologetically—into the whirl of American politics.[44]

Although the Age of Atlantic Revolutions heightened appeals for liberty, it also brought them to an end. As terror became the order of the day in France, many Americans backed away from calls for radicalism. On the one hand, the Terror played into the hands of Federalists who had argued, like Edmund Burke, that unfettered violence defined radical revolution. "For the French Revolution has been, from the first, hostile to all right and justice, to all peace and order in society," declared Fisher Ames in the year Jefferson assumed the presidency. In a eulogy for Washington, the Massachusetts Federalist bellowed "its very existence has been a state of warfare against the civilized world, and most of all against free and orderly republics, for such are never without factions, ready to be the allies of France, and to aid her in the work of destruction."[45] On the other hand, most Democratic-Republicans applauded popular sovereignty but did not relish a return to disorder. The French example proved that the rule of men of no property promised as much. Other issues also encouraged Americans to abandon the French revolutionary cause. The French ambassador, Edmond Genet, tried to play upon American Francophilia by encouraging citizens to arm a fleet of privateers for the French cause. The decision of the French directory to prey on American merchant ships carrying trade goods to Britain raised grave concerns as well. Therefore, Americans realized that events in France were revealing the limits of American revolutionary discourse while imperiling the emerging arrangement over political economy.[46]

Events in Saint-Domingue highlighted the limits of American support for Atlantic radicalism in even starker relief. Between 1790 and 1804, when the Republic of Haiti was declared, more than 300,000 men and women died violently in the largest slave revolution in human history. Refugees fled to America, particularly Philadelphia and Charleston, carrying tales of the horror of slave insurrection, of a racial revolution that had unleashed furies beyond imagination. More troublingly for Americans, some masters came to the United States with their slaves in tow, who knew firsthand of the links between violence and radicalism, leading American planters to fear that tales of insurrection in Saint-Domingue would lead to rebellion in their own communities. They were right to worry. In 1800, a slave known as Gabriel led a rebellion in Richmond. Hoping to unite blacks and lower class whites in a union sure to terrify the South's leaders, Gabriel was motivated, in part, by the Haitian example. Although northern merchants hoped to establish some sort of trading relationship with the people of Haiti, southern fears would not allow American recognition of the republic. Jefferson, who at first welcomed revolution in Haiti, came to dread it. He argued that the United States, along with Britain and France, should unite to contain the menace. The United States would, he argued, try to "confine this disease to its island." Virginians passed laws restricting manumission and dreamed up schemes to deport free blacks from the state. Slave insurrection, even imagining the end of slavery, would imperil America's revolution settlement.[47]

Fears of a return to chaos hemmed in the Democratic-Republican societies as well. Although they maintained their revolutionary forms and rhetoric, they eschewed radicalism, and by 1800, the most influential societies had disbanded.[48] For all their fascination with revolutionary France, Americans ultimately joined Democratic-Republican societies not to overturn the state but to watch over it. The liberty embodied in the public sphere, that imagined space that existed outside the state where people associated for causes, would not challenge but would balance the order imposed by the state. Dissent, therefore, increasingly took place within negotiated bounds, tacitly recognizing the new reality of the sovereignty manifested in the Constitution. Associational life also acted as a safety valve, giving those alienated from the Constitution the space to accept the new shape of sovereignty that was emerging while giving them a voice. The societies, however, blunted radical discourse as well. Members claimed to work within the framework of nation, decrying, for instance, violent separatism on the frontier.[49] They supported France but also made calls for vigilance and reform not to challenge the settlement but to secure it. Indeed, the distance an ocean afforded allowed them to celebrate French victories and violence vicariously while they condemned such violence at home or in Haiti.[50] They argued that if their voices were not heard and heeded, the nation would court disaster with the unraveling of the settlement. And they were right. The Jeffersonian victory, but more critically the peaceful transition from Federalist to Republican administrations, speaks to the persuasive power of these societies.

While the societies limited themselves, the state erected other limits. Radical émigrés, in particular, who did not shy away from the specter of radical revolution, by the late 1790s appeared as bogeys, harbingers of disorder, and most treated them as such. In the wake of the Terror in France, as violence became the defining characteristic of the revolutionary regime, they proved even more troubling, as Americans across the political spectrum, particularly those on the radical margins, found unity in the center. Indeed, in the wake of the French Revolution, a broad consensus was emerging about America's political culture. These years witnessed profound partisan struggle, as Federalists and Republicans saw each other as mortal enemies. Elites were not the only ones involved. All Americans, certainly those reading newspapers, which were proliferating in these years and becoming increasingly partisan, were engaged in political debates over what the revolution's legacy should mean in a tumultuous domestic environment and even more tempestuous international context. When rumors of war with France transfixed the nation, it seemed debate had reached a tipping point. Many feared the nation would pull itself apart.

The Alien and Sedition Acts, of course, are usually seen as markers of an unbridgeable political gulf between two rival factions; however, they also reveal the limits on political discourse that were emerging through a broad consensus. Passed by the Adams administration, a Federalist regime, the so-called Alien Acts were three measures passed to crack down on those radicals from abroad who had been streaming into the United States after the 1780s. Nationalistically minded leaders like John Adams believed that in the wake of the Terror in France, they had their opportunity to challenge political enemies at home, to keep foreign radicalism at bay, and to protect the nation. The Acts mandated a much longer period for natural-ization and allowed the state to deport those aliens deemed "dangerous to the peace and safety of the United States." The Sedition Act went a step further, targeting not only alien radicals, many of whom worked as editors of Republican newspapers, but also American citizens. Under the terms of the Act, the state could prosecute anyone who published anything "false, scandalous, and malicious" against the government of the United States. Both measures, passed by the smallest of margins, occasioned a firestorm.[51]

Democratic-Republican societies and their leaders criticized the Adams admin-istration for passing the Acts, pointing out how they could circumscribe legitimate dissent. Although Jefferson hoped what he called "the reign of the Witches" would pass, he worried over the nation's future if the group governing failed to appreci-ate what he considered central tenets of the revolution. But in other ways, the Acts captured the tenor of the times. Jefferson also had come to fear many of the radicals the Acts were aimed at. He worried, for instance, that foreigners might not know American ways and would thus play a detrimental role in its political culture. He had worried about those with monarchical principles, which he considered beyond the pale, yet he equally fretted over émigrés embracing what were regarded as Jacobin principles, which in the wake of the Terror also lay beyond the pale.[52] These two poles of loyalism and Jacobinism formed the limits of American discourse. What Americans feared more than losing their rights was losing their settlement. As Thomas Jefferson found the political center in the years after the Terror, or the polit-ical center found him, the radical fringes were peopled by radical émigrés, on the one hand, and arch-Federalists, on the other. Jefferson may have decried the Alien and Sedition Acts, but he tried to move away politically from those they were aimed at. Those who passed it, like Adams, were exiled to the political wilderness. In other words, one group on the margins became the target of the Acts; the other from the opposite end of the spectrum, which faded as a political force in the United States as soon as the Acts were passed, died of political natural selection. Both threatened the emerging settlement. In essence, the period broke the Federalists and tempered the Republicans, while Jefferson found the safe ground of political discourse that remained after the period.[53]

So unsurprisingly, when Thomas Paine retuned to America after his revolu-tionary adventures in France, no one accorded him a hero's welcome. The man who had composed *Common Sense* was not the same man who wrote *The Rights of Man*. More to the point, the America of 1800 did not resemble the America of 1776. When he arrived in Baltimore in 1802, few wanted to be seen with him. This man who helped define the nature of the struggle over sovereignty that had gripped the colonies in 1776 was now a pariah. Fittingly, when he died in 1809, few in America mourned him. His body was escorted from Greenwich to its resting place in New Rochelle by a Frenchwoman and, as she noted, her sons, "two Negroes...[and] a carriage loaded with six Irishmen," about the only sort of people who saw eye-to-eye with him. To add insult to injury, in 1819 a deranged disciple would dig up his bones, carry them to England, and lose them.[54] Radical émigrés like Paine, especially after

France's revolution began, promised to throw Americans back into the revolutionary crucible by bringing to light the nature of the trade-offs and negotiations that went into ending America's revolution. This idea, that radicalism would be hounded and bounded in the United States, represented the final piece of orderly settlement.

The turn toward the center, or better the recognition of the possible in America after revolution, reflected the ideas that propped up the "empire of liberty." Opportunity, for instance, had to become the watchword in America, not outcome.[55] In this case, an American necessity became an American virtue, as socioeconomic equality given the tensions that still existed in America, as well as the way revolution played itself out, could not be countenanced. People could and did call for it. Yet they lived on the margins. The answer to "why no socialism" in America, therefore, is found in the eighteenth, not the twentieth century. The cost of opening up the American Pandora's box was the undoing of the settlement.

The state secured the whole arrangement. The division of power between central government and the states, or the federal solution, did not so much diminish power or keep it in check but, in some ways, magnified it and made power particularly effective. The Virginia and Kentucky resolutions, in fact, demonstrated this. Written up to contest the Alien and Sedition Acts, they were in fact sewn from the same threads. The Resolutions, drafted by Jefferson and Madison, argued that the states should contest a law passed by Congress that was patently unconstitutional or even abhorrent. The resolutions, therefore, appear to be an instance when unfettered national power was challenged by the states. Viewed as protests against the power of the central government, they failed miserably. Only Virginia and Kentucky passed such resolutions, while many of the states condemned them. If the resolutions represented a call to arms for the rights of the states against federal power, they foundered as much as the Alien and Sedition Acts.[56]

From another vantage point, the measures were designed not so much to limit power as to define where its ultimate home should be. The states, the resolutions suggested, proved not only the safest places to store power but also the most efficacious. Closer to the people, the states could decide which measures made sense for a community, thus increasing the effectiveness of any measure through legitimacy. Order rested on the proper balance between efficacy and legitimacy, and each society, given its history and its distinctive tensions, should decide for itself how the state should function. The resolutions thus demonstrated how order in America could be sustained at multiple levels. In the instance of the resolutions, either the central government or the state could or should exercise sovereignty. The issue involved in the resolutions revolved around which would work the best. In other words, while it would seem that the dispute over the allotment of power in a federal system tried to address the ambiguous nature of sovereignty, power never fell between the stools. When states and the central government fought, ultimate power was exercised by one. When they did not, more often than not, power was exercised by both. The ambiguous nature of American sovereignty, therefore, meant that both ruled. The new state, with its many eyes and multiple fonts of sovereignty and designed to maintain order, was not a blunt instrument, but a finely crafted, multi-handled tool.[57]

The power of the multi-centered state, no doubt, contrasted with impotence abroad. Americans had developed nothing short of a fickle foreign policy, one premised on the idea of keeping the new nation away from disabling European power struggles and their penchant for fomenting domestic discord or harmony. Anglophiles not only wanted to use England as a model of American development but also hoped to foster closer relations with Britain. Francophiles figured that the two republics would become allies. Instead of coming up with a coherent policy, the government tried to negotiate between the rock of Britain and the hard place of France, but not in a particularly elegant fashion. The two warring nations tried to use American fickleness to their advantages, often with embarrassing results for American officials. Nonetheless, the warring factionalism in the United States, especially in the wake of the French Revolution, ensured that the new nation did not suffer a deathblow from the European behemoths. Isolationism based on necessity— but often masquerading as principle—defined the relationship of the United States to the rest of the world. Isolationism on the international front, therefore, offered the same hopes for internal stability and order that expansionism in the West did.[58] These apparent contradictions, then, went hand-in-hand just as they lay at the heart of the "empire of liberty."[59]

By 1800, Americans had achieved something miraculous and literally and figuratively awe-ful. They had created a society defined by the equality of whites and the unfreedom of blacks. Although persons could be equal in dignity, a spurious reading of the nature of reason disabled some from enjoying political participation. Americans could mouth platitudes about rights and freedom but at the same time steer clear of the radical implications of those ideas. Americans were building an empire of liberty at the expense of Indians and sustained by the movement of whites on eastern society's margins as well as by a second middle passage for slaves. The notion of politics that Americans had fashioned placed people at the heart of the sovereign state but consigned them to the polity's margins through a Constitution that contained antidemocratic elements. Sovereignty remained ambiguous but stealthily efficacious. A consensus had emerged over a capitalist system geared to agriculture, based on industry, and sustained by international trade. This notion of political economy enshrined opportunity but not outcome; have-nots would vie with haves for land out west and jobs in the cities earning wages. Americans were crafting an isolationist foreign policy within a state primed for territorial expansion. In fact, because securing their own liberty entailed expanding onto western territories held by other peoples, an imperial isolation defined what they had become.

The revolution, of course, transformed America. Episodic ideas about race, especially white attitudes toward Indians, and class, for instance, were hardening into more enduring ideals. Antiblack racism, which was by no means merely episodic before the revolution, was institutionalized. Deference, as a strategy for negotiating power relations, had dissolved as men and women had become self-sovereign. One state had collapsed; another had arisen. But in another way, things remained as they were. Women still inhabited a separate sphere, and the wealthy still inherited the land. The relationship between the endurance of old tensions and new ideas about sovereignty goes to the heart of what made this revolution American. As Kepler understood, revolution did not create something wholly new. Americans crafted the settlement they deserved, one that cohered to the hard realities of their colonial world, as well as the resulting ways in which the Furies played themselves out in the tumult of revolution. Conceiving of the settlement as Janus-faced or ambivalent misses the point that only this settlement could have sustained order.

While the settlement proved remarkably resilient given the power of the tensions it inscribed, contradictions did not represent the weak points of the settlement. In fact, the ways they related to each other made for strength. Two points of denial bound Americans together in a tacit agreement: the efficacious state that would appear weak; and the refusal of Americans to dwell on but accept contradictions. To live with the contradictions that defined them, as well as the state that underwrote those contradictions, required that Americans think of themselves as an exceptional people. In many ways, the idea of America as an exceptional place stemmed from its distant past. It was, after all, the "New World." As Locke famously said, "in the beginning, all was America." According to the earliest adventurers settling the Chesapeake, it appeared "a land as God made it," one primed for exploitation. To the Puritans, it resembled a "city upon a hill," a "shining beacon." Yet these older ideas gained a second birth with the revolution settlement, and because they proved critical in cementing the settlement, they endured and became tenacious. In fact, John Winthrop's famous sermon, *A Model of Christian Charity*, in which he had declared "we shall be as a city upon a hill," only became widely known and distributed after 1790. It had never been printed in the colonial period.[60]

Exceptionalist ideas were resurrected in part because Americans had to undo who and what they had been. First and foremost, they had to "unbecome British." More than nostalgia for a world that had been, for the political connection to Britain, or the blessings of Britishness, however, was at stake. The flight of loyalists put paid to such dreams. Rather, the tumult of revolution and war with Britain had tempered any American enthusiasm for British vanishing points. Yet, almost all white Americans were still attracted to Europe and many to Britain, seeing it as the touchstone of civility even if it had been corrupted. The postwar version of what had been the provincial dilemma that Americans struggled with in the years before revolution was now taking shape as a postcolonial dilemma rooted in the fear that untethered from the metropole they would degenerate. Becoming American, therefore, generated ambivalence. Despite winning constitutional independence from Britain, Americans still inhabited, for better or worse, a broader British Atlantic world, now as consolidated as ever even after the failure of British sovereignty to animate the system, of goods, peoples, and ideas centered in the archipelago. Although they shared "customs in common" with the British and saw Britain as the touchstone for expertise in an often-complex world, America had become a place apart. Such ambivalence encouraged Americans to craft stories of who they were based on the distinctive virtue of New World and new republic precisely because they fretted over the cultural implications of breaking the bonds with empire and the Old World. In other words, they displaced their anxieties about living in a marginal place, separated by an ocean and the civilizing influences of the center, by positing that they were exceptionally virtuous.[61] Displacement encouraged and allowed them to turn their backs on Britishness even while they maintained some links to Britain.

As one set of vanishing points disappeared, a new one came into focus. In other words, myth sustained the whole. Remembering and forgetting aspects of their revolution, or creating new vanishing points while unsigning old ones to oblivion, allowed Americans to accept contradictions that otherwise would have plunged them into the abyss. Myth explained the settlement, as well as the tortuous ways Americans had to conceive of themselves to maintain order in the nation. It rested on denial and tacit agreement, on the one hand, and relied on rituals and proclamation, on the other hand. And myth, too, cohered to the distinctive ways Americans had to conceive of themselves as they struggled to bring revolution to a close. At its heart, it centered on the founders. Americans heaped hope, scorn, responsibility, and culpability on their shoulders. In this way, the tensions that ever threatened to plunge Americans into tumult—and threatened sovereignty anew—were made manageable.

Americans extolled their founders as this settlement was taking shape. While Federalists, of course, lionized Washington, they were not alone since Americans of all stripes, even Republicans, made his birthday a holiday. He represented for most the idea of orderly virtue. In the first years after the Constitution was ratified, citizens made his birthday a day of toasts to honor those who had won the war and wrought order from chaos. In fact, the cult of Washington transfixed Americans by the 1790s because he served as a unifying figure, one in myth believed above the fray of political differences. On July 4, 1796, for instance, a group of Marylanders considering themselves Republicans raised their glasses to this: "George Washington: may the day of his nativity be marked in the calendar of time... and celebrated to the last ages."[62] From the early nineteenth century, when Parson Weems crafted such tales as Washington and the cherry tree, Americans wanted to get to know Washington's character, the imagined person beyond the man obsessed with formal bearing, especially how he personified classic virtues.[63] In other words, more than any other figure, he transcended tension.

So, too, did Benjamin Franklin, the man memorialized by postrevolutionary America as the embodiment of enlightened rule. After his death in 1790, Americans came to grieve for a man that they re-created. Although at first praise was muted—Franklin was, after all, a man apart: a diplomat, a scientist, a genius, and a Francophile—eventually, Americans reclaimed him. They did not hail his memory for his advances in science or the cosmopolitan identity he cultivated but saw him as one of their own, a shrewd, hard-working, virtuous everyman, a "poor Richard," happy to make his *Autobiography*, which preached such ideals, their own autobiographies. Here too Americans were memorializing less a man than the trade-offs of the revolution. Franklin embodied the idea that the United States was a land of opportunity and meritocracy—not of social equality. Genius and privilege, also aspects of Franklin's life, could not be memorialized in a society politicized and democratized by revolution. Forgotten also was his past as a slaveholder. Now he personified freedom. The person who styled himself the champion of the humble artisan had, in fact, been a devotee of the man who made Ireland safe for English planters and capital: Sir William Petty.[64]

Fittingly, Jefferson features in this discussion. The Fourth of July, in fact, became the celebration it would, as Republicans—in the midst of their opposition to Federalist rule and in the wake of their recoil from radicalism in France and

Haiti—made the holiday theirs. Throughout the 1770s and 1780s, Americans generally did not keep the day. The Society of Cincinnati organized small, local celebrations, in which common people had no role to play, except as spectators. The holiday, in fact, lionized Washington's martial virtues. Soon, it became a date of contestation, as Democratic-Republican societies tried to make the day theirs. Ultimately, they would conquer the day, turning it in a remarkably short time into the greatest and most popular holiday of the nation. Boisterous celebrations, in which common people played leading roles, popped up throughout the country, east and west, north and south. For many of these people, the Fourth celebrated the person of Thomas Jefferson, the author of the Declaration, and memorialized their loyalty to him. The cult of Washington, ultimately, was overshadowed by a fascination with Jefferson that focused on the Fourth.[65]

The veneration of Jefferson also served a unifying, not divisive, purpose. In coming in from out of the cold, in becoming the ruling party, Republicans had made their peace with the form of the new state. They also accepted the negotiations that had gone into creating a durable settlement. The Fourth of July became a day during which the rights of white men were celebrated. They, not blacks, Indians, or women, comprised part of the political nation. They took to the streets on this day not to overturn the revolutionary settlement or to usurp the standing of elites but to ratify their status in the new nation by letting their betters know that they would stand up for their political rights. The holidays they celebrated, focused on the person of Jefferson, reflected this reality. Ironically, the aristocrat from Virginia served as guardian of democracy.[66]

Although such celebrations, no doubt, centered on contests for who would rule at home, they did so within acceptable bounds, helping create a new national vanishing point, one that centered on the founders and the ideal of an "American Revolution." The Fourth of July, 1801, in the wake of Jefferson's inauguration, serves as a case in point. On that day, Americans touted both him and Washington. Throughout the country, citizens raised their glasses to the founders, toasting, for instance, "*The President of the United States*; may his wisdom consolidate the Republic and his virtues conciliate the feelings of all good men." In New York City, revelers declared, "we are now celebrating a double object, our ever memorable declaration of independence, and the restoration of our mangled constitution." Now safely dead, Washington could be celebrated by all. In Charleston, the Revolutionary Society hoped that "the immortal memory of George Washington" would "find a mausoleum in the breast of every good citizen." Others drank and toasted "to embalm his memory." Members of the Franklin Typographical Association feted Washington as "A Hero," both "Brave, as a Soldier—Virtuous, as a Man." Three times they cheered the words "let us feel happy and proud, that he was an American; and in that character, banished tyranny from his native soil." Six cheers rang out for "the executive of the United States—May those characters that *compose* it, faithfully fill their offices, and our Constitution stand *proof* against the *squabbles* of party." They reserved nine cheers for "THE PATRON OF OUR ART," Franklin. On this day, they commemorated an "American Revolution" that did not closely resemble America's revolution. "The establishment of civil liberty was the object, the felicity of man the end," as one group put it. "In this," they continued, "it differed from all other national revolutions."[67]

The ultimate vanishing point for the founders' American Revolution became 1776, the moment when history began anew. On this point, consensus emerged as soon as order was emerging. In 1789, a physician from South Carolina named David Ramsay published *The History of the American Revolution*. Ramsay's revolution started with the Puritans in the seventeenth century and ended when George Washington was "appointed" president. In *The History*, Ramsay views the revolution as the inevitable fulfillment of colonization. The people of New England, who had left England "by being denied the Rights of Men," decided to "pursue their own happiness in other regions." Although "exiled," they already, in fact, enjoyed a virtual independence. Their descendants just realized as much in 1776. The Declaration, then, established the basis for the "permanent security of American happiness." The rest was, literally, just details.[68]

Social upheaval does not feature in Ramsay's narrative. It is a story of inevitability. A native Pennsylvanian transplanted to the slave South, Ramsay had opposed the institution of slavery but came to change his mind. In his narrative, slaves matter insofar as they are potent bogeys. Dunmore's proclamation, what Ramsay considers ill conceived, proves an exception to this story. "The colonists," as he put it, "were struck with horror and filled with detestation of a government which was exercised in looseing the bonds of society." Dunmore also, he argued, was hatching a plan to foment Indian attacks on the frontier. It, too, was ill conceived. For Ramsay, these were exceptional moments, which providence delivered Americans from. Certainly, the Indians and the slaves had no agency of their own. In fact, the bonds of society held in this consensual revolution. "Where there were no royal troops, and where ordinary prudence was observed, the public peace was undisturbed," he reported. Ramsay's history is one of generals, armies in the abstract, and diplomacy. It did not involve the people.

The people were made invisible by 1776. For Ramsay, the significance of this date lay in the idea that "the revolution was not forced on the people by ambitious leaders grasping at supreme power." As a Federalist, Ramsay did not give Jefferson a prominent role; in fact, he is not mentioned in the drafting of the Declaration. In declaring independence, John Adams is given the lion's share of attention. Despite the omission, this is the founders' moment. "The anniversary of the day on which the great event took place," Ramsay declared, "has ever since been consecrated by the Americans to religious gratitude, and social pleasures. It is considered by them as the birth day of their freedom." With the Declaration, "every thing assumed a new form... [and] the dispute was brought to a single point." History turned on this moment, and the past was recast in the image of this narrative.

He conceded that there were bumps along the way. He argued that Pennsylvanians cooked up an unworkable and unfortunate state constitution, which "carried the spirit of discussion into every corner, and disturbed the peace and harmony of neighbourhoods." For Ramsay, order trumped liberty, and popular sovereignty had to be restrained by institutions and channeled in more productive directions. "By making the business of government the duty of everyman," he cautioned, Pennsylvania's experiment "drew off the attention of many from the steady pursuit of their respective businesses." The Articles, similarly, were ill conceived, "proposed at a time when the citizens of America were young in the science of politics, and when a commanding sense of duty, enforced by the pressure of a common danger, precluded the necessity of a power of compulsion." The Constitution remedied these concerns. And Washington's ascendancy would bring an end to a narrative of independence that was first grasped in 1776.

Stories of the Revolution differed in their focus, but not in their thrust, as upheavals were recast. In 1805, emboldened by Jefferson's ascendancy, Mercy Otis Warren published the *History of the Rise, Progress, and Termination of the American Revolution*. Born to one of the most influential families in Massachusetts, Warren had written plays, poems, and pamphlets before she turned her hand to history. Her political commitments differed from Ramsay. She was a Republican. Yet her history differed little from his, keeping a focus on battles and diplomacy and hinging on 1776. Warren starts the narrative with the Stamp Act crisis and casts the story as a family tale. "Great Britain the revered parent, and America the dutiful child," she argued, "had long been bound together by interest, by the sameness of habits, manners, law, and government." The British nation was a "home, the seat of happiness, the retreat to all the felicities of the human mind." Because of coercion beginning with the crisis of the 1760s and 1770s, strained bonds could not be "renounce[d] without pain, whether applied to the natural or the political parent." Warren ends her story with Washington as well, not his inauguration but when he metaphorically turned his sword over to Congress, after the "mutiny and insurrection" inspired by the Cincinnati. A short epilogue finishes as he left the office of president.[69]

Unlike Ramsay, Warren had to justify writing history. Like the narrative of the nation, her story centers on what it means for family. "The horrors of civil war was rushing to habitations not inured to scenes of rapine and misery; even to the quaint cottage where only concord and affection had reigned," she suggested. Experience in revolution, she added, "stimulated to observation a mind that had not yielded to the assertion, that all political attentions lay out of the road of female life." She had played a prominent role during the war years as many other women had, as had her family. Her husband fought but was cast into the political wilderness for his support of the Shaysites. A son in the navy was crippled. Another died in the Ohio country in a 1791 expedition against Indians. She did not, however, contest gender roles. She conceded, "there are certain appropriate duties assigned to each sex." Men fought, and men usually wrote about history. Revolution maintained the former but altered the latter. "Every domestic enjoyment depends on the unimpaired possession of civil and religious liberty," she declared. Therefore, she wrote her history "with a view of transmitting it to the rising youth of my country."

History turns on Jefferson, and 1776 serves as vanishing point. The Declaration "was drawn by the ingenious and philosophic pen of Thomas Jefferson, Esq." She did not have to remind her readers that "this wise and patriotic statesmen" would afterwards become "president of the United States of America." The Declaration divided those who hungered for liberty from those who sought power: "The timid trembled at the idea of final separation; the disciples of a passive obedience were shocked by a reflection of a breach of faith to their ancient sovereign; and the enemies to the general freedom of mankind, were incensed to madness, or involved in despair." With the Declaration, "every thing stood on a new and more respectable footing." For Warren, the system under the Constitution may have been flawed, but Jefferson redeemed it because he was author of liberty. Writing in 1805, a few years after the witches' reign, she prayed "May the hands of the executive of their choice, be strengthened more by the unanimity and affection of the people, than by the dread of penal inflictions, or any restraints that might repress free inquiry." In placing Washington and Jefferson at the center of American collective imagination, Ramsay and Warren did not deny the existence of tensions—far from it, by centering on founders, they acknowledged them, and in so doing, naturalized and comprehended them. In part, they accomplished this feat by centering narratives on 1776, enabling the conflation of the War of Independence with revolution, thus keeping the eyes of the nation on the finality and clarity of one at the expense of the unresolved ambiguities of the other.

Fittingly, Jefferson stands in the middle, not so much because he epitomized contradictions but because the programs and ideals he was most closely associated with brought revolution to a close. On one level, he tried to keep the forces at bay that would unravel the settlement, such as Indian land to the west and the unfreedom of blacks. On another level, Jefferson defined the limits and nature of the revolution. He stood in as the proxy for the common man, the champion in the eyes of urban workers and rural farmers of universal manhood suffrage, the right that was won through the competition and disorder of revolution. But he was a planter, an American aristocrat who wrapped himself in the language of austere republicanism, as well as a slave owner, who demonized Africans and African Americans, as inherently inferior. And he was the architect of Indian-removal policy, though he saw

Figure 9.3 John Trumbull, *Jefferson*, 1788. The Metropolitan Museum of Art.

Indians as redeemable. He was and is the flawed and enlightened founder, the author of the document that gave birth to the nation, who embodied American contradictions and who championed the cult of limited government.[70]

The founders' myth also obscured the stealthlike state that bound the settlement together. Only a powerful state could have held so many regions together with diverse histories and distinctive fault lines torn open by revolutionary unrest. Mythically, the founders, of course, created the antistate state, one born out of the fear of power. In reality, power and liberty, *imperium* and *libertas*, worked hand-in-hand, as sovereign power amenable to America's distinctive nature ensured liberty for some. The federal solution reflected this ideal. The American nation-state was an effective state that could address regional variations, histories, and fault lines within a broader union while wrapped in the rhetoric of impotence.

How this arrangement came to be reflects how revolution came to an end. Revolution ended with questions and contradictions, just where it had begun. Americans fastened onto the disjunction between power and liberty—categories rooted in Britain's seventeenth century—as they were caught in the grip of a seventeenth-century-like crisis over sovereignty. Such ideas gave structure and order to the chaos they were confronting and creating. But such constructs became increasingly dangerous as they tried to bring an end to revolution. In other words, seventeenth-century languages proved useful in making sense of origins; they were much more brittle in constructing order. The myth of the enfeebled state allowed Americans to believe that they leaned toward the liberty side of the equation, a conceit made necessary because of how men and women had become actors in the crucible of revolution. Therefore, just as Britons in the eighteenth century used the revolutionary language of the seventeenth century to create and sustain a stable state structure, so would Americans, and in doing so, would demonstrate an amazing capacity for adaptability. The process revolved around making legitimate government efficacious; or making efficacious government legitimate. The crucible of revolution both brought this state into being at the moment the state brought to an end the process of revolution. Miraculously, given the tensions the state managed, this arrangement would hold until the 1860s.

In 1817, Congress commissioned John Trumbull to paint a large version of *The Declaration of Independence* to hang in the rotunda of the Capitol building, then under construction. Although not the painter he was when he started collecting portraits, within a few years he completed a nearly perfect copy of his original. The completed painting made the rounds in the United States before coming to Washington, DC. In 1826, when the rotunda of the Capitol was completed, *The Declaration of Independence* was finally installed across from Trumbull's painting commemorating the day Washington handed his commission back to Congress. For all posterity, Jefferson would hang across from Washington.[71]

A critic for the *City of Washington Gazette* reported on its arrival in Washington. "We are pleased with this evidence of gratitude on the part of the government," the critic wrote, "to preserve and commemorate the striking incidents of that epoch, which resulted so gloriously to this country." To the critic, the Revolution was "that awful and interesting struggle, which was so happily terminated and which is still to give liberty and happiness to countless millions yet unborn." Artists like Trumbull, who engaged in that struggle that found happiness, had a responsibility "to commemorate some of the most striking events of our revolutionary contest." And Americans had produced some excellent painters: "We can boast of artists in this country not inferior to any in the world."[72]

The rendering of the scene did not please all. Although one critic applauded Trumbull's subject, the execution proved a different matter. He found fault with "the want of expression in the faces and the great stiffness in the attitudes of his figures." The founders "seem as if they were staring at vacuity," and "they are too stiff and prim." As he put it, "instead of seeming to attend with that deep and awful interest they must have felt to the presentation of that instrument which was to sever them from the mother country," some were talking to each other. Others stood "bolt upright like a lightning rod to an old chimney." With Franklin present at the scene, the pun had to be intended. Finally, the critic observed, "some of the figures are too gigantic for nature, or too large for their respective positions," especially those engaged in the central action. "Our countryman, West," he argued, "still retains the first rank among historical painters." While the critic suggested that Trumbull was no Benjamin West, he might have added that he was no Copley. Copley was more at home with the "interesting and awful" aspects of struggle, before they had been consigned to memory and hardened into the amber of myth.[73]

Jefferson looked beyond such criticism. What Trumbull commemorated mattered more than how it was represented. As the critics had their say, Jefferson wrote Trumbull a note of support. "I trust you have silenced the critic on your Declar. of Independence, as I am sure you must have satisfied every sound judge," Jefferson wrote. "Painters as well as poets," he believed, "have their license." What Jefferson called "the talent of imagination" had to animate art. Reality, he suggested, could be in the eye of the beholder, and critics had confounded accuracy with truth. They might as well have found fault with the painter "because you have not given his white wig and black stockings to Mr. Cushing, nor his real costume to Roger Sherman." In any event, Trumbull got Jefferson right. "As to the use you have made of my name," Jefferson concluded, "it did not need apology. It is always at your command for any service it can render you."[74]

When *The Declaration of Independence* was installed in the Capitol Building, the myths and arrangements that defined the revolution settlement threatened to come undone. Southerners clamored for the settlement, as it was, to stand. Many from the North countered that the nation and its myths could no longer contain certain contradictions. War was not yet spoken of, but some still remembered when animating myths could no longer sustain a vision of a society. At least two men did so, men who featured in Trumbull's epic. By the time Trumbull was commissioned to make the rotunda copy, Jefferson had retired to Monticello. John Adams once again lived in Massachusetts. The two had fallen out in the days since each had served as president, but afterwards the two had reconciled.

Jefferson was delighted that the two had patched up their differences. "A letter from you," he wrote in 1812 as their correspondence began anew, "calls up recollections very dear to my mind." The thoughts of what they had done, he continued, "carries me back to the times when, beset with difficulties and dangers, we were fellow laborers in the same cause, struggling for what is most valuable to man, his right to self government." Myth drifted away as he thought to what those years had meant. "Laboring always at the same oar," as he put it, "with some wave ever ahead, threatening to overwhelm us, and yet passing harmlessly under our bark, we knew not how we rode through the storm with heart and hand and made a happy port." In one sentence, Jefferson had written a history of what he, Adams, and all Americans had been through. Riding the storm out had brought a sort of redemption. But it had not brought perfection. "Still," he finished, "we did not expect to be without rubs and difficulties; and we have had them…and so we have gone on puzzled and prospering beyond example in the history of man." The process had ended, but the tensions remained.[75]

Of course, in the same year that the painting was unveiled in the Capitol's rotunda, both would die. Jefferson and Adams passed away 50 years to the day the scene the painting commemorated. These founders now loomed as archetypes of the North and South, and the settlement they had overseen was coming apart. These tensions, of course, would grow with time and eventually explode, as Frederick Douglass prophesied when he cast the Fourth of July—literally—as an African American anti-holiday. Ultimately, some of the fundamental contradictions of the American Revolution were finally resolved on the fields of Antietam and Gettysburg, when the most rotten aspect of the revolution settlement was finally expunged. Fittingly, Lincoln used the ideals of Jefferson's 1776 to make sense of civil war. But undoing one settlement and creating a new one would require levels of bloodshed no one dare imagine. Then, as now, the presence of tensions in the national consciousness reflects how we are the people of contradiction. This idea, rooted half in experience, half in hope, keeps the Furies at bay. They may reappear, as they did in the 1860s, but once put back in place, Americans revert to this idea of paradox. We have little choice; it is who we are.

Notes

PREFACE

1. The phrase is Pauline Maier's. See Pauline Maier, *American Scripture: Making the Declaration of Independence* (New York, 1997).

2. See James McPherson, *Battle Cry of Freedom: The Civil War Era* (New York, 1988); and Charles Royster, *The Destructive War: William Tecumseh Sherman, Stonewall Jackson, and the Americans* (New York, 1993). On Lincoln, Douglas, and the founders, see the excellent essay by Ralph Lerner, "Lincoln's Declaration—and Ours," *National Affairs* (Winter, 2011), http://www.nationalaffairs.com/publications/detail/lincolns-declaration-and-ours.

3. For a popular account of the sacredness of the Fourth of July, see Peter De Bolla, *The Fourth of July and the Founding of America* (New York, 2007).

4. See, for instance, Gordon Wood, *The Idea of America: Reflections on the Birth of the United States* (New York, 2011), 2-3.

5. Frederick Douglass, *Oration Delivered in Corinthian Hall, Rochester, July 5th, 1852* (Rochester, 1852), 14-21.

6. Carl Becker, *The History of Political Parties in the Province of New York, 1760-1776* (Madison, WI, 1909), 22. Also see Gary Nash, *The Unknown American Revolution: The Unruly Birth of Democracy and the Struggle to Create America* (New York, 2006); and Alfred Young, Ray Raphael, and Gary Nash, "Introduction: 'To Begin the World Over Again,'" in Young, Nash, and Raphael, eds., *Revolutionary Founders: Rebels, Radicals, and Reformers in the Making of the Nation* (New York, 2011), 3-15.

7. Jill Lepore, "Tea and Sympathy: Who Owns the American Revolution?" *The New Yorker* (3 May 2010), http://www.newyorker.com/reporting/2010/05/03/100503fa_fact_lepore.

8. Jill Lepore, *The Whites of Their Eyes: The Tea Party's Revolution and the Battle over American History* (Princeton, 2010).

9. Gordon Wood, "No Thanks for the Memories: Review of Jill Lepore's *The Whites of Their Eyes*," *New York Review of Books*, 13 January 2011.

10. Barack Obama, "Transcript of Barack Obama Speech," 13 May 2008, Politico, http://www.politico.com/news/stories/0308/9100.html; *The Audacity of Hope: Thoughts on Reclaiming the American Dream* (New York, 2006), 53, 95.

11. On vanishing points and history, see H. W. Smith, *The Continuities of German History: Nation, Religion, and Race across the Long Nineteenth Century* (Cambridge, 2008), 13–38. My thanks to John Deak for this reference.

12. Lynn Jacobs, "The Triptychs of Hieronymus Bosch," *The Sixteenth Century Journal*, 31, no. 4 (2000): 1009–41.

13. Samuel Johnson, *A Dictionary of the English Language*, Vol. II (London, 1755–56), 544.

PART I

1. On West and the painting, see John Dillenberger, *Benjamin West: The Context of His Life's Work* (San Antonio, 1977), 24–29; C. P. Stacey, "Benjamin West and 'The Death of Wolfe,'" *The National Gallery of Canada Bulletin*, 7 (1966): 1–5; Simon Schama, *Dead Certainties: (Unwarranted Speculations)* (New York, 1991); and the entry by Dorinda Evans in the *Oxford Dictionary of National Biography*. Also see Hugh Howard's *The Painter's Chair: George Washington and the Making of American Art* (New York, 2009); and Ann Uhry Abrams, *The Valiant Hero: Grand-Style History Painting* (Washington, DC, 1985). On philosophical history and art, see Thomas Keymer and John Mee, eds., *The Cambridge Companion to English Literature, 1740–1830* (London, 2004), 30; and J. G. A. Pocock, *Barbarism and Religion*, Vol. 1, *The Enlightenments of Edward Gibbon* (London, 1999), 280. My thanks to Felipe Fernandez-Armesto on this point.

2. Benjamin West, cited in Helmut von Erffa and Allen Staley, *The Paintings of Benjamin West* (New Haven, 1986), 57.

3. Douglas Fordham, *British Art and the Seven Years' War: Allegiance and Autonomy* (Philadelphia, 2010); Holger Hoock, *Empires of the Imagination: Politics, War, and the Arts in the British World, 1750–1850* (Washington, DC, 2010), 85–86.

4. There is some confusion over the identity of Adair. A physician named John Adair, present at the battle and one of Wolfe's chief surgeons, was listed as a member of the Society of Saint Andrew, and most likely was the man painted by Wolfe. See "Roster of Saint Andrew's Society of the State of New York with Biographical Data, Compiled by W. MacBean" (containing Scottish members of the British Army) in http://www.archive. org/stream/roster01stan/roster01stan_djvu.txt. On Adair's identity, see Archibald Malloch, "Robert and John Adair," *Bulletin of New York Academy of Medicine*, 10 (1937), 576–96. My thanks to Claire Lyons for this reference.

5. David Armitage, *Ideological Origins of the British Empire* (London, 2000).

6. Christopher Hodson, *The Acadian Diaspora: An Eighteenth-Century History* (New York, 2012), 44.

7. On the Acadian saga, see John Mack Faragher, *A Great and Noble Scheme: The Tragic Story of the Expulsion of the French Acadians from Their American Homeland* (New York, 2005).

8. On Fraser, see the entry from the *Oxford Dictionary of National Biography*.

9. There is some controversy over who this person in the painting is. Fintan O'Toole, however, makes a convincing case that West was portraying Johnson or an ideal of Johnson. See Fintan O'Toole, *White Savage: William Johnson and the Invention of America* (New York, 2005). The image may be, in fact, his nephew Guy Johnson, also born a Catholic in Ireland who succeeded Johnson as superintendent of Indian Affairs after his death in 1774. On this, see T. S. Abler, G. Hamell, and A. Einhorn, "Guy Johnson, Benjamin West, and Cohoes Falls: Issues of (Mis)Identification," *New York History*, 89, no. 2

(2008): 191–203. Regardless of the subject, the same message applies. For Johnson's life and career, see Daniel Richter's entry in the *Oxford Dictionary of National Biography*.

10. Stephen Brumwell, *Redcoats: The British Soldier and the War in the Americas, 1755–1763* (Cambridge, UK, 2002), 73, 318.

11. On Hendrick in the painting, and another West painting like *The Death of General Wolfe*, see Leslie Reinhardt, "British and Indian Identities in a Picture by Benjamin West," *Eighteenth-Century Studies*, 31, no. 3 (1988): 300. For the historical and imagined Hendrick, see Eric Hinderaker, *The Two Hendricks: Unraveling a Mohawk Mystery* (Cambridge, MA, 2010). For Hendrick in British clothes, see Timothy Shannon, "Dressing for Success on the Frontier," *William and Mary Quarterly*, 3rd ser., 53, no. 1 (1996): 13–42.

12. On this theme of savagery in the service of empire, see Geoffrey Plank, *Rebellion and Savagery: The Jacobite Rising of 1745 and the British Empire* (Philadelphia, 2006); and Chad Michael Jennings, "Savagery in Service of Empire: Scottish Highlanders and the Seven Years' War" (M.A. thesis, University of Virginia, 2007).

CHAPTER 1

1. A. Freeman, ed., *Conciliation with the Colonies: The Speech of Edmund Burke* (Boston, 1915), 56.

2. Thomas Paine, *Common Sense*, ed. Isaac Kramnick (New York, 1986), 81–82, 91.

3. Thomas Paine, *Rights of Man, Common Sense and Other Political Writings*, ed. Mark Philp (New York, 1995), 86.

4. On Byrd, see Jack Greene, introduction to *The Diary of Colonel Landon Carter of Sabine Hall, 1752–1778* (Charlottesville, VA, 1965).

5. On this theme of phases, see Daniel Richter, *Before the Revolution: America's Ancient Pasts* (Cambridge, MA, 2011).

6. William Byrd II to Hans Sloane, 10 September 1708, *The Correspondence of the Three William Byrds of Westover, Virginia, 1684–1776*, ed. Marion Tinling (Charlottesville, VA, 1977), 1:266.; William Byrd II to Hans Sloane, 31 May 1737, *Correspondence*, 2:513.

7. William Byrd II to Peter Collison, 18 July 1736, *Correspondence*, 2:493.

8. William Byrd II to James Wood, 10 March 1741, *Correspondence*, 2:584.

9. Kathleen M. Brown, *Good Wives, Nasty Wenches, and Anxious Patriarchs: Gender, Race, and Power in Colonial Virginia* (Chapel Hill, NC, 1996).

10. William Byrd II, *The Secret Diary of William Byrd of Westover, 1709–1712*, ed. Louis B. Wright and Marion Tinling (Richmond, VA, 1941), 79, 113, 205, 494.

11. See Trevor Burnard, *Mastery, Tyranny, and Desire: Thomas Thistlewood and His Slaves in the Anglo-Jamaican World* (Chapel Hill, NC, 2004). On Byrd and slave women, see Philip D. Morgan, *Slave Counterpoint: Black Culture in the Eighteenth-century Chesapeake and Lowcountry* (Chapel Hill, NC, 1998), 403.

12. On the colonies as English, see especially Carla Gardina Pestana, *The English Atlantic in an Age of Revolution, 1640–1661* (Cambridge, MA, 2004); and Alison Games, *Migration and the Origins of the English Atlantic World* (Cambridge, MA, 1999).

13. I owe this term to Nicholas P. Canny's *Making Ireland British, 1580–1650* (Oxford, 2001) and Jon Butler's *Becoming America: The Revolution before 1776* (Cambridge, MA, 2000). In some ways, the process described in this chapter brings the two approaches together. The idea ultimately comes from John M. Murrin, "Anglicizing an American Colony: The Transformation of Provincial Massachusetts" (Ph.D. diss., Yale University,

1966). He referred to the process as "anglicization," a convention most eighteenth-century American historians follow. The term "Britishization" is used in similar fashion by R. Taylor Stoermer, "Constitutional Sense, Revolutionary Sensibility: Political Cultures in the Making and Breaking of British Virginia, 1707–1776" (Ph.D. diss., University of Virginia, 2010).

14. On this point, see Richard Hofstadter, *America at 1750: A Social Portrait* (New York, 1973).

15. Edmund Burke, *Conciliation with the Colonies: The Speech by Edmund Burke*, ed. Archibald Freeman and Arthur W. Leonard (Cambridge, MA, 1915), 117.

16. Richard S. Dunn, *Sugar and Slaves: The Rise of the Planter Class in the English West Indies, 1624–1713* (1972; repr., Chapel Hill, NC, 2000).

17. Dafoe quoted in Richard Sheridan, "The Formation of Caribbean Plantation Society, 1689–1748," in P. J. Marshall, ed., *The Oxford History of the British Empire: The Eighteenth Century* (New York, 1998), 409.

18. Sheridan, "The Formation of Caribbean Plantation Society, 1689–1748"; and J. R. Ward, "The British West Indies in the Age of Abolition, 1748–1815," in P. J. Marshall, ed., *The Oxford History of the British Empire: The Eighteenth Century* (New York, 1998).

19. See Matthew Mulcahy, *Hurricanes and Society in the British Greater Caribbean, 1624–1783* (Baltimore, 2005).

20. The best narrative remains Edmund Morgan, *American Slavery, American Freedom: The Ordeal of Colonial Virginia* (New York, 1975). On the idea of Englishness in Virginia as a deformed variation of the metropolitan standard, see James Horn, *Adapting to a New World: English Society in the Seventeenth-Century Chesapeake* (Chapel Hill, NC, 1994).

21. Sir William Berkeley's Declaration, 10 May 1676, Egerton MS. 2395, f. 539, British Library, London; A Pardon granted unto the Governour and Assembly of his majestie's Plantation of Virginia, PL. 2582, f. 8, Pepys Library, Magdalene College, Cambridge University.

22. T. H. Breen and Stephen Innes, *"Myne Owne Ground": Race and Freedom on Virginia's Eastern Shore, 1640–1676* (New York, 1980); Ira Berlin, *Many Thousands Gone: The First Two Centuries of Slavery in North America* (Cambridge, MA, 1998); April Lee Hatfield, *Atlantic Virginia: Intercolonial Relations in the Seventeenth Century* (Philadelphia, 2007).

23. William Byrd I to Perry & Lane, 30 December 1684, *Correspondence*, 1:28; William Byrd I to Perry & Lane, 30 December 1684, *Correspondence*, 1:28–29.

24. At the same time, the Royal African Company, a British company that shipped slaves from Africa to the New World, lost its monopoly. Once it did, many independent British shippers went into the slaving business, driving the prices of human cargo down. As this happened, the population surge in England leveled off, making indentured servants more expensive and less inclined to travel to a troubled colony. On these themes, see Berlin, *Many Thousands Gone*; Morgan, *Slave Counterpoint*; Winthrop D. Jordan, *White over Black: American Attitudes toward the Negro, 1550–1812* (1968; repr., New York, 1977); Morgan, *American Slavery, American Freedom*; and William A. Pettigrew, "Free to Enslave: Politics and the Escalation of Britain's Transatlantic Slave Trade, 1688–1714," *William and Mary Quarterly*, 64, no. 1 (2007): 3–38.

25. In addition, the changing labor force allowed men like Byrd to style themselves as Englishmen, not only in terms of the structures they built but also in the ways that they treated the women in their lives. Unable to create a patriarchal society because of the skewed sex ratios of the seventeenth century, wealthy planters by the beginning of the

eighteenth century now had the social capital to ensure that they would rule all in this world, including their wives. White women would not toil in the fields. Instead, and further amplifying the racial divide, black men and black women would be degraded equally. The "feminine virtues" apparently only applied to white women. See Brown, *Good Wives*.

26. Peter H. Wood, *Black Majority: Negroes in Colonial South Carolina from 1670 through the Stono Rebellion* (New York, 1974); Morgan, *Slave Counterpoint*.

27. James H. Merrell, *The Indians' New World: Catawbas and Their Neighbors from European Contact through the Era of Removal* (Chapel Hill, NC, 1989), 55, 65–69; Alan Gallay, *The Indian Slave Trade: The Rise of the English Empire in the American South, 1670–1717* (New Haven, 2002).

28. Merrell, *Indians' New World*, 95.

29. On this idea of the marginality of New England, see Jack Greene, *Pursuits of Happiness: The Social Development of Early Modern British Colonies and the Formation of American Culture* (Chapel Hill, NC, 1988).

30. The classic accounts remain Perry Miller, *Orthodoxy in Massachusetts: A Genetic Study* (Cambridge, MA, 1933); *The New England Mind: The Seventeenth Century* (Cambridge, MA, 1939); and *The New England Mind: From Colony to Province* (Cambridge, MA, 1953).

31. On this theme as it pertains to race, see Jill Lepore, *The Name of War: King Philip's War and the Origins of American Identity* (New York, 1998); and as it pertains to the land, see William Cronon, *Changes in the Land: Indians, Colonists, and the Ecology of New England* (1985; rev. edn., New York, 2003).

32. This is an old story. There have been too many town studies published to mention, but for a very good representative book, see Kenneth A. Lockridge, *A New England Town: The First Hundred Years: Dedham, Massachusetts, 1636–1736* (New York, 1970).

33. William Blackstone, *Commentaries on the Laws of England* (Oxford, 1768), 3:326. On these themes, see Paul Langford, *A Polite and Commercial People: England 1727–1783* (London, 1989).

34. Stephen Innes, *Creating the Commonwealth: The Economic Culture of Puritan New England* (New York, 1995); Greene, *Pursuits of Happiness*.

35. David S. Lovejoy, *The Glorious Revolution in America* (New York, 1972). Also see Owen Stanwood, "The Protestant Moment: Antipopery, the Revolution of 1688–89, and the Making of an Anglo-American Empire," *Journal of British Studies*, 46, no. 3 (2007): 481–508.

36. Jeanne Boydston, *Home and Work: Housework, Wages, and the Ideology of Labor in the Early Republic* (New York, 1990).

37. On this, see Edwin G. Burrows and Mike Wallace, *Gotham: A History of New York City to 1898* (New York, 1999).

38. See Jill Lepore, *New York Burning: Liberty, Slavery, and Conspiracy in Eighteenth-Century Manhattan* (New York, 2005).

39. Lovejoy, *Glorious Revolution*, 252–55.

40. Bernard Bailyn, *The Origins of American Politics* (New York, 1968).

41. Daniel K. Richter, *The Ordeal of the Longhouse: The Peoples of the Iroquois League in the Era of European Colonization* (Chapel Hill, NC, 1992); Francis Jennings and others, eds., *The History and Culture of Iroquois Diplomacy: An Interdisciplinary Guide to the Treaties of the Six Nations and Their League* (Syracuse, NY, 1985); Richard White, *The*

Middle Ground: Indians, Empires, and Republics in the Great Lakes Region, 1650–1815 (Cambridge, UK, 1991).

42. Thomas M. Doerflinger, *A Vigorous Spirit of Enterprise: Merchants and Economic Development in Revolutionary Philadelphia* (Chapel Hill, NC, 1986); Joseph Illick, *Colonial Pennsylvania: A History* (New York, 1976); Gary Nash, *Quakers and Politics: Pennsylvania, 1681–1726* (Princeton, 1968).

43. Alexander Hamilton, 8 June 1744, "The Itinerarium of Dr. Alexander Hamilton," in Wendy Martin, ed., *Colonial American Travel Narratives* (New York, 1994), 191.

44. See Nash, *Quakers and Politics*.

45. James H. Merrell, *Into the American Woods: Negotiators on the Pennsylvania Frontier* (New York, 1999); Kevin Kenny, *Peaceable Kingdom Lost: The Paxton Boys and the Destruction of William Penn's Holy Experiment* (New York, 2009).

46. See Horn, *Adapting to a New World*.

47. Aaron Spencer Fogleman, *Hopeful Journeys: German Immigration, Settlement, and Political Culture in Colonial America, 1717–1775* (Philadelphia, 1996); William O'Reilly, "The Naturalization Act of 1709 and the Settlement of Germans in Britain, Ireland and the Colonies," in Randolph Vigne and Charles Littleton, eds., *From Strangers to Citizens: The Integration of Immigrant Communities in Britain, Ireland, and Colonial America* (London, 2001), 492–502.

48. Marianne Sophia Wokeck, *Trade in Strangers: The Beginnings of Mass Migration to North America* (University Park, PA, 1999).

49. Council Held at the Courthouse of Philadelphia, 21 September 1727, *Minutes of the Provincial Council of Pennsylvania* (Philadelphia, 1852), 3:283. See also Philadelphia Council, 17 September 1717, *Minutes of the Provincial Council of Philadelphia*, 3:29.

50. On this, see A. G. Roeber, *Palatines, Liberty, and Property: German Lutherans in Colonial British America* (Baltimore, 1993).

51. Thomas Martin Devine, *Scotland's Empire, 1600–1815* (London, 2003), 97–108. On the influence of the Scots, see Ned C. Landsman, *From Colonials to Provincials: American Thought and Culture, 1680–1760* (New York, 1997); *Scotland and Its First American Colony, 1683–1765* (Princeton, 1985); and Ned C. Landsman, ed., *Nation and Province in the First British Empire: Scotland and the Americas, 1600–1800* (Lewisburg, PA, 2001).

52. Devine, *Scotland's Empire*, 119–31.

53. Patrick Griffin, *The People with No Name: Ireland's Ulster Scots, America's Scots Irish, and the Creation of a British Atlantic World, 1689–1764* (Princeton, 2001).

54. Testimony of Teedyuscung, 23 June 1762, *The Papers of Sir William Johnson*, ed. James Sullivan (Albany, NY, 1921), 3:779.

55. Richard R. Beeman, *The Evolution of the Southern Backcountry: A Case Study of Lunenburg County, Virginia, 1746–1832* (Philadelphia, 1984).

56. Warren R. Hofstra, *The Planting of New Virginia: Settlement and Landscape in the Shenandoah Valley* (Baltimore, 2004).

57. Benjamin Franklin, "Observations Concerning the Increase of Mankind and the Peopling of Countries" (1751), in *The Autobiography & Other Writings*, ed. Peter Shaw (New York, 2008), 294.

58. These themes are developed in the work of T. H. Breen. See his articles, including "An Empire of Goods: The Anglicization of Colonial America, 1690–1776," *Journal of British Studies*, 25, no. 4 (1986): 467–99; "'Baubles of Britain': The American and Consumer Revolutions in the Eighteenth Century," *Past and Present*, 119 (1988): 73–104.

59. Ward, "The British West Indies in the Age of Abolition, 1748–1815," 415–21.

60. Benjamin Franklin to Deborah Franklin, 19 February 1758, *The Writings of Benjamin Franklin*, ed. Albert Henry Smyth (New York, 1907), 3:433.

61. See, for instance, George Washington to Robert Cary and Company, 1 May 1759, *The Writings of George Washington*, ed. Worthington Chauncey Ford (New York, 1889), 2:128–29.

62. Paul Staiti, "Character and Class," in C. Rebora et al., eds., *John Singleton Copley in America* (New York, 1995), 53–64, 184; T. H. Breen, "The Meaning of 'Likeness': American Portrait Painting in an Eighteenth-century Consumer Society," *Word and Image* (1990): 325–50.

63. Warren Cox, "Palladio and Libraries in Eighteenth Century America," and Calder Loth, "Palladio's Legacy to America," in Charles Hind and Irena Murray, eds., *Palladio and His Legacy: A Transatlantic Journey* (Venice, Italy, 2011), 114–18, 142. On the Irish and Anglo-Palladianism and the parallels to American experience, see Toby Barnard, *Making the Grand Figure: Lives and Possessions in Ireland, 1641–1770* (New Haven, 2004), 21–29.

64. David P. Handlin, *American Architecture* (1985; 2nd edn., London, 2004), 22–32; James Coltrain, "The Structures of Provincialism: Britain's Many Voices in the Colonies," *Atlantic Studies*, 6, no. 1 (2009): 11–36.

65. Brown, *Good Wives*.

66. On Scottish factors and the tobacco trade, see Devine, *Scotland's Empire*, 70–89.

67. Susan Klepp and Billy Smith, eds., *The Infortunate: The Voyage and Adventures of William Moraley, an Indentured Servant* (1992; 2nd edn., University Park, PA, 2005), 95.

68. Ward, "The British West Indies in the Age of Abolition, 1748–1815," 429.

69. Henry F. May, *The Enlightenment in America* (New York, 1976), 34–36; Joyce Chaplin, *The First Scientific American: Benjamin Franklin and the Pursuit of Genius* (New York, 2006); John E. Crowley, *The Invention of Comfort: Sensibilities & Design in Early Modern British & Early America* (Baltimore, 2001).

70. For the idea of provincialism, I am indebted to Miller, *From Colony to Province*; Bernard Bailyn and John Clive, "England's Cultural Provinces: Scotland and America," *William and Mary Quarterly*, 3rd ser., 11, no. 2 (1954): 200–213; and more recently, Landsman, *From Colonials to Provincials*.

71. On this, see especially Joyce Chaplin, "The British Atlantic"; J. R. McNeill, "The Ecological Atlantic"; William O'Reilly, "Movements of People in the Atlantic World"; David Eltis, "Africa, Slavery, and the Slave Trade, Mid-Seventeenth to Mid-Eighteenth Centuries," in Nicholas Canny and Philip Morgan, eds., *The Oxford Handbook of the Atlantic World c. 1450–c. 1850* (New York, 2011).

72. On this general phenomenon, see Jon Butler, *Awash in a Sea of Faith: Christianizing the American People* (Cambridge, MA, 1990); and Thomas S. Kidd, *The Great Awakening: The Roots of Evangelical Christianity in Colonial America* (New Haven, 2007).

73. Paul Boyer and Stephen Nissenbaum, *Salem Possessed: The Social Origins of Witchcraft* (Cambridge, MA, 1974).

74. Jonathan Edwards, "Sinners in the Hands of an Angry God" (1739), in *The Works of Jonathan Edwards*, Vol. 22, *Sermons and Discourses, 1739–1742*, ed. Harry S. Stout and Nathan O. Hatch (New Haven, 2003), 411.

75. On Edwards, see George Marsden, *Jonathan Edwards: A Life* (New Haven, 2003).

76. T. H. Breen and Timothy D. Hall, "Structuring Provincial Imagination: The Rhetoric and Experience of Social Change in Eighteenth-Century New England," *American Historical Review*, 103, no. 5 (1998): 1411–39.

77. Gilbert Tennant, *The Danger of an Unconverted Ministry, Consider'd in a Sermon on Mark VI.34* (Philadelphia, 1740), 4.

78. Timothy D. Hall, *Contested Boundaries: Itinerancy and the Reshaping of the Colonial American Religious World* (Durham, NC, 1994); Griffin, *People with No Name*.

79. Whitefield to _____, 9 July 1757, in *The Works of the Reverend George Whitefield* (London, 1771), 3:207. My thanks to Peter Choi for this reference.

80. On his career, see Harry S. Stout, *The Divine Dramatist: George Whitefield and the Rise of Modern Evangelicalism* (Grand Rapids, MI, 1991).

81. Franklin, *Autobiography*, 130.

82. Frank Lambert, *"Pedlar in Divinity": George Whitefield and the Transatlantic Revivals, 1737–1770* (Princeton, 1994).

83. Rhys Isaac, *The Transformation of Virginia, 1740–1790* (Chapel Hill, NC, 1982).

84. Whitefield, quoted in Hofstadter, *America at 1750*, 252. On how the Great Awakening fostered a greater sense of toleration among Protestants, see Chris Beneke, *Beyond Toleration: The Religious Origins of American Pluralism* (New York, 2008).

85. On other provincial responses to becoming British, see James Livesey, *Civil Society and Empire: Ireland and Scotland in the Eighteenth-Century Atlantic World* (New Haven, 2009); and Bailyn and Clive, "England's Cultural Provinces."

86. Sheridan, "The Formation of Caribbean Plantation Society, 1689–1748," 405.

87. Bailyn, *Origins of American Politics*, 15–60; quote from 59.

88. Bailyn, *Origins of American Politics*, 62–97; quote from 87; Richard Beeman, *The Varieties of Political Experience in Eighteenth-Century America* (Philadelphia, 2004).

89. Jack Greene, *The Quest for Power: The Lower Houses of Assembly in the Southern Royal Colonies, 1689–1776* (Chapel Hill, NC, 1964).

90. For this portrait of Franklin, see Gordon S. Wood, *The Americanization of Benjamin Franklin* (New York, 2004).

91. The phrase is Lawrence Henry Gipson's. See Lawrence Henry Gipson, "The American Revolution as an Aftermath of the Great War of Empire, 1754–1763," *Political Science Quarterly*, 65, no. 1 (1950): 86–104.

92. For the Seven Years' War and the events leading up to it, I have relied on Fred Anderson, *The Crucible of War: The Seven Years' War and the Fate of Empire in British North America, 1754–1766* (New York, 2000).

93. See Richter, *Ordeal of the Longhouse*; and Francis Jennings, *Empire of Fortune: Crowns, Colonies, and Tribes in the Seven Years War in America* (New York, 1988).

94. Easton Council Records, 31 July 1756, in *Minutes of the Provincial Council of Pennsylvania* (Harrisburg, PA, 1851), 7:218.

95. Michael N. McConnell, *A Country Between: The Upper Ohio Valley and Its Peoples, 1724–1774* (Lincoln, NE, 1992).

96. On the French-allied Indians, see White, *Middle Ground*.

97. On Washington, see Fred Anderson and Andrew Cayton, *The Dominion of War: Empire and Liberty in North America, 1500–2000* (New York, 2005).

98. Timothy Shannon, *Indians and Colonists at the Crossroads of Empire: The Albany Congress of 1754* (Ithaca, NY, 2000), 241; Anderson, *Crucible of War*, 78.

99. Anderson, *Crucible of War*, 80. On squabbling and self-interestedness, see also Jennings, *Empire of Fortune*; and Stanley Katz, *Newcastle's New York: Anglo-American Politics, 1732–1753* (Cambridge, MA, 1968).

100. Shannon, *Indians and Colonists at the Crossroads*, 211–19; quote from 205. See also Andrew Beaumont, "'Ambitious Men of Modest Means': Colonial Administration under the Earl of Halifax, 1748–1761" (D.Phil. thesis, Oxford University, 2007).

101. Franklin, *Autobiography*, 172.

102. Duncan Cameron, *The Life, Adventures, and Surprizing Deliverances, of Duncan Cameron, Private Soldier in the Regiment of Foot, Late Sir Peter Halket's*, 3rd edn. (Philadelphia, 1756), 11–12.

103. Anderson and Cayton, *Dominion of War*.

104. Jonathan Mayhew, *Two Discourses Delivered October 25th, 1759: Being the Day Appointed by Authority to Be Observed as a Day of Public Thanksgiving, for the Success of His Majesty's Arms, More Particularly in the Reduction of Quebec* (Boston, 1759), 29.

105. Mayhew, quoted in Fred Anderson, *The War That Made America: A Short History of the French and Indian War* (New York, 2005), 207–8. Mayhew, *Two Discourses*, 61.

CHAPTER 2

1. On the mapping of Ireland, as well as its implications for conquest, see William Smyth, *Map-Making, Landscapes and Memory: A Geography of Colonial and Early Modern Ireland, c. 1530–1750* (Notre Dame, IN, 2006). For Petty's life, see Toby Barnard's excellent summary in the *Oxford Dictionary of National Biography*.

2. "An Act for the Satisfaction of the Adventurers for Lands in Ireland, 1653," in *The History of the Survey of Ireland*, ed. T. A. Larkom (Dublin, 1851), 378–79.

3. On Hobbes and Memories of Ireland, see Burke Griggs, "The Memory of Rebellion and Civil War in British Political Argument, 1646–1721" (Ph.D. diss., Yale University, 1998).

4. See, for instance, a deposition of Richard Baker signed by Petty on 14 December 1678 in a dispute between Irish and English merchants over a shipment of tobacco, Ormande Mss. 82, f. 143, National Library of Ireland, Dublin.

5. Sir William Petty, "A Treatise of Ireland, 1687," in *Economic Writings of Sir William Petty*, ed. John Graunt (Cambridge, 1899), 2:551.

6. On the role of Parliament in the British Isles, see Jim Smyth, *The Making of the United Kingdom, 1660–1800: State, Religion and Identity in Britain and Ireland* (Harlow, UK, 2001). David Armitage suggests that the ideology of state formation in Britain informed the ideology of empire in *The Ideological Origins of the British Empire* (Cambridge, UK, 2000). For Shelburne's life, see John Cannon's entry in the *Oxford Dictionary of National Biography*.

7. Shelburne, cited in R. A. Humphreys, "Lord Shelburne and the Proclamation of 1763," *The English Historical Review*, 49, no. 194 (1934): 242.

8. On a similar dynamic from an earlier period, one that informs my approach, see Ken MacMillan, *Sovereignty and Possession in the English New World: The Legal Foundations of Empire, 1576–1640* (Cambridge, UK, 2006).

9. On situating America within a British context from the perspective of "new" British history, see Eliga H. Gould, *The Persistence of Empire: British Political Culture in the Age of the American Revolution* (Chapel Hill, NC, 2000); T. H. Breen, "Ideology and Nationalism on the Eve of the American Revolution: Revisions *Once More* in Need of

Revising," *Journal of American History*, 84, no. 1 (1997): 13–39; Nicholas Canny, *The Origins of Empire*, Vol. 1 of *The Oxford History of the British Empire* (Oxford, 2001); P. J. Marshall, *The Eighteenth Century*, Vol. 3 of *The Oxford History of the British Empire* (Oxford, 2001); and especially, the AHR Forum on "The New British History in Atlantic Perspective," *American Historical Review*, 104, no. 2 (1999): 426–500.

10. For a very different approach to the consolidation of Britain than the consensual model that prevails within the "new" British history, see Michael Hechter, *Internal Colonialism: The Celtic Fringe in British National Development* (New Brunswick, NJ, 1999). The idea here was influenced by Andrew Fitzmaurice, *Humanism and America: An Intellectual History of English Colonization, 1500–1625* (Cambridge, UK, 2003).

11. This is the characterization of John Murrin, "A Roof Without Walls: The Dilemma of American National Identity," in Richard Beeman, Stephen Botein, and Edward C. Carter II, eds., *Beyond Confederation: Origins of the Constitution and American National Identity* (Chapel Hill, NC, 1987), 333–48.

12. P. J. Marshall, *The Making and Unmaking of Empires: Britain, India, and America c. 1750–1783* (New York, 2005), 207; C. A. Bayly, "The Age of Revolutions in Global Context: An Afterword," in David Armitage and Sanjay Subrahmanyam, eds., *The Age of Revolutions in Global Context, c. 1760–1840* (London, 2010), 209.

13. On these themes, see Gabriel Paquette, *Enlightenment, Governance, and Reform in Spain and Its Empire, 1759–1808* (London, 2010); Michael Kwass, *Politics of Taxation in Eighteenth-Century France: Liberté, Égalité, Fiscalité* (Cambridge, 2000); John Garrigus, *Before Haiti: Race and Citizenship in French Saint-Domingue* (New York, 2006). For the British, on the global level, see Philip Stern, *The Company State: Corporate Sovereignty and the Early Modern Foundations of the British Empire in India* (New York, 2011).

14. Nicholas Canny argues that although global factors influenced Atlantic societies, all people could not see things from a global perspective. See "Writing Atlantic History, or Reconfiguring the History of Colonial British America," *Journal of American History*, 86 (1999): 1093–1114.

15. Benjamin Franklin to Peter Collinson, n.d., 1748, cited in James Delbourgo, *A Most Amazing Scene of Wonders: Electricity and Enlightenment in Early America* (Cambridge, MA, 2006), 129–30.

16. Brendan McConville, *The Kings' Three Faces: The Rise & Fall of Royal America, 1688–1776* (Chapel Hill, NC, 2006).

17. Karen O'Brien, *Narratives of Enlightenment: Cosmopolitan History from Voltaire to Gibbon* (New York, 2005); J. G. A. Pocock, *Barbarism and Religion*, Vol. 3, *The First Decline and Fall* (New York, 2005). On Augustus, see David Womersley, "Introduction," to Edward Gibbon, *The History of the Decline and Fall of the Roman Empire* (New York, 1994).

18. Gould, *Persistence of Empire*.

19. For a more consensual understanding of the creation of Britishness, see Linda Colley, *Britons: Forging the Nation, 1707–1837*, 3rd edn. (New Haven, 2009).

20. For a study of the origins of the American Revolution that stresses the idea of parliamentary sovereignty, see Edmund S. Morgan, *The Birth of the Republic, 1763–89*, 3rd edn. (Chicago, 1992).

21. Paquette, *Enlightenment, Governance, and Reform in Spain*; Pocock, *Barbarism and Religion*, Vol. 3.

22. Bernard Bailyn, *The Ideological Origins of the American Revolution*, enl. edn. (Cambridge, MA, 1992); J. G. A. Pocock, ed., *Three British Revolutions, 1641, 1688, 1776* (Princeton, 1980).

23. John Morrill, "Three Kingdoms and One Commonwealth?: The Enigma of Mid-seventeenth-century Britain and Ireland," in Alexander Grant and Keith Stringer, eds., *Uniting the Kingdom?: The Making of British History* (London, 1995).

24. On British attempts to unite the two kingdoms, see Brian P. Levack, *The Formation of the British State: England, Scotland, and the Union, 1603–1707* (Oxford, 1987).

25. For an excellent and readable summary of James I and the subsequent period, one on which this narrative is based, see Mark A. Kishlansky, *A Monarchy Transformed: Britain, 1603–1714* (London, 1996).

26. On the virtues and drawbacks of dynastic union, see Smyth, *Making of the United Kingdom*.

27. My reading of this period has been shaped by Nicholas Canny, *Making Ireland British, 1580–1650* (Oxford, 2001); and Sean J. Connolly, *Contested Island: Ireland, 1460–1630* (Oxford, 2007).

28. Rory Rapple, *Martial Power and Elizabethan Political Culture: Military Men in England and Ireland, 1558–1594* (Cambridge, UK, 2009); D. B. Quinn, *The Elizabethans and the Irish* (Ithaca, NY, 1966); Nicholas P. Canny, *The Elizabethan Conquest of Ireland: A Pattern Established, 1565–76* (New York, 1976).

29. "The Life of Sir Walter Raleigh," n.d., Add. Ms. 4231, v–vi, British Library, London.

30. "Certyn Notes and Observations Touching the Deducing and Planting of Colonies," n.d., Cotton Mss., Titus BX, f. 402, British Library.

31. On these themes, see Ciaran Brady and Jane Ohlmeyer, "Making Good: New Perspectives on the English in Early Modern Ireland," in Ciaran Brady and Jane Ohlmeyer, eds., *British Interventions in Early Modern Ireland* (Cambridge, UK, 2005).

32. On the emergence of Parliament, see Mark A. Kishlansky, *Parliamentary Selection: Social and Political Choice in Early Modern England* (Cambridge, UK, 1986).

33. On this, see Conrad Russell, *The Fall of the British Monarchies, 1637–42* (Oxford, 1991).

34. Depositions concerning Murders and Robberies committed in the Queen's County, 1641 Depositions, Trinity College Dublin, MS. 815, f. 85, 322. See also Nicholas Canny, "England's New World and Old," in *Origins of Empire*, Vol. 2 of *Oxford History of the British Empire*, ed. Nicholas Canny, 161.

35. Deposition of Richard Newberrie, MS 836, f. 60–61, 27 June 1642. These depositions are now available at http://1641.eneclann.ie/index.php.

36. John Booker, *A Bloody Irish Almanack, or, Rebellious and Bloody Ireland* (London, 1646), 7, 11.

37. *A Solemn League and Covenant, for Reformation; and Defence of Religion, the Honour and Happiness of the King, and the Peace & Safetie of the Three Kingdoms* (Aberdeen, 1643), 11.

38. For the Levellers, see the classic work of Christopher Hill, *The World Turned Upside Down: Radical Ideas during the English Revolution* (1972; repr., London, 1991).

39. For this period, see Steven C. A. Pincus, *1688: The First Modern Revolution* (New Haven, 2009).

40. John Locke, *The Two Treatises of Government* (1689; London, 1821), II.viii.102, II.x.135.

41. Colley, *Britons*.

42. Holger Hoock, *Empires of the Imagination: Politics, War, and the Arts in the British World, 1750–1850* (London, 2010), 86–87.

43. On this theme, see Bernard Bailyn and John Clive, "England's Cultural Provinces: Scotland and America," *William and Mary Quarterly*, 3rd ser., 11, no. 2 (1954): 200–213;

and most recently, James Livesey, *Civil Society and Empire: Ireland and Scotland in the Eighteenth-Century Atlantic World* (New Haven, 2009).

44. Defoe, *The History of the Union of Great Britain* (Edinburgh, 1709), 20–21, 28–30.

45. Jim Smyth, "'A Victory Best Forgotten'?: Constructing Culloden" (unpublished paper). See also Colin Kidd, *Subverting Scotland's Past: Scottish Whig Historians and the Creation of an Anglo-British Identity, 1689–c. 1830* (Cambridge, UK, 1993); Geoffrey Plank, *Rebellion and Savagery: The Jacobite Rising of 1745 and the British Empire* (Philadelphia, 2006); Allan I. Macinnes, *Clanship, Commerce, and the House of Stuart, 1603–1788* (East Linton, UK, 1996).

46. Ebenezer Latham, *Great Britain's Thanks to God; to Her Governours, and the People, that Offer'd Themselves Willingly in Defence of Their Dear Country, against the Late Attempt by France and Rome* (Derby, 1746), 4.

47. See Toby Barnard, *A New Anatomy of Ireland: The Irish Protestants, 1649–1770* (New Haven, 2003); R. F. Foster, *Modern Ireland, 1600–1972* (London, 1988).

48. Sir William Domville's Disquisition, 1668, Mss. 40, National Library of Ireland, Dublin.

49. William Molyneux, *The Case of Ireland's Being Bound by Acts of Parliament in England, Stated* (Dublin, 1698), 170.

50. Jonathan Swift, *Fraud Detected: Or, The Hibernian Patriot, Containing, All the Drapier's Letters to the People of Ireland, on Wood's Coinage, & c.* (Dublin, 1725), 64.

51. Swift, "A Letter to the Whole People of Ireland," in *The Drapier's Letters to the People of Ireland*, ed. Herbert Davis (Oxford, 1935), 70, 68.

52. S. J. Connolly, *Religion, Law, and Power: The Making of Protestant Ireland* (1992; repr., Oxford, 2002).

53. See Patrick Griffin, "America's Changing Image in Ireland's Looking-Glass: Provincial Construction of an Eighteenth-Century British Atlantic World," *Journal of Imperial and Commonwealth History*, 26, no. 3 (1998): 32–33. On Wilkes, refer to Peter D. G. Thomas, *John Wilkes: A Friend to Liberty* (New York, 1996); and Arthur Cash, *The Scandalous Father of Civil Liberty* (New Haven, 2006).

54. Patrick Griffin, *The People with No Name: Ireland's Ulster Scots, America's Scots Irish, and the Creation of a British Atlantic World* (Princeton, 2001).

55. Breandán Ó Buachalla, "'James Our True King': The Ideology of Irish Royalism in the Seventeenth Century," in D. George Boyce, Robert Eccleshall, and Vincent Geoghegan, eds., *Political Thought in Ireland since the Seventeenth Century* (London, 1993), 7–35; Foster, *Modern Ireland*; Éamonn Ó Ciardha, *Ireland and the Jacobite Cause, 1685–1766: A Fatal Attachment* (Dublin, 2002).

56. Jonathan Scott, *When the Waves Ruled Britannia: Geography and Political Identities, 1500–1800* (London, 2011).

57. For the ideology of empire, see Armitage, *Ideological Origins*. For the identity of empire, including Wilkes's campaigns, see Colley, *Britons*.

58. Richard Hofstadter, *America at 1750: A Social Portrait* (New York, 1973), 3–9.

59. See Fred Anderson, *A People's Army: Massachusetts Soldiers and Society in the Seven Years' War* (Chapel Hill, NC, 1984).

60. Benjamin Franklin, *The Interest of Great Britain Considered, with Regard to Her Colonies* (London, 1760), 45, 14, 13.

61. Fred Anderson, *The Crucible of War: The Seven Years' War and the Fate of Empire in British North America, 1754–1766* (New York, 2000), 562. John Brewer puts the debt

at £132 million in *The Sinews of Power: War, Money, and the English State, 1688–1783* (New York, 1988).

62. Anderson, *Crucible of War*, 563. On financing interest, see John J. McCusker and Kenneth Morgan, eds., *The Early Modern Atlantic Economy* (Cambridge, UK, 2000). For a worldwide understanding of the meaning of 1763, see Colin G. Calloway, *The Scratch of a Pen: 1763 and the Transformation of North America* (Oxford, 2006).

63. Thomas Gage to Henry Bouquet, 15 October 1764, in *The Papers of Henry Bouquet*, ed. Louis Waddell (Harrisburg, PA, 1994), 6:663.

64. On this episode, see Elizabeth A. Fenn, *Pox Americana: The Great Smallpox Epidemic of 1775–82* (New York, 2001).

65. Jeffrey Amherst Memorandum, 16 July 1763, *Papers of Henry Bouquet*, 6:315.

66. On Amherst's career in Scotland, see Geoffrey Plank, *An Unsettled Conquest: The British Campaign against the Peoples of Acadia* (Philadelphia, 2000). On the ways the British approach differed from the French, see Richard White, *The Middle Ground: Indians, Empires, and Republics in the Great Lakes Region, 1650–1815* (Cambridge, UK, 1991). Also see Eric Hinderaker, *Elusive Empires: Constructing Colonialism in the Ohio Valley, 1673–1800* (Cambridge, UK, 1997). On the similar ways the English considered Scots and Indians, see Colin G. Calloway, *White People, Indians, and Highlanders: Tribal Peoples and Colonial Encounters in Scotland and America* (Oxford, 2008).

67. The best works on Pontiac's War are Gregory Evans Dowd's two books: *A Spirited Resistance: The North American Indian Struggle for Unity, 1745–1815* (Baltimore, 1992); and *War under Heaven: Pontiac, the Indian Nations, & the British Empire* (Baltimore, 2002).

68. Richter, *Facing East from Indian Country*, 201–2.

69. Mark Noll, "Canada, 1759–1815," in Vol. 1 of *The Cambridge History of Religions in America*, ed. Stephen Stein (Cambridge University Press, forthcoming in June 2012).

70. See Patrick Griffin, *American Leviathan: Empire, Nation, and Revolutionary Frontier* (New York, 2007).

71. On these themes, and as they pertain to Johnson and Stuart, see Fintan O'Toole, *White Savage: William Johnson and the Invention of America* (New York, 2005); Linda Colley, *Captives: Britain, Empire, and the World, 1600–1850* (London, 2002); and J. Russell Snapp, *John Stuart and the Struggle for Empire on the Southern Frontier* (Baton Rouge, LA, 1996).

72. *By the King, a Proclamation* (London, 1763).

73. Colin G. Calloway, *White People, Indians, and Highlanders*; Margaret Connell Szasz, *Scottish Highlanders and Native Americans: Indigenous Education in the Eighteenth-Century Atlantic World* (Norman, OK, 2007).

74. The region was "terra nullius." On this see Gould, *Persistence of Empire*.

CHAPTER 3

1. James McCullough, Journal, 1748–1758, in Kerby A. Miller et al., eds., *Irish Immigrants in the Land of Canaan: Letters and Memoirs from Colonial and Revolutionary America* (New York, 2003), 172–78.

2. *Pennsylvania Gazette*, 27 October 1763. On the Paxton affair, see Kevin Kenny, *Peaceable Kingdom Lost: The Paxton Boys and the Destruction of William Penn's Holy Experiment* (New York, 2009).

3. Matthew Smith, *A Declaration and Remonstrance of the Distressed and Bleeding Frontier Inhabitants of the Province of Pennsylvania* (Philadelphia, 1764), 3–5.

4. "The Conduct of the Paxton-Men Impartially Represented" (Philadelphia, 1764), in *The Paxton Papers*, ed. John R. Dunbar (The Hague, 1957), 272, 293, 297.

5. On this theme, see James Merrell, *Into the American Woods: Negotiators on the Pennsylvania Frontier* (New York, 1999).

6. Edmund S. Morgan and Helen Morgan, *The Stamp Act Crisis: Prologue to Revolution*, rev. edn. (Chapel Hill, NC, 1953), 21–28.

7. Ibid., 27–35.

8. Ibid., 58, 72.

9. John Brewer, *The Sinews of Power: War, Money, and the English State, 1688-1783* (Cambridge, MA, 1990).

10. Peter D. G. Thomas, *The Townshend Duties Crisis: The Second Phase of the American Revolution* (London, 1987), 1–50; Morgan and Morgan, *Stamp Act Crisis*.

11. "Instructions of the Town of Boston to Its Representatives in the General Court," 18 September 1765, in *The Writings of Samuel Adams*, ed. Harry Alonzo Cushing (New York: G. P. Putnam's Sons, 1904), 1:8, 9.

12. Thomas Hutchinson to Richard Jackson, 30 August 1765, quoted in George P. Anderson, "Ebenezer McIntosh: Stamp Act Rioter and Patriot," *Publications of the Colonial Society of Massachusetts*, 26 (1927): 32–33. On Mackintosh as a man who united the better, middling, and upper sort, see Alfred Young, "Ebenezer Mackintosh: Boston's Captain General of the Liberty Tree," in Alfred Young, Gary Nash, and Ray Raphael, eds., *Revolutionary Founders: Rebels, Radicals, and Reformers in the Making of the Nation* (New York, 2011), 15–33.

13. Gary B. Nash, *Urban Crucible: Social Change, Political Consciousness, and the Origins of the American Revolution* (Cambridge, MA, 1979), 185. On these rituals, see Peter Messer, "Stamps and Popes: Rethinking Violence in the Coming of the American Revolution," forthcoming in Patrick Griffin and Peter Onuf, eds., *Violence and the American Revolution* (Charlottesville, VA).

14. James Otis, *A Vindication of the British Colonies, against the Aspersions of the Halifax Gentleman, in His Letter to a Rhode-Island Friend* (Boston, 1765), 5, 15.

15. Patrick Henry, "Stamp Act Resolutions," in William Wirt Henry, *Patrick Henry: Life, Correspondence and Speeches* (New York: Charles Scribner's Sons, 1891), 1:80–81.

16. Daniel Dulany, *Considerations on the Propriety of Imposing Taxes in the British Colon[i]es, for the Purpose of Raising a Revenue, by Act of Parliament* (New York, 1765), 5–6. The best work on these pamphlets remains Bernard Bailyn, *The Ideological Origins of the American Revolution*, enl. edn. (Cambridge, MA, 1992).

17. Andrew O'Shaughnessy, "The Stamp Act Crisis in the British Caribbean," *William and Mary Quarterly*, 3rd ser., 51 (1994): 203–26.

18. Douglas Hamilton, *Scotland, the Caribbean, and the Atlantic World, 1750-1820* (Manchester, UK, 2005).

19. Rebecca Starr, *A School for Politics: Commercial Lobbying and Political Culture in Early South Carolina* (Baltimore, 1998); Benjamin Carp, *Rebels Rising: Cities and the American Revolution* (New York, 2007); Russell Menard, "Slavery, Economic Growth, and Revolutionary Ideology in the South Carolina Lowcountry," in Ronald Hoffman et al., eds., *The Economy of Early America: The Revolutionary Period, 1763-1790* (Charlottesville, VA, 1988).

20. Carp, *Rebels Rising*.

21. Isaac Barré, cited in Morgan and Morgan, *Stamp Act Crisis*, 69.

22. On this idea, see E. P. Thompson, *Customs in Common* (New York, 1991).

23. Eliga Gould, *The Persistence of Empire: British Political Culture in the Age of the American Revolution* (Chapel Hill, NC, 2000), 120.

24. Sir William Blackstone, cited in Jack Rakove, *Revolutionaries: A New History of the Invention of America* (Boston, 2010), 21.

25. Nash, *Urban Crucible*, 147–59.

26. Nash, *Urban Crucible*, 149–64. On smuggling, see Thomas M. Truxes, *Defying Empire: Trading with the Enemy in Colonial New York* (New Haven, 2008).

27. Bailyn, *Ideological Origins of the American Revolution.*

28. Thomas Kidd, *God of Liberty: A Religious History of the American Revolution* (New York, 2010), 15–16, 32–33.

29. Kidd, *God of Liberty*, 24, 38–39, 52–53; Jon Butler, "James Ireland, John Leland, John 'Swearing Jack' Waller, and the Baptist Campaign for Religious Freedom in Revolutionary Virginia," in Alfred Young, Gary Nash, and Ray Raphael, eds., *Revolutionary Founders: Rebels, Radicals, and Reformers in the Making of the Nation* (New York, 2011), 172–74.

30. Isaac, *The Transformation of Virginia*; Woody Holton, *Forced Founders: Indians, Debtors, Slaves and the Making of the American Revolution in Virginia* (Chapel Hill, NC, 1999), 197–98.

31. John Ragosta, *Wellspring of Liberty: How Virginia's Religious Dissenters Helped Win the American Revolution and Secured Religious Liberty* (New York, 2010).

32. Peter Doll, *Revolution, Religion, and National Identity: Imperial Anglicanism in British North America, 1745–95* (Madison, NJ, 2000); Ned Landsman, "The Episcopate, the British Union, and the Failure of Religious Settlement in Colonial British America," in Chris Beneke and Christopher Grenda, eds., *The First Prejudice: Religious Tolerance and Intolerance in Early America* (Philadelphia, 2011), 75–97. See especially Robert Ingram, *Religion, Reform, and Modernity in the Eighteenth Century: Thomas Secker and the Church of England* (London, 2007). Secker quoted on p. 211.

33. Ingram, *Religion, Reform, and Modernity*, 246, 251, 253; Doll, *Revolution, Religion, and National Identity*; Patricia Bonomi, *Under the Cope of Heaven: Religion, Society, and Politics in Colonial America* (New York, 2003).

34. Bernard Bailyn, *The Origins of American Politics* (New York, 1968), 98; Rakove, *Revolutionaries*, 34; Bernard Bailyn, *The Ordeal of Thomas Hutchinson* (Cambridge, MA, 1974), 2, 12.

35. Patrick Griffin, "America's Changing Image in Ireland's Looking Glass: Provincial Construction of an Eighteenth Century British Atlantic World," *Journal of Imperial and Commonwealth History*, 26, no. 3 (1998): 28–49; George Rudé, *Wilkes and Liberty: A Social Study of 1763 to 1774* (Oxford, 1962); Pauline Maier, *From Resistance to Revolution: Colonial Radicals and the Development of American Opposition to Britain, 1765–1776* (New York, 1972).

36. Pauline Maier, *The Old Revolutionaries: Political Lives in the Age of Samuel Adams* (New York, 1980), 102–15, 164–200.

37. Douglas Adair and John Schutz, eds., *Peter Oliver's Origin and Progress of the American Rebellion: A Tory View* (San Marino, CA, 1961), xiii, 3, 39, 145, 9.

38. This is the gist of the idealist perspective on the American Revolution. See, in particular, the work of Bernard Bailyn and Edmund Morgan.

39. Jonathan Swift, *A Proposal for the Universal Use of Irish Manufacture, in Cloaths and Furniture of Houses, & c. Utterly Rejecting and Renouncing Every Thing Wearable that Comes from England* (Dublin, 1720), 6.

40. Fred Anderson, *The Crucible of War: The Seven Years' War and the Fate of Empire in British North America, 1754–1766* (New York, 2000), 562; Sean Connolly, *Divided Kingdom: Ireland 1630–1800* (New York, 2010), 386. On this dynamic, see Jim Smyth, *The Making of the United Kingdom, 1660–1800: State, Religion, and Identity in Britain and Ireland* (Harlow, UK, 2001). Pauline Maier makes the case that there was nothing unusual about riot in Boston or in the Atlantic world. See *From Resistance to Revolution*.

41. Brendan McConville, *The King's Three Faces: The Rise and Fall of Royal America, 1688–1776* (Chapel Hill, NC, 2006), 1–2, 58–59; Messer, "Stamps and Popes."

42. Robert M. Calhoon, "Loyalism and Neutrality," in Jack Greene and J. R. Pole, eds., *A Companion to the American Revolution* (Malden, MA, 2000), 235.

43. Gordon S. Wood, *The Americanization of Benjamin Franklin* (New York, 2004).

44. For Franklin's misunderstandings, see Edmund S. Morgan, *Benjamin Franklin* (New Haven, 2002). On the repulsion Americans felt toward taxation in general, see Morgan, *The Birth of the Republic, 1763–89* (Chicago, 1992).

45. Lewis Namier and John Brooke, *Charles Townshend: His Character and Career* (Ann Arbor, MI, 1959); Cornelius Foster, *The Uncontrolled Chancellor: Charles Townshend and His American Policy* (Providence, RI, 1978); Peter D. G. Thomas, *The Townshend Duties Crisis:* 1–50; Thomas Bartlett, "The Townshend Viceroyalty, 1767–1772," in D. W. Hayton and Bartlett, eds., *Penal Era and Golden Age: Essays in Irish History, 1690–1800* (Belfast, 2005).

46. Jack Greene, *The Constitutional Origins of the American Revolution* (New York, 2010). On rule of India as yet another sovereign arrangement, see Philip Stern, *The Company-State: Corporate Sovereignty and the Early Modern Foundations of the British Empire in India* (New York, 2011).

47. T. H. Breen quotes this list in *The Marketplace of Revolution: How Consumer Politics Shaped American Independence* (Oxford, 2004), 236.

48. Maya Jasanoff, "Revolutionary Exiles: The American Loyalist and French Émigré Diasporas," in David Armitage and Sanjay Subrahmantam, eds., *The Age of Revolutions in Global Context, c. 1760–1840* (London, 2010), 42.

49. Rakove, *Revolutionaries*, 23.

50. "Divide & Impera. *Divide and Tyrannize*," *Pennsylvania Gazette*, 14 April 1768.

51. Breen, *Marketplace of Revolution*; Colin Kidd, "North Britishness and the Nature of Eighteenth-Century British Patriotisms," *Historical Journal*, 39, no. 2 (1996): 361–82.

52. John Adams certainly read and admired Swift. See John E. Ferling, *John Adams: A Life* (Knoxville, TN, 1992), 174.

53. James Otis, *The Rights of the British Colonies Asserted and Proved* (Boston, 1764), in *Pamphlets of the American Revolution*, ed. Bernard Bailyn (Cambridge, MA, 1965) 1:456.

54. *New-Hampshire Gazette, and Historical Chronicle*, 19 August 1768. On the contradiction between liberty and slavery, see Edmund S. Morgan, *American Slavery, American Freedom: The Ordeal of Colonial Virginia* (New York, 1975).

55. Rakove, *Revolutionaries*, 20, 33; T. H. Breen, *American Insurgents, American Patriots: The Revolution of the People* (New York, 2010), 99, 102, 170, 173.

56. Dickinson, *Letters from a Farmer in Pennsylvania to the Inhabitants of the British Colonies* (New York, 1768), 19.

57. Bailyn, *Ideological Origins*.

58. Theodore Draper, *A Struggle for Power: The American Revolution* (New York, 1996); Andrew Jackson O'Shaughnessy, *An Empire Divided: The American Revolution and the British Caribbean* (Philadelphia, 2000).

59. Oliver, *Origin & Progress*, 65, 70.

60. Thomas Hutchinson, cited in Bailyn, *Ordeal of Thomas Hutchinson*, 85.

61. For the balance between liberty and power, see Bailyn, *Ideological Origins*, 58.

62. Benjamin Franklin, *Narrative of the Late Massacres, in Lancaster County, of a Number of Indians, Friends of This Province, by Persons Unknown*, in *The Writings of Benjamin Franklin*, ed. Albert Henry Smyth (New York, 1906), 4:310, 295.

63. Gordon S. Wood, *The American Revolution: A History* (New York, 2002).

64. Warren R. Hofstra, *The Planting of New Virginia: Settlement and Landscape in the Shenandoah Valley* (Baltimore, 2004); James T. Lemon, *The Best Poor Man's Country: Early Southeastern Pennsylvania* (Baltimore, 2002).

65. Bailyn, *Origins of American Politics*, 99; Rhys Isaac, *Transformation of Virginia 1740–1790* (Chapel Hill, NC, 1982).

66. Colin G. Calloway, *White People, Indians, and Highlanders: Tribal Peoples and Colonial Encounters in Scotland and America* (Oxford, 2008); Geoffrey Plank, *Rebellion and Savagery: The Jacobite Rising of 1745 and the British Empire* (Philadelphia, 2006). For reluctance, see John Oliphant's entry for James Grant in the *Oxford Dictionary of National Biography*.

67. "Copy of a Remonstrance Presented to the Commons House of Assembly in South Carolina, by the Upper Inhabitants of the Said Province," November 1767, in *The Carolina Backcountry on the Eve of the Revolution: The Journal and Other Writings of Charles Woodmason, Anglican Itinerant*, ed. Richard J. Hooker (Chapel Hill, NC, 1953), 215.

68. John Oliphant, *Peace and War on the Anglo-Cherokee Frontier, 1756–63* (Baton Rouge, LA, 2001); Rachel Klein, "Ordering the Backcountry: The South Carolina Regulation," *William and Mary Quarterly*, 3rd ser., 38, no. 4 (1981): 661–80.

69. Marjoleine Kars, *Breaking Loose Together: The Regulator Rebellion in Pre-Revolutionary North Carolina* (Chapel Hill, NC, 2002), 1–7, 111.

70. William Johnson to Henry Moore, 22 October 1767, *The Papers of Sir William Johnson*, ed. Alexander C. Flick (Albany, NY, 1927), 5:741.

71. Wood, *Americanization of Benjamin Franklin*.

72. For these events, see Dowd, *War under Heaven*; and Kenny, *Peaceable Kingdoms Lost*.

73. Benjamin Franklin to John Ross, 8 June 1765, *Writings of Benjamin Franklin*, 4:385.

74. Sir William Johnson to the Lords of Trade, 22 November 1765, *Documents Relative to the Colonial History of the State of New York*, 7:790.

75. Kenny, *Peaceable Kingdom Lost*.

76. Robert V. Hine and John Mack Faragher, *The American West: A New Interpretive History* (New Haven, 2000).

77. See Richard White, *The Middle Ground: Indians, Empires, and Republics in the Great Lakes Region, 1650–1815* (Cambridge, UK, 1991); Eric Hinderaker, *Elusive Empires: Constructing Colonialism in the Ohio Valley, 1673–1800* (New York, 1997).

78. Lord Hillsborough to Sir William Johnson, 4 January 1769, *Documents Relative to the Colonial History of the State of New York*, 8:145.

79. Oliver, *Origin and Progress*, 70.
80. Thomas Gage to Lord Barrington, 28 June 1768, *Correspondence of Thomas Gage*, 2:479–480.
81. Samuel Adams to James Warren, 7 January 1776, *Writings of Samuel Adams*, 3:250.
82. Thomas Gage quoted in Griffin, *American Leviathan*, 94.

PART II

1. Carrie Rebora Barratt and Paul Staiti, eds., *John Singleton Copley in America* (New York, 1995), 41.
2. Jill Lepore, *The Whites of Their Eyes: The Tea Party's Revolution and the Battle over American History* (Princeton, 2010).
3. On the transatlantic interpretations, see Jennifer Roberts, "Copley's Cargo: Boy with a Squirrel and the Dilemma of Transit," *American Art*, 21 (2007), 21–41.
4. Copley to Henry Pelham, 11 July 1774, "Letters and Papers of John Singleton Copley and Henry Pelham," *Collections of the Massachusetts Historical Society*, 71 (Boston, 1914): 226. For Copley's life, as well as the views of Reynolds and West, see Paul Staiti's entry on Copley in *Oxford Dictionary of National Biography*. Also see Hugh Howard's *The Painter's Chair: George Washington and the Making of American Art* (New York, 2009); and Ann Uhry Abrams, *The Valiant Hero: Grand-Style History Painting* (Washington, DC, 1985).
5. Emily Ballew Neff, *John Singleton Copley in England* (London, 1995), 102, 113. On Watson and tea, see Benjamin Carp, *Defiance of the Patriots: The Boston Tea Party and the Making of America* (New Haven, 2010), 78, 211; and the Staiti entry in the *Oxford Dictionary of National Biography*.
6. Irma Jaffe, "John Singleton Copley's *Watson and the Shark*," *The American Art Journal*, 9 (1977), 15–25.
7. Staiti entry in the *Oxford Dictionary of National Biography*.
8. For a reading of the painting that discusses some of these themes, see Louis Masur, "Reading *Watson and the Shark*," *The New England Quarterly*, 67, no. 3 (1994): 427–54.
9. Copley to Henry Pelham, 6 August 1775, "Letters and Papers," 348.
10. Holger Hoock, *Empires of the Imagination: Politics, War, and the Arts in the British World, 1750–1850* (London, 2010), 93–94.

CHAPTER 4

1. Samuel Adams to John Scolley, 30 December 1780, in *The Writings of Samuel Adams*, ed. H. A. Cushing (New York, 1908), 4:236–38.
2. Elizabeth Murray cited in Patricia Cleary, *Elizabeth Murray: A Woman's Pursuit of Independence in Eighteenth-Century America* (Amherst, MA, 2000), 137.
3. Ibid.
4. T. H. Breen, *The Marketplace of Revolution: How Consumer Politics Shaped American Independence* (Oxford, 2004), 286–88.
5. Thomas Hobbes, *Leviathan*, ed. Richard Tuck, rev. edn. (Cambridge, UK, 1996), 153.
6. John Locke, *The Second Treatise of Government*, in *Political Writings*, ed. David Wootton (Indianapolis, 2003), 348. On the idea of the appeal to heaven, see Breen, *Marketplace of Revolution*.
7. Gordon S. Wood, *The Radicalism of the American Revolution* (New York, 1992).

8. For events in the West in the wake of the Fort Stanwix Treaty, see Patrick Griffin, *American Leviathan: Empire, Nation, and Revolutionary Frontier* (New York, 2007); Eric Hinderaker, *Elusive Empires: Constructing Colonialism in the Ohio Valley, 1673–1800* (New York, 1997); and Richard White, *The Middle Ground: Indians, Empires, and Republics in the Great Lakes Region, 1650–1815* (Cambridge, UK, 1991).

9. George Rogers Clark to Jonathan Clark, 9 January 1773, in *George Rogers Clark Papers, 1771–1781*, ed. James Alton James (Springfield, IL, 1912), 1:2.

10. "Delawares, Munsies and Mohicans to Governors of Pennsylvania, Maryland and Virginia," 4 December 1771, *Documents of the American Revolution, 1770–1983: Colonial Office Series* ed. R.G. Davies (Dublin, 1974), 3:255.

11. Griffin, *American Leviathan.*

12. Gary Nash, *Unknown American Revolution, The Unruly Birth of Democracy and the Struggle to Create America* (New York, 2005), 92–93, 97.

13. See the essays in Ronald Hoffman et al., eds., *The Economy of Early America: The Revolutionary Period, 1763–1790* (Charlottesville, VA, 1988).

14. Robert Middlekauff, *The Glorious Cause: The American Revolution, 1763–1789*, rev. edn. (Oxford, 2005), 200–209; Hiller B. Zobel, *The Boston Massacre* (New York, 1970), 102–3; Richard Archer, *As If an Enemy's Country: The British Occupation of Boston and the Origins of Revolution* (Oxford, 2010), 128–29.

15. Nash, *Unknown American Revolution*, 97; Pauline Maier, *The Old Revolutionaries: Political Lives in the Age of Samuel Adams* (New York, 1980), 3–18.

16. Pauline Maier, *From Resistance to Revolution: Colonial Radicals and the Development of American Opposition to Britain, 1765–1776* (New York, 1972).

17. Middlekauff, *Glorious Cause*, 203–7.

18. John Adams, 4 December 1770, Boston Massacre Trial, in *American State Trials*, ed. John D. Lawson (St. Louis, 1918), 10:486.

19. Frederic Kidder, ed., *History of the Boston Massacre, March 5, 1770* (Albany, 1870).

20. Gary B. Nash, *The Urban Crucible: Social Change, Political Consciousness, and the Origins of the American Revolution* (Cambridge, MA, 1979), 163–64; Ray Raphael, *A People's History of the American Revolution: How Common People Shaped the Fight for Independence* (New York, 2001).

21. See E. P. Thompson, *The Making of the English Working Class*, new edn. (Harmondsworth, UK, 1972).

22. Nash, *Urban Crucible.*

23. T. H. Breen, *American Insurgents, American Patriots: The Revolution of the People* (New York, 2010), 25–27. On Petty and Franklin, see Joyce Chaplin, *The First Scientific American: Benjamin Franklin and the Pursuit of Genius* (New York, 2006).

24. Robert A. Gross, *The Minutemen and Their World* (New York, 1976), 10–29, 76–93.

25. Gregory Nobles, *Divisions throughout the Whole: Politics and Society in Hampshire County, Massachusetts, 1740–1775* (New York, 1983). On revivals in this period, see Thomas S. Kidd, *The Great Awakening: The Roots of Evangelical Christianity in Colonial America* (New Haven, 2007).

26. Peter Oliver, *Peter Oliver's Origin and Progress of the American Rebellion: A Tory View*, ed. Douglas Adair and John Schutz (San Marino, CA, 1961), 35, 93.

27. James Bowdoin, Joseph Warren, and Samuel Pemberton, *A Short Narrative of the Horrid Massacre in Boston* (1770; repr., New York, 1849), 7–8.

28. Maier, *From Resistance to Revolution.*

29. Carol Berkin, *Revolutionary Mothers: Women in the Struggle for America's Independence* (New York, 2005), 13–21; Mary Beth Norton, *Liberty's Daughters: The Revolutionary Experience of American Women, 1750–1800* (1980; repr., Ithaca, NY, 1996), 160–61.

30. Cleary, *Elizabeth Murray*, 101, 133.

31. Norton, *Liberty's Daughters*.

32. Linda Kerber, *Women of the Republic: Intellect and Ideology in Revolutionary America* (Chapel Hill, NC, 1980).

33. Breen, *Marketplace of Revolution*; Nash, *Unknown American Revolution*.

34. Thomas Gage to Hillsborough, 10 April 1770, in *The Boston Massacre: A History with Documents*, ed. Neil L. York (New York, 2010), 103.

35. I owe this idea of "deference" to a forum in *Early American Studies*, 2 (2005). See especially Gregory Nobles, "A Class Act: Redefining Deference in Early American History," 287–300; Richard Beeman, "The Varieties of Deference in Eighteenth-Century America,"313–39; and Barbara Clark Smith, "Beyond the Vote: The Limits of Deference in Colonial Politics," 342–62.

36. Maier, *From Resistance to Revolution*, 121–22.

37. Edmund S. Morgan, *The Birth of the Republic, 1763–1789*, 3rd edn. (Chicago, 1992), 53. Middlekauff, *Glorious Cause*, 212–15.

38. On this, see Rhys Isaac, *The Transformation of Virginia, 1740–1790* (Chapel Hill, NC, 1982); Robert Ingram, *Religion, Reform, and Modernity in the Eighteenth Century: Thomas Secker and the Church of England* (London, 2007), 256; Thomas Kidd, *God of Liberty: A Religious History of the American Revolution* (New York, 2010), 64–65.

39. P. J. Marshall, *The Making and Unmaking of Empires: Britain, India, and America, c. 1750–1783* (Oxford, 2005).

40. Benjamin Carp, *Defiance of the Patriots: The Boston Tea Party and the Making of America* (New Haven, 2010), 8, 14; Marshall, *The Making and Unmaking of Empires*, 211. Edmund Burke, "Speech on American Taxation," 1774, in *Burke's Speeches on American Taxation*, ed. F. G. Selby (London, 1917), 10–11.

41. Carp, *Defiance of the Patriots*, 15, 19.

42. Burke, "Speech on American Taxation," 9.

43. John W. Tyler, *Smugglers & Patriots: Boston Merchants and the Advent of the American Revolution* (Boston, 1986), 186–98. For the context of these events, as well as the bind Hutchinson found himself—in and what the narrative that follows is based on—see Bernard Bailyn, *The Ordeal of Thomas Hutchinson* (Cambridge, MA, 1974), 259–62; and Carp, *Defiance of the Patriots*, 122–29.

44. Copley to Jonathan and Isaac Winslow Clarke, 1 December 1730, in "Letters and Papers of John Singleton Copley and Henry Pelham," *Collections of the Massachusetts Historical Society*, 71 (Boston, 1914): 211–12; Carp, *Defiance of the Patriots*, 95–108.

45. Bailyn, *The Ordeal of Thomas Hutchinson* 259–62; Carp, *Defiance of the Patriots*, 122–24, 129.

46. On the fine line, see Maier, *From Resistance to Revolution*.

47. Burke, "Speech on American Taxation," 59.

48. Locke, *Second Treatise*, 272. Edmund Burke, "Speech on Moving His Resolutions for Conciliation with the Colonies," 22 March 1775, in *Burke's Speeches*, ed. Selby, 130.

49. Breen, *American Insurgents, American Patriots*, 83.

50. Ibid., 110–19.

51. Nicholas Creswell, 19 October 1774, *The Journal of Nicholas Cresswell, 1774–1777*, ed. Samuel Thornely (Port Washington, NY, 1968), 43–44.

52. Jack Rakove, *Revolutionaries: A New History of the Invention of America* (Boston, 2010), 54–56; Breen, *American Insurgents*, 129, 152.

53. Peter Thompson, "Waging War against a Distant People: The Logic of the Associations Adopted in 1774," forthcoming in Patrick Griffin and Peter Onuf, eds., *Violence and the American Revolution* (Charlottesville, VA).

54. Earl of Dunmore to Lord Dartmouth, 24 December 1774, *Documents of the American Revolution*, 8:265–66.

55. Breen, *American Insurgents*, 160–75. Dunmore quoted on 175.

56. Mark Noll, "Canada, 1759–1815," in Vol. 1 of *The Cambridge History of Religions in America*, ed. Stephen Stein (Cambridge University Press, forthcoming in June 2012).

57. Andrew Jackson O'Shaughnessy, *An Empire Divided: The American Revolution and the British Caribbean* (Philadelphia, 2000).

58. *Pennsylvania Packet*, 15 August 1774; *Norwich Packet*, 1 September 1774; 8 September 1774. For Charles I and the unconstitutional nature of what he was doing, at least as far as Puritans were concerned, see Edmund S. Morgan, *The Puritan Dilemma: The Story of John Winthrop*, 3rd edn. (New York, 2007).

59. On the switchboard metaphor, see Bernard Bailyn, *The Ideological Origins of the American Revolution*, enl. edn. (Cambridge, MA, 1992).

60. O'Shaughnessy, *An Empire Divided*, 4, 8–9, 15–30.

61. Ibid., 99.

62. Nicholas Creswell, 14 September 1774, *Journal*, 39.

63. Jack P. Greene "Identity in the British Caribbean," in Nicholas Canny and Anthony Pagden, eds., *Colonial Identity in the Atlantic World, 1500–1800* (Princeton, 1987), 261.

64. Jack P. Greene, "The Caribbean Connection," in Jack P. Greene, *Imperatives, Behaviors, and Identities: Essays in Early American Cultural History* (Charlottesville, VA, 1992).

65. John K. Thornton, "African Dimensions of the Stono Rebellion," *American Historical Review*, 96, no. 4 (1991): 1101–1113.

66. William Ryan, *The World of Thomas Jeremiah: Charles Town on the Eve of the American Revolution* (New York, 2010); J. William Harris, *The Hanging of Thomas Jeremiah: A Free Black Man's Encounter with Liberty* (New Haven, 2010).

67. Woody Holton, *Forced Founders: Indians, Debtors, Slaves, and the Making of the American Revolution in Virginia* (Chapel Hill, NC, 1999).

68. Isaac, *Transformation of Virginia*.

69. T. H. Breen, *Tobacco Culture: The Mentality of the Great Tidewater Planters on the Eve of Revolution* (1985; repr., Princeton, 2001), 209.

70. On Dunmore, see Holton, *Forced Founders*; and Hinderaker, *Elusive Empires*.

71. On Dunmore's War, see Fred Anderson and Andrew Clayton, *The Dominion of War: Empire and Liberty in North America, 1500–2000* (New York, 2005).

72. On this dynamic, see Arno Meyer, *The Furies: Violence and Terror in the French and Russian Revolutions* (Princeton, 2000).

73. Burke, "Speech on American Taxation," 60.

74. Burke, "Conciliation with the Colonies," 117–18.

75. Adam Smith, *The Wealth of Nations, Books IV–V*, ed. Andrew Skinner (London, 1999), 206.

76. Joseph Galloway, *A Candid Examination of the Mutual Claims of Great-Britain, and the Colonies: With a Plan of Accommodation on Constitutional Principles* (New York, 1775), 54.

77. Petition of the Continental Congress to the King, 26 October 1774, *Documents of the American Revolution*, 8:219.

78. See Rakove, *Revolutionaries*, for the marginalization of the moderates.

CHAPTER 5

1. Dunmore, *Proclamation, 7 November 1775* (Norfolk, 1775); Douglas R. Egerton, *Death or Liberty: African Americans and Revolutionary America* (Oxford, 2009), 66. On Dunmore and Virginia's elite, see Woody Holton, *Forced Founders: Indians, Debtors, Slaves, and the Making of the American Revolution in Virginia* (Chapel Hill, NC, 1999).

2. Holton, *Forced Founders*, 159.

3. Sylvia Frey, *Water from the Rock: Black Resistance in a Revolutionary Age* (Princeton, 1991).

4. Ibid. On this ruling and its implications, see George Van Cleve, "Founding a Slaveholders' Union, 1770–1797," in Matthew Mason and John Craig Hammond, eds., *Contesting Slavery: The Politics of Bondage and Freedom in the New American Nation* (Charlottesville, VA, 2011), 118–21.

5. On these remarkable stories, see Simon Schama, *Rough Crossings: The Slaves, the British, and the American Revolution* (New York, 2006), 18–19.

6. Egerton, *Death or Liberty*, 46–57, 68–69; Woody Holton, *Black Americans in the Revolutionary Era: A Brief History with Documents* (Boston, 2009), 4–10.

7. Michael Lee Lanning, *African Americans in the Revolutionary War* (New York, 2000); Schama, *Rough Crossings*.

8. Maya Jasanoff, *Liberty's Exiles: American Loyalists in a Revolutionary World* (New York, 2011), 49.

9. For these events, and what followed, see David Hackett Fischer, *Paul Revere's Ride* (New York, 1994), which focuses on contingency; and Arthur Tourtellot, *Lexington and Concord: The Beginning of the War of the American Revolution* (New York, 1959).

10. Robert Middlekauff, *The Glorious Cause: The American Revolution, 1763–1789*, rev. edn. (Oxford, 2005), 279.

11. On this narrative, see Robert A. Gross, *The Minutemen and Their World* (New York, 1976).

12. For the nature of this early army, see Charles Royster, *A Revolutionary People at War: The Continental Army and American Character, 1775–1783* (Chapel Hill, NC, 1979). On the ideas of imagined communities, see Benedict Anderson, *Imagined Community: Reflections on the Origin and Spread of Nationalism* (New York, 2006).

13. Edmund Burke, "Speech on Moving His Resolutions for Conciliation with the Colonies," 22 March 1775, in *Burke's Speeches on American Taxation*, ed. F. G. Selby (London, 1956), 122.

14. Ray Raphael, *A People's History of the American Revolution: How Common People Shaped the Fight for Independence* (New York, 2001), 51–52. Also see Gross, *Minutemen*; Gary Nash, *The Unknown American Revolution: The Unruly Birth of Democracy and the Struggle to Create America* (New York, 2005).

15. Mercy Otis Warren, *The Blockheads: Or, the Affrighted Officers: A Farce* (Boston, 1776), 6.

16. On loyalists, see Jasanoff, *Liberty's Exiles*, 6–9.

17. Mary Beth Norton, *The British Americans: The Loyalist Exiles in England, 1774–1789* (Boston, 1972); Ruma Chopra, "Loyalist Persuasions: New York City, 1776–83" (Ph.D. diss., University of California, Davis, 2008).

18. Jack Rakove, *Revolutionaries: A New History of the Invention of America* (Boston, 2010), 89–93.

19. John Adams to Abigail Adams, 17 June 1775, in *The Letters of John and Abigail Adams*, ed. Frank Shuffleton (1876; repr., New York, 2004), 43. For this choice, see Middlekauff, *Glorious Cause*.

20. Letter to the Canadians, 29 May 1775, *Journals of Continental Congress* (1905), 2:68. On the "continental" aspirations of Americans in naming Congress and the Army, as well as the idea that a continental struggle included Canada, see James Drake, *The Nation's Nature: How Continental Presumptions Gave Rise to the United States of America* (Charlottesville, VA, 2011).

21. Middlekauff, *Glorious Cause*, 304–7; Royster, *Revolutionary People at War*.

22. Elizabeth A. Fenn, *Pox Americana: The Great Smallpox Epidemic of 1775–82* (New York, 2001), 3, 9, 62–64.

23. Ibid., 66–69.

24. Piers Mackesy, *The War for America, 1775–1783* (Lincoln, 1964; repr. 1993).

25. Robert G. Parkinson, "From Indian Killer to Worthy Citizen: The Revolutionary Transformation of Michael Cresap," *William and Mary Quarterly*, 63, no. 1 (2006): 97–122; Royster, *Revolutionary People at War*.

26. "The Letter to the Inhabitants of the Province of Canada," in *Journals of Continental Congress* (1906), 4:86.

27. Mark Noll, "Canada, 1759–1815," in Vol. 1 of *The Cambridge History of Religions in America*, ed. Stephen Stein (Cambridge University Press, forthcoming in June 2012).

28. "Extract of a Letter from Weathersfield, in Connecticut, to a Gentleman in New York," 23 April 1775, in *American Archives*, 4th ser., ed. Peter Force (Washington, DC, 1839), 2:363. On this theme, see Thomas S. Kidd, *The Great Awakening: The Roots of Evangelical Christianity in America* (New Haven, 2007).

29. On these ideas, see T. H. Breen, *American Insurgents, American Patriots: The Revolution of the People* (New York, 2010), 31–35, 244–51.

30. Ibid., 46–50.

31. Wayne Lee, *Crowds and Soldiers in Revolutionary North Carolina: The Culture of Violence in Riot and War* (Gainesville, FL, 2001), 152.

32. On this, see T. M. Devine, *Scotland's Empire, 1600–1815* (London, 2003).

33. Mackesy, *War for America*, 43–45.

34. Lee, *Crowds and Soldiers*, 152–56; Donald MacDonald, "A Manifesto," February 1776, in *American Archives*, 4th ser. (Washington, DC, 1843), 4:983.

35. Thomas Paine, *Common Sense*, ed. Isaac Kramnick (London, 1986), 63–64, 86.

36. Sophia Rosenfeld, *Common Sense: A Political History* (Cambridge, MA, 2011), 136–50.

37. Eran Shalev, *Rome Reborn on Western Shores: Historical Imagination and the Creation of the American Republic* (Charlottesville, VA, 2009), 67–71, 104, 219; Jeremy Black, "Gibbon and International Relations," in Rosamond McKittrick and Roland Quinault, eds., *Edward Gibbon and Empire* (New York, 1997); J. G. A. Pocock, *Barbarism and Religion*, Vol. 3, *The First Decline and Fall* (New York, 2005); J. G. A. Pocock, *Barbarism and Religion*, Vol. 4, *Barbarians, Savages and Empires* (New York, 2005).

38. Nicholas Creswell, 26 January 1776, *The Journal of Nicholas Cresswell, 1774–1777*, ed. Samuel Thornely (Port Washington, NY, 1968), 136.

39. On Inglis, see Jasanoff, *Liberty's Exiles*, 30.

40. Garry Wills, *Inventing America: Jefferson's Declaration of Independence* (Garden City, NY, 1978). The best treatment of the Declaration is Pauline Maier's *American Scripture: Making the Declaration of Independence* (New York, 1997).

41. David Armitage, *The Declaration of Independence: A Global History* (Cambridge, MA, 2007).

42. Carl Lotus Becker, *The Declaration of Independence: A Study in the History of Political Ideas* (1942; repr., New York, 1966).

43. Thomas Jefferson, Draft of the Declaration of Independence, 28 June 1776, *Journals of Continental Congress* (1906), 5:498.

44. Thomas Jefferson, "Notes of Debates," 7 June 1776, *Journals of Continental Congress* (1906), 6:1093.

45. Colin Calloway, *The American Revolution in Indian Country: Crisis and Diversity in Native American Communities* (Cambridge, MA, 1995); Jack M. Sosin, *The Revolutionary Frontier, 1763–1783* (New York, 1967).

46. Edwin Burrows and Mike Wallace, *Gotham: A History of New York City to 1898* (New York, 1999), 232; Brendan McConville, *The Kings Three Faces: The Rise and Fall of Royal America, 1688–1776* (Chapel Hill, NC, 2006), 308–9.

47. Richard White, *The Middle Ground: Indians, Empires, and Republics in the Great Lakes Region, 1650–1815* (Cambridge, MA, 1991).

48. Calloway, *American Revolution in Indian Country.*

49. Claudio Saunt, *A New Order of Things: Property, Power, and the Transformation of the Creek Indians, 1733–1816* (New York, 1999), 59–67; Calloway, *American Revolution in Indian Country*, 45.

50. On popular sovereignty, see Edmund S. Morgan, *Inventing the People: The Rise of Popular Sovereignty in England and America* (New York, 1988); and Gordon S. Wood, *The Radicalism of the American Revolution* (New York, 1991).

51. Gordon S. Wood, *The Creation of the American Republic, 1776–1787* (1969; repr., Chapel Hill, NC, 1998), 131, 329–30. See also Nash, *Unknown American Revolution.*

52. Bradley J. Birzer, *American Cicero: The Life of Charles Carroll* (Wilmington, DE, 2010); Wood, *Creation*, 251; Rakove, *Revolutionaries*, 187–89.

53. Wood, *Radicalism.* Kenneth Owen, "Pennsylvania Politics and the American Revolution" (D.Phil., Oxford University, 2011); Jessica Roney, *Revolution by Association: Philadelphia and the American Founding* (University of Pennsylvania Press, forthcoming).

54. Wood, *Creation*, 227.

55. Nash and Wood agree on these points, although Wood sees Pennsylvania as an aberration.

56. Pauline Maier, *From Resistance to Revolution: Colonial Radicals and the Development of American Opposition to Britain* (New York, 1972).

57. Jasanoff, *Liberty's Exiles*, 7, 21–23.

58. Wood, *Radicalism.*

59. Abigail Adams to John Adams, 11 April 1776, quoted in Joyce Lee Malcolm, *Peter's War: A New England Slave Boy and the American Revolution* (New Haven, 2009), 96.

60. Laurel Ulrich, *Good Wives: Images and Realities in the Lives of Women in Northern New England, 1650–1750* (New York, 1991).

61. Alfred F. Young, *Masquerade: The Life and Times of Deborah Sampson, Continental Soldier* (New York, 2004).

62. See Mary Beth Norton, *Liberty's Daughters: The Revolutionary Experience of American Women, 1750–1800* (1980; repr., Ithaca, NY, 1996).

63. Carol Berkin, *Revolutionary Mothers: Women in the Struggle for America's Independence* (New York, 2005), 29, 41, 36.

64. Ibid., 32.

65. See Nash, *Unknown American Revolution*.

66. Judith Apter Klinghoffer and Lois Elkins, "'The Petticoat Electors': Women's Suffrage in New Jersey, 1776–1807," *Journal of the Early Republic*, 12 (1992), 159–93.

67. Norton, *Liberty's Daughters*.

68. Royster, *Revolutionary People at War*; Fred Anderson, *A People's Army: Massachusetts Soldiers and Society in the Seven Years' War* (Chapel Hill, NC, 1984).

69. James Thacher, January 1775, *A Military Journal during the Revolutionary War, from 1775 to 1783*, 2nd edn. (Boston, 1827), 11, 13.

70. Amos Farnsworth, 21 May 1775, *Amos Farnsworth's Journal*, in *Three Military Diaries Kept by Groton Soldiers in Different Wars*, ed. Samuel A. Green (Groton, MA, 1901), 85; Samuel Langdon, *Government Corrupted by Vice, and Recovered by Righteousness: A Sermon Preached before the Honorable Congress of the Colony of the Massachusetts-Bay in New England, Assembled at Watertown, on ... the 31ˢᵗ Day of May, 1775* (Watertown, MA, 1775), 28.

71. Ambrose Serle, 12 and 14 August 1776, *The American Journal of Ambrose Serle, Secretary to Lord Howe 1776–1778* (New York, 1969), 62–63.

72. Mackesy, *War for America*, 87.

73. For this series of events, see Middlekauff, *Glorious Cause*.

74. Serle, *American Journal*, 78–79.

75. On British strategy, see Middlekauff, *Glorious Cause*.

76. Mackesy, *War for America*, 33–34, 36.

77. Stephen Kemble, 18 October 1776, 21 February 1777, "Journals of Lieut.-Col. Stephen Kemble," in *Collections of the New York Historical Society* (New York, 1884), 94, 110.

78. David Hackett Fischer, *Washington's Crossing* (New York, 2004).

79. Matthew Spring, *With Zeal and With Bayonets Only: The British Army on Campaign in North America* (Norman, OK, 2008). My thanks to Will Hay for bringing this book to my attention.

80. Stephen Conway, *The British Isles and the War of American Independence* (Oxford, 2000), 11–44; Jasanoff, *Liberty's Exiles*, 44–45.

81. Serle, 1 September 1776, *American Journal*, 87. Frederick Mackenzie, June 1778, *Diary of Frederick Mackenzie* (Cambridge, MA, 1930), 1:299.

82. Mackesy, *War for America*, 111, 117, 121, 126–28.

83. Stephen Taaffe, *The Philadelphia Campaign, 1777–1778* (Lawrence, KS, 2003), 84, 88–90, 102–4; Mackesy, *War for America*, 129.

84. Taaffe, *Philadelphia Campaign*, 2–3, 229–33.

85. Richard Buel, *In Irons: Britain's Naval Supremacy and the American Revolutionary Economy* (New Haven, 1998).

86. Mackesy, *War for America*, 30.

87. James Kirby Martin et al., *A Respectable Army: The Military Origins of the Republic, 1763–1789* (Arlington Heights, IL, 1982).

88. Serle, 2 September 1776, *American Journal*, 88.

89. Cresswell, 14 December 1776, *Journal*, 176.

90. David Noel Doyle, *Ireland, Irishmen, and Revolutionary America, 1760–1820* (Dublin, 1981), 109–11.

91. Egerton, *Death or Liberty*, 75; Royster, *Revolutionary People at War*, 241–42; Holton, *Black Americans*, 10–11.

92. Michael McDonnell, "'The Spirit of Levelling': James Cleveland, Edward Wright, and the Militiamen's Struggle for Equality in Revolutionary Virginia," in Alfred Young,

Gary Nash, and Ray Raphael, eds., *Revolutionary Founders: Rebels, Radicals, and Reformers in the Making of the Nation* (New York, 2011), 135–45. Also see McDonnell, *The Politics of War: Race, Class, and Conflict in Revolutionary Virginia* (Chapel Hill, NC, 2007).

93. Joseph Plumb Martin, *Private Yankee Doodle, Being a Narrative of Some of the Adventures, Dangers and Sufferings of a Revolutionary Soldier*, ed. George F. Scheer (Boston, 1962), 135, 197–98.

94. Berkin, *Revolutionary Mothers*, 50–58.

95. Nancy Loane, *Following the Drum: Women at the Valley Forge Encampment* (Dulles, VA, 2009), 3–4, 115–16.

96. Cresswell, 13 September 1776, *Journal*, 160; 13 July 1777, *Journal*, 251–52.

CHAPTER 6

1. For this series of events, see Patrick Griffin, *American Leviathan: Empire, Nation, and Revolutionary Frontier* (New York, 2007); Richard White, *The Middle Ground: Indians, Empires, and Republics in the Great Lakes Region, 1650–1815* (New York, 1991).

2. George Rogers Clark to Patrick Henry, 3 February 1779, *George Rogers Clark Papers, 1771–1781*, Virginia Series, Vol. 3, ed. James Alton James (Springfield, IL, 1912), 97.

3. John Burgoyne, quoted in Robert Middlekauff, *The Glorious Cause: The American Revolution, 1763–1789*, rev. edn. (Oxford, 2005), 379.

4. Peter Silver, *Our Savage Neighbors: How Indian War Transformed Early America* (New York, 2008), 245–46.

5. June Namias, *White Captives: Gender and Ethnicity on the American Frontier* (Chapel Hill, NC, 1993), 117–33; Silver, *Our Savage Neighbors*, 245–46.

6. Entries for 2 October 1777 and 11 August 1777, in *The Specht Journal: A Military Journal of the Burgoyne Campaign*, trans. Helga Doblin, ed. Mary C. Lynn (Westport, CT, 1995), 85, 66.

7. On the campaign, see Middlekauff, *Glorious Cause*, 366–84. On Fraser, see *Oxford Dictionary of National Biography*.

8. Muenchhausen, 26 September 1777, *At General Howe's Side 1776–1778: The Diary of General William Howe's Aide de Camp, Captain Friedrich von Muenchheusen*, trans. Ernst Kipping (Monmouth Beach, NJ, 1974), 47. On the occupation, see Stephen R. Taaffe, *The Philadelphia Campaign, 1777–1778* (Lawrence, KS, 2003), esp. 169–70, 172–73.

9. David M. Ludlum, *Early American Winters 1604–1820* (Boston, 1966), 102, 103, 105.

10. Thomas Paine, "The Crisis, Number 1" (1776), in *Thomas Paine: Political Writings*, ed. Bruce Kuklick (1989; repr., Cambridge, UK, 1997), 49.

11. Ibid., 56.

12. Howard Jones, *Crucible of Power: A History of American Foreign Relations to 1913* (Lanham, MD, 2009), 1–17; Jonathan Dull, *A Diplomatic History of the American Revolution* (New Haven, 1985); Stacy Schiff, *A Great Improvisation: Franklin, France, and the Birth of America* (New York, 2005). On the economic implications, see Richard Buel, *In Irons: Britain's Naval Supremacy and the American Revolutionary Economy* (New Haven, 1998).

13. For these themes, see Jack Rakove, *Revolutionaries: A New History of the Invention of America* (Boston, 2010).

14. Piers Mackesy, *The War for America, 1775-1783* (Lincoln, NE, 1993), 182–83; George Herring, *From Colony to Superpower: U.S. Foreign Relations since 1776* (New York, 2008), 11, 23.

15. John Ferling, *Setting the World Ablaze: Washington, Adams, Jefferson, and the American Revolution* (Oxford, 2000), 196–97.

16. Paul Lockhart, *The Drillmaster of Valley Forge: The Baron de Steuben and the Making of the American Army* (New York, 2008), 114–15, 190–94.

17. Matthew Spring, *With Zeal and with Bayonets Only: The British Army on Campaign in North America, 1775-1783* (Norman, OK, 2008).

18. Mackesy, *War for America*, 185, 215.

19. Ferling, *Setting the World Ablaze*, 197–98.

20. Nancy K. Loane, *Following the Drum: Women at the Valley Forge Encampment* (Washington, DC, 2008), 115–16.

21. Middlekauff, *Glorious Cause*, 420–28; Lockhart, *Drillmaster*, 165, 211.

22. P.J. Marshall, *The Making and Unmaking of Empires: Britain, India, and America c. 1750-1783* (New York, 2007), 363.

23. Mackesy, *War for America*, 99.

24. H. M. Scott, *British Foreign Policy in the Age of the American Revolution* (Oxford, 1990); Mackesy, *War for America*, 186–89.

25. Howard Jones, *Crucible of Power: A History of American Foreign Relations to 1913* (Lanham, MD, 2009), 1–17; Thomas Chavez, *Spain and the Independence of the United States: An Intrinsic Gift* (Albuquerque, NM, 2002); Mackesy, *War for America*, 378.

26. Mackesy, *War for America*, 166, 249, 251; Chavez, *Spain and the Independence of the United States*.

27. William M. Fowler, *Rebels under Sail: The American Navy during the Revolution* (New York, 1976), 10–42.

28. Fowler, *Rebels under Sail*, 42–124.

29. Mackesy, *War for America*, 212.

30. Fowler, *Rebels under Sail*, 141–68.

31. John Paul Jones, *John Paul Jones' Memoir of the American Revolution Presented to King Louis XVI of France*, trans. and ed. Gerard W. Gawalt (Washington, DC, 1979); A. T. Q. Stewart, *A Deeper Silence: The Hidden Origins of the United Irish Movement* (London, 1993).

32. Marshall, *Making and Unmaking of Empires*, 355. Also see Vincent Morley, *Irish Opinion and the American Revolution, 1760–1783* (Cambridge, 2002), 204.

33. Sung Bok Kim, *Landlord and Tenant in Colonial New York: Manorial Society, 1664–1775* (Chapel Hill, NC, 1978).

34. Ray Raphael, *A People's History of the American Revolution: How Common People Shaped the Fight for Independence* (New York, 2001), 26–27. Also see Gary Nash, *The Unknown American Revolution: The Unruly Birth of Democracy and the Struggle to Create America* (New York, 2005); and Sung Bok Kim, *Landlord and Tenant*.

35. Raphael, *People's History*, 28–30; Michael Bellesiles, *Revolutionary Outlaws: Ethan Allen and the Struggle for Independence on the Early American Frontier* (Charlottesville, VA, 1993).

36. Raphael, *People's History*, 28–30; Bellesiles, *Revolutionary Outlaws*.

37. Alan Taylor, *Liberty Men and Great Proprietors: The Revolutionary Settlement on the Maine Frontier, 1760–1820* (Chapel Hill, NC, 1990), 6–15.

38. See Benjamin L. Carp, *Rebels Rising: Cities and the American Revolution* (Oxford, 2007).

39. Edwin G. Burrows and Mike Wallace, *Gotham: A History of New York City to 1898* (New York, 1999), 245–48.

40. Ibid., 249–54.

41. Middlekauff, *Glorious Cause*, 541–43; Taaffe, *The Philadelphia Campaign*, 169–74.

42. Marquis de Chastellux, *Travels in North America in the Years 1780, 1781 and 1782 by the Marquis de Chastellux*, ed. Howard C. Rice (Chapel Hill, NC, 1963), 130.

43. Gary Nash, *Unknown American Revolution*, 314–19.

44. Jacqueline Carr, *After the Siege: A Social History of Boston, 1775–1800* (Boston, 2005), 88–146.

45. Boston Town Records, 19 March 1777, *A Report of the Record Commissioners of the City of Boston* (Boston, 1887), 18:276.

46. Frederick Mackenzie, June, 1778, *Diary of Frederick Mackenzie* (Cambridge, MA, 1930), 1:298.

47. Nathaniel Greene, quoted in Rakove, *Revolutionaries*, 112–13.

48. Brendan McConville, *These Daring Disturbers of the Public Peace: The Struggle for Property and Power in Early New Jersey* (Ithaca, NY, 1999), 223–45. Also see Raphael, *People's History*, 26.

49. Douglas R. Egerton, *Death or Liberty: African Americans and Revolutionary America* (Oxford, 2009), 65–67; Woody Holton, *Black Americans in the Revolutionary Era: A Brief History with Documents* (Boston, 2009), 58.

50. On the mindset of loyalists, see Maya Jasanoff, *Liberty's Exiles: American Loyalists in the Revolutionary World* (New York, 2011); Bernard Bailyn, *The Ordeal of Thomas Hutchinson* (Cambridge, MA, 1974); and Mary Beth Norton, *The British-Americans: The Loyalist Exiles in England, 1774–1789* (Boston, 1972).

51. Norton, *British-Americans*.

52. On this see, Mackesy, *War for America*.

53. Advertisement, *Royal Georgia Gazette*, 16 August 1781.

54. Marjoleine Kars, *Breaking Loose Together: The Regulator Rebellion in Pre-Revolutionary North Carolina* (Chapel Hill, NC, 2002), 212–14; Wayne E. Lee, *Crowds and Soldiers in Revolutionary North Carolina: The Culture of Violence in Riot and War* (Gainesville, FL, 2001).

55. Dan L. Morrill, *Southern Campaigns of the American Revolution* (Baltimore, 1993), 96.

56. Middlekauff, *Glorious Cause*, 438–49; John C. Dann, ed., *The Revolution Remembered: Eyewitness Accounts of the War for Independence* (Chicago, 1980), 183.

57. Middlekauff, *Glorious Cause*, 449.

58. Carol Berkin, *Revolutionary Mothers: Women in the Struggle for America's Independence* (New York, 2005), 39.

59. Deposition of William Gipson, in Dann, *Revolution Remembered*, 188–89.

60. Middlekauff, *Glorious Cause*, 450–57.

61. Ronald Hoffman and Peter J. Albert, eds., *Arms and Independence: The Military Character of the American Revolution* (Charlottesville, VA, 1984); Hoffman and Thad Tate, ed., *An Uncivil War: The Southern Backcountry during the American Revolution* (1985).

62. Mackenzie, 5 August 1781, *Diary*, 2:581–82.

63. Dann, *Revolution Remembered*, 202.

64. For a breakdown of how people chose the sides they did based on their position on Regulation, see Richard Maxwell Brown, *The South Carolina Regulators*

(Cambridge, MA, 1963), 123–26. My thanks to Andrew Brown for pointing out these data.

65. James Collins, *Autobiography of a Revolutionary Soldier*, ed. John M. Roberts (Clinton, LA, 1859), 53. My thanks again to Andrew Brown for this reference.

66. Berkin, *Revolutionary Mothers*, 65–66.

67. Mackenzie, 5 August 1781, *Diary*, 2:582.

68. See T. H. Breen, *American Insurgents, American Patriots: The Revolution of the People* (New York, 2010).

69. Simon Schama, *Rough Crossings: Britain, the Slaves, and the American Revolution* (London, 2005).

70. Orderly Book of 71st Highland Regiment, 9 May 1779, Huntington Library, San Marino, CA.

71. Cassandra Pybus, "Jefferson's Faulty Math: The Question of Slave Defections in the American Revolution," *William and Mary Quarterly*, 3rd ser., 62, no. 2 (2005): 243–64.

72. Ferling, *Setting the World Ablaze*, 245–46.

73. Egerton, *Death or Liberty*, 82; Ira Berlin, *Many Thousands Gone: The First Two Centuries of Slavery in North America* (Cambridge, MA, 1998), 291–93.

74. This is one the essential points of Sylvia Frey's *Water from the Rock: Black Resistance in a Revolutionary Age* (Princeton, 1992). See especially p. 63. Henry Laurens to Provincial Council of Wilmington, 2 January 1776, *Colonial and State Records of North Carolina*, ed. Walter Clark (Goldsboro, NC, 1895), 11:268; Henry Laurens to Richard Caswell, 26 September 1778, *Colonial and State Records of North Carolina*, ed. Walter Clark (1896), 13:235; Pybus, "Jefferson's Faulty Math." On the increasing number and vigilance of slave patrols during the war, see Sally E. Hadden, *Slave Patrols: Law and Violence in Virginia and the Carolinas* (Cambridge, MA, 2001), 155–57.

75. Edmund S. Morgan, *American Slavery, American Freedom: The Ordeal of Colonial Virginia* (New York, 1975).

76. For strategies in the West, see Jack M. Sosin, *Whitehall and the Wilderness: The Middle West in British Colonial Policy, 1760–1775* (Lincoln, NE, 1961). On the West in general during these years, see Griffin, *American Leviathan*.

77. John Grenier, *The First Way of War: American War Making on the Frontier* (New York, 2008).

78. On the different strategies adopted by Indians during the Revolution, see Colin G. Calloway, *The American Revolution in Indian Country: Crisis and Diversity in Native American Communities* (Cambridge, UK, 1995).

79. Daniel Brodhead to Washington, 17 October 1780, in *Correspondence of the American Revolution; Being Letters of Eminent Men to George Washington, from the Time of His Taking Command of the Army to the End of His Presidency*, ed. Jared Sparks (Boston: Little, Brown, 1853), 3:120. On these dynamics, see Calloway, *American Revolution in Indian Country*.

80. For the campaign, see Joseph T. Glatthaar and James Kirby Martin, *Forgotten Allies: The Oneida Indians and the American Revolution* (New York, 2006); Washington to Horatio Gates, 6 March 1779, *Writings of George Washington*, ed. Wothington Chauncey Ford (New York, 1890), 7:354.

81. Washington to the Marquis de Lafayette, 12 September 1779, *Writings of George Washington*, 8:49.

82. Daniel K. Richter, *The Ordeal of the Longhouse: The Peoples of the Iroquois League in the Era of European Colonization* (Chapel Hill, NC, 1992); Alan Taylor, *The Divided Ground: Indians, Settlers, and the Northern Borderland of the American Revolution* (New York, 2006).

83. Calloway, *American Revolution in Indian Country*.

84. Henry Stuart to John Stuart, 26 August 1776, *Colonial and State Records of North Carolina*, 10:764.

85. Henry Stuart to John Stuart, 26 August 1776, *Colonial and State Records of North Carolina*, 10:773–79.

86. For the nature of these communities, see White, *Middle Ground*; and Gregory Dowd, *A Spirited Resistance: The North American Indian Struggle for Unity, 1745–1815* (Baltimore, 1993). For the Cherokee story, see Calloway, *American Revolution in Indian Country*.

87. On violence in Kentucky, see Stephen Aron, *How the West Was Lost: The Transformation of Kentucky from Daniel Boone to Henry Clay* (Baltimore, 1996).

88. John Mack Faragher, *Daniel Boone: The Life and Legend of an American Pioneer* (New York, 1992).

89. William Irvine to Ann Irvine, 29 December 1781, Irvine Correspondence, Vol. 5, Historical Society of Pennsylvania, Philadelphia (hereinafter HSP), 31; Daniel Brodhead to Ephraim Blaine, 22 January 1781, Brodhead Letterbook, HSP, 43.

90. For a narrative of the massacre, see Daniel K. Richter, *Facing East from Indian Country: A Native History of Early America* (Cambridge, MA, 2001), 221–23; and especially Thomas Slaughter, *The Whiskey Rebellion: Frontier Epilogue to the American Revolution* (New York, 1986), 75–78.

91. William Moore, president of the Council in Philadelphia, to William Irvine, 13 April 1782, Irvine Correspondence, Vol. 5, HSP, 78.

92. Arent DePeyster to Frederick Haldimand, 7 January 1783, Haldimand Add. Mss. 21756, 94, British Library, London.

93. Irvine to Moore, 9 May 1782, Irvine Correspondence, Vol. 5, HSP, 104.

94. Humble petition of Frontier Inhabitants, 13 April 1782, Irvine Correspondence, Vol. 5, HSP, 77.

95. Dann, *Revolution Remembered*, 310–14; DePeyster to Haldimand, 8 April 1782, Haldimand Add. Mss 21762, 13; John Turney, Lt. of Corps of Rangers, to DePeyster, 7 June 1782; William Campbell, Capt. Commander at Sanduskey, to DePeyster, 11 June 1782, Haldimand Add. Mss., 21762, 66, 62. Edmond Polk put the number killed and missing at 40. See Polke to Irvine, 11 June 1782, Irvine Correspondence, Vol. 6, HSP, 22.

96. John Knight, *Narrative of a Late Expedition against the Indians* (Philadelphia, 1783), 5–10.

97. Ibid., 11–12. Ephraim Douglas to Irvine, 26 July 1782, *Pennsylvania Magazine of History and Biography*, 1, no. 1 (1877): 46.

98. Extract of a Letter from Captain Caldwell to DePeyster, 13 June 1782, Haldimand Add. Mss. 21762, 80.

99. William Irvine to Ann Irvine, 12 April 1782, Irvine Correspondence, HSP, Vol. 5, 76; Griffin, *American Leviathan*, 172–75. Alan Taylor covers this growing sentiment in *Divided Ground*, 107.

PART III

1. Holger Hoock, *Empires of the Imagination: Politics, War, and the Arts in the British World, 1750-1850* (London, 2010).

2. Helen A. Cooper, "John Trumbull: A Life," in Cooper, ed., *John Trumbull: The Hand and Spirit of a Painter* (New Haven, 1982).

3. Trumbull and other painters of the period are the subject of Hugh Howard's *The Painter's Chair: George Washington and the Making of American Art* (New York, 2009). Also see, Ann Uhry Abrams, *The Valiant Hero: Grand-Style History Painting* (Washington, DC, 1985). For Trumbull's life and *The Declaration of Independence*, see Irma B. Jaffe, *Trumbull: The Declaration of Independence* (New York, 1976), as well as Jaffe's entry in *American National Biography* and the entry by Theodore Sizer in the *Dictionary of American Biography*. Also See, Hoock, *Empires of the Imagination*, 110-11.

4. Theodore Sizer, ed., *The Autobiography of Col. John Trumbull* (New Haven, 1953), 146-47.

5. Hoock, *Empires of the Imagination*, 112.

6. Trumbull to Thomas Jefferson, 11 June 1789, in Sizer, *Autobiography*, 158-59.

CHAPTER 7

1. See John Shy's excellent summary in *American National Biography*.

2. John E. Ferling, *Setting the World Ablaze: Washington, Adams, Jefferson, and the American Revolution* (Oxford, 2000), 230–40.

3. Arthur Schrader, "'The World Turned Upside Down': A Yorktown March, or Music to Surrender By," *American Music*, 16, no. 2 (1998), 183.

4. Piers Mackesy, *The War for America, 1775-1783* (Lincoln, NE, 1993).

5. Washington, quoted in Ferling, *Setting the World Ablaze*, 250.

6. Joseph Plumb Martin, *Private Yankee Doodle: Being a Narrative of Some of the Adventures, Dangers, and Sufferings of a Revolutionary Soldier*, ed. George F. Scheer (Boston, 1962), 232.

7. James Thacher, quoted in Joyce Lee Malcolm, *Peter's War: A New England Slave Boy and the American Revolution* (New Haven, 2009), 221.

8. Johann Ewald, *Diary of the American War: A Hessian Journal*, ed. and trans. Joseph P. Tustin (New Haven, 1979), 334–36.

9. On Yorktown and the surrender, see Robert Middlekauff, *The Glorious Cause: The American Revolution, 1763-1789* (New York, 2005); and Ferling, *Setting the World Ablaze*, 247–52.

10. Schrader, "World Turned Upside Down," 180–216.

11. Christopher Hill, *The World Turned Upside Down: Radical Ideas during the English Revolution* (New York, 1972), 380–81.

12. Garry Wills, *Cincinnatus: George Washington and the Enlightenment* (Garden City, NY, 1984), 13.

13. Eran Shalev, *Rome Reborn on Western Shores: Historical Imagination and the Creation of the American Republic* (Charlottesville, VA, 2009), 220–21.

14. See Gordon Wood, *Revolutionary Characters: What Made the Founders Different* (New York, 2006).

15. Mackesy, *War for America*, 435.

16. Maya Jasanoff, *Liberty's Exiles: American Loyalists in the Revolutionary World* (New York, 2011), 55.
17. For a good narrative of peace negotiations, and on which much of this is based, see Jack Rakove, *Revolutionaries: A New History of the Invention of America* (Boston, 2010).
18. Robert Morris, *The Peacemakers* (New York, 1965).
19. George III to Thomas Townshend, 9 November 1782, Townshend Papers, Henry E. Huntington Library, San Marino, CA.
20. Holger Hoock, *Empires of the Imagination: Politics, War, and the Arts in the British World, 1750–1850* (London, 2010), 89.
21. P. J. Marshall, *The Making and Unmaking of Empires: Britain, India, and America, c. 1750–1783* (New York, 2007), 353.
22. P. J. Marshall, *Remaking the British Atlantic: The United States and the British Empire after American Independence* (New York, 2012), 47–49.
23. Alan Taylor, *The Civil War of 1812: American Citizens, British Subjects, Irish Rebels, and Indian Allies* (New York, 2010), 22, 30; Morris, *The Peacemakers*, 285.
24. See entry in *Oxford Dictionary of National Biography*; Jonathan Dull, *A Diplomatic History of the American Revolution* (New Haven, 1985), 150.
25. Morris, *The Peacemakers*, 412; Hoock, *Empires of the Imagination*, 96.
26. See Gordon S. Wood's contribution in Bernard Bailyn et al., *The Great Republic: A History of the American People*, Vol. 1 (Independence, KY, 1991). See also Alan Taylor, *The Divided Ground: Indians, Settlers, and the Northern Borderland of the American Revolution* (New York, 2006).
27. Minor Myers, Jr., *Liberty without Anarchy: A History of the Society of the Cincinnati* (Charlottesville, VA, 1983), 259.
28. Gordon S. Wood explores Washington's character, his faith in deference but also in the revolution, as well as his support of the Cincinnati. See *Revolutionary Characters*, 43–44.
29. What follows is based on Edward Skeen and Richard Kohn, "The Newburgh Conspiracy Reconsidered," *William and Mary Quarterly*, 3rd ser., 31, no. 2 (1974): 291–92, 285, 289, 288. See also Middlekauff, *The Glorious Cause*, 582–84.
30. George Washington to the Officers of the Army, 10 March 1783, *The American Revolution: Writings from the War of Independence* (New York, 2001), 775.
31. Hoock, *Empires of the Imagination*, 89.
32. Jasanoff, *Liberty's Exiles*, 67–81, 99.
33. Jasanoff, *Liberty's Exiles*, 85–87; Maya Jasanoff, "Revolutionary Exiles: The American Loyalist and French Émigré Diasporas," in David Armitage and Sanjay Subrahmantam, eds., *The Age of Revolution in Global Context, c. 1760–1840* (London, 2010), 54.
34. Robert M. Calhoon, "Loyalism and Neutrality," in Jack P. Greene and J. R. Pole, eds., *A Companion to the American Revolution* (Malden, MA, 2004), 246; Mary Beth Norton, *The British-Americans: The Loyalist Exiles in England, 1774–1789* (Boston, 1972). On numbers to Canada, as well as the creation of Upper Canada, see Taylor, *The Civil War of 1812*, 22.
35. Jasanoff, *Liberty's Exiles*, 6.
36. Edwin G. Burrows and Mike Wallace, *Gotham: A History of New York City to 1898* (New York, 1999).
37. Simon Schama, *Rough Crossings: Britain, The Slaves, and the American Revolution* (London, 2005).

38. Stanley Elkins and Eric McKitrick, *The Age of Federalism: The Early American Republic, 1788–1800* (New York, 1993).

39. Rush, "Address to the People of the United States, 1787," in Hezekiah Niles, ed., *Centennial Offering: Republication of the Principles and Acts of the Revolution in America* (New York, 1876), 234.

40. The statisics in this section are based on Robert Becker, "Currency, Taxation, and Finance, 1775–1787," in Greene and Pole, eds., *A Companion to the American Revolution*, 392–95; Middlekauff, *Glorious Cause*, 596.

41. John McCusker and Russell Menard, *The Economy of British America, 1607–1789* (Chapel Hill, NC, 1985), 361–74.

42. Woody Holton, *Unruly Americans and the Origins of the Constitution* (New York, 2007); Gordon S. Wood, *Empire of Liberty: A History of the Early Republic, 1789–1815* (Oxford, 2009), 16–19.

43. Alan Taylor, *Liberty Men and Great Proprietors: The Revolutionary Settlement on the Maine Frontier, 1760–1820* (Chapel Hill, NC, 1990); Robert A. Gross, ed., *In Debt to Shays: The Bicentennial of an Agrarian Revolution* (Charlottesville, VA, 1993).

44. On the postwar sectional strife, see Thomas P. Slaughter, *The Whiskey Rebellion: Frontier Epilogue to the American Revolution* (New York, 1986); and Patrick Griffin, *American Leviathan: Empire, Nation, and Revolutionary Frontier* (New York, 2007).

45. Taylor, *Divided Ground*.

46. On Congress and the Articles—and concepts of sovereignty—in this light, see Peter S. Onuf, "Sovereignty," in Greene and Pole, eds., *A Companion to the American Revolution*, 676–77, as well as *The Origins of the Federal Republic: Jurisdictional Controversies in the United States, 1775–1787* (Philadelphia, 1983). See especially, Jack Rakove, *The Beginnings of National Politics* (New York, 1979).

47. On this idea, see Wood, *Empire of Liberty*, 7.

48. David Ramsay, quoted Wood, Empire of Liberty, 7.

49. On this dynamic, see Benedict Anderson, *Imagined Communities: Reflections on the Origin and Spread of Nationalism* (New York, 2006).

50. On the templates and challenges to deference, see Bernard Bailyn, *Ideological Origins of the American Revolution*, enl. edn. (Cambridge, MA, 1992); and Gordon S. Wood, *The Radicalism of the American Revolution* (New York, 1991).

51. What follows is based on the work of a number of scholars, which is distilled in Carol Berkin, *Revolutionary Mothers: Women in the Struggle for America's Independence* (New York, 2005), 149–56.

52. Martin, *Private Yankee Doodle*, 241.

53. Chevalier de Verger, quoted in Malcolm, *Peter's War*, 223.

54. Johann Ewald, 14 October 1781, *Diary*, 335.

55. Cassandra Pybus, "Jefferson's Faulty Math: The Question of Slave Defections in the American Revolution," *William and Mary Quarterly*, 3rd ser., 62, no. 2 (2005): 256.

56. Richard Saunders, "Genius and Glory: John Singleton Copley's 'The Death of Major Peirson,'" *American Art Journal*, 22 (1990): 4–39; Paul Staiti, entry for Copley in the *Oxford Dictionary of National Biography*; Hoock, *Empires of the Imagination*, 94–95.

57. Ira Berlin, *Many Thousands Gone: The First Two Centuries of Slavery in North America* (Cambridge, MA, 1968), 256–89.

58. Ibid., 290–324.

59. Ibid., 228–55.

60. Ibid., 237; Aaron Fogleman, "From Slaves, Convicts, and Servants to Free Passengers: The Transformation of Immigration in the Era of the American Revolution," *Journal of American History*, 85, no. 1 (1998): 43–76.

61. James Oakes, *Slavery and Freedom: An Interpretation of the Old South* (New York, 1990).

62. Thomas Jefferson, *Notes on the State of Virginia: With Related Documents*, ed. David Waldstreicher (New York, 2002), 178.

63. Ibid., 177.

64. See Alexander Broadie, *A History of Scottish Philosophy* (Edinburgh, 2009), 235–300; Sophia Rosenfeld, *Common Sense: A Political History* (Cambridge, MA, 2011), 233–34.

65. Oakes, *Slavery and Freedom*.

66. Jefferson, *Notes*, 145. On repatriation, see Christa Dierksheide, "The Amelioration of Slavery in the Anglo-American Imagination, 1770–1840" (Ph.D. diss., University of Virginia, 2009).

67. Jefferson, *Notes*, 65–66.

68. Colin G. Calloway, *The American Revolution in Indian Country: Crisis and Diversity in Native American Communities* (Cambridge, UK, 1995); Joseph T. Glatthaar and James Kirby Martin, *Forgotten Allies: The Oneida Indians and the American Revolution* (New York, 2006).

69. Anthony F. C. Wallace, *Jefferson and the Indians: The Tragic Fate of the First Americans* (Cambridge, MA, 1999); *The Death and Rebirth of the Seneca* (New York, 1970).

70. Taylor, *Divided Ground*.

71. Calloway, *American Revolution in Indian Country*; Griffin, *American Leviathan*.

72. William Christian, quoted in Calloway, *American Revolution in Indian Country*, 58.

73. James H. Merrell, *The Indians' New World: Catawbas and Their Neighbors from European Contact through the Era of Removal* (Chapel Hill, NC, 1989), 223–25.

74. Claudio Saunt, *A New Order of Things: Property, Power, and the Transformation of the Creek Indians, 1733–1816* (New York, 1999), 75–82.

75. See Griffin, *American Leviathan*.

76. Robert A. Gross, *The Minutemen and Their World* (New York, 1976), 162–69, 177.

77. Ray Raphael, *A People's History of the American Revolution: How Common People Shaped the Fight for Independence* (New York, 2001); Jacqueline Barbara Carr, *After the Siege: A Social History of Boston, 1775–1800* (Boston, 2005), 147–59.

78. Burrows and Wallace, *Gotham*, 265–80.

79. Martin, *Private Yankee Doodle*, xxiv.

80. J. R. Pole, "Law: Continuity and Reform," in Greene and Pole, eds., *A Companion to the American Revolution*, 453.

81. Jim Smyth, *The Men of No Property: Irish Radicals and Popular Politics in the Late Eighteenth Century* (Dublin, 1992); A. T. Q. Stewart, *A Deeper Silence: The Hidden Origins of the United Irish Movement* (London, 1993).

82. Maurice Bric, *Ireland, Philadelphia and the Re-Invention of America, 1760–1800* (Dublin, 2008), 71, 74–75, 123, 146. See also David A. Wilson, *United Irishmen, United States: Immigrant Radicals in the Early Republic* (Ithaca, NY, 1998).

83. Michael Durey, *Transatlantic Radicals and the Early American Republic* (Lawrence, KS, 1997), 1–12, 50, 174.

84. Seth Cotlar, "In Paine's Absence: The Trans-Atlantic Dynamics of American Popular Political Thought, 1789–1804" (Ph.D. diss., Northwestern University, 2000).

85. On these themes, see especially the Gross, Ernst, Buels, and Chu essays in Gross, ed., *In Debt to Shays.* "Profound upheaval" is Gross's characterization (p. 18).

86. On this see, Holton, *Unruly Americans,* 160–61.

87. Gregory Nobles, "'Satan, Smith, Shattuck, and Shays': The People's Leaders in the Massachusetts Regulation of 1786," in Al Young, Gary Nash, and Ray Raphael, eds., *Revolutionary Founders: Rebels, Radicals, and Reformers in the Making of the Nation* (New York, 2012), 215–30.

88. William Pencak, "'The Fine Theoretic Government of Massachusetts Is Prostrated to the Earth': The Response to Shays's Rebellion Reconsidered," in Gross, ed., *In Debt to Shays,* 121–44. For this interpretation, see Leonard Richards, *Shays's Rebellion* (Philadelphia, 2002).

89. Wood, *Empire of Liberty,* 14.

90. Richard Price, Anne-Robert-Jacques Turgot (baron de l'Aulne), and Charles-Joseph Mathon de La Cour, *Observations on the importance of the American Revolution, and the Means of Making it a Benefit to the World* (Philadelphia, 1785), 85.

91. *Independent Gazetteer,* 27 September 1787.

CHAPTER 8

1. *Massachusetts Centinel,* 14 April 1787, in John P. Kaminski, Gaspare J. Saladino, Richard Leffler, Charles H. Schoenleber, and Margaret A. Hogan, eds., *The Documentary History of the Ratification of the Constitution Digital Edition* (Charlottesville, VA, 2009).

2. James Madison, "Note on Benjamin Franklin's Speech against Executive Salaries," 2 June 1787, in Ralph Ketcham, ed., *The Anti-Federalist Papers and the Constitutional Convention Debates,* (New York, 2003), 47; Benjamin Franklin, "Speech on the Signing of the Constitution," 17 September 1787, in ibid., 176.

3. One newspaper published a poem "On Dr. Franklin's Shedding a Tear, While Signing the Federal Constitution." See David Waldstreicher, *In the Midst of Perpetual Fetes: The Making of American Nationalism, 1776–1820* (Chapel Hill, NC, 1997), 87.

4. Edmund S. Morgan, *Benjamin Franklin* (New Haven, 2002).

5. For the period after the war as counterrevolution, see Terry Bouton, *Taming Democracy: "The People," the Founders, and the Troubled Ending of the American Revolution* (New York, 2007).

6. For good narratives of the convention, which this study draws upon, see Robert Middlekauff, *The Glorious Cause: The American Revolution, 1763–1789* (Oxford, 2005); and especially Richard Beeman, *Plain, Honest Men: The Making of the American Constitution* (New York, 2009).

7. Madison to George Muter, 7 January 1787, in Lyon G. Tyler, ed., *Tyler's Quarterly Historical and Genealogical Magazine* (Richmond, VA, 1920), 1:30.

8. David Waldstreicher, *Slavery's Constitution: From Revolution to Ratification* (New York, 2009), 71.

9. James Madison, "Notes on Roger Sherman's Comments," 31 May 1787, in Gaillard Hunt, ed., *The Debates in the Federal Convention of 1787: Which Framed the Constitution of*

the United States of America (1920; repr., Clark, NJ, 2005), 31–32; "Notes on Elbridge Gerry's Comments," 31 May 1787, in ibid., 32.

10. Richard Brookhiser, Gentleman Revolutionary: Gouverneur Morris, the Rake Who Wrote the Constitution (New York, 2003).

11. On Morris, see Clarence Ver Steeg, Robert Morris: Revolutionary Financier (New York, 1972).

12. James Madison, "Federalist Paper No. 54," 12 February 1788, in The Federalist, 344.

13. Samuel Adams to Richard Henry Lee, 24 August 1789, in The Writings of Samuel Adams, ed. Harry Alonzo Cushing (New York, 1908), 4:334.

14. James Madison, "Notes on William Patterson's Comments," 16 June 1787, in Debates of the Federal Convention of 1787, 106.

15. Ira Berlin, Generations of Captivity: A History of African-American Slaves (Cambridge, MA, 2003).

16. General Pinckney, Federal Convention, 21–22 August 1787, in The Anti-Federalist Papers and the Constitutional Convention Debates, 163; John Rutledge, ibid., 161.

17. James Madison, Federal Convention, 5 July 1787, Debates in the Federal Convention of 1787, 207.

18. Benjamin Franklin, Federal Convention, 25 July 1787, in Debates in the Federal Convention of 1787, 325.

19. For an excellent analysis of slavery and the Constitution, see George Van Cleve, A Slaveholder's Union: Slavery, Politics, and the Constitution in the Early American Republic (Chicago, 2010).

20. John Rutledge, Federal Convention, 21 August 1787, Debates in the Federal Convention of 1787, 442.

21. Van Cleve, Slaveholder's Union, 229; Beeman, Plain, Honest Men, 326–27; Douglas R. Egerton, Death or Liberty: African Americans and Revolutionary America (Oxford, 2009), 243–45.

22. Berlin, Generations of Captivity; Van Cleve, Slaveholder's Union.

23. Gouverneur Morris, Federal Convention, 8 August 1787, in Notes of Debates in the Federal Convention of 1787 (1966; repr., New York, 1987), 411.

24. David Waldstreicher, Slavery's Constitution: From Revolution to Ratification (New York, 2009), 84–85, 92; Beeman, Plain, Honest Men.

25. Sylvia Frey, Water from the Rock: Black Resistance in a Revolutionary Age (Princeton, 1991), 283–84.

26. These ideas are based on Van Cleve, Slaveholder's Union. David Waldstreicher makes the point about "self-aware" sections and how the institution was not explicitly mentioned in Slavery's Constitution, 88, 98–99.

27. James Wilson, Federal Convention, 13 July 1787, Debates in the Federal Convention of 1787, 250; Mark David Hall, The Political and Legal Philosophy of James Wilson, 1742-1798 (Columbia, MO, 1997), 96; James Wilson, "Of Man, as a Member of Society," in The Works of the Honourable James Wilson, L.L.D., ed. Bird Wilson (1804; repr., Clark, NJ, 2004), 308.

28. Judith Apter Klinghoffer and Lois Elkins, "'The Petticoat Electors': Women's Suffrage in New Jersey, 1776-1807," Journal of the Early Republic, 12 (1992): 159–93.

29. Carol Berkin, Revolutionary Mothers: Women in the Struggle for America's Independence (New York, 2005), 153–55.

30. On the idea of virtue, see J. G. A. Pocock, The Machiavellian Moment: Florentine Political Thought and the Atlantic Republican Tradition (Princeton, 1975). On men and

their roles in shaping sons, see T. H. Breen, *Puritans and Adventurers: Change and Persistence in Early America* (New York, 1980); and Kathleen M. Brown, *Good Wives, Nasty Wenches, and Anxious Patriarchs: Gender, Race, and Power in Colonial Virginia* (Chapel Hill, NC, 1996).

31. Jan Lewis, "'Of Every Age Sex & Condition': The Representation of Women in the Constitution Author," *Journal of the Early Republic*, 15 (1995): 359–87.

32. Nancy Cott, *The Bonds of Womanhood: "Women's Sphere" in New England, 1780–1835* (New Haven, 1977).

33. Hendrik Hartog, *Man and Wife in America: A History* (Cambridge, MA, 2000); Sandra VanBurkleo, *"Belonging to the World": Women's Rights and American Constitutional Culture* (New York, 2001).

34. On these ideas, see Rosemarie Zagarri, *Revolutionary Backlash: Women and Politics in the Early American Republic* (Philadelphia, 2007); and Ruth Bloch, *Gender and Morality in Anglo-American Culture, 1650–1800* (Berkeley, CA, 2003).

35. Berkin, *Revolutionary Mothers*, 155–57. On the complicated Abigail Adams, who ultimately resisted patriarchy, see Woody Holton, *Abigail Adams* (New York, 2010).

36. Sheila Skemp, "America's Mary Wollstonecraft: Judith Sargent Murray's Case for the Equal Rights of Women," in Alfred Young, Gary Nash, and Ray Raphael, eds., *Revolutionary Founders: Rebels, Radicals, and Reformers in the Making of the Nation* (New York, 2011), 289–302.

37. On this idea, see Gordon S. Wood, *The Creation of the American Republic, 1776–1787* (Chapel Hill, NC, 1969).

38. James Wilson, Pennsylvania Convention, 1 December 1787, *Documentary History of the Ratification of the Constitution Digital Edition*.

39. Robert McCloskey, ed., *The Works of James Wilson*, Vol. 1 (Cambridge, MA, 1967), 80–81. My thanks to Howard Pashman for this reference.

40. Gordon S. Wood, *Empire of Liberty: A History of the Early Republic* (Oxford, 2009), 15–19.

41. Ibid., 31.

42. Stanley M. Elkins and Eric McKittrick, *The Age of Federalism: The Early American Republic, 1788–1800* (New York, 1993), 31–32.

43. Saul Cornell, *The Other Founders: Anti-Federalism and the Dissenting Tradition in America, 1788–1828* (Chapel Hill, NC, 1999), 23; Elkins and McKittrick, *Age of Federalism*, 31. For these debates and the process of ratification, see Pauline Maier, *Ratification: The People Debate the Constitution, 1787–1788* (New York, 2010).

44. Maier, *Ratification*, ix, 73, 122.

45. Ibid., xiii, 130, 132, 187, 207

46. Ibid., 45, 59, 93.

47. Ibid., 324.

48. James Madison, "Federalist Paper No. 51," 8 February 1788, in *The Federalist*, 322.

49. On the differences between Madison and Hamilton on these issues, see Max M. Edling, *A Revolution in Favor of Government: Origins of the U.S. Constitution and the Making of the American State* (Oxford, 2003).

50. Maier, *Ratification*, 392.

51. Michael Merrill and Sean Wilentz, *The Key of Liberty: The Life and Democratic Writings of William Manning, "a Laborer," 1747–1814* (Cambridge, MA, 1993), 1–28. On artisans, see Richard Beeman, *The Varieties of Political Experience in Eighteenth-Century America* (Philadelphia, 2004).

52. Cornell, *Other Founders*, 28, 22.

53. Maier, *Ratification*, 195.
54. Ibid., 264–66.
55. Pauline Maier, *The Old Revolutionaries: Political Lives in the Age of Samuel Adams* (New York, 1980), 280–89.
56. Maier, *Ratification*, 35.
57. Ibid., 39.
58. Cornell, *Other Founders*, 12, 110–20, 70.
59. Elkins and McKittrick, *Age of Federalism*, 32–62.
60. John Howe, *Language and Political Meaning in Revolutionary America* (Amherst, MA, 2004).
61. On the contradictions between antistatist realities and the Federalist quest for powerful government and the "light" and "inconspicuous" government that took shape because of them, see Edling, *Revolution in Favor of Government*.
62. Alison L. LaCroix, *The Ideological Origins of American Federalism* (Cambridge, MA, 2010), 3, 7, 175, 216.
63. Eric Slauter, *The State as a Work of Art: The Cultural Origins of the Constitution* (Chicago, 2009). For a similar interpretation, but one that focuses on the shared experiences in horticulture, as well as in horticultural imagery, see Andrea Wulf, *Founding Gardeners: The Revolutionary Generation, Nature, and the Shaping of the American Nation* (New York, 2011).
64. Bouton, *Taming Democracy*. Douglas Bradburn, *The Citizenship Revolution: Politics and the Creation of the American Union, 1774–1804* (Charlottesville, VA, 2009).
65. For the West in these years, see Patrick Griffin, *American Leviathan: Empire, Nation, and Revolutionary Frontier* (New York, 2007); and Gregory Nobles, *American Frontiers: Cultural Encounters and Continental Conquest* (New York, 1998).
66. *Pittsburgh Gazette*, 17 November 1787, in Bernard Bailyn, ed., *The Debate on the Constitution: Federalist and Anti-Federalist Speeches, Articles, and Letters during the Struggle over Ratification* (New York, 1993), 1:324.
67. On the history of the Northwest Ordinance, see Peter Onuf, *Statehood and Union: A History of the Northwest Ordinance* (Bloomington, IN, 1992).
68. On this, see Peter Onuf, *Jefferson's Empire: The Language of American Nationhood* (Charlottesville, VA, 2001).
69. On this group, see Patrick Griffin, "Reconsidering the Ideological Origins of Indian Removal: The Case of the Big Bottom 'Massacre,'" in Andrew R. L. Clayton and Stuart D. Hobbs, eds., *The Center of a Great Empire: The Ohio Country in the Early American Republic* (Athens, OH, 2005), 11–35.
70. On conditions here, see Bouton, *Taming Democracy*; and especially, Terry Bouton, "A Road Closed: Rural Insurgency in Post-Independence Pennsylvania," *Journal of American History*, 87 (2000), 855-87.
71. Bouton, *Taming Democracy*.
72. See Thomas P. Slaughter, *The Whiskey Rebellion: Frontier Epilogue to the American Revolution* (New York, 1986).
73. Hamilton to George Washington, 2 August 1794, in *The Papers of Alexander Hamilton*, ed. Harold C. Syrett and Jacob E. Cooke (New York, 1972), 17:17; Hamilton to George Washington, 1 September 1792, in *Papers of Alexander Hamilton* (New York, 1967), 11:312.
74. Bouton, *Taming Democracy*.

75. Bradburn, *Citizenship Revolution*.

76. Michael Bellesiles, *Revolutionary Outlaws: Ethan Allen and the Struggle for Independence on the Early American Frontier* (Charlottesville, VA, 1993), 245–60.

77. This vision of government, one that was powerful but appeared weak, through an associative distribution of privileges and responsibilities suggested that Americans would be happy in the nineteenth century with a government that was unseen. On this, see Brian Balogh, *A Government Out of Sight: The Mystery of National Authority in Nineteenth-Century America* (New York, 2009).

CHAPTER 9

1. Gordon Wood, *The Idea of America: Reflections on the Birth of the United States* (New York, 2011), 216–17.

2. Eric Foner, *Tom Paine and Revolutionary America*, rev. edn. (1976; New York, 2005), 258; Seth Cotlar, "In Paine's Absence: The Trans-Atlantic Dynamics of American Popular Political Thought, 1789–1804" (Ph.D. diss., Northwestern University, 2000), 1–4.

3. On the English equivalent, see E. P. Thompson, *The Making of the English Working Class* (Harmondsworth, UK, 1972). On the revolutionary effects of the American Revolution on American religious life, see Nathan O. Hatch, *The Democratization of American Christianity* (New Haven, 1989).

4. *Gazette of the United States*, 19 June 1802.

5. Cotlar, "In Paine's Absence," 1–4; David Freeman Hawke, *Paine* (New York, 1974), 353–63.

6. Alan Taylor, *The Civil War of 1812: American Citizens, British Subjects, Irish Rebels, and Indian Allies* (New York, 2010).

7. On this contradiction, see Max M. Edling, *A Revolution in Favor of Government: Origins of the U.S. Constitution and the Making of the American State* (Oxford, 2003).

8. P. J. Marshall, *Remaking the British Atlantic: The United States and the British Empire after American Independence* (New York, 2012).

9. John J. McCusker and Russel R. Menard, *The Economy of British America, 1607–1789* (Chapel Hill, NC, 1985), 369–71.

10. James Fichter, *So Great a Proffit: How the East Indies Trade Transformed Anglo-American Capitalism* (Cambridge, MA, 2010).

11. McCusker and Menard, *Economy of British America*, 372–77.

12. John Taylor to Thomas Jefferson, 15 February 1799, *The Papers of Thomas Jefferson Digital Edition*, ed. Barbara B. Oberg and J. Jefferson Looney (Charlottesville, VA, 2008).

13. Drew R. McCoy, *The Elusive Republic: Political Economy in Jeffersonian America* (New York, 1982).

14. Adam Smith, *An Inquiry into the Nature and Causes of the Wealth of Nations*, ed. Edwin Cannan (1904; repr., Chicago, 1976), 405.

15. Alexander Hamilton, "Report on Manufactures" (1791; repr., Washington, DC, 1913), 14.

16. Stanley Elkins and Eric McKitrick, *The Age of Federalism: The Early American Republic, 1788–1800* (New York, 1993), 262.

17. Ibid., 258–61.

18. Hamilton, "Report on Manufactures," 14.

19. McCoy, *Elusive Republic*; John Lamberton Harper, *American Machiavelli: Alexander Hamilton and the Origins of U.S. Foreign Policy* (Cambridge, UK, 2004).

20. Joyce Appleby, *The Relentless Revolution: A History of Capitalism* (New York, 2010), 174–75.

21. Jefferson to William Ludlow, 6 September 1824, in *The Writings of Thomas Jefferson*, ed. H. A. Washington (New York, 1859), 7:377.

22. Appleby, *Relentless Revolution*, 176.

23. See James McPherson, *Battle Cry of Freedom: The Civil War Era* (New York, 1988). On how the original ideas developed over the course of the early nineteenth century, see Daniel Walker Howe, *What Hath God Wrought: The Transformation of America, 1815–1848* (Oxford, 2007).

24. See Gordon S. Wood, *The Radicalism of the American Revolution* (New York, 1991).

25. Gordon S. Wood, *Empire of Liberty: A History of the Early Republic, 1789–1815* (Oxford, 2009), 142.

26. Howe, *What Hath God Wrought*.

27. Andrew R. L. Cayton, *Ohio: The History of a People* (Columbus, OH, 2002), 21–22, 30–31, 50–51. For how governments sponsored such projects, see Carol Sheriff, *The Artificial River: The Erie Canal and the Paradox of Progress, 1817–1862* (New York, 1996).

28. D. W. Meinig, *The Shaping of America: A Geographical Perspective on 500 Years of History*, Vol. 1, *Atlantic America, 1492–1800* (New Haven, 1986); and Vol. 2, *Continental America, 1800–1867* (New Haven, 1992).

29. Adam Rothman, *Slave Country: American Expansion and the Origins of the Deep South* (Cambridge, MA, 2005); Ira Berlin, *Generations of Captivity: A History of African-American Slaves* (Cambridge, MA, 2003).

30. Appleby, *Relentless Revolution*, 175–76; James Oakes, *Slavery and Freedom: An Interpretation of the Old South* (New York, 1990).

31. On Jefferson and Indians, see Bernard W. Sheehan, *Seeds of Extinction: Jeffersonian Philanthropy and the American Indian* (Chapel Hill, NC, 1973).

32. Berlin, *Generations of Captivity*; Christopher Hitchens, *Thomas Jefferson: Author of America* (New York, 2005).

33. Eran Shalev, *Rome Reborn on Western Shores: Historical Imagination and the Creation of the American Republic* (Charlottesville, VA, 2009), 2, 3, 104-5. The most penetrating analysis of the empire of liberty is Peter Onof, *Jefferson's Empire: The Language of American Nationhood.* (Charlottesville, VA, 2000).

34. On the many fault-lines in France and the resulting violence, see William Doyle, *The Oxford History of the French Revolution* (New York, 2003).

35. Simon Newman, "American Political Culture and the French and Haitian Revolutions: Nathaniel Cutting and the Jeffersonian Republicans," in David Geggus, ed., *The Impact of the Haitian Revolution in the Atlantic World* (Columbia, SC, 2001), 74.

36. Ibid., 74.

37. Matthew Rainbow Hale, "Neither Britons Nor Frenchmen: The French Revolution and American National Identity" (Ph.D. diss., Brandeis University, 2002).

38. See Cotlar, "In Paine's Absence."

39. Alfred F. Young, *The Democratic Republicans of New York: The Origins, 1763–1797* (Chapel Hill, NC, 1967).

40. Ibid., 392–95.

41. Sean Wilentz, *The Rise of American Democracy: Jefferson to Lincoln* (New York, 2006), 40–42.

42. Ibid., 53–58; Wood, *Empire of Liberty*, 162–63.

43. Maurice J. Bric, *Ireland, Philadelphia, and the Re-Invention of America, 1760–1800* (Dublin, 2008); David A. Wilson, *United Irishmen, United States: Immigrant Radicals in the Early Republic* (Ithaca, NY, 1998). On the radical nature of the poorer sort, see Jim Smyth, *The Men of No Property: Irish Radicals and Popular Politics in the Late Eighteenth Century* (Dublin, 1992).

44. Cotlar, "In Paine's Absence."

45. Fisher Ames, "Eulogy on Washington," 8 February 1800, in *Works of Fisher Ames* (Boston, 1809), 126. For the idea of the age of Atlantic Revolution, see R. R. Palmer, *The Age of Democratic Revolution: A Political History of Europe and America, 1760–1800* (Princeton, 1970). For a recent reevaluation of the utility of the idea, see Wim Klooster, *Revolutions in the Atlantic World: A Comparative History* (New York, 2009).

46. On the ways events in France and Haiti curtailed radicalism in the United States, see the excellent essay by Newman, "American Political Culture."

47. Laurent Dubois, *Avengers of the New World: The Story of the Haitian Revolution* (Cambridge, MA, 2004), 8, 225, 304. David Brion Davis, "Impact of the French and Haitian Revolutions," in Geggus, ed., *The Impact of the Haitian Revolution in the Atlantic World*, 3–9; and Seymour Drescher, "The Limits of Example," in ibid., 6, 10.

48. Wilentz, *Rise of American Democracy*, 68–69.

49. Ibid., 63; Patrick Griffin, *American Leviathan: Empire, Nation, and Revolutinary Frontier* (New York, 2007).

50. On the lure of vicarious violence, see Hale, "Neither Britons Nor Frenchmen."

51. Wood, *Empire of Liberty*, 249, 259.

52. Ibid., 248.

53. Cotlar, "In Paine's Absence."

54. Hawke, *Paine*, 399–401.

55. This is the central point made by Wood in *Radicalism of the American Revolution* and *Empire of Liberty*, though Wood suggests that the idea of a middling, Republican or liberal sort pursuing its own happiness was an American virtue that emerged from the Revolution.

56. Wilentz, *Rise of American Democracy*, 78–81.

57. For an interpretation of Jefferson that suggests he did not fear power, see Peter S. Onuf, *The Mind of Thomas Jefferson* (Charlottesville, VA, 2007).

58. Hitchens, *Thomas Jefferson*, 187.

59. For two different versions of this idea, one steeped in paradox and the other less so, see Onuf, *Jefferson's Empire;* and Wood, *Empire of Liberty*. The gulf is pointed out by John L. Brooke, review of Wood, *Empire of Liberty*, in *William and Mary Quarterly*, 67, 3rd series (2010): 549–57.

60. David Hall, *Ways of Writing: The Practice and Politics of Text-Making in Seventeenth-century New England* (Philadelphia, 2008), 28. My thanks to Abram VanEngen for this reference.

61. Kariann Akemi Yokota, *Unbecoming British: How Revolutionary America Became a Postcolonial Society* (New York, 2011), 238–39; Marshall, *Remaking the British Atlantic*.

62. Waldstreicher, *In the Midst of Perpetual Fetes: The Making of American Nationalism, 1776–1820* (Chapel Hill, NC, 1997), 117–19, 139. Also see Simon Newman, *Parades and*

the Politics of the Street: Festive Culture in the Early American Republic (Philadelphia, 1997), 60.

63. Edward Lengel, *Inventing George Washington: America's Founder, in Myth and Memory* (New York, 2011).

64. Waldstreicher, *In the Midst of Perpetual Fetes*, 76–77. On Franklin, see Gordon S. Wood, *The Americanization of Benjamin Franklin* (New York, 2004), 232–46; and Joyce Chaplin, *The First Scientific American: Benjamin Franklin and the Pursuit of Genius* (New York, 2006), 340–45. On Franklin and slavery and Petty, and how they defined him, see David Waldstreicher, *Runaway America: Benjamin Franklin, Slavery, and the American Revolution* (New York, 2004).

65. See Newman, *Parades and Politics*, 79, 83–87. The same held for the day of his inauguration: 4 March 1801. Each March 4th, Republicans marked the beginning of a new republican age. As much as Federalists embraced the idea of Washington, Jefferson became their deity. The Fourth of March celebrations focused on Jefferson, on his virtues, policies, and persona. See Waldstreicher, *In the Midst of Perpetual Fetes*, 187, 192; Newman, *Parades and Politics*, 80–81.

66. Newman, *Parades and the Politics*, 95–115; Waldstreicher, *In the Midst of Perpetual Fetes*, 352.

67. *American Mercury*, 9 July 1801; *American Citizen and General Advertiser*, 3 July 1801, 8 July 1801; *City Gazette*, 6 July 1801.

68. This and the paragraphs that follow are drawn from David Ramsay, *The History of the American Revolution*, Vol. 1, ed. Lester Cohen (Indianapolis, 1990), 228, 233, 311–13, 318, 322, 327, 333.

69. For Warren's history, see Mercy Otis Warren, *History of the Rise, Progress, and Termination of the American Revolution*, Vol. 1, ed. Lester Cohen (Indianapolis, 1994), 165–66, 169–70, xx–xxi, xli–xliv.

70. On Jefferson and our fixation with contradiction, see Onuf, *Mind of Thomas Jefferson*.

71. Architect of the Capitol, http://www.aoc.gov/cc/art/rotunda/declaration_ independence. cfm (accessed 4 January 2011).

72. "Col. Trumbull's Painting," *City of Washington Gazette*, 8 May 1819.

73. "Col. Trumbull's Painting," *City of Washington Gazette*, 8 May 1819.

74. Jefferson to John Trumbull, 11 November 1818, *Papers of Thomas Jefferson*, Library of Congress, http://memory.loc.gov/master/mss/mtj1/051/0000/0053.jpg.

75. Jefferson to John Adams, 21 January 1812, quoted in *George Dangerfield, The Era of Good Feelings* (Chicago, 1952), 15–16. My thanks to Dan Graff for this reference.

Index

Note: Page numbers followed by the italicized letter "*f*" indicate figures.